CORPORATE CRIME UNDER ATTACK

THE FORD PINTO CASE AND BEYOND

Francis T. Cullen
William J. Maakestad
Gray Cavender

CJ
anderson

D0059260

CORPORATE CRIME UNDER ATTACK: THE
FORD PINTO CASE AND BEYOND

Copyright 1987 Anderson Publishing Co.

Library of Congress Cataloging-in-Publication Data

Cullen, Francis T.
© Corporate crime under attack.

Includes index.
1. Ford Motor Company—Trials, litigation, etc. 2. Trials
(Homicide)—Indiana—Winamac. 3. Trials (Products liability)
—Indiana—Winamac. 4. Pinto automobile. 5. Criminal liability of
juristic persons—United States. I. Maakestad, William J.
II. Cavender, Gray, 1947- . III. Title.
KF224.F67C85 1987   345.73'0268   87-1762
ISBN 0-87084-177-7   347.305268

 Criminal Justice Studies
Anderson Publishing Co.
Cincinnati, Ohio

Kelly Humble *Managing Editor*

For:

Paula J. Dubeck
Jean Brummer
Catherine and Gray Cavender, Jr.

Table of Contents

Preface

On August 10, 1978, three teenage girls perished when a rear-end collision caused their Ford Pinto to burst into flames. Unfortunately, as we know, this was not the first time a crash had claimed the lives of a group of youths; nor were these girls the first victims of a Pinto-related fire. Yet the teenagers' deaths were unique in the legal reactions they evoked. Scarcely a month after the accident, an Indiana grand jury indicted Ford Motor Company on three charges of reckless homicide, and a local prosecutor embarked on a vigorous crusade to see that Ford paid for its alleged "crime."

This book tells the story of the Ford Pinto trial. Making this story understandable, however, requires more than simply relaying the facts of the case. To be sure, the details are fascinating in themselves: the story's characters are strong-willed and interesting; there is a David-and-Goliath appeal in a county prosecutor taking on a major American corporation; and the plot is sufficiently dramatic and its ending sufficiently uncertain to make the case suspenseful.

Yet a simple account of the facts does not explain why a *criminal* prosecution of this sort was undertaken. Certainly, other options existed. The drivers—or fate—could have been blamed for the tragic accident. Why even consider holding a corporation culpable for the teenagers' deaths? And why contemplate labeling a major American corporation a reckless killer? To some extent, the answers lie in the unique history of the Pinto, which includes allegations that the subcompact had a defective fuel system. But more is involved; indeed, the idea that a broader perspective is needed to address questions of this sort is the central premise of our book.

Thus, throughout our analysis, we attempt to demonstrate that the Ford Pinto trial is best understood as a sign of the times—the product of a general movement against white-collar and corporate illegality. We argue further that this attack on corporate crime—whether by prosecutors, politicians, or intellectuals—is itself a manifestation of broad legal, social-structural, and ideological changes that have taken place over the past two decades.

In a sense, this very book supports our claim. The authors' social backgrounds differ widely: one of us was raised in the northeast, one in the midwest, and one in the south. We also have taken different academic paths: one of us is a sociologist who teaches in a department of criminal justice, another is a lawyer who teaches in a business school, and the other is a lawyer/criminologist on the faculty of a school of justice studies. Not surprisingly, our personal styles differ markedly and we do not share precisely the same views of politics, the law, justice, or, for that matter, baseball. Nonetheless, even before meeting and working on this project, each of us had developed a concern about a realm of illegality that the previous generation of scholars had largely neglected: white-collar crime. This convergence of intellectual interests may be a coincidence, but a sociological explanation seems more compelling: just as the Ford Pinto trial is a product of the prevailing context, we believe that this book, too, grew from the current social climate.

We realize that our intellectual labors are embedded in and shaped by our social experiences; as a result, we are particularly sensitive to the ways in which our biases may have influenced our objectivity. Reflexiveness is no guarantee that we have insulated our writings against our values. Indeed, we make no claim that this book is value-free in the sense that it is uninformed by an underlying political ideology. We have taken pains, however, to avoid rhetoric and to let the "facts"—as we know them—tell the Pinto story. Our goal is not to write an antibusiness tract or to single out Ford Motor Company and accuse its officials of wrongdoing. We leave to the reader the task of drawing conclusions about Ford or any other corporation. Instead, our purpose is to provide some understanding of why corporations such as Ford have come under attack by the criminal law at this point in history when similar conduct would have escaped criminal prosecution little more than a decade earlier. At the very least, we hope that our analysis sensitizes scholars to the importance of this question and to the implication it has for studying the relationship between corporations and criminal law.

The organization of the book reflects our conviction that the Pinto case assumes significance when it is placed within a larger context and seen as a product of that context. Thus we wait until Part II of the book to present the actual account of the case—why an Indiana prosecutor blamed Ford for the teenagers' deaths (Chapter 4), what obstacles had to be overcome before Ford could be prosecuted for reckless homicide (Chapter 5), and what occurred at the trial (Chapter 6). By contrast, Part I sets the context for understanding why the prosecution transpired and why it earned national attention—important to news reporters, lawyers, and academicians alike.

We have attempted to write this first part so that the uninitiated reader can negotiate it without too much difficulty; yet we have incorporated enough new material so that this section should prove useful to those more familiar with the field of corporate criminality. In all, Part I contains three chapters: the first details the emergence of a social movement against white-collar crime; the second reviews the nature of the corporate crime problem; and the third shows how corporations increasingly have been held criminally liable for their actions. The seventh and final chapter of the book ties together Parts I and II by highlighting what the Pinto trial teaches us about corporate illegality and its control. This chapter also explores how the Ford case helps us to understand the growing number of corporate criminal prosecutions—especially for violent offenses—that have taken place in the aftermath of the 1980 Pinto trial.

It is also appropriate to disclose that one of the authors—William Maakestad—was an active participant in the Pinto trial. A lawyer and a (half) brother of the prosecutor (Michael Cosentino), Bill attended many sessions of the trial, lived with the prosecution team during the trial, and made substantive contributions to the prosecution's efforts. Admittedly, his involvement carries both a benefit and a risk. We benefit by first-hand knowledge of public testimony in the trial and of events behind the scenes. We run the risk, however, that our in-depth knowledge of the prosecution's members and their perspectives will inadvertently bias our account of the trial. Only the reader can judge whether we have committed this error, but we are reassured by the precautions we have taken to avoid presenting a slanted story.

Finally, we are pleased to engage in the custom of thanking those who have helped us to complete this project. The good people at Anderson Publishing Co. must be singled out for their continued support and patience as deadlines passed unmet; we hope their wait will prove worthwhile. Karen Feinberg, our copy editor, had the unenviable task not only of cleaning up our prose but also of creating a uniform tone for a book written by three authors. We are so confident in her abilities that we suspect that most readers will have difficulty determining which authors wrote which sections. We must also express our appreciation for the assistance given by our colleagues at our respective academic homes: the Department of Criminal Justice at the University of Cincinnati, the Department of Management at Western Illinois University, and the School of Justice Studies at Arizona State University. To other individuals, too, we owe debts of all sorts—intellectual, emotional, and practical. The specific contributions are too numerous to describe in detail, but we trust they know what these contributions are and how much they have helped. We feel obliged, in the best sense of the word, to list their names: Richard Abrams, John

Borntrager, M.A. Bortner, Velmer Burton, John Braithwaite, Brent Fisse, Nancy Jurik, Russ Morey, Joanne Nigg, Howard Nudd, and John Wozniak.

We dedicate this book to Paula J. Dubek, to Jean Brummer, and to Catherine and Gray Cavender, Jr.

Francis T. Cullen
University of Cincinnati

William J. Maakestad
Western Illinois University

Gray Cavender
Arizona State University

PART I

CORPORATE CRIME
UNDER ATTACK

Chapter 1
The Movement Against White-Collar Crime

The headlines above and others like them are standard fare in the morning newspaper or the weekly news magazine. They are noteworthy for two reasons. First, they preview an array of interesting stories that feature crime as their connecting the men. Crime news is always sensational, and these stories are especially dramatic because they recount fascinating crimes which were committed by powerful individuals and organizations. Stories about celebrities and other figures in the "upperworld" seem to elicit a certain voyeurism, which grows even more pronounced when the theme is crime and the melodrama it entails. The crimes of political and business leaders make for good copy.

Second, the very appearance of these stories contradicts conventional wisdom about such crimes. Such diverse commentators as journalists, academics who study the media, and criminologists usually agree that the pub-

1

lic prefers the lurid and gory details that characterize street crime over reports about the supposedly sedate and sophisticated wrongdoing of the powerful. Perhaps the public is simply cynical about the nature of politics and business, dismissing the significance of corruption in these institutions with the comment, "Everyone knows they're all a bunch of crooks." On the other hand, it may be that certain practices, although morally problematic, are not viewed as crimes. The descriptive comment is "That's just politics" or "That's just business." Some authorities note that historically, for a variety of reasons, many questionable activities that are relatively common to the powerful have seldom been defined as crime, and hence have not mobilized the state machinery that redresses criminal behavior. In any case, the conventional view is that the depredations of political and business elites arouse neither the ire of the state nor the moral indignation of the public.

Yet, over the past decade, we have been confronted with an increasing number of such stories, and their appearance can not be explained as just another news theme created by the media. These stories depict crimes and criminals that seldom appeared in typical crime news in the past. More important, they describe actual criminal cases initiated by the state. Conventional wisdom notwithstanding, the public now learns regularly about the crimes of political and business elites and the efforts of the state to redress them. The appearance of these stories and the cases they report suggests that something has changed with respect to the delicts of the powerful.

Much of the argument in this book rests on the premise that something has indeed changed—changed to such an extent that many of the political and economic institutions of our society have seemingly "come under attack," especially by the legal system, but on a number of other fronts as well. In addition to criminal prosecutions, the citizen interest generated by media exposure and criminological research also reflects a concern with "white-collar crime" in general and "corporate crime" in particular. We suggest that the emerging concern over malfeasance within political and economic institutions is seen most accurately as a manifestation of certain changes in the prevailing social and political context, which have sensitized people on all these fronts to the crimes of the powerful.

These considerations are also essential for understanding why a conservative county prosecutor charged Ford Motor Company with reckless homicide for the deaths of three young women in 1978. To be sure, the Ford Pinto trial had its peculiarities, and, as a celebrated incident, contained unique legal and policy implications. But as will be argued throughout, the Pinto case was as much a product of the times as it was special. Indeed, scarcely a decade before, the deaths of the three teenagers would probably have been labeled an unfortunate, tragic accident and then forgotten by all but their families and friends. Instead, the accident was followed by a criminal prosecution and by months of national attention that may be traced through such headlines as "Ford Indicted in Crash," "The Pinto, the Girls, the Anger," "Ford Seeks Dismissal of Criminal Charges," "Pinto Criminal Trial of Ford Motor Co. Opens Up Broad Issues," "Pinto Death Case About to Begin," and, in the end, "Three Cheers in Dearborn."[2]

Our initial purpose here is to illuminate why white-collar crime and, more specifically, corporate crime have come under attack. Accordingly, we will suggest that America has experienced a broad social movement against white-collar criminality. We will then consider the source of this movement, how it has fostered a flurry of academic research on lawlessness in the upperworld, and what path the campaign against white-collar illegality is likely to take in the future. After this examination we will devote the remaining chapters in Part I to a more comprehensive background for assessing the importance and implications of the Pinto trial. We will review the nature of America's corporate crime problem and the legal response traditionally invoked to control this form of unlawful behavior.

In Part II we will set forth the specifics of the Ford Pinto case. This interesting trial serves a useful heuristic function, offering an actual case as a vantage point from which we may assess the potential of the criminal sanction as a mechanism for suppressing corporate misbehavior.

The Social Movement Against White-Collar Crime

Something *has* changed in our society with respect to the crimes of the powerful. The best indicator of this change is the increased attentiveness to white-collar crime on a number of fronts, including the media, academic research, and the legal system.

To support this view, we must examine the social movement concept, which is an analytic vehicle for understanding the nature and the breadth of social change. We offer two definitions of the concept.

> A social movement is a collectivity acting with some continuity to promote or resist a change in the society or group of which it is a part. [To paraphrase], the salient characteristics include shared values that are sustained by an ideology, a sense of membership, norms, and division of labor.[3]

> A social movement is a set of actions of a group of people. These actions have the following characteristics: they are self-consciously directed toward changing the social structure and/or ideology of a society, and they either are carried on outside of

ideologically legitimate channels of change or use those channels in innovative ways.[4]

A synthesis of these definitions suggests that the focal concern of a social
movement is social change: change that is resisted or promoted by a group
of people motivated by shared values or an ideology. Herbert Blumer, a sociologist and a pioneer in the field of social movements, has emphasized a
sense of collectivity or "we-consciousness" as a definitive characteristic of
such a group with its shared values. He has suggested that social movements typically emerge from a background of general unrest or dissatisfaction and that they evidence a concern with individuals' rights and privileges.[5] In more recent formulations, the background of social movements
has been depicted as a generalized sense of injustice and a pursuit of equal
justice that serves as the motivating ideology for social change or resistance
to change.[6]

Blumer has identified several types of social movements; two of these
seem to be most relevant to our analysis. The first is a "specific" social
movement and especially one of its subtypes—the "reform movement."
Reform movements are parsimonious in their aim, which is simply to effect
change in some restricted portion of the existing social order. The foundations of the prevailing order, such as power and resources and their distribution throughout society, go unchallenged by this sort of movement. As
one scholar has put it, those who constitute a reform movement assent to
the political institutions of the state, and the means whereby they attempt
reform are within those prescribed by the state.[7] Accordingly they employ
only legitimate methods, such as making public speeches or lobbying legislators, to accomplish their goal. Reliance on legitimate methods often guarantees an aura of respectability for a reform movement. The reform movement in Blumer's typology exemplifies the characteristics of a social movement in their purest form. In the reform movement we find a definite organization that includes membership, leadership, a division of labor, "we-consciousness," and sustaining values (e.g., the Temperance Movement,
MADD).[8] Although the reform movement is limited in its methods and
goals, this category is defined by rigorous criteria.

Blumer's second category, the "general social movement," is characterized by more flexible criteria and is more accommodating for our analysis.
A general social movement, according to Blumer, is unorganized in both
structure and identity, is composed of people in different areas, and is essentially "an aggregation of individual lines of action based on individual
decisions and selection."[9] In the view of some scholars, the general movement is so diffuse and so seriously lacking in the important element—identity—that it is not a social movement at all. In Blumer's view,

however, the general movement is the background from which specific social movements, such as reform movements, develop with their defining
characteristics, including an organizational identity.[10]   A general social
movement is an emergent focus of a shift in cultural values that has yet to
converge into a well-defined reform movement. This type of movement will
provide the framework for our analysis.

The Social Movement Framework Applied

Sociologist Jack Katz has applied this framework in a recent paper, arguing that over the past ten years or so America has experienced a social
movement against white-collar crime. He has supported his thesis by delin-
eating the significant increase in the number of political and business elites
that have been prosecuted since the 1970s.

> In the area of political corruption, in addition to the unprece-
> dented cases against federal officials, charges for the criminal
> use of gubernatorial powers have been brought in Illinois
> (Kerner), Oklahoma (Hall), Maryland (Agnew, Mandel), and
> Tennessee (Blanton). Scores of the nation's largest corpora-
> tions admitted to criminal political contributions in the 1972
> campaign; hundreds acknowledged bribes, or "sensitive pay-
> ments," to foreign officials. Law enforcement agencies from the
> FBI to local police departments have been charged with system-
> atic criminal violations of civil rights.[11]

For Katz, an important aspect of this movement has been the increasing
displacement of conventional criminality or street crime as a political issue
by a concern with white-collar crime. As evidence of the shifting political
emphasis, Katz has suggested that one need only contrast the late 1960s and
the state's "war on crime" in the streets with the 1970s and the Watergate
proceedings, candidate Jimmy Carter's attack of the Nixon pardon, the
politicization of white-collar crime as a general campaign issue, and the subsequent commitment of the Carter administration to make the crimes of the
rich and powerful a top priority for the Justice Department.[12]

Katz has suggested that this movement focuses on the prosecution of individual cases and stems from the enforcement activities of governmental
agencies such as the Justice Department. According to Katz, the Justice
Department has made some effort to assume leadership, especially during
the Carter administration, although he has depicted this effort as a largely
decentralized movement that is propelled by the attorneys who staff the

governmental agencies. These attorneys, acting in a quasi-legislative capacity, have expanded the scope of criminal law to include activities of the politicians and business executives that have not traditionally been covered by criminal law.[13] They have prosecuted certain types of defendants who previously enjoyed an unofficial, if not a legal, immunity from criminal prosecutions. In a sense, it is the federal prosecutors, operating on a case-by-case basis, who are the catalysts or moral entrepreneurs of the movement: that is, people who take the initiative to create or enforce rules. Morals entrepreneurs are a driving force behind social movements and they attempt to produce some socially beneficial outcome, although they may pursue individual, self-serving ends as well.[14]

These prosecuting attorneys illustrate both sorts of goals. According to Katz, their efforts represent a commitment to equal justice, but at the same time they are motivated to prosecute white-collar offenders by the pragmatic prospect of gaining professional prestige and mobility. Katz has observed, however, that in many respects these activities differ somewhat from earlier social movements. For example, the movement against white-collar crime, unlike notable social movements of the past, has generated little corrective legislation or other major institutional reform (although, as we shall see in Chapter 7, such reform may yet be undertaken).[15] Further, the decentralized nature and individual-case motif of the prosecutions impedes any sense of collectivity and probably works against the development of a division of labor within a collectivity.

Thus the activities detailed by Katz vary from the criteria that typically define social movements in other analyses. It must be noted, however, that he has limited his analysis expressly to the prosecutions that are initiated by federal enforcement agencies. If we expand his argument to include a broader spectrum of activities, Katz's analysis becomes a compelling point of embarkation for a thorough investigation of the social movement against white-collar crime. Such an expansion seems warranted because in addition to the federal prosecutors, other sources of agitation contribute to a general milieu in which white-collar crime has become an issue of public concern. Moreover, these other sources of agitation are reminiscent of earlier social movements.

For example, Katz has downplayed any public involvement with respect to white-collar crime, perhaps because he has also dismissed the importance of the media on the subject. The media played a key role in earlier social movements; muckraking journalists mobilized the public through stories that condemned whole institutions and advocated sweeping reforms. In Katz's view, however, reporters today have abandoned broad institutional themes and focus instead on narrow issues or cases. Yet there are indications that the public is more aware and less tolerant of these crimes than ever.[16] The increased salience of this issue is no doubt due to the media spotlight on white-collar crime, as reflected by the headlines with which we opened this chapter. Though there is a tendency toward individualization in current media stories, such reports are nonetheless important, and they frequently address the condition of an entire industry through the vehicle of a specific example. Thus stories about a disaster in a coal mine or a defective make of automobile raise issues of corporate responsibility that go beyond the individual case.[17]

The media made similar contributions to social reforms in the past. *The Jungle*, Upton Sinclair's popular novel, aroused public indignation about deplorable conditions in the meat-packing industry and contributed to the passage of pure-food laws during the early 1900s.[18] Some stories are limited to a specific case, but even they may mobilize or contribute to a series of larger actions. More recently, several media reports about gas tanks in the Ford Pinto focused attention on problems with the automobile that culminated in an investigation of the Pinto by the National Highway Traffic Safety Administration, a recall of Pintos by Ford, a number of successful personal-injury suits against Ford, and eventually a criminal prosecution of the Ford Motor Company by the State of Indiana for reckless homicide.[19] Investigative reporters may pursue a different tack today, but, as the Ford Pinto case demonstrates, their stories may facilitate the emergence of a social movement and the reform-oriented efforts of others within such a movement.

The Ford Pinto scenario is instructive because it sensitizes us to the role of other moral entrepreneurs and their interactions with one another with respect to white-collar crime. The most obvious of these is Ralph Nader, a prominent figure whose long-term involvement in a variety of consumer issues resembles the activities of the devoted Progressive reformers of an earlier era. His credits as a reformer include attacks on the auto industry and on corporations in general, and he has addressed the issue of crime by business executives as well.[20] Nader used his reputation as a nationally known reformer to publicize one of the early media exposés about the Pinto gas tank. That additional publicity and Nader's credibility contributed to the series of actions against the Ford Motor Company described in the preceding paragraph. These actions involved a network of people that included private plaintiffs' lawyers, expert witnesses, county prosecutors, volunteer law professors and law students, and the media. The interaction of these contributors combined with the larger social milieu to produce the Ford Pinto trial, one event in the larger movement against white-collar crime.[21]

One other area of related activity has contributed to the general social movement against white-collar crime: criminological research on the topic. This research constitutes another source of agitation against business and organizational illegality and corresponds to similar activities that occurred in earlier social movements. Students of social movements have suggested the likelihood that intellectuals, either as individuals or as an entire discipline, may formulate and/or disseminate the sustaining ideology or shared norms that are essential to the organizational identity of a movement.[22] The academic, who lends a sense of credibility to the practical side, establishes the terms of discourse and the agenda for reform during the emergence of a social problem topic or in the early phases of a social movement. For example, the American Social Science Association, later the American Sociological Association, was created as a professional organization of social scientists oriented toward social reform during the Progressive era at the turn of the century.[23] Speaking through the collective voice of their newly created professional association, they lobbied for a variety of reforms. Although these sociologists joined other reform-minded individuals and groups, they claimed a certain expertise as academics who studied social problems and they lent a sense of scientific credibility to the agenda for reform.

The discipline of criminology enjoys a similar heritage. Indeed, many reforms of the Progressive era addressed issues of crime and delinquency, and the activist, social-science stance that prevailed in those days probably contributed to the development of criminology as a spinoff perspective. Thus criminology has often been characterized as an academic discipline that is steeped in the tradition of activist, liberal reform.[24] It is not surprising that today criminology might contribute to a movement that is designed to eradicate corruption.

Katz neglected academic criminology in his analysis, probably because he has attributed the movement to the personnel—primarily career-oriented prosecution attorneys—who staff the federal enforcement agencies. Nevertheless, his analysis seems especially fertile for a consideration of academic criminology as a contributor to the general movement because white-collar crime has emerged as such an important topic within the discipline. Concurrent with the increase in prosecutions documented by Katz, there has been a virtual explosion of criminological research on the subject of white-collar crime. We stress the concurrence of prosecutions and research to avoid the implication that one caused the other. They represent diverse aspects, the practical and the academic, of the same issue: the general social movement against white-collar crime.

In summary, we have suggested that the concept of general social movement accommodates our analysis of the increased salience of white-collar crime. In this chapter our attention is directed primarily at two aspects of this movement—the initiation of criminal prosecutions and the production of relevant academic research. While neither activity by itself constitutes a social movement, both may be understood as part of the larger context of such a movement. This observation is especially salient if we cast these activities as a purported change of orientation in the legal profession and in academic criminology, which has occurred within a milieu of shifting values.

The remainder of this chapter is organized around three themes that pertain to the general social movement against white-collar crime and one of its subcategories, corporate crime. We suggest (1) that the emergence of this movement is a reflection or product of a crisis of legitimacy; (2) that the movement has essentially revitalized the legal system and academic criminology; and (3) that this movement has produced effects that have been largely symbolic up to this point. The meaning and significance of these three themes will be revealed in detail in our analysis of the social movement against white-collar crime.

Genesis of the Movement

Katz has cited three interrelated factors that explain the emergence of the social movement against white-collar crime, as he conceptualized this crusade. The first is the long-term development of several relatively autonomous federal enforcement agencies, including the Justice Department, that provide an institutional setting for the movement. Second, the attorneys who staff the agencies have a pronounced careerist orientation that is furthered by the prosecution of notable cases, such as those involving political and business leaders. And third, Watergate and similar scandals frequently implicated and weakened the leadership of these agencies, thereby creating a political power vacuum that permitted advancement when aggressive staff attorneys battled political and business corruption.[25]

Katz has situated his social movement within the context of the political crisis that followed the Watergate affair, a view that conforms to the literature on social movements. Scholars portray social movements as arising from a background of general dissatisfaction about individual rights or a generalized sense of injustice.[26] A period of political unrest certainly followed in the wake of Watergate. But while Katz's explanation provides a plausible rationale for the efforts of attorneys whom he has portrayed as moral entrepreneurs or catalysts of the attack on white-collar crime, it is insufficient for our analysis because it fails to address the role of academic criminologists within a more broadly based movement. Accordingly, we offer an alternative explanation, building upon Katz's, that includes a rationale for both the prosecutions and the research and is also compatible with the literature on social movements.

We suggest that the notion of a "legitimation deficit" or "crisis" is central to this analysis. "Legitimation" refers to the justification (or authority) of the state as it exercises political power, and to the public's acceptance of the state as it acts. In this sense, legitimation connotes both a process and an output dimension.[27] A process exists whereby the state produces its legitimacy, and legitimation is the product or output of this process. Our consideration of legitimation deficits and crises provides a structure for understanding the shifts in orientation that have purportedly occurred within the legal apparatus and within academic criminology. Moreover, this notion facilitates our more inclusive analysis because it focuses attention on the general background of unrest and on the sense of injustice that is the larger milieu of this movement.

Over the past twenty years we have experienced a seemingly endless flow of events that has repeatedly challenged our faith in major social institutions or the ideals on which they are based. The list of events is long and often cited; it includes the efforts of women, ethnic and racial minorities, gays, and many others first to sensitize us to and then to erase the disturbing inequities in the social, political, and economic spheres that have plagued their lives. It includes the realization that because of the distribution of power and resources throughout society, there is not an equal opportunity to achieve "the good life," and that for many, even minimal subsistence is problematic. The list includes the severe disruptions that accompanied our involvement in Vietnam and the continuing national demoralization that is the aftermath of that stupid and wasteful venture. It includes the disclosure of business practices that are shocking in their illegality and all too often reprehensible in their immoral disregard for life. And finally, the list includes the Watergate affair and all the related political activities of those fallen leaders who appealed to lofty ideals but were corrupted by simple greed. Yet these political and business criminals appear to have enjoyed special privileges and immunities because the state has only infrequently mobilized the machinery of the criminal law to redress such serious wrongs. The result of these events, and of the inadequate response to them, has been the substitution of cynicism for national purpose and an erosion of confidence in law and in many of our political and economic institutions.

Some academics who study the erosion of confidence in the state's authority stress the significance of triggering events in the production of a legitimation crisis—that is, events that produce a crisis and then generate reform activities such as legislation or revolution. Others see such a crisis as a tendency inherent in our political economy. (We use "political economy" as a corrective term that reflects the interdependence rather than the independence of the political and the economic realms. These interconnections will be discussed in detail in Chapter 3.) In either case the academics' ideas are derived at least partially from Max Weber, the German sociologist whose influential scholarly works appeared during the late 1800s and the early 1900s. Weber's intellectual interests were wide-ranging, although his most persistent concern was the development of capitalism in the western world and the contribution of religious and political institutions to that development. He was especially interested in the appearance of an autonomous or independent legal order and its relationship to the emergence of capitalism.

Much of Weber's work addresses the interconnections between capitalism as an advanced economic system and the centralized state with its autonomous legal order. In Weber's view capitalism is distinguished by the methodical and predictable routine of the political economy. The dominant business form is the rational, permanent enterprise, which is characterized by rational capital accounting. The modern bureaucratic state facilitates these routines by guaranteeing calculability in the political sector. Predictable laws and their administration via the legal apparatus are unique features of this rational political organization.[28]

The modern state, according to Weber, enjoys a virtual monopoly on the use of coercive force to maintain the political economy, although it governs most effectively when citizens accede to its legitimacy. The state's assertion of legitimate authority rests to a significant degree on law and on several characteristics of the legal order. Law, in turn, enjoys its own sense of legitimacy because of these characteristics, which supposedly include neutrality (one person or group is not favored over another), autonomy (the legal apparatus is not influenced by either the political or the economic system), and formal rationality (the legal apparatus is autonomous and applies its own decision criteria, which can be generalized and therefore predicted).[29] Thus law contributes to the legitimacy of the state in capitalist society.

Today, however, the legitimacy of the political system becomes increasingly problematic as the state continues to extend its sphere of influence ever deeper into all facets of social existence. The state, for example, is heavily involved in the economic sector. Its activities in this sector have displaced many of the steering functions that in earlier days were left to the market forces. These activities range from the fiscal and monetary policies that are designed to smooth out disruptive economic cycles to government loans that bail out faltering businesses. The state has also become more integrally involved in aspects of the sociocultural sphere, including health care and regulation, a variety of social welfare services, and virtual control of the educational system.

Of course, there are many interpretations of the state's expansion into these areas. Some consider the state's growing role to be an abomination; others regard it as a social necessity. In either case, the deeper penetration by the state into the social fabric produces a greater demand for legitimation of the state's authority. Jurgen Habermas, a German scholar and a contemporary authority on legitimation, has suggested that the expansion of state activity into the sociocultural realm necessitates increased legitimation to justify the state's incursion into this new area. Ironically, however, the traditional cultural techniques of legitimation are largely ineffective because they have been displaced by the state's growing intervention into the sociocultural realm—the very action that created the need for greater legitimation in the first place. Thus, in the past, sociocultural legitimation was nonpolitical and largely unquestioned, a private matter for such institutions as the family, the church, or education at the local level. Yet, as Habermas has observed, attempts by the state to enhance legitimacy through other means, such as some form of administrative governmental control (e.g., centralized curriculum planning, health-care legislation, or sex education), are not particularly effective in the sociocultural area.[30] This expansion into the sociocultural sphere tends to stir up matters that were taken for granted, to politicize them, and thereby to increase the need to legitimate the state's actions. Moreover, once the state has intervened, it creates the expectation that it will continue relevant activities (such as government regulation and social programs). Recently, however, these demands have sometimes gone unsatisfied because of the fiscal crisis that confronts government at all levels[31] and because of ideological questions posed by conservatives about the propriety of the state's role in this sphere. Thus the intervention into the sociocultural realm is complicated by the state's ability (or inability) to meet the demands it has created and to legitimate its intervention. As a result, the legitimacy of the state tends to be least when its need for legitimacy is greatest. As Habermas has noted,

> If governmental crisis management fails, it lags behind programmatic demands that it has placed on itself. The penalty for this failure is withdrawal of legitimation. Thus, the scope for action contracts precisely at those moments in which it needs to be drastically expanded.[32]

Similarly, the demand for legitimation increases as the state expands into the economic sector, but this situation, too, contains irony and poses a dilemma. The state must legitimate its intervention into the economic sector amid the continued private appropriation of public wealth; as Habermas has put it, the state's legitimation problem is "how to distribute the...social product inequitably and legitimately."[33]

Thus, even in the best of situations, inherent contradictions exist in the political economy and foster a tendency toward deficits or crises of legitimation. And in light of the list given earlier, these are not the best of times; they are characterized by the campaign for civil rights, Vietnam, Watergate, and seemingly insatiable demands for minimal social services that the government is either unable or unwilling to meet. These events may be seen as the trigger for a legitimation crisis or, alternatively, as manifestations of such a crisis. In either case, they have called into question broad political and economic policies by drawing attention to basic contradictions in our political economy.

More important for our analysis, these events have challenged the legitimacy of law and the legal apparatus and ultimately the legitimacy of the social order. Law and the legal apparatus have been hit especially hard by the various disclosures on the list. We have witnessed a challenge to the efficacy of law and the legal system as a mechanism for assuring compliance to the value system that underlies our social order. For a variety of reasons, such as the sophistication and the grand scale of the crimes or the transformation of criminality into good politics and good business, law, especially criminal law, has not been particularly effective in regulating the crimes among elite groups. But another issue is far more serious: when members of elites who had violated the law were caught, they either received no sanction or one that was disproportionately lenient when compared to the penalty for conventional criminals. The legal apparatus was playing favorites; disclosures of that bias undermined the law's neutrality and thus challenged its legitimacy.

In a sense, then, Katz's analysis is correct when it situates the prosecutions of business and political leaders within the context of a post-Watergate political crisis. The prosecutions, especially if they result in convictions, reaffirm the efficacy of the legal apparatus with respect to the crimes of the powerful. But far more important, these prosecutions reassert the ideology of equal justice and the neutrality of law. Thus it is not surprising that these prosecutions appear as part of a general movement with a crisis of legitimation as background. First, in a situation where a legitimation deficit clearly exists, the state may be expected to respond with actions that vindicate its claims to legitimacy. The prosecutions of white-collar offenders are just such a response because they demonstrate the efficacy, autonomy, and neutrality of law and thereby contribute to the legitimacy of the state's authority. They are evidence, in short, against allegations that in the United States "the rich get richer and the poor get prison." Second, the very agencies that were implicated in the scandals and to some extent generated the crisis are often the instigators of the prosecutions. Thus the law is legitimated in a general sense, and specific units of the legal apparatus that had become suspect are exonerated as well. Finally, these prosecutions reflect the careerist motivation of the prosecuting attorneys, but only within the larger social context that has produced a shift of professional orientation—the legal profession's recommitment to equal justice. For Katz, the background of the prosecutions of political and business elites is a post-Watergate crisis in government; for us, it is a more deep-seated crisis of legitimation.

Similarly, the contribution of academic criminology to the general movement against white-collar crime may also be understood as a professional reorientation that is set against the background of a legitimation crisis. Because criminologists and prosecuting attorneys share a social milieu, they experienced the same disturbing events that challenged many of our institutions and produced a crisis of legitimation. And because their professional environment is concerned directly with law and crime, criminologists were also affected deeply by the disclosure of serious wrongdoing by political and business elites. As an academic discipline, criminology furnishes the framework within which crime-related matters are considered. Traditionally, however, the discipline has provided little in the way of an intellectual agenda for systematically addressing the crimes of the powerful. As a result, repeated revelations of such crime not only undermined the legitimacy of law, but also threatened the intellectual legitimacy of criminology; they jeopardized the discipline's "ownership" of crime as a public problem.[34]

The recent outpouring of criminological research on white-collar crime might be seen, then, as the academic side of a general social movement. In one respect this academic activity is directly linked to the government's greater emphasis on white-collar crime. The federal government is frequently a source of funding for scholarly research, and during this period of increased prosecution, criminologists often have been able to secure grant support for research into white-collar criminality, thereby furthering their careers. This criminological activity is the result of a professional reorientation that reflects intellectual tension or dissatisfaction during a disciplinary crisis of legitimacy. (We do not mean to imply that criminology as an academic discipline is confronting a legitimation crisis. This concept, as used by Habermas and others, suggests a more deep-seated societal malady. Rather, because criminology has neglected the crimes of elites, it has suffered a threat to its credibility as an academic discipline, although this threat occurred within the context of the larger societal crisis of legitimation.)

This crisis of intellectual legitimacy has bred a certain uneasiness in academic criminology during the past fifteen years, as evidenced by the criticism of much that was conventional wisdom, the exploration of alternative paradigms, and an attentiveness to emergent topics such as white-collar crime. Criminologists have critiqued criminology; some have advocated new paradigms or at least new intellectual agendas for criminological inquiry. Notably, neither the sense of uneasiness nor the call for a new agenda was confined to criminologists of a particular bent or political ideology, but were spread throughout the discipline, which suggests the pervasive drift that Herbert Blumer describes as the background of a general movement.[35]

Criminologists on the political right, for example, criticized the long-standing interest in the etiology or causation of criminal behavior. They suggested that criminology's fascination with the root causes of crime (e.g. poverty and family disorganization) had focused the research agenda on certain fundamental social conditions. Even if these factors ultimately "caused" crime, they were so deeply ingrained in the very structure of society as to be virtually immutable. Criminology, having become fixated on these unalterable structural factors, had rendered itself irrelevant for the formulation of public policy on crime.[36] As a solution to this problem, these criminologists suggested that criminology's intellectual agenda be redirected to make it policy-relevant; the focus of research should be on factors and conditions that could be manipulated to reduce crime. Deterrence research, for instance, would be a priority on such an agenda[37] because it emphasizes the severity, certainty, and swiftness of penalties as a vehicle for reducing crime.

Scholars on the political left were also critical of criminology, but they were concerned with the assumption, implicit in prior theoretical research, that crime was largely a phenomenon of the lower class.[38] They argued that there was too much deterrence research; criminology had essentially abdicated its intellectual autonomy to become a tool (i.e., a purveyor of information and rationalization) of the repressive state that maintained the capitalist order.[39] Their solution to this problem was to redirect criminology's intellectual agenda to focus on capitalism as a mode of production and on its connection to criminal behavior. An analysis of the relationship between the political economy and criminality, for example, would be a priority on such an agenda.[40] Some criminologists on the left agreed that theoretical criminology had become too abstract and that input on policy matters had been abdicated to the political right. Accordingly, they advocated a variety of strategies that might guide the formulation of public policy on crime.[41]

Liberal criminologists also reproved the discipline. Their criticisms addressed scientific positivism as the theoretical underpinning of criminology and challenged the assumptions that criminal behavior was caused by factors beyond the control of the individual, which could be identified and cured through the application of scientific principles. They debunked the companion myths of humanitarianism and scientific expertise, demonstrating that these myths had justified an unwarranted expansion of state control over the lives of vulnerable populations (e.g., the length of prison sentences for juvenile offenders). The state had accomplished this intervention under the guise of good intentions, and criminology had rationalized it. Liberal criminologists were also concerned with policy implications because it was the transformation of theory into practice that had produced the expansion of social control. Their solution to this problem was to redirect criminology's intellectual agenda in one of two ways: either criminology should pursue an interactionist approach (that is, attempt to understand criminality from the criminal's perspective rather than attempt to "cure" the offender),[42] or, alternatively, criminology should adopt a legalistic stance that emphasized due process and procedural rights rather than the needs of the offender, a focus that did little good and much harm.[43] An analysis of the adverse, potentially crime-producing effects of the criminal justice system would be a priority on the interactionist agenda;[44] a concern with the abuse of discretion would be a priority on the legalistic agenda.[45]

The sense of uneasiness within the discipline reflected a concern about the relevance of criminology to the formulation of public policy on crime. Criminology has always cultivated something of an "applied" image, and doubt about its policy relevance posed a threat to that aspect of its intellectual credibility; even theoretical critique was infected with such a concern. On the one hand, criminology was condemned for an alleged failure to generate theory and practice that would help reduce crime; on the other hand, it was criticized for its inexcusable neglect of crimes by the powerful. Research on white-collar crime emerged amid this disciplinary tension. With this focus, criminology manifested a new policy relevance that was directed toward the control of white-collar crime and, at the same time, addressed the crimes of political and business leaders.

Thus academic criminology, like the legal apparatus, underwent a professional reorientation in response to its own crisis of intellectual legitimacy. That reorientation contributed to and was fueled by a general social movement against white-collar crime.

White-Collar Crime As A Revitalization Movement

An endless stream of disclosures about the crimes of the powerful, occurring as they did with other events that revealed serious contradictions in our social order, threatened the legitimacy of the legal apparatus and academic criminology. The members of these professions responded to this crisis with prosecutions against white-collar criminals and research into this type of illegality. As they began to address the phenomenon, however, lawyers and criminologists proceeded in a manner that was consistent with the ideals and customs of their respective professions. They expanded their professional agendas to include white-collar crime, but this reorientation was informed by well-established traditions. In a sense, the social movement against white-collar crime took the form of a revitalization movement rather than a commitment to a genuinely new direction in these professions.

The term "revitalization movement," which we have borrowed from anthropological literature, denotes "any conscious, organized effort by members of a society to construct a more satisfying culture."[46] Revitalization movements clearly resemble social movements in some respects (e.g., they represent an effort to effect significant changes or reforms in a society), although anthropologists typically use the term in a fairly specific fashion to describe reformative religious movements that arise in disorganized societies. Such movements, which originate in situations of social and cultural stress, are attempts to devise a new culture that will resolve existing conflicts. While the new culture exhibits its own dogma, myth, and ritual, some of these elements may be carried over from the conflict-ridden society and transformed to fit within the new order.[47] We employ this concept in our analysis because it highlights the continuity that exists between old traditions and a new culture.

Anthropologist Anthony F.C. Wallace, who coined the term "revitalization movements," likened them to chemical reactions that produce new compounds. In Wallace's analogy, just as certain substances will combine to form a new compound when mixed with a catalyst and heated, independent and sometimes incompatible social traits will synthesize into a new culture when catalyzed by the prophet of a revitalization movement and heated by social disorder.[48] We may extend his analogy to include the activities recently directed against white-collar lawlessness. A social movement against white-collar crime has arisen, fueled by disturbing contradictions in our society and by crises of legitimacy, and catalyzed through the entrepreneurial efforts that we have described. At this stage, the movement consists primarily of prosecutorial and research activities that draw heavily upon the extant customs and ideologies of the legal order and academic criminology. Much as a troubled society is reinvigorated by a revitalization movement, the movement against white-collar crime has been directed at revitalizing the legal order and academic criminology. The movement and the new form it entails exhibit a certain dogma, myth, and ritual; these elements reflect the traditions of the respective professions. Thus the customs and ideologies of the legal order and academic criminology receive new life and legitimacy.

The continuity of customs and ideology is readily apparent in the prosecutorial activity that is directed against white-collar crime. While Katz discounted any particular *political* ideology, he nonetheless described an underlying commitment to "equal justice" as a partial motivation for the federal prosecutors:

> The movement to prosecute white-collar crime has been justi-
> fied in the name of equal justice. [Later, he noted] that the ad-
> vance of American governmental commitments toward equal
> justice has not flowed steadily from the implications of a gener-
> ally embraced political ideology but sporadically, out of contexts
> of societal crises....[49]

In terms of a social movement, this commitment gives the prosecutors a
sustaining ideology that is grounded in a generalized sense of injustice and
the pursuit of equal justice. The American tradition of jurisprudence is
steeped in the notion of equal justice, so the assertion of that ideology by
the legal profession maintains a fundamental, historical link. More important, the revival of the ideology of equal justice, especially when applied to
the crimes of the powerful, has contributed to the legitimacy of law by ostensibly reaffirming the neutrality and autonomy of the legal order at a time
when these traits were in doubt. The focus on white-collar crime has
tended to negate a crisis of legitimacy and to revitalize the ideological tradition of the legal system.

Similarly, the case motif of individual prosecutions as the vehicle for attacking white-collar crime reflects long-standing customs of the federal legal
apparatus. These customs include investigations of alleged wrongdoing by
federal law-enforcement agencies and grand juries, criminal indictments,
and, in many instances, trials of members of political and business elites.[50]
These activities tend to demonstrate the efficacy of law and its administration. Moreover, the reliance on statutes and the precedent value of case law
maintains the traditions of the legal order and contributes to its legitimacy
by reaffirming the formally rational character of law.

In like fashion, the reorientation within academic criminology has revitalized ideals and customs that were traditional in that profession. Research on white-collar crime is consistent with the predominant liberal ideology of the discipline and actually resolves a dilemma with respect to this
ideology. This dilemma involved a contradiction between two strands of
criminology: one was rather legalistic and informed by the notion of equal
justice and the responsibility of rational agents; the other was a sometimes
sympathetic, sometimes scientific criminology that focused on the "needs"
of individual offenders and on the conditions that gave rise to those "needs"
and mitigated an offender's culpability. As we have noted, contemporary
criminology has been informed by the tenets of a positivism that is both
humanitarian and scientific. Once these tenets were discredited, at least
partially, criminology was confronted by an intellectual gap. Research into
white-collar crime has filled this gap by revitalizing the legalistic variant of

criminology. This focus redirects the research agenda to the crimes of political and business leaders, who are the epitome of rational and responsible
agents. Moreover, these offenders merit little sympathy because their
"needs" have been satisfied more than adequately through their positions of
privilege. Thus ideological tension within the discipline is resolved while the
predominant liberal ideology is maintained.

At the same time, the reorientation maintains the customs of the profession. In the nascent days of the discipline, Edwin Sutherland, perhaps the
dean of U.S. criminologists in this century, defined criminology as a body of
knowledge about crime as a social phenomenon that addressed the process
of making laws, breaking laws, and reactions to the breaking of laws.[51] His
definition appeared in an early criminology textbook, but it endured, and
over the years established the agenda for social scientists engaged in criminological research. Several decades ago that agenda included white-collar
crime research by Sutherland and others. However, interest in the topic
waned rather quickly in favor of research on more conventional forms of
crime; even so, the recent proliferation of white-collar crime research constitutes a refurbished area of inquiry, and is consistent with the orienting
themes of the discipline that Sutherland developed half a century ago. In a
sense, the current focus on white-collar crime maintains the traditional
dogma, myth, and ritual of the criminological enterprise.

Some researchers focus on the process of law-making with respect to
white-collar crime. Their work addresses such issues as the distinction between civil and criminal wrongs and the attempt to redefine as criminal certain behaviors of political and business leaders.[52] They also direct attention
to the related matter of who is a criminal, an important question in light of
the prior reluctance to apply criminal definitions to the behavior of elites.
Sutherland originally introduced this topic during criminology's earlier consideration of white-collar crime.[53]

A second line of criminological inquiry pertains to lawbreaking and includes a consideration of the nature, extent, and costs of white-collar crime,
as well as theoretical explanations. These studies often address traditional
issues such as the rationality and hence the responsibility of offenders, and
they are consistent with an important theme in criminological research, the
etiology of criminal behavior.[54]

Finally, criminologists discuss the reactions to lawbreaking by elites. This
topic ranges from a discussion about how the legal apparatus might prevent
these crimes to a consideration of the standard philosophical justifications
for the criminal sanction and their applicability to white-collar crime and
criminals.[55]

These studies represent only a sample of a much larger body of work that
reflects the expansion of criminology into an area virtually neglected over

the past several decades. This research has contributed valuable data about white-collar crime and has helped to broaden thinking about the true nature of America's crime problem. Accordingly, our intention is not to denigrate these studies but to show that they are informed by the heritage of criminological research.

Thus criminology, like the legal order, experienced a professional reorientation that rendered white-collar crime a salient topic. Like the lawyers, criminologists responded in a manner that was consistent with their profession and actually reinforced the ideals and customs. They contributed to a social movement against white-collar crime while revitalizing traditional ideologies of the legal order and academic criminology.

The Symbolic Movement Against White-Collar Crime

We situate the recent prosecutorial and research activity within the framework of a general social movement, and, more specifically, as a professional reorientation that has taken place in response to a crisis of legitimacy. The prosecution of political and business elites and the development of a research agenda that addresses their crimes give the appearance of a responsible new direction that shores up the legitimacy of the legal order and academic criminology.

This activity is predictable when we consider the literature that pertains to such a crisis within the legal system. The literature suggests that three potentially irreconcilable demands confront the legal system in a crisis situation: it must preserve the social order, uphold the formally rational character of law, and maintain the integrity of the legal apparatus in an organizational sense. Reform-oriented and/or prosecutorial activities are likely attempts at resolution.[56] Prosecutions reaffirm the legal order when the problem of individual or group morality arises. Reform activity occurs when the threat to legitimacy reaches a more general level, such as when the credibility of an entire institution or an academic discipline is called into question.

Though these activities are predictable, we do not claim that they have produced widespread substantive reform either in the affected professions or in the larger society. With respect to the prosecutions, Katz has noted that *institutional* reforms were never sought; our designation of all this activity as a "general" social movement is compatible with his position. The movement against white-collar crime consists of a set of relatively uncoordinated activities that evidence almost no agenda for organized social reform. Moreover, the character of these activities, especially the revitalization of the ideals and customs of the legal order and academic criminology, tends to work against genuine social reform in theory and practice.

Consider the legal apparatus. During the 1970s, when white-collar crime became a salient political issue, federal prosecutions against white-collar criminals increased significantly. Yet the ideals and customs of the legal order are such that these crimes were actually depoliticized by the operation of the legal system. The ideology of equal justice and the customary case motif direct the law's attention to the *individual* white-collar criminal and away from the organizational dimension of such crimes and the political economy that encourages them. Even when the prosecutions are successful, the individualistic focus detaches white-collar criminality from the very features that produce it.

We may also question the commitment of the federal legal apparatus to address the crimes of the affluent. Because of vestigial issues related to the definition of crime, the sophistication of the crimes, or the continuing power that privilege begets, political and business elites too often remain immune to criminal prosecutions, both personally and organizationally. The difficulty may simply be a lack of resources; although the number of cases reported may be increasing, data indicate that the Justice Department still devotes relatively little of its budget to combating white-collar crime.[57]   On the other hand, the problem may be definitional. According to the definition proffered by the U.S. Attorney General in 1980,

> White-collar offenses shall constitute those classes of non-violent illegal activities which principally include traditional notions of deceit, deception, concealment, manipulation, breach of trust, subterfuge or illegal circumvention.[58]

This definition is obviously so broad that it permits nonelites to be prosecuted for white-collar offenses, and thus siphons off the scarce resources that might otherwise be directed against the crimes of the powerful. Then again, the problem may reflect an organizational dimension. With respect to corporate crime, for example, a variety of organizational pressures encourage employees to violate the law to further corporate interests. Corporate leaders, however, may be able to arrange internal matters so that these pressures, the violations they compel, and prosecutions for the violations are greatest at lower levels of the corporation.[59]   Corporate interests and corporate leaders are thereby protected by these organizational dynamics.

For whatever reasons, only a relatively small proportion of all federal prosecutions are undertaken against high-level executives or corporations for white-collar crime; when such prosecutions do occur, the record reveals some interesting patterns that are at variance with political rhetoric.

Notwithstanding an occasional "big-name" defendant (such as E.F. Hutton) much of the activity that U.S. attorneys label "white-collar crime prosecution" is not directed at executives but at lower-echelon personnel who do not enjoy the protection of political or economic power.

There is some evidence, then, that nonelite persons are more likely than elites to be charged with white-collar crimes. The data indicate further that the nonelite are typically prosecuted for offenses such as mail fraud or embezzlement, suggesting that the legal order is still concerned primarily with crimes that are indiviualistic or committed against the corporation, and not those committed for or by it.[60] This pattern of enforcement may be due to a cyclical downswing in the economic sector and the response of corporate leaders to this adversity. During economic troughs, such as those which occurred during the last decade or so, we might expect corporate leaders to push for the prosecution of these individualistic crimes because they are costly at a time when corporations cannot afford them. Further, we might expect the executives of powerful corporations to advocate more stringent enforcement against white-collar and corporate crime as a strategy for harassing competitors who are less secure economically and must commit such crimes to survive. A similar argument is advanced with respect to corporate support for regulatory legislation. Several authorities have suggested that it is usually the more powerful corporations that endorse regulatory legislation because they are better able to weather costly constraints than their less advantaged competitors.[61]

In any case, it is the nonelite who traditionally have borne the brunt of federal law enforcement. Prosecutions for "upperworld" offenses such as bribery and restraint of trade are rare, and the politicians and executives who are convicted of such violations usually receive lenient sentences.[62] Perhaps these offenders and their offenses are still viewed as qualitatively different from conventional crime and thus deserving of special consideration.[63] Alternatively, it may be argued that the criminal law is applied less frequently and less harshly to business and political leaders. The powerful members of society can offer the greatest rewards for nonenforcement and can create the greatest organizational strain when enforcement against them is attempted.[64]

Thus the legal order mounted an aggressive campaign against white-collar crime, which resulted in successful prosecutions in several sensational cases and promoted the idea that all offenders—rich and poor alike—should meet with equal justice before the law. "Things changed" in this important sense, and the notion of sanctioning elites criminally was no longer out of place. At the same time, the effect of much of this activity was more symbolic than real. Although its legitimacy was bolstered somewhat and its ideals and customs were revitalized, the legal apparatus did not undergo the kind of institutional transformation that would allow it to address elite lawlessness systematically and on a large scale. In many instances, the criminal justice system still maintains a respectful distance from the powerful and their crimes.

Similarly, academic criminology took up the topic of white-collar crime in a manner consistent with its ideals and customs. Researchers have thereby reasserted the policy relevance and hence the intellectual legitimacy of criminology while maintaining the traditional themes of the discipline. As suggested earlier, the current research on white-collar crime is consistent with the orienting themes originally proposed by Sutherland as he defined the agenda for criminological inquiry: making laws, breaking laws, and the reaction to the breaking of laws. As in the past, however, adherence to these themes tends to minimize criminology's intellectual obtrusiveness with respect to the crimes of the powerful.

Despite the recent profusion of relevant research, in several significant senses the study of white-collar crime has advanced little since Sutherland introduced the topic more than forty years ago. The debate over what is a crime and who is a criminal, first addressed by Sutherland, remains unresolved, and serious definitional ambiguities about the very phenomena under investigation continue to taint much of the research.[65] The confusion is largely due to the treatment of law and lawmaking in criminological research, a matter that is especially problematic in the area of white-collar crime.

Many criminologists ascribe an almost sacred quality to law, accepting as "givens" the legal definitions of crimes that are formulated by legislators and interpreted by the keepers of the law—legal scholars and/or the legal apparatus. Many socially harmful behaviors are not crimes when performed by the powerful simply because they have never fallen within the ambit of the criminal law as defined and interpreted by the legal profession.[66] When criminologists probe deeper, they typically portray the law and its administration as a reflection of the will of the people. They explain the absence or presence of criminal responsibility for misbehavior by the elite as a function of the changing nature of moral sentiment with respect to that behavior. Certain economic wrongs, for example, are not considered criminal because they are not morally reprehensible in the eyes of the public.[67] Conversely, in the Pinto case, a definition of the Ford Motor Company "as a criminal" emerged supposedly because the moral sentiment of the public shifted.[68]

Unfortunately, this type of analysis contains a potential tautology because it neglects the degree to which public moral sentiment is shaped by official definitions of crime. Moreover, these analyses tend to be ahistorical, detaching the law and the legal apparatus that administers it from the specific sociohistorical milieu of which it is a part. Criminological studies only occasionally address the historical development of large-scale business organizations, the historical development of the legal apparatus as a part of an increasingly centralized state, or the relationship of these phenomena to conceptualizations of corporate criminal responsibility. We will explore these relationships in a later chapter.

Etiological studies often fare no better. Several researchers apply existing theoretical explanations of criminal behavior to white-collar criminality, while others pursue a traditional interest in the creation of typologies of white-collar crime and criminals.[69] Some criminologists suggest that white-collar criminality is qualitatively different from conventional criminality, a conclusion that permits the adaptation of old ideas about criminal penalties to the supposedly new topic. The traditional justifications for the criminal sanction and the extant alternatives to punishment are then considered applicable to white-collar criminals and, in some instances, to entire organizations, even though some have been largely discredited for conventional crime.[70] Finally, in spite of a growing number of important exceptions,[71] most criminologists tend to separate white-collar crime and their explanations for it from the organizational context and the political economy of which it is a part.

Thus criminologists have expanded their research agenda to include white-collar crime. This research restores the intellectual credibility of the discipline because it addresses policy matters in a long-neglected area. Criminology, however, like the legal order, responded to a crisis of legitimacy in a manner that revitalized professional ideals and customs and in important respects maintained a "business-as-usual" orientation. Today, as in the past, these ideals and customs are such that the crimes of the powerful too often remain beyond the reach of federal prosecutions and outside truly innovative and critical criminological inquiry. In this sense, the social movement against white-collar crime has been largely symbolic.

Conclusion

Over the past decade there has been an increased awareness that white-collar crime is a socially harmful phenomenon, which poses a serious problem for our society. Concern about this problem has been manifested in several ways and on a number of fronts, and we have proposed the sociological concept of a social movement as a useful vehicle for understanding the emergent concern. With such a framework, we can analyze both the movement's components and the whole that they constitute, as well as the reasons why the attack on white-collar crime has emerged at this particular time.

According to one application of this sociological framework, the recent interest in white-collar crime may be seen as a social movement that was initiated by the prosecuting attorneys who staff key federal enforcement agencies. This discussion serves as a good starting point for our own analysis, although we have modified and expanded it in several respects. First, we suggest that the concern with white-collar crime constitutes a particular type of movement—a "general" social movement. Our characterization includes the various activities that are directed against white-collar crime and, in light of their uncoordinated nature, is perhaps more consistent with the relevant academic literature on social movements. Second, we suggest that this general social movement enjoys a base of support that goes beyond the U.S. Attorneys who staff federal enforcement agencies. In addition to federal prosecutors, the movement includes contributions from state prosecutors, private attorneys, prominent citizen reformers, the media, and criminologists. Our analysis has focused on two components of this movement: the litigation against and the criminological studies of white-collar criminality. Finally, we suggest that this movement involves a professional reorientation that occurred in response to a crisis of legitimacy. A series of embarrassing disclosures concerning crimes by members of political and business elites challenged the legitimacy of both the legal order and academic criminology. In response, U.S. Attorneys and research criminologists expanded their respective agendas to include white-collar crime.

In doing so, however, they addressed white-collar criminality in a manner that was consistent with the long-standing ideals and customs of their professions. For the lawyers, this entailed a recommitment to the ideology of equal justice and the individual case motif. For criminologists it involved a reaffirmation of the dominant liberal ideology, adherence to the agenda for research prescribed years ago by noted criminologist Edwin Sutherland, and a renewed concern with the policy implications of that research. The response of the legal order and of academic criminology to the crisis of legitimacy maintained continuity with the past through the revitalization of traditions that have historically excluded a consideration of the crimes of the powerful. As a result, despite important exceptions, the bulk of federal prosecutions have been against the nonelite for individualistic crimes that victimize the organization, and criminological research has continued to detach white-collar crime from the organization and the political economy. We must conclude that, to date, the impact of the prosecutions and the research often has been more symbolic than real with respect to the crimes of the powerful.

Even so, we must not underestimate the importance of the symbolic dimension of these activities. With respect to law in general, for example, a public commitment to enforce existing statutes or a debate that attends the passage of new legislation is an intrinsically significant gesture, regardless of the consequences that actually follow. Symbolic gestures contribute to the legitimacy of the state and its laws through the affirmation of social ideals and norms and the appeasement of critics on issues of public morality.[72] The prosecutions and the research that address white-collar crime operate in this fashion. They reaffirm important ideals and convey the appearance that the legal system and the intellectual discipline that studies crime are "on the job." The symbolic dimension of these activities thereby shores up the legitimacy of the legal order and academic criminology.

Our analysis may be viewed with some disillusionment. After all, we have argued that the recent focus on white-collar crime has essentially revitalized the legitimacy of the legal order and an academic discipline through symbolic gestures. Accordingly, the ideology of equal justice will be empty rhetoric so long as most of the crimes of political and business elites remain beyond the pale of criminal law and intellectual inquiry.

Some commentators have argued that this outcome is virtually inevitable, especially with respect to corporate crime. As a social institution, law is a component of a larger political economy that places a high premium on corporate profits. As we will see in Chapter 3, corporations have historically enjoyed a virtual immunity from criminal prosecutions and from certain categories of civil cases as well. The ideology of equal justice notwithstanding, these authorities have warned that we should not expect the deployment of the criminal law to stifle business practices that contribute to profitability in the economic sector, even when the practices are socially harmful.[73]

On the other hand, there is a reason for guarded optimism in the matter of equal justice for the crimes of the powerful. To be sure, political and business leaders have enjoyed a degree of immunity from the criminal law over the years, but this immunity has always created a tension between the equal treatment that the law promises and the unequal treatment that it delivers. If perpetually unchecked, the disparity between promise and practice would threaten the neutrality and thus the legitimacy of law and, ultimately, the legitimacy of the larger social order. But the legitimacy of law has been and continues to be fairly well established, primarily because the legal order sometimes does live up to its promises. The noted historian E.P. Thompson has addressed this issue:

> The essential precondition for the effectiveness of law, in its function as ideology, is that it shall display an independence from gross manipulation and shall seem to be just. It cannot seem to be so without upholding its own logic and criteria of equity; indeed, on occasion, by actually being just.[74]

Another scholar of legal history has offered a more dramatic comment on this point, observing that the legitimacy of the law has been maintained by the occasional hanging of a nobleman.[75]

The point here is that the legitimacy of law is sometimes called into question, especially today, in light of the publicity that surrounds the crimes of political and business elites. Research into white-collar crime and prosecutions against a few "big-name defendants" are manifestations of this concern, the equivalent of occasionally hanging a nobleman. These activities, however, are merely a response to—not a resolution of—a much deeper crisis of legitimation. As we noted earlier, this issue is increasingly problematic because the modern state has continually extended its sphere of authority into all realms of social existence, thereby creating greater demands for legitimation.

As Habermas has observed, formally democratic institutions and procedures are defining features of the modern state, a political apparatus that enjoys generalized mass loyalty by virtue of the universal rights of citizenship it has granted.[76] The ideological foundation of these rights is the notion of equal justice, a popular ideology to which the public is strongly committed. Given the strength and diffusion of this commitment throughout society, we should anticipate that the public will demand the fulfillment of these ideological promises, especially those such as equal justice, which are the essence of the state's claim to legitimacy.[77] Because the law is an important institution for effectuating such ideological promises, it is an essential component of the state's legitimation, but only so long as it operates effectively and within prescribed ideological bounds. In other words, the state must use the law to regulate socially harmful behavior regardless of who commits it, at least some of the time.

Throughout this analysis we have emphasized that the recent prosecutorial and research activity is part of a general social movement against white-collar crime. The defining characteristics of all such movements are a background shift in cultural values, a generalized sense of injustice, and the pursuit of equal justice. Although these concerns remain diffuse and largely symbolic, they are clearly on the agenda of public problems. Public-opinion research now suggests that people are concerned about white-collar crime and, more specifically, about corporate criminality. Other surveys indicate that the prestige of corporate executives has declined; that the public is more aware than ever that corporate criminality is socially harmful behavior, often in a physical sense; and that the public is increasingly intolerant of such conduct. Thus we note a shift in cultural values about corporate misbehavior, and, at the same time, a strong commitment to equal justice as the ideological underpinning of the legal order.

These considerations suggest the need for a balanced perspective on the relationship between corporations and the criminal law. On the one hand, we must acknowledge that the movement against white-collar crime has produced little fundamental institutional reform. Moreover, despite the increasing publicity given to corporate misconduct, only a fraction of the defendants who come before our courts wear white collars; fewer still are drawn from the upper echelon of corporate America. Corporations as criminal defendants remain the exception, not the rule. Therefore we have been careful not to claim too much from the movement against white-collar crime. Yet it seems equally incorrect to dismiss as inconsequential the corporate crime prosecutions that have occurred, or the social conditions that stimulated them. As we will argue in later chapters, this emergent climate has made prosecutions like Ford's possible to an unprecedented degree, thereby enhancing future efforts to bring corporations within the reach of criminal law. The attack on corporate crime will encounter substantial obstacles and meet with uneven success, but we anticipate that it will continue to grow, perhaps markedly and in important ways, in the time ahead.

Notes

1   These headlines are taken from the following sources: "Crime in the Suites: A Spree of Corporate Skulduggery Raises Questions and Concerns," *Time* (June 10, 1985), p. 56; "Execs Sentenced to 25 Years in Corporate Murder," *Chicago Sun-Times* (July 2, 1985), p. 2; "Coliseum Official Put on Probation," *Cincinnati Post* (February 25, 1983), p. 1; "Stealing $200 Billion 'The Respectable Way,'" *U.S. News and World Report* (May 20, 1985), p. 83; "Highway Robbery: The War on Big Riggers," *U.S. News and World Report* (February 16, 1981), p. 49; "Corporate Crimes: Criminal Prosecution Gaining More Favor," *Chicago Tribune* (September 9, 1984), Section 7, p. 1; "Pin Stripes to Prison Stripes," *Industry Week* (August 4, 1986), pp. 54-55; "Justice for White-Collar Crooks," *Chicago Tribune* (December 3, 1976); "Public Gives Executives Low Marks for Honesty and Ethical Standards," *Wall Street Journal* (November 2, 1983), p. 31; "White-Collar Crime: Booming Again," *New York Times* (June 9, 1985), Section 3, p. 1; "Corporate '10 Most Wanted' Proposed," *Peoria Journal Star* (1979).

2   "Ford Indicted in Crash," *Peoria Journal Star* (September 14, 1978) p. C-13; Dennis Byrne, "The Pinto, the Girls, the Anger," *Chicago Sun-Times* (September 17, 1978), pp. 5, 50; "Ford Seeks Dismissal of Criminal Charges," *Peoria Journal Star* (October 25, 1978) p. D-3; Andy Pasztor, "Pinto Criminal Trial of Ford Motor Co. Opens Up Broad Issues," *Wall Street Journal* (January 4, 1980), pp. 1, 23; Dennis M. Royalty, "Ford on Trial: Pinto Death Case About to Begin," *Indianapolis Star* (December 2, 1979), Section 3, p. 15; "Three Cheers in Dearborn," Time (March 24, 1980), p. 24.

3   Ralph Turner and Lewis M. Killian, *Collective Behavior*. Second edition. Englewood Cliffs, N.J.: Prentice-Hall, 1972, p. 246; Lewis Killian, "*Social Movements*: A Review of the Field," in R. Evans (ed.), Social Movements. Chicago: Rand McNally, 1973, p. 16

4   Roberta Ash Garner, *Social Movements in America*. Second edition. Chicago: Rand McNally, 1977, p. 1.

5   Herbert Blumer, "Collective Behavior," in A. M. Lee (ed.), *Principles of Sociology*. New York: Barnes and Noble, 1951, pp. 200-202.

[6] Ralph Turner, " The Public Perception of Protest," *American Sociological Review* 34 (December 1969), p. 819; Turner and Killian, *Collective Behavior*, p. 259.

[7] Blumer, "Collective Behavior," p. 212; Garner, *Social Movements in America*, p. 6.

[8] Blumer, "Collective Behavior," p. 202.

[9] *Ibid.*, pp. 200-201.

[10] *Ibid.*, p. 202.

[11] Jack Katz, "The Social Movement Against White-Collar Crime," in Egon Bittner and Sheldon Messinger (eds.), *Criminology Review Yearbook*. Volume 2. Beverly Hills, Ca.: Sage Publications, 1980, p. 162.

[12] *Ibid.*, p. 161.

[13] *Ibid.*, p. 167.

[14] Howard Becker, *Outsider: Studies in the Sociology of Deviance*. New York: The Free Press, 1963, pp. 147-163.

[15] Katz, "The Social Movement Against White-Collar Crime," pp. 165-169

[16] Francis T. Cullen, Bruce G. Link, and Craig W. Polanzi, The Seriousness of Crime Revisited: Have Attitudes Toward White-Collar Crime Changed?" *Criminology* 20 (May 1982), pp. 83-102.

[17] Harry M. Caudill, "Manslaughter in a Coal Mine," *The Nation* 224 (April 23, 1977), p. 224; L. Kramer, "Nader: Vega's Gas Tank as Dangerous as Pinto's," *Washington Post* (August 31, 1978), p. D-5.

[18] Upton Sinclair, *The Jungle*. New York: Signet Classic, 1905.

[19] Mark Dowie, "Pinto Madness," *Mother Jones* 2 (September-October 1977), pp. 18-32; Jack Anderson and Les Whitten, "Auto Maker Shuns Safer Gas Tank," *Washington Post* (December 30, 1976), p. B-7.

[20] Ralph Nader, *Unsafe At Any Speed: The Designed-In Dangers of the American Automobile*. New York: Grossman, 1965; Ralph Nader and

Mark Green, "Crime in the Suites: Coddling the Corporations," *New Republic* 166 (April 29,1972), pp. 18-21; Ralph Nader and Mark Green, *Corporate Power in America*. New York: Grossman, 1973.

[21] Francis T. Cullen, William J. Maakestad, and Gray Cavender, "The Ford Pinto Case and Beyond: Corporate Crime, Moral Boundaries, and the Criminal Sanction," in Ellen Hochstedler (ed.), *Corporations as Criminals*. Beverly Hills: Sage Publications, 1984, pp. 107-130

[22] Turner and Killian, *Collective Behavior*, p. 265.

[23] Blake McKelvey, *American Prisons: A Study in American Social History Prior to 1915*. Revised and reprinted edition. Montclair, N.J.: Patterson Smith, 1968 (originally published in 1936), pp. 118-119.

[24] John Galliher, "The Life and Death of Liberal Criminology," *Contemporary Crises* 2 (1978).

[25] Katz, "The Social Movement Against White-Collar Crime," pp. 167-175.

[26] Blumer, "Collective Behavior," pp. 172-200; Turner, "The Public Perception of Protest," p. 819; Turner and Killian, *Collective Behavior*, p. 259.

[27] David O. Friedrichs, "The Legitimacy Crisis in the United States: A Conceptual Analysis," *Social Problems* 27 (June 1980), pp. 540-541.

[28] Randall Collins, "Weber's Last Theory of Capitalism: A Systematization," *American Sociological Review* 45 (December 1980), pp. 925-928.

[29] David Trubeck, "Max Weber on Law and the Rise of Capitalism," *Wisconsin Law Review* (Summer 1972), pp. 715-729; David Trubeck, "Complexity and Contradiction in the Legal Order: Balbus and the Challenge of Critical Social Thought About Law," *Law and Society Review* 11 (Winter 1977), pp. 538-541.

[30] Jurgen Habermas, *Legitimation Crisis*. Boston: Beacon Press, 1975, pp. 69-72.

[31] For a more detailed discussion of the fiscal crisis that confronts the state, see James O'Connor, *The Fiscal Crisis of the State*. New York: St. Martin's Press, 1973.

[32] Habermas, *Legitimation Crisis*, p. 69.

[33] *Ibid.*, pp. 47-48; Thomas McCarthy, The *Critical Theory of Jurgen Habermas.* Cambridge: MIT Press, 1978, p. 368.

[34] Joseph R. Gusfield, *The Culture of Public Problems: Drinking-Driving and the Symbolic Order.* Chicago: University of Chicago Press, 1981, p. 10

[35] Blumer, "Collective Behavior" p. 200.

[36] James Q. Wilson, *Thinking About Crime.* New York: Vintage Books, 1975, pp. 52-57.

[37] *Ibid.*, pp. 58-70.

[38] Ian Taylor, Paul Walton, and Jock Young, *The New Criminology: For a Social Theory of Deviance.* New York: Harper and Row, 1973, pp. 268-281.

[39] David M. Gordon, "Capitalism, Class, and Crime in America," *Crime and Delinquency* 19 (April 1973), pp. 163-186; Steven Spitzer, "Toward a Marxian Theory of Deviance," *Social Problems* 22 (June 1975) pp. 638-651

[40] William Chambliss, "Toward a Political Economy of Crime," *Theory and Society* 2 (Summer 1975), pp. 149-170.

[41] Ian Taylor, *Law Against Order: Arguments for Socialism.* London: Macmillan, 1981; Stanley Cohen, "Guilt, Justice and Tolerance: Some Old Concepts for a New Criminology," in D. Downes and P. Rock (eds.), *Deviant Interpretations.* New York: Barnes and Noble, 1979, pp. 20-49.

[42] David Matza, *Becoming Deviant.* Englewood Cliffs, N. J.: Prentice-Hall, 1969.

[43] Frederick Kellog, "From Retribution to Desert," *Criminology* 15 (August 1977), pp. 179-192.

[44] Edwin Schur, *Radical Non-Intervention: Rethinking the Delinquency Problem.* Englewood Cliffs, N.J.: Prentice-Hall, 1973.

[45] Norval Morris, *The Future of Imprisonment.* Chicago: University of Chicago Press, 1974.

[46] Anthony F.C. Wallace, *Religion: An Anthropological View*. New York: Random House, 1966, p. 30.

[47] Anthony F.C. Wallace, "Revitalization Movements," *American Anthropologist* 58 (March 1956).

[48] Wallace, *Religion: An Anthropological View*, pp. 210-211.

[49] Katz, "The Social Movement Against White-Collar Crime," p. 165.

[50] *Ibid.*, pp. 167-169.

[51] Edwin Sutherland, *Principles of Criminology*. Second edition. Philadelphia: Lippincott, 1934, p. 3.

[52] Christopher D. Stone, *Where the Law Ends: The Social Control of Corporate Behavior*. New York: Harper and Row, 1975; John E. Conklin *"Illegal But Not Criminal": Business Crime in America*. Englewood Cliffs, N.J. : Prentice-Hall, 1977; Stephen Blum-West and Timothy Carter, "Bringing White-Collar Back In: An Examination of Crimes and Torts," *Social Problems* 30 (June 1983), pp. 545-554.

[53] Leonard Orland, "Reflections on Corporate Crime: Law in Search of Theory and Scholarship," *American Criminal Law* Review 17 (1980), pp. 501-520.

[54] Stephen Yoder, "Criminal Sanctions for Corporate Illegality," *Journal of Criminal Law and Criminology* 69 (Spring 1978), pp. 40-58; John Braithwaite, "Inegalitarian Consequences of Egalitarian Reforms to Control Corporate Crime," *Temple Law Quarterly* 53 (1980), pp. 1127-1146.

[55] John Braithwaite and Gilbert Geis, "On Theory and Action for Corporate Crime Control," *Crime and Delinquency* 28 (April 1982) pp. 292-314; John Braithwaite, "The Limits of Economism in Controlling Harmful Corporate Conduct," *Law and Society Review* 16 (No. 3, 1981-1982), pp. 481-504; M. David Ermann and Richard Lundman, *Corporate Deviance*. New York: Holt, Rinehart and Winston, 1982.

[56] Issac Balbus, *The Dialectics of Legal Repression: Black Rebels Before the American Criminal Courts*. New York: Russell Sage Foundation, 1973, p. 24; David O. Friedrichs, "The Law and the Legitimacy Crisis: A Critical Is-

sue for Criminal Justice," in R.G. Iacovetta and D.H. Chang (eds.), *Critical Issues in Criminal Justice*. Durham: Carolina Academic Press, 1979, pp. 300-301.

[57] David Simon and Stanley Swart, "The Justice Department Focuses on White-Collar Crime: Promises and Pitfalls," *Crime and Delinquency* 30 (January 1984), p. 110.

[58] Quoted in Simon and Swart, "The Justice Department Focuses on White-Collar Crime: Promises and Pitfalls," p. 109.

[59] John Braithwaite, "Paradoxes of Class Bias in Criminological Thinking," in Harold E. Pepinsky (ed.), *Rethinking Criminology*. Beverly Hills: Sage Publications, 1982.

[60] John Hagan, Ilene Nagel (Bernstein), and Celesta Albonetti, "Differential Sentencing of White-Collar Offenders," *American Sociological Review* 45 (October 1980), pp. 814-815.

[61] Kevin Wright, "Economic Adversity, Reindustrialization, and Criminality," in K. Wright (ed.), *Crime and Criminal Justice in a Declining Economy*. Cambridge: Oelgeschlater, Gunn and Hain, Publishers, 1981, p. 61; Lawrence Friedman and Jack Ladinsky, "Social Change and the Law of Industrial Accidents," *Columbia Law Review* 67 (January 1967); James Inverarity, Pat Lauderdale, and Barry Feld, *Law and Society: Sociological Perspectives on Criminal Law* Boston: Little, Brown and Company, 1983, pp. 216-237.

[62] John Hagan and Ilene Nagel, "White-Collar Crime, White-Collar Time: The Sentencing of White-Collar Offenders in the Southern District of New York," *American Criminal Law Review* 20 (No. 2, 1982), pp. 259-301.

[63] Kenneth Mann, Stanton Wheeler, and Austin Sarat, "Sentencing the White-Collar Offender," *American Criminal Law Review* 17 (Spring 1980), pp. 479-500.

[64] William Chambliss and Robert Seidman, *Law, Order, and Power*. Reading, Ma.: Addison-Wesley Publishing, 1971, p. 266.

[65] See Orland, "Reflections on Corporate Crime: Law in Search of Theory and Scholarship"; Hagan, Nagel (Bernstein), and Albonetti, "Differential Sentencing of White-Collar Offenders," pp. 806-807; Ronald L. Kramer,

"Corporate Criminality: The Development of an Idea," in Ellen Hochstedler (ed.), *Corporations as Criminals*. Beverly Hills: Sage Publications, 1984.

[66] See Orland, "Reflections on Corporate Crime: Law in Search of Theory and Scholarship"; Jerome Hall, *Principles of Criminal Law*. Indianapolis: Bobbs-Merrill, 1947, pp. 247-257; Nancy Frank, "From Criminal to Civil Penalties in the History of Health and Safety Laws," *Social Problems* 30 (June 1983), pp. 532-544.

[67] Sandford Kadish, "Some Observations on the Use of Criminal Sanctions in Enforcing Economic Regulations," *University of Chicago Law Review* 30 (Spring 1963), pp. 423-449; Harry Ball and Lawrence Friedman, "The Use of Criminal Sanctions in the Enforcement of Economic Legislation: A Sociological View, *Stanford Law Review* 17 (January 1965), pp. 197-223.

[68] Victoria Lynn Swigert and Ronald A. Farrell, "Corporate Homicide: Definitional Processes in the Creation of Deviance," *Law and Society Review* 15 (No. 1, 1980-1981), pp. 161-182.

[69] Michael Hughes and Timothy Carter, " A Declining Economy and Sociological Theories of Crime: Predictions and Explications." in Kevin Wright (ed.), *Crime and Criminal Justice in a Declining Economy*. Cambridge: Oelgeschlager, Gunn and Hain, Publishers, 1981; Herbert Edelhertz, "White-Collar and Professional Crime: The Challenge for the 1980s," *American Behavioral Scientist* 27 (September 1980), pp. 109-128.

[70] Yoder, "Criminal Sanctions for Corporate Illegality"; Braithwaite and Geis, "On Theory and Action for Corporate Crime Control"; Brent Fisse, "Community Service as a Sanction Against Corporations," *Wisconsin Law Review* (No. 5, 1981), pp. 970-1017.

[71] Laura Shill Schrager and James F. Short, Jr., "Toward a Sociology of Organizational Crime," *Social Problems* 25 (April 1978), pp. 407-419; Harold C. Barnett, "Corporate Capitalism, Corporate Crime," *Crime and Delinquency* 27 (January 1981, pp. 4-23; David R. Simon and D. Stanley Eitzen, *Elite Deviance*. Boston: Allyn and Bacon, 1982; Albert Cohen, "Criminal Actors: Natural Persons and Collectives." Unpublished manuscript.

[72] Joseph R. Gusfield, "Moral Passage: The Symbolic Process in Public Designations of Deviance," *Social Problems* 15 (Fall 1967), pp. 176-178.

[73] Barnett, "Corporate Capitalism, Corporate Crime"; Ball and Friedman, "The Use of Criminal Sanctions in the Enforcement of Economic Legislation: A Sociological View," p. 199; H. J. Glasbeek, "Why Corporate Deviance Is Not Treated As Crime: The Need to Make 'Profits' a Dirty Word," *Osgood Hall Law* Journal 22 (Fall 1984), pp. 393-439.

[74] E.P. Thompson, *Whigs and Hunters: The Origin of the Black Act.* New York: Pantheon Books, 1975, p. 263.

[75] Douglas Hay, "Property, Authority and the Criminal Law," in D. Hay, P. Linebaugh, J. Rule, E.P. Thompson, and C. Winslow (eds.), *Albion's Fatal Tree: Crime and Society in Eighteenth-Century Europe.* New York: Pantheon Books, 1975, pp. 33-34.

[76] Habermas, *Legitimation Crisis*, p. 36.

[77] Frances Fox Piven and Richard A. Cloward, *The New Class War: Reagan's Attack on the Welfare State and Its Consequences.* New York: Pantheon Books, 1982, p. 128.

Chapter 2
The Corporate
Crime Problem

"How lawless are big companies?" asked a 1980 *Fortune* article. *Fortune*'s investigation of legal infractions by 1,043 major corporations revealed an unsettling answer: "A look at the record since 1970 shows that a surprising number of them have been involved in blatant illegalities." Aside from firms whose violations escaped detection by government enforcement officials, fully 11 percent of the businesses in the sample committed at least "one major delinquency," a statistic that *Fortune* termed "pretty startling."[1]

These observations and those offered by other commentators suggest that corporate lawlessness is extensive. But are the crimes of "big companies" costly? Too often, the actual consequences of this type of illegality are concealed from the public. Yet the veil of corporate secrecy is lifted on special occasions, such as the recent scandal at E.F. Hutton and the notorious electrical-equipment conspiracy of the 1950s, and we gain a fuller view of the true costs of crime in the business world. The results of these exposés have generally proved to be disquieting.

The production of the Pinto automobile by the Ford Motor Company presents such an opportunity to look into the corporate world. In the chapters that follow, we will see what happens when the fourth largest corporation in the world markets a product that many allege to be dangerously defective. We will also explore the successes and failures surrounding subsequent attempts to sanction Ford criminally, and then evaluate how this case sheds light on the central controversies involved in the control of corporate lawlessness.

In this chapter we present a general overview of the "corporate crime problem," with emphasis on the ways in which business entities may illegally force financial burdens upon society, damage the social fabric, and physically assault unsuspecting citizens (as some believe was the case in the Ford Pinto incident). We do not intend to paint a uniformly dark picture of all business enterprises; such a picture would weaken credibility by ignoring the complexity and variability of economic undertakings and would suffer the shortcomings of any stereotype. Nonetheless, the customary manner of thinking about crime has often blinded the public to the full dimensions—especially the violent aspects—of America's corporate crime problem. Therefore this chapter will seek to broaden the traditional view of "serious crime" by showing the magnitude of the costs incurred when corporations move beyond prevailing legal boundaries.

Before embarking upon this task, we will set a context for our discussions by considering two issues. First we will explain what we mean when we call corporate behavior "criminal." Then we will examine how corporate illegality (as noted above) frequently remained a secondary concern—particularly before the recent events that brought corporations under attack—when criminologists and other citizens contemplated the problem of crime in America.

Corporate Crime as White-Collar Crime: Definitional Issues

In the 1940s, Edwin Sutherland introduced and popularized the concept of "white-collar crime."[2] This idea had the revolutionary effect of sensitizing subsequent students of crime and, ultimately, those outside academic circles to a range of behaviors that had previously escaped careful scrutiny: the illegal activities of the affluent.[3]

Although Sutherland's own research concentrated on the pervasiveness of the unlawful actions of corporations, he proposed a considerably more comprehensive definition of white-collar criminality, which encompassed all offenses "committed by a person of respectability and high social status in the course of his occupation."[4] The very breadth of this definition has been a source of the concept's vitality and ambiguity. The major advantage is that it prompted social commentators to investigate the full range of criminal offenses emanating from the occupations of the rich, including crimes by politicians, crimes by professionals such as physicians, tax cheating, crimes against businesses, such as employee theft or embezzlement, and crimes by corporate organizations themselves. On the other hand, while these various offenses share a common thread—if nothing else, they fall well outside traditional categories of street crime—important qualitative differences exist among them. Thus the use of a catchall term like "white-collar crime" risks obscuring the differences among many of these offenses: for example, the act of a physician who defrauds the government by billing for false Medicaid payments and that of a multimillion-dollar corporation that markets a defective product. Therefore, when analysts speak generally of "white-collar crime," it is not always clear what they have in mind.[5]

In short, Sutherland's selection of the term "white-collar" to demarcate a realm of occupational behavior was not free of limitations. More controversial, however, was his tendency to characterize the occupational transgressions of the upperworld as "crime." The controversy centered around the reality that most of the actions subsumed under Sutherland's concept of white-collar crime are not often defined by the state as criminal. Although important changes are now taking place, criminal sanctions traditionally have been employed only sparingly in the social control of the business, political, and professional deviance of the affluent. Civil courts, where monetary damages can be won, and administrative agencies, which develop and enforce regulations for industry, have been relied upon to control the occupational behavior, particularly the corporate behavior, of those in the upper strata. Critics have thus questioned whether the behavior included in Sutherland's definition can rightly be called "crime."[6]

The most notable criticism, because it was both an early and a forceful critique of Sutherland's view of white-collar criminality, was the 1947 essay by lawyer-sociologist Paul Tappan, titled "Who is the criminal?"[7] Tappan's chief concern was that Sutherland's concept was frequently used to encompass any means of accumulating profits that commentators might see as socially injurious or morally reprehensible, whether or not the conduct violated existing criminal codes. Therefore, whether an act was defined as a "crime" depended less upon the applicability of legal standards than upon the ideology or idiosyncracies of any given scholar. Not surprisingly, this state of affairs, in Tappan's view, caused the term "white-collar criminality" to lose its conceptual rigor and to "spread into vacuity, wide and handsome."[8] Such confusion meant that it was impossible to demarcate what constituted a "crime" among the occupationally advantaged, a condition that precluded systematic scientific investigation. For Tappan, the only solution was to restrict criminological analysis to that set of behaviors which met the criteria imposed by a narrow, legalistic definition of crime. Being more a lawyer than a sociologist, Tappan concluded, "Only those are criminals who have been adjudicated as such by the courts. Crime is an intentional act in violation of the criminal law (statutory and case law), committed without defense of excuse, and penalized by the state as a felony or misdemeanor."[9]

In reaction to Tappan and similar critics of that time, Sutherland was able to make a persuasive argument for the legitimacy of a broad definition of white-collar crime and for the inclusion of a wide range of business violations within criminology. First, he noted that the failure of criminal sanctions to regulate the behavior of the rich and powerful was largely a reflection of the elite's ability to use their position to avoid exposure to prosecution. "White-collar criminals," he stated, "are relatively immune because of the class bias of the courts and the power of their class to influence the implementation and administration of the law."[10] Thus the absence of criminal convictions among the rich cannot be taken as evidence for the absence of criminality. Second, Sutherland observed that much occupational deviance could ultimately be punished by criminal penalties. In some instances, the exercise of such penalties is contained as a possible option in the legislation proscribing particular business activities (e.g., price fixing); in others, criminal sanctions are available when injunctions to obey the rulings of an administrative agency are ignored. Sutherland included injunctions because such penalties were, by law, "part of the procedure for enforcement"; consequently their use involved "decisions that the corporations committed crimes."[11] In any event, Sutherland proposed that the appropriate criterion for determining the criminality of an act—whether by someone wearing a white collar or by someone unemployed—is its *potential* to be criminally sanctioned. "An unlawful act is not defined as criminal by the fact that it is punished," he asserted, "but by the fact that it is punishable."[12]

Our review of Sutherland's attempt to delineate a new realm of criminality serves as a necessary prelude for understanding what is implied by "corporate crime," a term often used but not always defined in the literature. Corporate crime is conceived most accurately as a form of white-collar crime; it is thus a "crime of the rich" or part of "upperworld criminality." Corporate violations, however, differ from other forms of white-collar illegality. The most distinctive feature of corporate crime is that it is *organizational*, not individualistic. This is not to suggest that corporate acts are not the product of individuals; after all, a corporation cannot do anything but through the acts of its agents. The crucial point, however, is that the individuals involved in corporate criminality are acting in behalf of the organization and not primarily for direct personal gain—although higher corporate profits, including those obtained illegally, may bring executives such personal benefits as promotions, bonuses, and salary increases. Thus an executive who participates in a price-fixing scheme to stabilize a company's market position is committing a corporate offense; an executive who embezzles funds or profits from an insider-trading scheme is not.

Corporate crimes are organizational in another sense as well: the activation of nearly all corporate policies—whether legal or illegal—requires the coordination of diverse elements within a corporation. Thus few violations of the law could be committed without the involvement (though not necessarily the culpability) of many persons within the corporate structure.[13]

Corporate illegality is an organizational phenomenon, but in what sense can it be considered a "crime"? We must emphasize again that civil courts and regulatory agencies (like the FTC or FDA) are the traditional mechanisms for the social control of corporate conduct, and that the use of criminal sanctions remains relatively infrequent. Yet, as Sutherland has reminded us, "crime" is distinguished from other types of behavior by its potential to be punished under the criminal law, not by the actual application of a sanction. Later scholars also embraced this conception of criminality, and it will serve to guide our work as well. In this study, corporate crime will be defined as *illegal acts potentially punishable by criminal sanction and committed to advance the interests of the corporate organization.*[14]

Images of the Crime Problem

The Traditional Image

Since the 1930s, the FBI has issued the *Uniform Crime Reports*, a statistical compendium that assesses both the magnitude and the changes in the nation's crime rate. In this annual report, the FBI provides special information on eight offenses that constitute the "Crime Index," the nation's measure of "serious" crime.   These offenses are murder/non-negligent manslaughter, rape, robbery, aggravated assault, larceny-theft, motor vehicle theft, and arson.

Many scholars have warned that such "official statistics" may be a major source of misconception about the nation's crime problem. One potentially significant bias concerns us here: the kinds of offenses that were selected—*and not selected*—to compose the Crime Index. The offense categories constituting the Index share a common element; they rarely include the illegalities committed in corporate surroundings. Thus we learn how many citizens were robbed or had their cars stolen each year, but we are not told how often corporations sold us defective automobiles or defrauded the public by fixing prices illegally. Even if only inadvertently, the statistical reports of the FBI send a distinct message: street crime, not white-collar or corporate lawlessness, is the real source of the crime problem in America.

Social scientists acknowledge the importance of FBI statistical indices in defining what constitutes society's crime problem. These indices have long been aired regularly in the media and used by politicians to demonstrate the urgent need to reestablish "law and order" in the nation's communities.[15] At the same time, the very selection of the offenses that appeared initially in the Crime Index represents deep-seated cultural and political conceptions about the origins of serious crime. Since the onset of immigration and the concentration of foreign and minority peoples in urban centers, slum neighborhoods have been viewed as dangerous places and their residents as a dangerous class; the poor, not the rich, are to be feared as society's criminals.

A number of ideological movements in the latter part of the nineteenth century consolidated this image in the American mind. Social Darwinist thought, which emerged in the final quarter of the 1800s, portrayed the disadvantaged as falling to the bottom levels of society because they were the least fit among the combatants in the struggle for survival. Their inability to stay within the strictures of the law was seen in turn as an outgrowth of their biological inferiority and innate moral defects.[16]

Closer to the turn of the century, the liberally oriented Progressives offered a more optimistic view of offenders, suggesting that criminality was not a product of innate and irreversible defects, but of defects in the social order, which were amenable to reforms. Yet even though criminogenic forces were no longer seen to rest within the poor themselves, they were not far removed. The origin of society's crime problem was now the pathology or disorganization of slum life. In the words of Anthony Platt, "the city was suddenly found to be a place of scarcity, disease, neglect, ignorance, and 'dangerous influences.' Its slums were the 'last resorts of the penniless and criminal'; here humanity reached the lowest level of degradation and misery."[17]

This image of the "crime problem" remains with us today; to a great degree, the public continues to embrace the view that street crimes and poor criminals pose the gravest dangers for society. This is not to say, however, that corporate or alternative forms of white-collar crime are regarded as morally neutral or acceptable behaviors. Indeed, public attitudes toward business violations are complex, changing, and frequently misread. As such, they deserve further attention.

The Public Image of the Crime Problem

Social commentators have long asserted that white-collar crime does little to excite moral indignation in the general public. As early as 1907, E.A. Ross decried the lack of concern about the evils of "new varieties of sins"—business violations—when he remarked that "in today's warfare on sin, the reactions of the public are about as serviceable as gongs and stinkpots in a modern battle."[18] Three decades later, Edwin Sutherland maintained that white-collar criminality flourishes "because the community is not organized solidly against that behavior,"[19] and in 1968 a President's Commission concluded that "the public tends to be indifferent to business crime or even to sympathize with the offenders who have been caught."[20] Even today, many commentators continue to portray the public as unconcerned about the effects of white-collar lawlessness.[21]

A growing body of research evidence, however, questions the accuracy of these and similar claims, and suggests that the public is far from indifferent to the crimes of the advantaged. Opinion surveys reveal that Americans believe that white-collar crime is widespread and should not be taken lightly.[22] Business violations that cause or threaten substantial physical injury are of particular concern and receive considerable social disapproval.[23] In these cases, there is pervasive support for punishing culpable executives; after all, citizens state, everyone should be equal before the law and should be held accountable for their misdeeds.[24]

Consistent with our discussion in Chapter 1, it also appears that concern about white-collar and corporate crime has grown in recent times. Studies indicate that the public now judges white-collar criminality to be more serious than it had in the past,[25] has lost confidence "in the people running major companies,"[26] and believes that "most American corporate executives are not honest."[27] In this context, it is not surprising that citizens see the law as an appropriate means to establish order in the business community; they support—sometimes vigorously—attempts by criminal justice officials to get tough with the occupational crimes of the rich. Indeed, this set of attitudes is one reason why we believe that, to an unprecedented degree, flagrant affronts to morality by corporations are vulnerable to criminal prosecution.

Even so, this assessment should not be taken to imply that the public now appreciates fully the complexity or the magnitude of the "corporate crime problem"; nor does it mean that people have relinquished fully their traditional ideas of where the "real crime problem" rests. Meaningful changes have occurred in public attitudes about white-collar crime, but it would be an overstatement to assert that most citizens' thinking has undergone a complete transformation.

It is necessary to distinguish between rating corporate transgressions as serious and understanding the true prevalence and costs of these offenses. Although citizens disapprove strongly of business illegalities that endanger human life and believe that the criminal law should be invoked in these instances, they typically do not know how violent such violations can be. Though public consciousness has been raised both by celebrated civil and criminal cases (such as the Ford Pinto trial) and by the prevailing social context, people still tend to assume that white-collar crime—particularly corporate crime—is primarily an economic phenomenon: occasions on which companies inflict physical harm are serious and deserve a punitive response, but they are, "after all," infrequent and episodic. The rich may use shady business means to line their pockets, the thinking goes, but it is the poor who take our lives, accost us in the streets, violate the sanctity of our homes, and make us afraid and mistrustful of strangers.[28] A 1980 newspaper editorial titled "Dangerous Criminals" is instructive:

> The idea that we should be easier on people whose crimes mark them as brutal and dangerous to life and limb is crazy. Yet, that is the notion that goes with the idea that somebody who broke the latest rule invented by the bureaucrats committed the worst crime. Even as we sizzle about the public officials grabbing for bribes in the latest FBI "Sting" exposé, we ought to face the facts. They are crooked bums but they aren't axe murderers. Neither one deserves much sympathy, perhaps, but reality demands a sane priority between people clearly capable of blow-torch murder and bloody abuse to get what they want and the guy who has a chance to pick up some extra cash effortlessly and can't resist it....We cannot afford to indulge in fantasies that tickle our prejudices. We need to be realistic about dealing with all types of crime and the record speaks for itself. Crime inflicted with a total disregard for the physical well-being of the victim are the most dangerous to us all...and those who commit such are the most persistent criminals among us. Those are proven facts—not ideological fancies.[29]

Soon we will examine exactly what are "the proven facts" and what are the "ideological fancies" surrounding the actions of those who merely "break the latest rule invented by the bureaucrats." For now it is enough to repeat that many citizens still view corporate and other types of white-collar crime as predominantly economic ventures which result in the victimization of human life only on inadvertent and exceptional occasions. By contrast, the physical harm that results from street crime is readily manifest and is thrust vividly and daily upon the public consciousness. Thus Americans fear these offenses most and tell researchers that they consider them most serious. What was true at the turn of the century remains true in large measure today: the public believes that the crimes of the poor—the "dangerous class"—and not those of the rich form the basis of America's crime problem.

If you have some reservations about this conclusion, consider the following questions. What is your immediate mental image when you are asked, "Who is the typical criminal?" Is this person middle-aged or young? White or black? Rich or poor? Does this person live in a suburb or a slum? Dress for success or have a rough look? Hold a pen or a gun? Not many of us could readily escape the powerful image of crime and criminals long entrenched in the American consciousness, and comfortably select the first alternative answer offered for each question.[30]

Revisionist Images of the Crime Problem

For many years, the great majority of criminologists joined the public in embracing the idea that crime is fundamentally a lower-class phenomenon.[31] Yet, over the years, some researchers have challenged the accepted wisdom that the poor alone constitute the criminal element in society. One notable assault on the lowerclass image of criminality was launched by researchers armed with a novel statistical tool for measuring crime rates: "self-report" scales that asked respondents to state how many times and in what ways they had violated the law. This technique, it was argued, would assess more accurately the actual amount of crime in society; it would detect a range of "hidden" illegal acts that do not appear in "official statistics" compiled by the state, either because the offenses are not reported or because the police do not arrest a suspect. Researchers also contended that the assessment would be unbiased by factors affecting the likelihood that certain offenses (e.g., rape) would be reported or by the proclivity of the police to arrest members of disadvantaged populations.

The data drawn from self-report studies painted a picture of criminality that differed dramatically from the image presented by official statistics. As a result, some commentators claim that they "can now speak of the myth of social class and criminality...class and criminality are not now, and probably never were related, at least not in the recent past."[32] Other scholars dispute this sweeping contention, claiming instead that serious street crimes and chronic street offenders are more prevalent among lower-class urban populations.[33] Nonetheless, self-report researchers have succeeded in challenging the traditional views that poverty and crime are linked ineluctably and that affluence insulates against criminal involvement. At least among academic criminologists, the lower-class image of crime has been transformed from a part of their social reality into an empirical controversy.

A second attempt to revise the perspective on the nature of the crime problem—and the one that concerns us most in this chapter—was made by social commentators like Edwin Sutherland, who sought to illuminate the criminality of business people. Where self-report research questioned the link between social class and the commission of street crime, students of business (and other occupational) offenses performed a very different function: they focused on *behaviors that were typically not prosecuted as crime or initially thought by many to constitute crime.* Under Sutherland's guidance, this diverse yet distinct realm of lawlessness would eventually come to be known as "white-collar crime."

Concerted efforts to expose the damaging and sometimes ruthless conduct of business people first emerged in the early years of this century during the Progressive Era. Termed "muckrakers" by Theodore Roosevelt,
such authors as Upton Sinclair, Lincoln Steffens, Ida Tarbell, and Charles
Russell passionately dramatized the social misery wrought by the burgeoning of large industrial enterprises and by the capitalistic obsession with
profit at the expense of human needs that guided them. Historian Vernon
Parrington captured the essence of this Progressive tradition when he observed that these social critics:

> were read eagerly because they dealt with themes that many
> were interested in—the political machine, watered stock, Stan-
> dard Oil, the making of great fortunes....There was a vast
> amount of nosing about to discover bad smells, and to sensitive
> noses the bad smells seemed to be everywhere. Evidently some
> hidden cesspool was fouling American life, and as the inquisitive
> plumbers tested the household drains they came upon the
> source of infection—not one cesspool but many, under every city
> hall and beneath every state capitol—dug secretly by politicians
> in the pay of respectable businessmen....It was a dramatic dis-
> covery and when the corruption of American politics was laid
> on the threshold of business...a tremendous disturbance re-
> sulted.[34]

It is notable that these remarks suggest a certain duality in Progressive
thinking. On the one hand, we observe a clear sensitivity to the evils of "big
business." On the other hand, as we recall from our earlier discussions,
commentators of this era—particularly those who embraced the emerging
social sciences—also did much to strengthen the idea that lower-class conditions were the prime breeding grounds of criminality. According to historian David Rothman, the link between these two positions is found in the
Progressives' belief that by instituting reforms aimed at curbing the excesses
of business, it would be possible to broaden economic opportunities and
thus facilitate the process of elevating the poor into the noncriminogenic
middle class.[35] In addition, it may be fair to conclude that the legacy of the
Progressives is twofold: they fostered mistrust simultaneously toward corporations and toward the poor. The powerful are corrupt and should be
treated with suspicion; the powerless are dangerous and should be
feared—at least until efforts to transform them into "respectable" citizens
prove successful.

Much like the Muckrakers, reformist academics who wrote in this period
also attempted to cast a spotlight on the scandals of big business. In 1912,

for example, Thorsten Veblen likened the captains of industry to the juvenile delinquent in his "unscrupulous conversion of goods and persons to his own ends, and a callous disregard of the feelings and wishes of others, and of the remoter effects of his actions."[36]

Perhaps the most forceful denunciation of corporate social irresponsibility can be found in the 1907 Progressive tract of sociologist E.A. Ross, *Sin and Society: An Analysis of Latter-Day Inequity.* Ross began his attack on corporate industrialism with the observation that new economic relationships create opportunities for "new varieties of sin;" that is, the emergence of a corporate economy opens the way for fresh approaches to victimizing the public.

Anticipating many themes that would be embellished by later critics of big business, Ross set out to define the distinctive features of this developing area of immorality. For one thing, he stated, these new sinners do not fit the traditional image of those who prey on society; they occupy positions of influence and are "respectable" members of the community. Further, in contrast to the direct interpersonal nature of crimes like robbery, the businessman plans his transgressions "leagues or months away from the evil he causes. Upon his gentlemanly presence the eventual blood and tears do not obtrude themselves....The current methods of annexing the property of others are characterized by a pleasing indirectness and refinement."[37] As a consequence, Ross believed, the public had not yet come to realize the full magnitude of the social harms emanating from the "moral insensitivity" of big business, and thus failed to display "the flood of wrath and abhorrence that rushes down upon the long-attainted sins."[38] Yet, in Ross's opinion, the harms engendered by the trickery of the industrialist class were immense, and far outweighed those stemming from the immoralities of the poor.

Ross's moral outrage led him to attach the stigma of "crime" to the new varieties of sin, and he branded as "criminaloids" the rich and powerful businessmen who preyed on the unsuspecting public. Despite their malfeasance, these criminaloids had succeeded in hiding behind the "anonymity of the corporation" and in remaining immune from punitive measures. Ross argued that only the threat of prison would constrain their behavior. Indeed, criminal sanctions should be aimed at the very top of the corporate ladder. "The directors of a company," urged Ross, "ought to be individually accountable for every case of misconduct of which the company receives the benefit, for every preventable deficiency or abuse that regularly goes on in the course of the business."[39]

Just over three decades after E.A.Ross attempted to identify as criminal the corrupt business practices of corporate leaders, Edwin H. Sutherland introduced his now-classic concept of "white-collar crime." His initial essay on this topic, titled "White-Collar Criminality" and published in 1940, began with the sentence, "This paper is concerned with crime in relation to business",[40] and over the course of the subsequent decade he continued to champion the idea that the unlawful occupational behavior of the affluent could rightly be considered criminal. Unlike Ross, however, Sutherland maintained that he was not a reformer embarking on a moral crusade against the sins of the captains of industry. His efforts, he argued, were "for the purpose of developing theories of criminal behavior"—specifically, for showing the advantages of his own theory of differential association—and "not for the purpose of muckraking or of reforming anything except criminology."[41] Some commentators have suggested that Sutherland was disingenuous in making this disclaimer; that because he was writing in an academic context, which displayed a strong preference for "value-free" social science, he saw a need to conceal his real ideological leanings in order to sustain the legitimacy of his work.[42] Whatever his motivations, Sutherland's contributions played a major role in opening up the study of crime by the rich and in revising the notion that crime is exclusively a lower-class phenomenon.

In his essay "White-Collar Criminality," Sutherland observed that existing "criminal statistics show unequivocally that crime, *as popularly conceived and officially measured*, has a high incidence in the lower class and a low incidence in the upper class" (emphasis in original).[43] Even so, he cautioned, these official statistics foster a mistaken image of the crime problem because they "are biased in that they have not included vast areas of criminal behavior of persons not in the lower class."[44] Sutherland emphasized that "one of these neglected areas is the criminal behavior of business and professional men"—a glaring omission given that the criminality of those in the upperworld "has been demonstrated again and again in the investigations of land offices, railways, insurance, munitions, banking, public utilities, stock exchanges, the oil industry, real estate, reorganization committees, receiverships, bankruptcies, and politics."[45]

Not until the end of the 1940s, however, could Sutherland present systematic empirical data aimed at verifying his earlier impressions that white-collar crime is a pervasive feature of American society. He reported the data in his 1949 classic *White Collar Crime*. Despite this broad title, Sutherland focused exclusively on corporate crime. In doing so, he completed the first and, until recently, the only large-scale quantitative study of this mode of white-collar criminality.

Sutherland analyzed the practices of the 70 largest industrial and commercial corporations in the United States, whose life span averaged 45 years. To measure the extent of their criminality, Sutherland "attempted to collect all the records of violations of law by each of these corporations, so far as these violations have been decided officially by courts and commissions."[46]   He recognized that some critics might dispute his use of the judgments passed down by civil courts and administrative regulatory agencies as evidence of criminality; yet, as discussed earlier in this chapter, he remained firm in asserting that "violations of law which were attested by decisions of equity and civil courts and by administrative commissions are, with very few exceptions, crimes."[47] Sutherland did note, however, that his use of official statistics would underestimate substantially the true prevalence of illegality in his corporate sample, because "only a fraction of the violations of law by a particular corporation result in prosecution, and only a fraction of the corporations which violate the law are prosecuted." In general, he contended, "few corporations are prosecuted for behavior which is industry-wide."[48]

Despite this observation, even the incomplete official records available to Sutherland revealed that the largest and most powerful businesses in the land operate regularly outside legal boundaries. On the basis of these records, he found that the corporations in his sample had violated the law 980 times. The data also indicated that "every one of the 70 corporations has a decision against it, and the average number of decisions is 14.0."[49] Using language traditionally reserved for discussions of street criminals, Sutherland reported that 98 percent of his sample were "recidivists," bearing "two or more adverse decisions."[50]   In keeping with the image of the street criminal, he proposed that most of the corporations could be considered "habitual criminals." After noting that states had enacted laws that "define an habitual criminal as a person who has been convicted four times of felonies," he stated, "If we use this number and do not limit the convictions to felonies, 90 percent of the 70 largest corporations in the United States are habitual criminals."[51] Even if this analysis were limited to adverse criminal decisions, the majority of the sample would still qualify as chronic offenders, in that 60 percent were "convicted in criminal courts and have an average of approximately four convictions each."[52]

As suggested earlier in this chapter, Sutherland's conceptual and empirical contributions have had the enduring effect of sensitizing criminologists to a new realm of criminality—the occupational offenses of the affluent, particularly corporate illegality—and thus of revising dramatically the image of crime. The full impact of his work, however, was not immediately apparent. Although his concept of white-collar crime quickly entered the established lexicon of criminologists and his book has been called "the publishing highlight of the 1940s in criminology,"[53] the initial influence of Sutherland's writing was not great enough to inspire a sustained paradigm for research on lawlessness in the business world. He did lay the groundwork for several notable inquiries, but most of these studies were conducted either by his students and/or shortly after his works were published. Following that initial wave of interest, a long hiatus occurred in the study of corporate criminality.[54]

Within the past fifteen years, however, interest in this subject has revived. The same social context that reshaped the public's thinking about crime—only partially, but in important ways—has influenced the thinking of the current generation of criminologists. As proposed in Chapter 1, the events of this period heightened the crisis of legitimacy in the discipline and provided a context in which insights like Sutherland's took on new meaning and life.[55] As a result, an increasing number of scholars joined the movement against white-collar crime, and turned their attention from the crimes of the poor to the crimes of the privileged.

The efforts of these scholars, as well as those of popular writers, have produced a growing body of research which has helped us to understand how, and to what extent, corporate offenses victimize citizens and contribute to the nation's "crime problem." Let us now consider these patterns of victimization in greater detail.

The Prevalence of Corporate Crime

As we noted in introducing this chapter, an investigation by *Fortune* found that 11 percent of a sample of 1,043 companies committed at least "one major delinquency" between 1970 and 1980. In 1982, *U.S. News and World Report* furnished a similar account in its article, "Corporate Crime: The Untold Story." The reporters discovered that "of America's 500 largest corporations, 115 have been convicted in the last decade of at least one major crime or have paid civil penalties for serious misbehavior." The picture was even bleaker when the conduct of the nation's twenty-five biggest companies was examined. Since 1976, seven had been convicted on criminal charges, and "seven more have been forced into settlements of major non-criminal charges—a total of 56 percent linked to some form of serious misbehavior." On a broader level, the magazine reported that from 1971 to 1980 "2,690 corporations of all sizes were convicted of federal criminal offenses."[56]

Although these figures indicate that corporate illegality is widespread, it appears that they underestimate the true prevalence of lawlessness in the business community. A more detailed search of records and rulings by a team of researchers headed by Marshall B. Clinard and Peter C. Yeager paints an even darker picture. These researchers calculated the number of criminal, civil, and administrative actions either initiated or completed by 25 federal agencies against the 477 largest publicly owned manufacturing corporations in the United States during 1975 and 1976. For these two years alone, they discovered that "approximately three-fifths of the...corporations had at least one action initiated against them."[57] When offenses were classified according to seriousness, it was found that one-fourth of the firms "had multiple cases of non-minor violations."[58] Further, some corporations were found to be far worse than others: only 8 percent of the corporations in the sample "accounted for 52 percent of all violations charged in 1975-1976, an average of 23.5 violations per firm."[59]

Clinard and Yeager's data also provide a point of comparison with the earlier research of Edwin Sutherland. As noted, Sutherland's study of 70 corporations over a 45-year period led him to conclude that nearly all corporations recidivate and that most are "habitual criminals." Clinard and Yeager reached a similar conclusion on the basis of the number of actions successfully completed (not simply initiated) against the corporations sampled, the criterion of corporate crime employed by Sutherland. In the two years covered by their study, 44 percent of the companies were repeat offenders. Moreover, "if one could extrapolate the number of sanctions over the average equivalent time period used by Sutherland, the result would far exceed his average of 14 sanctions."[60]

Finally, Clinard and Yeager were careful to observe that their statistics represent "only the tip of the iceberg of total violations."[61] Because they could not obtain access to agency records that detailed all actions taken against corporations, the researchers estimated that their figures may undercount such allegations by as much as one-fourth to one-third. In addition, the figures are based only on actions undertaken by federal agencies, and thus do not include transgressions detected by state and local administrators and investigators. Beyond these considerations, Clinard and Yeager relied on "official statistics" to measure illegal corporate behavior: actions initiated or completed by federal agencies. As noted, official statistics invariably underestimate actual violations because they do not reflect the many cases in which court or enforcement officials do not know that an offense was committed. At present we have no way of learning the exact dimensions of the "hidden delinquency" of corporations. When we realize, however, that major corporate misdeeds (such as price fixing) have continued undetected for a decade or more, we have reason to believe that the "hidden" or "dark" figures of corporate lawlessness are substantial.

In conjunction with Sutherland's *White Collar Crime*, Clinard and Yeager's research remains the most systematic analysis of illegal corporate conduct. Subsequent empirical studies, though more limited in scope, reinforce the view that law and order have yet to be established in the business community.

Some scholars, however, disagree with Clinard and Yeager's conclusions. Favoring a strict legalistic definition of corporate crime rather than the broad definition used by researchers of the Sutherland tradition, Leonard Orland questions whether Clinard and Yeager's study can be used to "support the claim of widespread corporate crime in America." He revives the Tappan-Sutherland debate and chides Clinard and Yeager for trying to assert "that corporate crime is prevalent by pointing to a large number of incidents that have nothing to do with criminal law and even less to do with crime." Instead, he says, the "tabulation of recorded crime should be the starting point for determining the actual extent of crime."[62]

Despite this criticism, Orland does not dispute that corporate crime—even when defined by strict legalistic criteria—is a frequent and troubling occurrence: he reports that for the fiscal years 1976-1979, 574 corporate criminal convictions were obtained in federal courts.[63] He also inspected filings to the Securities Exchange Commission to determine the number of corporations that had reported being involved in "material legal proceedings." Because criminal cases are not automatically "presumed to be material," SEC filings constitute only a "minimal estimate of corporate criminal convictions." Even so, for 1978 alone, "fourteen of the 100 largest industrial corporations disclosed criminal convictions to the SEC."[64]

A more recent study, in the *Academy of Management Journal*, analyzed violations of antitrust laws and the Federal Trade Commission Act by Fortune 500 companies between 1980 and 1984. Corporate illegality was measured by the "total number of instances in which firms were found guilty in litigated cases, were parties to nonlitigated consent decrees, or involved in unsettled cases in which the court found substantial merit to the charges against the cited firms." Even though the researchers investigated only a limited area of corporate conduct, they found that the companies in their sample averaged nearly one violation apiece, and "that the mean for those firms which were involved in some type of illegal activity was three acts."[65]

Recent media reports provide similar evidence of corporate lawlessness. Revelations of misconduct have become so common that, as a *Time* article titled "Crime in the Suites" observes, "the way things are going, *Fortune* may have to publish a 500 Most Wanted List"; according to another *Time* writer, "during 1985 the business pages often looked like the police blotter as investigators uncovered case after case of corporate crime."[66] Newspapers across the nation also voiced concern about the prevalence of corporate brushes with the law. The *New York Times* concluded that "a corporate crime wave appears to be exploding," while the *Peoria Journal Star* ran the headline, "Corporate Crime Was Big Business in 1985."[67] To be sure, talk of a "crime wave" may reflect the increased sensitivity of the media to corporate illegality rather than an escalation in real rates of such misdeeds.[68]

Nonetheless, it appears that in the future, the media will suffer no shortage of newsworthy material. "It's not going to stop," comments Robert W. Ogren, head of the fraud section for the Department of Justice. "We have a terrific pipeline of cases," adds Joseph H. Sherick, former chair of the Securities and Exchange Commission.[69]

Some readers might object that the data and news report cited here present an excessively bleak and potentially misleading image of corporate management—that most executives do not violate the law repeatedly, if at all. Although studies suggest that some managers' ethics in economic matters are questionable, we have no reason to believe that executives are any more or less moral than other men and women.[70] We also recognize that of the thousands who make and implement policy in a large corporation, only a few corrupt or harried executives are needed to involve a company in illegal activities.[71] Yet, even though such statements are useful in balancing our view of the corporate manager, two considerations should be kept in mind.

First, readers should be careful not to apply a double standard, even unwittingly, when examining scholarly research on unlawful conduct in the business community. "If a criminologist undertakes a study of mugging or murder," observes one scholar of corporate crime, "no one expects a 'balanced' account which gives due credit to the fact that many muggers are good family men...or perhaps generous people who have shown a willingness to help neighbors in trouble." Nonetheless, "criminologists are expected to provide such 'balance' when they study corporate criminals."[72]

Second, an evaluation of corporate lawlessness ultimately is less a matter of individual morality than of organizational consequences. It is not so important to know whether most executives abide by laws and regulations most of the time if the organizational environment produces *a rate of corporate crime that continues to exact huge and unwarranted costs from society*—and nearly every student of corporate illegality agrees that business crime is widespread and enormously costly. Later we will examine the extent of these costs, showing how corporate offenses illegally redistribute wealth, undermine the nation's moral and social fabric, and inflict injury, illness, and death of unsuspecting victims.

Before we do, however, we must address another concern. In proposing that corporate illegality is prevalent and an important dimension of the crime problem, we do not mean to imply that street crimes should be considered inconsequential. Even a brief review of the facts about street crimes is disquieting: FBI records indicate that in any given year, over one million serious violent crimes and eleven million serious property offenses are committed. In 1984 alone there were nearly 19,000 homicide victims, and over a quarter of the nation's households were "touched by a crime of violence or theft."[73]   The economic costs associated with FBI Crime Index offenses are also troubling. For these offenses (excluding homicide), the Bureau of Justice Statistics reported an annual cost of $10.9 billion in terms of "the value of cash and property taken, property damage, and medical expenses sustained."[74] Further, these figures do not capture all the hurt and social disruption caused by street crime. They do not tell of the deep and sometimes permanent psychological scars that plague crime victims; nor do they tell how fear of victimization burdens too many citizens and diminishes the quality of life in too many communities.[75]

Street crime damages property, lives, and the social fabric, but deep concern about these consequences, though deserved, should not lessen our concern about the damage inflicted by corporate lawlessness. As students of white-collar crime have warned, it is erroneous to identify the crime problem as simply a "dangerous class problem"—street crimes committed by the urban poor. We cannot afford to neglect the capacity of corporations, the most powerful actors in society, to victimize society. Although corporate crime is usually less spectacular than the typical homicide or robbery, it still does significant harm, and in many respects this harm may far exceed the damage wrought by more traditional modes of criminality. This harm can be divided into three categories: economic costs, social costs, and physical costs.

The Economic Costs of Corporate Crime

The exact costs of corporate crime are unknown, but by every indication the annual financial loss runs into many billions of dollars. Social commentators agree that the amount of money accumulated illegally by America's corporations dwarfs the amount appropriated through traditional street crimes. They agree that Sutherland may have understated this difference when he asserted that the cost of business criminality "is probably several times as great as the financial cost of the crimes which are customarily regarded as the 'crime problem.'"[76]

The tremendous economic impact of corporate lawlessness results in part from the extensive involvement of business in unlawful activities, but it is also due to the reality that the costs of even a single corporate offense are often immense. Data reported by Stanton Wheeler and Mitchell Rothman illustrate this point vividly. In an analysis of presentence reports on offenders convicted in federal courts during the fiscal years 1976, 1977, and 1978, they found that the median economic loss for "eight presumptively white-collar offenses" committed by "organizational offenders" was $387,274. By contrast, the "median take" for individuals who did not use an "organizational role" to commit white-collar offenses barely exceeded $8,000.[77]

The gap becomes even more pronounced when the losses due to organizational crimes are compared with those incurred in traditional street offenses. According to FBI statistics, in 1984 the average economic loss per crime was $609 for robbery, $900 for burglary, $376 for larceny-theft, and $4,418 for motor vehicle theft.[78] Viewed together, these data suggest, in the words of Wheeler and Mitchell, that "just as the organizational form has facilitated economic and technological development on a scale far beyond that achieved by individuals, so that form has permitted illegal gains on a magnitude that men and women acting alone would find hard to attain." They seem correct in concluding that the "organization [is] the white-collar criminal's most powerful weapon."[79]

The huge losses that may attend an individual corporate offense are evident in the fraud perpetrated by the Equity Funding Corporation of America (EFCA). Beginning in the early 1960s, the executives of EFCA introduced a novel concept called the "equity funding program." In this somewhat complex program the company offered its mostly middle-class clientele the opportunity first to purchase mutual-fund shares and then to use these shares as collateral to secure a company loan to buy an EFCA life insurance policy. The rising value of the mutual-fund shares, it was hoped, would exceed the interest due on the loan and defray at least a portion of the insurance premiums. As early as 1964, top corporate executives began to report exaggerated sales figures and profits. The purpose of this continuing fraud was to inflate artificially the value of EFCA stock, which then could be used as a resource to back the company's plans to expand by acquiring other firms. The executives were successful in achieving these goals, but a nagging question arose: How could they make up the bogus earnings they were reporting and thus balance the company's books?

Initially, loans were obtained, laundered through foreign holdings, and subsequently claimed as profits rather than liabilities. But this solution only worked temporarily because payment on the loans soon came due. As an alternative, officials legally began to "reinsure" EFCA life insurance policies with other companies. That is, in exchange for a cash settlement, EFCA in effect would sell its customers' policies to another firm. While this plan had the benefit of providing much-needed immediate income, it also engendered a new difficulty: in the years to come, EFCA would not receive premium payments from what would have been its regular policyholders; the payments would go to the reinsuring company.

Faced with a severe and unresolved cash-flow problem, the EFCA executives embarked on their most shocking scheme. They created totally fictitious policies and reinsured or sold these policies to other insurance firms.

Eventually, 50 to 100 workers were assigned to manufacture these bogus policies. Before a disgruntled ex-employee exposed this undertaking in 1973, 64,000 phony policies had been sold; EFCA executives had even "killed off" 26 "policyholders" and collected on their claims. In the end, 22 executives were convicted; most received prison sentences. The price tag for this one corporate crime proved to be an astounding $2 *billion*.[80]

E.F. Hutton's much-publicized fraud provides another example of the costs associated with corporate lawlessness. For a twenty-month period beginning in July 1980, Hutton engaged in a complex check-kiting scheme in which officials at branch offices consistently wrote checks that exceeded funds on deposit in more than four hundred commercial banks. By shifting money from one bank account to another, company executives kept their checks from bouncing. The delay between the writing of the initial checks and the time when the overdrafts were covered provided Hutton with the equivalent of interest-free loans. The total operation involved nearly $10 billion; on some days the company enjoyed $250 million in illegal "loans." In a 1985 plea bargain with the Justice Department, Hutton eventually pleaded guilty to 2,000 felony counts of mail and wire fraud, paid the maximum fine allowable under law ($2 million), and established an $8 million restitution fund to repay the banks it victimized.[81]

The banking industry itself provides still another example of the size of the transactions involved when corporations violate existing statutes. The respected First National Bank of Boston recently paid a criminal fine of $500,000 for failing to notify federal authorities of cash deposits of more than $10,000. In all, $1.2 billion in deals with foreign financial institutions went unreported. Underlying this charge was the fear that a variety of banks were "laundering" money for organized crime, that is, providing underworld offenders with easily negotiable checks and other financial instruments in exchange for large amounts of cash. The lending institutions, of course, benefit by the opportunity to use these illegal funds in investments and in interest-earning loans. Indeed, the incentives may be strong enough to make nonreporting and laundering widespread. Investigations have been launched against 140 other banks on the suspicion that they, too, failed to notify the government of substantial cash or currency transactions.[82]

As these cases indicate, corporations employ a variety of illegal means to accumulate profits. Below, we will outline five general ways in which corporations transgress the law in search of financial benefits. We do not contend that these five methods make up a complete catalog of corporate offenses, but they should serve to illustrate our proposition: the economic costs of corporate crime constitute a serious dimension of the nation's crime problem.

Financial Fraud

In her book *Wayward Capitalists*, Susan Shapiro notes that trust is the foundation of our economic system:

> Trust—the impersonal guarantee that representation of exper-
> tise or risk or financial condition can be taken at face value and
> the fiduciaries are not self-interested—is truly the foundation of
> capitalism. This taken-for-granted social technology makes it all
> work. It serves as the laxative that loosens money in the pockets
> and mattresses and bank accounts of potential investors and
> moves it along into the coffers of our nation's corporations.
> With the demise of trust, this one-and-a-half-trillion-dollar capi-
> talist fund would surely dry up.[83]

"But," Shapiro has asked, "how secure is this foundation, this premise of trust?" It would be inaccurate to assume that the foundation is crumbling; after all, most citizens learn that most of the time their money is handled honestly, even if not with the desired expertise. Violations of financial trust are sufficiently frequent, however, that confidence in the system has diminished; in notorious cases of corporate financial fraud—such as the Equity Funding and E.F. Hutton scandals discussed above—the cracks in the system's foundation widen and threaten the integrity of our economic institutions. As we have suggested, this is one reason why corporations have come under attack.

Shapiro's statistics reveal the extent of the economic costs associated with corporate financial frauds—crimes committed by or against corporations. Her research focuses on offenses investigated by the Securities and Exchange Commission, such as misrepresenting the worth of stocks or of the company issuing them, stock manipulation, self-dealing, and insider trading. Shapiro estimates that the mean cost to victims of SEC offenses was $100,000, with 19 percent of the cases incurring losses in excess of $500,000.[84] For cases that end in a criminal conviction, the costs are even higher. Recall Wheeler and Rothman's study of presentence reports on white-collar offenders in federal courts; they found that the "median take for persons convicted of SEC fraud was almost half a million dollars"; 20 percent of these cases incurred losses greater than $2.5 million.[85]

The collapse of ESM Government Securities—a small but ostensibly thriving corporation dealing in government bonds, notes, and bills—is a recent example of the possible ramifications of a securities fraud. Over a period of several years, ESM officials engaged in "repo" agreements, in which investors purchased securities with the understanding that ESM would repurchase them at a higher price on a later, specified date. Between the times of purchase and repurchase, ESM used the investors' cash to make a profit through other financial transactions. Although "repos" are legal transactions, several unprofitable deals placed ESM under great strain. To remain solvent, company executives allegedly began to sell the same securities to different investors and then bribed an accountant $125,000 to certify false ESM financial statements. When this scheme unraveled in late February and early March 1985, the news of the fraud rocked ESM's investors, which included nearly seventy cities, counties, and financial institutions. A total of $300 million could not be repaid. Beaumont, Texas lost $20 million; Toledo, Ohio lost $19 million.

The hardest hit investor was Cincinnati's Home State Savings Bank, which had engaged in "reverse repos" with ESM. In these transactions, the bank gave ESM $814 million in securities, which ESM was then free to use in its dealings with other clients; in exchange for the securities, the bank received a loan of only $670 million. Home State intended to purchase more securities with this money, sell them at a later date, repay the loan, and regain control of the securities it had put up as collateral. The demise of ESM derailed this plan; as a result, no resources were available to cover the difference between the $670 million loan and the $814 million worth of securities. Thus, Home State lost $144 million; when the loss was announced, it triggered a three-day run on deposits by worried customers, which led to the bank's collapse. Home State was rescued only when the Ohio legislature allocated over $80 million to induce another bank to purchase the troubled company. Fearing that runs on accounts would leave other thrifts in disarray, Ohio's Governor Celeste closed sixty-eight of the state's savings and loan institutions until they could acquire adequate federal insurance. Because of these new restrictions, some banks did not reopen for several months, leaving depositors either unable to use their savings accounts or with only limited access. The disclosure of ESM's improprieties resulted in numerous guilty pleas to criminal charges carrying prison terms.[86]

Of course, numerous financial frauds occur outside the securities industry. One of these, the "OPM scandal," shows vividly their potential costs. For ten years OPM Leasing Services, Inc. engaged in a variety of fraudulent schemes, engineered by the firm's two top executives, that transformed the company into one of the nation's foremost computer-leasing operations. In this complex intrigue loans were secured from several banks to finance the same leasing transaction, the value of leasing agreements was inflated, fictitious leasing agreements were created to obtain financial backing, false financial statements were prepared, and employees of clients were paid off. From 1972 to 1977, OPM received over $15 million in fraudulent loans. In the latter part of 1978, however, the funds accrued through illegal ventures began to increase rapidly, and in little more than two years, OPM used leasing agreements with Rockwell International—the giant electronics and aerospace company—to secure nearly $200 million in fraudulent loans from nineteen lending institutions. The scheme collapsed in February 1981, and as a result of subsequent prosecutions more than a dozen people employed by OPM or its clients received prison sentences; OPM's top two executives were sentenced to terms of ten and twelve years. At their sentencing the presiding judge commented, "For ten years OPM perpetrated a series of commercial frauds which in length of time and amounts stolen from their victims are without parallel in the recent annals of this court."[87]

Closing the Enterprise System

In theory, America's economic system is based on free and fair competition, but on a number of occasions corporations have endeavored to create what has been called a "closed enterprise system."[88]   Attempts to close the free market take many forms, such as monopolization, price fixing, price discrimination, and conspiring to divide markets. The goal is to limit competition, thereby inflating profits and insulating a business against the economic fluctuations that often accompany a free but less stable market. As a general category, practices aimed at closing the enterprise system are termed "antitrust violations." They are illegal because they transgress antitrust statutes—the Sherman Act, the Clayton Act, and the Federal Trade Commission Act—which prohibit business activities that restrain open competition.[89]

By all accounts, antitrust infractions are widespread and costly. In the *Fortune* article that focused on the prevalence of business lawlessness, it was reported that antitrust regulations had been violated in 60 percent of the major corporate delinquencies uncovered.[90]   Clinard and Yeager also illuminate the extensiveness of this crime: one antitrust or trade violation was detected for every three corporations in their sample. In 1975-1976, 161 actions were initiated against the 477 manufacturing firms chosen for investigation; of these, 118 were prosecuted successfully and 40 were still pending in court. In only three cases was the corporation exonerated.[91] The cost of these illegal restraints on the market is difficult to gauge precisely, but the annual price tag is high; economists' estimates range from $32 billion to as much as $265.2 billion.[92]

Price fixing has probably received the most publicity and the greatest number of criminal prosecutions, largely because the practice is ubiquitous and because the culpability of corporate officials can often be established in such conspiracies. The pervasiveness of such practices can be seen in a 1971 survey of the presidents of leading companies. Sixty percent of the respondents agreed that many fellow executives fix prices.[93]   More concrete evidence exists as well; scandals have been detected, as Ralph Nader and Mark Green observe, in "nearly every conceivable industry...from milk and bread to heavy electrical equipment, from lobster fishing and the cranberry industry to steel sheets and plumbing fixtures."[94]   Indeed, conspiring to set prices has become a way of life in some industries. In the words of one executive indicted in a price-fixing arrangement in the paper industry, "It's always been done in this business, and there's no real way of ever being able to stop it—not through Congress, not the Justice Department. It may slow for a few years. But it will always be there."[95]

These pricing arrangements are immensely costly to consumers: $35 million in overcharges in the Seattle-Tacoma area because of collusion by bread companies; losses of as much as $9 million in a three-year period, when Arkansas dairy companies set prices on milk sold to public schools and other state institutions; millions lost from a plot to rig prices of plumbing fixtures; a cost of $51 for 100 tetracycline tablets which dropped to $5 after the exposure of a price conspiracy; savings to consumers of over $225 million after a price-fixing case was launched against a blue-jeans company; a massive bid-rigging scheme by highway and paving contractors that resulted in millions of dollars in overcharges and in fines of $50 million, 400 convictions, and 141 prison sentences. Practices such as these may inflate the prices of consumer goods up to 25 percent above what they would be in a genuinely free market.[96]

Perhaps the most celebrated and revealing instance of price fixing is the "incredible electrical conspiracy."[97]   Throughout most of the 1950s, companies in the electrical industry conspired to fix the prices of as many as twelve different products. The executives who managed their company's division of heavy electrical equipment (which involved such expensive items as turbogenerators) arranged a series of clandestine meetings, in which they agreed to sell their goods at artificially inflated prices and to apportion various percentages of the market among themselves. The strategy was quite simple and highly profitable: before submitting supposedly sealed bids on potential contracts, the parties would consult to determine how high the price would be set, and which firm would be allowed to "win" the "competition." When the conspiracy was finally unmasked at the end of the decade, 45 corporate officials were fined a total of $136,000 and seven were imprisoned for a month apiece. The 29 corporations involved in the numerous price-fixing agreements received fines of nearly $2 million, with the stiffest penalties imposed on GE ($437,500) and Westinghouse ($372,500).

On the surface these economic sanctions may appear substantial, but they are insignificant in comparison to the costs of this corporate crime. According to Justice Department calculations, the prices of the nearly $7 billion worth of goods sold while the price-fixing schemes were in progress would have been 40 percent lower had a free and not a closed enterprise system been permitted to function.   The profits reaped by the corporate conspirators from these criminal arrangements—money illegally taken from the public—approached the "incredible" figure of $3 billion.[98]   Gilbert Geis, a criminologist who studied the scandal, noted that "the heavy electrical equipment price-fixing conspiracy alone involved more money than was stolen in all of the country's robberies, burglaries, and larcenies during the years in which the price fixing occurred."[99]

Letting the Buyer Beware

Corporate fraud and deception have also prevailed in the intimately associated areas of advertisement and product quality.   In a number of instances, companies have used false advertisements to induce the public to purchase goods and services that deliver few of the publicized benefits.   In an attempt to assess the legitimacy of television commercials, Ralph Nader and Aileen Cowan sent letters to 58 companies, requesting test results that documented the effects claimed for a variety of products.   No company supplied clear statistical proof to verify the quality of its merchandise.   Nader and Cowan concluded that "advertisers make vague claims which give consumers no real understanding of the products' performance, invoke clinical tests with little scientific basis to substantiate claims, and otherwise deliberately mislead and confuse the consumer."[100]

Examples of product misrepresentation are not difficult to find.   One case that received extensive publicity is General Motors' substitution of Chevrolet motors for specially advertised "Rocket V-8" engines in over 87,000 Oldsmobile cars.[101]   Another example is a citrus company's practice of adulterating orange juice and then marketing it as "100 percent pure."   The loss to consumers through excessive corporate profits from this operation approximated $1 million.[102]   In the pharmaceutical industry, the Food and Drug Administration (FDA) has indicated that as many as one-third of the American firms that manufacture prescription drugs may be defying federal regulations against false and misleading advertisements.[103]   The annual toll is considerable: consumers waste $500 million on worthless and misrepresented drugs and cures.[104]

Consumers also pay less obvious costs.   As we will discuss below, corporations have a long record of recklessly marketing dangerously defective products. Sometimes these practices result in extensive physical injuries and deaths, and exact economic costs in medical fees and lost wages.   In addition, corporations have fought attempts to recall hazardous merchandise. Although many of these companies believe that their products do not pose excessive risks to consumers, some refusals to undertake recalls stem from an excessive desire to avoid the loss of profits. Other companies have attempted to delay recalls in hopes that the products will wear out in the interim or that the replacement value of the product will be reduced. Officials at Firestone, for instance, apparently were aware that their radial "Series 500" tires were defective. An internal company memorandum noted, "We are making an inferior quality radial...subject...to belt-edge separation at high mileage."[105] Despite this information, it has been alleged that Firestone delayed recalling the dangerous radials, an action that reportedly saved the company and cost customers $1.7 million per week.[106]

Violation of Workplace Safety Standards

Later in this chapter we will discuss the extent to which corporate actions inflict injury, illness, and death on their employees. Our purpose here, however, is to note that these violent practices also incur economic costs. In 1978 alone, it was estimated that in terms of lost wages, medical expenses, insurance payments, and delays in productivity, the toll for occupational injuries was $23 billion. A Department of Labor study indicated that the cost of treating diseases caused by toxic agents in the workplace could range from $30 billion to $50 billion.[107]

Some occupational accidents and occupationally induced diseases are caused by dangers inherent in the work, some by workers' negligence, and other by misguided but presently legal corporate policies. Even so, a substantial portion of these misfortunes, and hence of the subsequent financial costs (perhaps 30 percent or more), can be attributed to corporate violations of safety standards.[108] In these instances it can be said that unlawful corporate violence contributes to the crime problem by creating unwarranted expenses for workers, their families, and other social participants (such as insurance companies or consumers, who may be forced to pay higher prices to offset these production-related costs).

Burdening the Public

Taxpayers are often called upon to subsidize the illegal pursuits of wayward corporations. When businesses fail to abide by tax laws, for example, the public must shoulder an unfair load of the tax burden. The Internal Revenue Service assesses at $1.2 billion the yearly cost in unreported corporate taxes.[109]

More recently, corporations in the defense industry have been accused of defrauding the American taxpayer. In May 1985, General Electric pleaded guilty to submitting $800,000 in false claims for payment on a Minuteman missile contract. The company was given the maximum allowable fine of $1.04 million and was forced to repay all fraudulently obtained funds.[110] GE was not the only defense contractor under fire; General Dynamics was compelled to settle $75 million in disputed overcharges stemming from practices that Navy Secretary John Lehman claimed "call into question the integrity and responsibility of the corporation."[111] Later, another investigation led to the indictment of General Dynamics officials on charges that they defrauded the government of $7.5 million from 1978 to 1981, while developing a weapons system.[112] By mid-1985, half of the 100 largest defense contractors were under criminal investigation.[113]

Another case of corporate impropriety burdening the public involves Revco Drug Stores, Inc., one of the largest discount drug chains in the country. In 1977, Revco was convicted of fraudulently obtaining more than $500,000 in Medicaid payments from the Ohio Department of Public Welfare, an agency funded by taxpayers. Revco's problems began when more than 50,000 claims were rejected by the computers at the Welfare Department. Company personnel believed that the prescriptions were filled in good faith and went unpaid only because of computer glitches. Revco officials determined, however, that the labor needed to correct and resubmit the rejected claims would cost more than the value of the claims, so they sought unlawful solutions to this dilemma. Two executives hired a clerical staff of six and instructed them to fabricate claims that would satisfy Welfare Department standards in order to obtain the reimbursements that Revco claimed it deserved. After the scheme was uncovered, the company pleaded no contest to ten counts of falsification (a first-degree misdemeanor), was fined $50,000, and agreed to pay restitution of more than $500,000. The two executives also pleaded no contest to two counts of falsification and were fined $2,000 apiece. In a footnote to this case, in 1981 a Franklin County Court granted Revco's application to have its criminal record expunged. This innovative ruling allowed a corporation to benefit from an expungement statute that had been created for individual first-time offenders.[114]

Perhaps the most devastating financial cost borne by the public is that of repairing the environmental damage caused by illegal corporate pollution. The price tag is immense, as in the case of Allied Chemical's unlawful discharge of the pesticide Kepone into the waterways of Virginia. Eventually Allied pleaded no contest to 940 counts of water pollution and was fined $13.24 million. Although this is a heavy sanction, the cleanup costs to be paid by public tax monies may total between $100 million and $2 billion.[115] If we include other items, such as lost productivity (as when commercial fishing areas are destroyed) and medical fees to treat chemically induced diseases, the yearly national price of corporate disregard for the environment is over $10 billion for water pollution[116] and another $16 billion for air pollution.[117]

Finally, we cannot ignore the enforcement costs of corporate illegality—the sums of money that must be spent to keep businesses within the confines of the law. Some commentators have argued that regulatory agencies are less effective than they might be in reducing corporate lawlessness because they are not allocated enough funds to investigate properly and to sustain a fight against wealthy corporations. Whether or not this contention is accurate, the cost of running nine major federal agencies for 1982 alone was estimated at nearly $7 billion.[118] Further, the legal expenses involved in prosecuting a corporate offense can mount endlessly. These are passed on twice to the public: directly by the government in the form of higher taxes and indirectly by the accused companies through higher prices charged to consumers.

We could provide many more examples, but the figures cited here should be sufficient to convince the reader that corporate lawlessness exacts a tremendous financial toll. The monies lost to "suite crime" far exceed the costs of "street crime," but it would be wrong to assume that this brand of white-collar illegality is "merely" or exclusively an economic problem. Corporate crime also penetrates and undermines the social order and, most significantly, does violence to the American public.

The Social Costs of Corporate Crime

When people think of the "costs of crime," they often think of losing valued property or sustaining bodily harm. Yet crime also takes its toll in another important respect; it exacts "social costs" in the sense that it weakens the social order and detracts from the quality of life that people might otherwise enjoy. These effects may be more obvious with regard to conventional street crimes than in the case of corporate lawlessness; senseless homicides or robberies are difficult to overlook and prevent citizens from enjoying the benefits of a safe community. The social costs of business crime are often (though not always) more subtle, damaging the social fabric covertly. Notably, such criminality has the capacity to erode public confidence in the economic system and to threaten the moral foundations of our society.

A number of social commentators have asserted that the debilitating impact of business crime on our nation's moral character is among the most serious costs that any crime could exact. In 1940, Edwin Sutherland observed that "the financial loss from white-collar crime, great as it is, is less important than the damage to social relations. White-collar crimes violate trust and therefore create distrust, which lowers social morale and produces social disorganization on a large scale. Other crimes produce relatively little effect on social institutions or social organizations."[119] Former Attorney General Ramsey Clark expressed similar sentiments when he commented that business crime "is the most corrosive of all crimes. The trusted prove untrustworthy; the advantaged, dishonest...As no other crime, it questions our moral fiber."[120]

The public's lack of faith in the morality of big business also spawns related social ills. By tarnishing the images of corporations, it diminishes the willingness of the public to purchase certain consumer goods and to invest needed capital in the market.[121] Further, the belief that corporate executives violate the law regularly but with impunity—the notion that the "rich get richer and the poor get prison"—may serve the less advantaged as a justification for entering crime. As one *Fortune* editor asked, "How much crime in the streets is connected with the widespread judgment that the business economy itself is a gigantic rip-off?"[122]

Corporations damage the quality of social life in still other ways. Through illegal labor practices ranging from safety violations to wage discrimination, they make the "good life" less attainable for their employees at work and at home. Through illegal pollution of air and water, they rob the general public of healthy and pleasing surroundings and of enjoyable recreational facilities. Through illegal intrusion into the political process, such as bribing elected officials or making unlawful campaign contributions, they insure that corporate rather than public needs will take precedence. And when intimate criminal bonds between corporate and political elites are unmasked, public cynicism about both institutional spheres grows accordingly.[123]

Finally, corporate irresponsibility may not just weaken the moral order and diminish quality of life but in extreme cases—such as Buffalo Creek, West Virginia—may lead to the complete deterioration of a community. Shortly before eight o'clock in the morning of February 26, 1972, after a night of rain, a mining-company dam that sat precariously above Buffalo Creek Valley collapsed and unleashed 130 million gallons of water and coal waste products. A mixture of water and sludge rushed down the slopes at speeds of up to thirty miles an hour. The devastation was sudden and immense: 125 people were drowned or crushed to death, 1,000 homes were ruined, 16 small communities lining the valley were washed away. The flood destroyed "everything in its path."[124]

Officials of Pittston, the parent company of Buffalo Mining, which constructed and maintained the dam, immediately declared the regrettable disaster "an act of God." Those closer to Buffalo Creek voiced different sentiments. One flood victim remarked, "You can blame the Almighty, all

right—the almighty dollar";[125] another said, "All I call the disaster is murder. The coal company knew the dam was bad, but...they did not care about
the good people that lived up Buffalo Creek."[126] An investigative commission convened by the governor agreed in part, finding that "The Pittston
Company, through its officials, has shown flagrant disregard for the safety of
residents of Buffalo Creek and other persons who live near coal-refuse im-
poundments."[127] In the face of a civil suit launched on behalf of several
hundred flood victims by Gerald Stern and a staff of fellow lawyers, Pittston
agreed to an out-of-court settlement of $13.5 million; eventually the com-
pany paid over $30 million to dispose of claims related to the disaster.[128]

The clearest evidence that Pittston had acted in a reckless manner was
uncovered by Gerald Stern and his associates as they prepared their civil
case against the giant company. The dam at Buffalo Creek had been constructed by dumping huge piles of solid waste products from the nearby
mining operation across the creek bed. This mound of refuse was supposed
to contain the large quantities of water that the company disposed of daily
after it had been used to clean coal in preparation for shipment to market.
Stern learned, however, that the dam had a crucial engineering flaw: it possessed no emergency spillway that could absorb excess water should the
need arise—such as on the rainy night preceding the disaster. His investigations also disclosed that other Pittston-managed dams had runoff systems,
and that corporate executives apparently were aware that the lack of a spillway at the Buffalo Creek impoundment was potentially dangerous.[129]

The survivors at Buffalo Creek lost much more than their property and
belongings. Many who had barely escaped the flood and who had watched
as friends and relatives were swept away by the onrushing wave of debris
and coal-blackened water suffered intense psychic trauma. Kai Erikson, a
sociologist who studied the disaster and its aftermath, commented, "Two
years after the flood, Buffalo Creek was almost as desolate as it had been
the day following, the grief as intense, the fear as strong, the anxiety as
sharp, the despair as dark."[130] There was another scarring cost as well:
what Erikson has called "collective trauma...a blow to the basic tissues of
social life that damages the bonds attaching people together and impairs the
prevailing sense of communality."[131] After the flood, people were thrown
together hurriedly into emergency trailer-court camps, where few of the old
communities and communal bonds could be reconstructed. For most residents, life would never be the same. The words of one survivor paint a dis-
heartening but typical portrait:

> This whole thing is a nightmare, actually. Our life-style has been
> disrupted, our home destroyed. We lost many things we loved,
> and we think about those things. We think about our neighbors

and friends we lost. Our neighborhood was completely destroyed, a disaster area. There's just an open field there now
and grass planted where there were many homes and many people lived.[132]

The Physical Costs of Corporate Crime

Physical costs—the toll in lives lost, injuries inflicted, and illnesses suffered—are perhaps the gravest and certainly the most neglected of the damages that corporate lawlessness imposes on the American people. The
events at Buffalo Creek should help to dispel the misconception that corporations "might take some of our money but at least no one gets hurt." Yet
it would be wrong to assume from the Buffalo Creek incident that corporate
negligence causes injury or death only in unusual circumstances. Every day,
in unpublicized and often latent ways, corporations illegally victimize the
bodies of workers, consumers, and members of society in general.

Significantly, the *physical costs of violent corporate crime may outstrip the
injuries and deaths sustained at the hands of street criminals.* Indeed, a
growing number of social commentators have suggested that corporate
lawlessness costs more than street crime not only in dollars and cents but
also in life and limb.[133]

Workers as Victims

A decade ago, Ralph Nader made the alarming pronouncement that "as
a form of violence, job casualties are statistically at least three times more
serious than street crime."[134] In raw figures, the National Institute for Occupational Safety and Health (NIOSH) has estimated that each year workers suffer at least 10 million traumatic injuries, 3 million of which are classified as "severe." Approximately 6,000 employees are killed in occupational
accidents.[135] Further, NIOSH has indicated that exposure to chemicals and
other toxic agents in the workplace may cause as many as 100,000 deaths
and 390,000 cases of disease per year.[136]

Admittedly, it would be neither accurate nor fair to indict corporations
for all of these casualties. Some job tasks are inherently dangerous, and
employees are occasionally negligent about their own well-being. In some
areas, too, the government condones the sacrifice of a measure of worker
safety and protection in hopes of lowering consumer costs, increasing corporate efficiency, and improving the vitality of the economy. The endangering practices that result might strike some as insensitive, if not immoral,
but they are not necessarily illegal.

It is equally clear, however, that a substantial portion of workers' deaths, injuries, and diseases are caused by the violation of prevailing laws and regulations. Reports indicate that 30 percent of all industrial accidents are caused by illegal safety violations (and another 20 percent by legal but unsafe conditions).[137] The record may be much worse in some segments of the business world, notably the coal mining industry, in which mishaps have claimed 100,000 lives and injured 1.5 million people since 1930.[138] Indeed, NIOSH data reveal that mining and quarrying workers have a higher "occupational traumatic death rate" (55 per 100,000 workers) than members of any other job category.[139]

The 1976 catastrophe in Letcher County, Kentucky, in which 26 people perished, is a tragic illustration of the hazards faced by miners. The disaster began when a malfunction in the mine's ventilation system allowed dangerous quantities of volatile methane gas to accumulate in a shaft two thousand feet below the surface. Supervisors had failed to monitor the air quality in accordance with established guidelines, and unsuspecting workers entered a section filled with methane. They died in a ball of flame when sparks from machinery ignited the lethal gas.

Before the explosion, the mining operation had been cited for 652 safety violations, including 60 for inadequate ventilation. Moreover, 500 new citations for safety infractions were issued in the following thirteen months. In this light, commentary published in *The Nation* seems credible:

> Twenty-six men died under circumstances that reek of carelessness, lack of skill, illegality, incompetence and official neglect, but no noteworthy changes have been induced by the tragedy....If sleepless nights have been endured, it was because of the profits lost during the months when the coal vein was sealed, not because outraged justice demanded it.[140]

The consequences of illegally disregarding employees' health and well-being appear even more profound when we consider the deadly and crippling *diseases* caused by the workplace. Toxic agents are especially dangerous. Typically they do not take their toll suddenly and openly; they kill silently, over the course of many years, and often in ways that seem indistinguishable from other ailments. Workers do not die dramatically on the job; they simply become ill, and all too often never regain their health.[141]

"Statistics," as Paul Brodeur notes, "are human beings with the tears wiped off"; they do not capture the "agonizing human consequences" of occupationally induced illnesses.[142] With this consideration in mind, we find special significance in the statistics on the effects of toxic agents in the workplace. As noted above, the annual toll is disquieting: 100,000 deaths and nearly 400,000 cases of disease.

Lung disease is a common danger of toxic exposure. Inhalation of cotton, flax, or hemp dusts can lead to byssinosis, a condition that causes "chest tightness" and severely impairs lung function. NIOSH has estimated that byssinosis, also known as "brown lung disease," has "disabled 35,000 current and retired textile workers."[143] Another disabling ailment is silicosis, which results from contact with silica dust generated in foundries, abrasive blasting operations, and stone or glass manufacturing. Each year as many as 1.2 million workers are exposed to silica dust. NIOSH also reports that approximately 4.5 percent of all coal miners suffer from "black lung disease," and that each year 4,000 deaths can be attributed to this disorder.[144]

Exposure to asbestos appears to have especially damaging effects. One outcome is asbestosis, a lung disease that can surface 10 to 20 years after initial exposure and for which there is no specific treatment. Victims suffer from "extensive scarring of the lung and progressive shortness of breath." Approximately 11.5 million Americans—most of whom worked in asbestos plants, insulation operations, and shipyards during World War II—have been exposed to asbestos. Longitudinal studies indicate that 10 to 18 percent of these people will die from asbestosis.[145] The effects of asbestos exposure are not limited to asbestosis; according to NIOSH, "as many as 6,000 asbestos-related lung cancers occur annually." Moreover, "up to 11 percent of workers exposed to asbestos" may eventually develop cancerous mesothelial tumors.[146]

Asbestos is not the only carcinogenic toxic agent. Each year, over 400,000 Americans die of cancer. Although precise figures cannot be determined, NIOSH concludes that "little doubt remains that occupational factors are significantly related to an increased risk of cancer." The estimated proportion of cancers attributed to occupational conditions ranges from less than 4 percent to over 20 percent.[147]

Occupational exposure to toxic agents has also been implicated in the causation of asthma, cardiovascular diseases, and adverse reproductive outcomes. The potential impact of toxic exposure on reproductive functioning is particularly dismaying because the effects of unhealthy work conditions may be passed on to the next generation. NIOSH notes that occupational exposures may not only reduce fertility and heighten spontaneous abortions but also increase the probability of birth defects. Although research on adverse reproductive outcomes is still in the early stages, NIOSH cautions that available data suggest that "the problem is both widespread and serious."[148]

No reliable statistics exist for the proportion of occupationally induced illnesses and deaths that can be attributed to corporate illegality. Even when corporations comply in good faith with existing safety regulations, toxic exposures may take place because of a lack of scientific evidence warning of potential hazards. Yet enough instances of executives' disregard for workers' health have been documented to justify the allegation that corporate negligence is responsible for many health and safety violations; in some cases these laws are broken intentionally.[149]

The plight of asbestos workers appears to support the conclusion that business places profits above workers' safety. In his book *Outrageous Misconduct*, Paul Brodeur alleges that although manufacturers had evidence for the deleterious effects of asbestos exposure, they either failed to explore the implications of this evidence or decided consciously to hide this information from their employees. For nearly half a century, the extent of the corporations' knowledge about the inherent dangers of asbestos remained largely secret. Since the early 1970s, however, workers have brought numerous lawsuits against asbestos manufacturers, and the probing of the plaintiffs' lawyers has unearthed widespread evidence of corporate irresponsibility. A number of juries were convinced that asbestos manufacturers had been "guilty of outrageous and reckless misconduct" in suppressing information from workers. In ten cases against one company, decided in 1981 and 1982, juries awarded plaintiffs not only compensatory damages but also punitive damages averaging over $600,000 a case.[150] It is estimated that of thousands of lawsuits will be filed in the future and that the cost of compensating asbestos victims may eventually total several billion dollars.

The relationship between corporate illegality and workplace victimization emerged into the national spotlight in a case involving Stefan Golab, a 61-year-old Polish immigrant working for Film Recovery Systems, Inc. (FRS), a company located in the northwest Chicago suburb of Elk Grove Village.[151] FRS was a recycling operation that extracted silver from film negatives by dipping them in a cyanide solution. By 1981, the company was grossing $13 million a year.

The day after Christmas 1982, FRS hired Stefan Golab to clean the vats containing the cyanide solution. On February 10, 1983, Golab staggered from the plant floor into the workers' lunchroom. Collapsing into a chair, he began to shake violently and foam at the mouth; then he lapsed into unconsciousness. A life squad soon arrived, but Golab could not be revived. He died before reaching the hospital.

At first it was believed that Golab had died of a heart attack, but an autopsy showed that the cause of death was poisoning by the plant's cyanide fumes. Subsequent investigations revealed, in the view of Cook County State's Attorney Richard A. Daley, that Golab had worked in "a huge gas chamber."[152] A prosecution team headed by Daley's assistant Jay Magnuson charged that conditions at FRS were so hazardous that Golab had been murdered. The prosecution argued that company officials had ignored repeated instances of workers becoming nauseous and vomiting; had hired mostly illegal aliens who could not speak English and had failed to warn them of the dangers of cyanide; had scraped skull-and-crossbones warnings off drums of cyanide; had clearly violated safety regulations by equipping employees with only paper facemasks and cloth gloves before assigning them to work over open vats containing cyanide; and had such inadequate ventilation that the plant's air was a thick yellow haze with a distinct cyanide odor, which exceeded safety standards by containing four times the accepted level of cyanide.

Magnuson sought and received homicide indictments against FRS as well as five corporate officials, claiming that "exposing workers to something as dangerous as cyanide gas is no different than firing a weapon into a crowd. You have created a strong probability of death. No intention is needed at that point."[153]   After a two-month bench trial, Judge Ronald J.D. Banks agreed that the prosecution had proven its contentions: Stefan Golab's death "was not an accident but in fact murder."[154]   On June 14, 1985, Judge Banks found three FRS officials guilty of murder and of 14 counts of reckless conduct. (Midway through the trial, he had dismissed the case against one other official; the governor of Utah refused to extradite the fifth company executive who had been indicted). Banks also convicted Film Recovery Systems and Metallic Marketing Systems, Inc., which owned one half of FRS's stock, of involuntary manslaughter and of 14 counts of reckless conduct. Two weeks later, he sentenced the three executives to 25 years in prison and fined them $10,000 apiece. The companies were fined $24,000 each. In rendering his decision, Banks commented, "This is not a case of taking a gun and shooting someone. It is more like leaving a time bomb in an airport and then running away. The bomb kept ticking...until Stefan Golab died."[155]

Consumers as Victims

Corporate violence extends not only to workers who produce goods but also to those who purchase them. Many products, even when used as recommended by the manufacturers, injure or kill thousands of consumers every year. Statistics on consumer casualties confirm this conclusion: dangerous products result annually in approximately 28,000 deaths and 130,000 serious injuries.[156]

Again, it is difficult to calculate exactly what proportion of these physical costs can be attributed directly to corporate illegality. Evaluations of product quality and safety, however, lend credence to the assessment that the unlawful victimization of consumers is widespread.[157] A Consumer Product Safety Commission analysis demonstrated that 147 out of 847 fabrics failed to meet flammability standards, 8 out of 15 models of baby cribs were defective, 753 out of 1,338 toys were hazardous, and 117 out of 148 products were unsafely packaged.[158]   In the same vein, the U.S. General Accounting Office found "gross contamination" in 35 of 65 poultry operations it examined, while inspections of meat-processing factories revealed that 18 of 216 plants in North Dakota and 31 of 57 plants in Massachusetts were characterized by unsanitary conditions.[159]   These statistics, especially with reference to the meat-packing industry, have led some scholars to conclude that Upton Sinclair's descriptions of conditions in the early 1900s are all too often still valid. Specific examples support this assessment:

> In 1984, Nebraska Beef Processors and its Colorado subsidiary, Cattle King Packing company—the largest supplier of ground meat to school lunch programs and also a major supplier of meat to the Defense Department, supermarkets, and fast-food chains—was found guilty of: (1) regularly bringing dead animals into its slaughterhouses and mixing rotten meat into its hamburgers; (2) labeling old meat with phony dates; and (3) deceiving U.S. Department of Agriculture inspectors by matching diseased carcasses with the healthy heads from larger cows....In 1979, a New Jersey firm was convicted of making pork sausage with an unauthorized chemical which masks discoloration of spoiled meat. And in 1982, a California company used walkie-talkies to avoid inspectors while doctoring rotten sausage.[160]

Data on the extent of product recalls also point to corporate culpability in the marketing of defective goods. Between 1966 and 1971 alone, the FDA was forced to recall nearly 2,000 different drug products, including "806 because of contamination or adulterations, 752 because of subpotency or superpotency, and 377 because of label mixups."[161]   In the decade following its inception in 1972, the Consumer Product Safety Commission (CPSC) recalled over 300 million dangerously defective products. According to one source, the agency's action may have prevented as many as 1.25 million serious injuries and deaths in a five-year period.[162]

Further, when it has been possible to penetrate corporate defenses and obtain more than a cursory look into corporate operations, commentators have seen that even leading corporations are sometimes willing to place profits above consumer safety. GM's Corvair, first exposed by Ralph Nader's *Unsafe At Any Speed*,[163] is one of the most celebrated of these cases. From its inception, the Corvair was plagued by rear-end suspension difficulties that caused it to become directionally unstable and to overturn at high speeds. As revealed by John DeLorean, a GM executive of that era who would later have legal difficulties of his own, "these problems with the Corvair were well documented inside GM's Engineering Staff long before the Corvair was offered for sale."[164] Nevertheless, the company launched the Corvair in 1959 and initially resisted attempts by its own staff to introduce a stabilizing bar capable of reducing the car's hazards; at an additional cost of $15 per vehicle, it was deemed "too expensive." DeLorean offers a telling summation of this episode:

> To date, millions of dollars have been spent in legal expenses and out-of-court settlements for those killed or maimed in the Corvair. The corporation steadfastly defends the car's safety, despite the internal engineering records which indicated it was not safe, and the ghastly toll in deaths and injury it recorded.[165]

Another example of corporate insensitivity to consumers' well-being surfaced in an exposé by a former B.F. Goodrich engineer. He recounted how superiors ordered him to falsify test results and to help construct an elaborate document indicating that a company-designed brake for a new Air Force attack plane had satisfied all qualification standards. The deficiencies in the brake assemblies were revealed only after several near-crashes.[166]

Similar scandals have prevailed in the pharmaceutical industry. A study of 17 pharmaceutical companies, for example, disclosed that over a two-year period each company violated the law at least once, and two drug companies committed more than 20 violations; when compared with firms in other industries, the pharmaceutical companies committed 2.5 times their share of total violations.[167] Case studies add further documentation of illegalities in the pharmaceutical industry.[168] One case frequently cited as an example of egregious corporate conduct involves the anti-cholesterol drug MER/29. Employees of the William S. Merrell Company (a subsidiary of Richardson-Merrell) falsified laboratory findings in order to secure FDA approval of MER/29. After the drug was marketed, numerous users suffered negative side effects, including cataracts and loss of hair. Eventually, both the William S. Merrell Company and Richardson-Merrell, as well as three corporate officials (two doctors and a vice-president), pleaded no contest to a variety of criminal charges. The companies were also named in nearly 500 civil suits that reportedly awarded nearly $200 million in damages to victims.[169]

In his book *At Any Cost*,[170] Morton Mintz details the problems associated with another pharmaceutical product: the "Dalkon Shield," an IUD manufactured by A.H. Robbins. According to Mintz, the company marketed 4.5 million Shields in 80 countries on the basis of exaggerated claims for the device's effectiveness and safety. Although advertisements claimed that those wearing the IUD had a pregnancy rate of only 1.1 percent, the actual rate was five times as high. In addition, the Dalkon Shield caused more miscarriages than other IUDs among women who became pregnant, and was more likely to cause potentially lethal septic spontaneous abortions. In the United States at least fifteen women died from such abortions; in Third World countries, where the antibiotics needed to treat this condition often are not available, the toll is unknown but suspected to be much higher, amounting in Mintz's view to "hundreds—possibly thousands—of women."[171] The Shield also caused pelvic infections that subjected thousands of its consumers to extended periods of chronic pain and in some instances irrevocably harmed their reproductive systems. One consultant estimated that of the 2.2 million American women who used this IUD, approximately 87,000 may have suffered physical harm.[172]

The Dalkon Shield remained on the market for over three years, from January 1971 to June 28, 1974. Mintz alleges that A.H. Robbins failed to recall the device despite growing evidence that it was a safety hazard; the company continues to maintain that its product was no more dangerous than other IUDs. It appears, however, that Dalkon Shield victims and juries have found Mintz's interpretation more compelling. By 1985, over 14,000 victims had filed either civil suits or nonlitigated claims for compensation, while juries had awarded plantiffs $24.8 million in punitive damages.[173] The prospect of sustaining losses in future lawsuits moved A.H. Robbins to file for reorganization under Chapter 11 of the Bankruptcy Code, "so that it could be protected from lawsuits by creditors—Shield victims, above all—while it devised a plan to pay its debts."[174]

Is the Dalkon Shield case an isolated incident of corporate lawlessness? What, Mintz asks, does this "catastrophe teach us?"

> Not that the A.H. Robbins Company was a renegade in the pharmaceutical industry. Yes, Robbins—knowingly and willfully—put corporate greed before human welfare, suppressed scientific studies that would ascertain safety and effectiveness, concealed hazards from consumers, the medical profession and government, assigned a lower value to foreign lives than to American lives, behaved ruthlessly toward victims who sued, and hired outside experts who would give accommodating testimony. Yet almost every other major drug company has done one or more of these things, and some have done them repeatedly or routinely, and continue to do so. Some have even been criminally prosecuted and convicted, and are recidivists.[175]

The Public as Victims

Participants in a corporate society need not produce or consume goods to risk victimization by corporate violence. Each day, business practices occur that endanger the lives of the general public. Sometimes these physical costs are exacted dramatically, as when the dam collapsed at Buffalo Creek and 125 residents perished. More often, however, the toll is taken by the more silent means of environmental pollution. A *Time* magazine article captures this fact:

> Natural disasters and wars do their damage spectacularly and quickly—shaking, crushing, burning, ripping, smothering, drowning. The devastation is plain; victims and survivors are clearly distinguished, causes and effects easily connected. With the unnatural disasters caused by environmental toxins, however, the devastation is seldom certain or clear or quick. Broken chromosomes are unseen; carcinogens can be slow and sneaky. People wait for years to find out if they or their children are victims. The fears, the uncertainties, and the conjectures have a corrosive quality that becomes inextricably mingled with the toxic realities.[176]

The risks posed increasingly by the nation's air, earth, and water are linked directly with our dependence on industrial processes and chemicals that generate toxic pollutants but also, ironically, provide us with the products, technological advances, cures, and employment that sustain the quality of our lives. The magnitude of this dependence is seen in these statistics: there are "160 million tons of air pollution emitted annually, 225 million tons of hazardous waste generated, [and] 4 million tons of toxic chemicals discharged into waterways and streams."[177]

In recent years, public consciousness has been raised regarding the immense dangers posed by releasing these pollutants into the environment. Environmental groups are responsible in part for focusing attention on the growing health risks created by current disposal practices, but several highly publicized toxic disasters have also helped to identify environmental victimization as a major social problem. The catastrophe in Bhopal, India forced attention on the possibility that an industrial chemical disaster could take life quickly and on a large scale. The leak of 45 tons of methyl isocyanate from a Union Carbide pesticide plant claimed the lives of over 2,000 citizens. "Human progress came up against human frailty," commented Roger Rosenblatt. "The air was poisoned, and the world gasped."[178]

The American public has not had to look abroad to see the dangers of pollution. The words "Love Canal" signify the capacity of toxic agents to pose such a severe risk that citizens are driven from their homes.

From the early 1940s to the 1950s, the Hooker Chemical Company dumped 20,000 tons of chemical waste residues in a 15-acre trench located in Niagara Falls, New York. The site was called "Love Canal" after William T. Love, who had started and then abandoned excavations on a canal designed to bypass the falls and join the Niagara River to Lake Ontario. In 1953, Hooker sold the dump site to the city's school board for the token fee of $1, noting in the deed that the "premises have been filled...with waste products resulting from the manufacturing of chemicals by the grantor" and that it was transferring liability "for injury to a person or persons, including death therefrom...in connection with or by reason of the presence of said industrial wastes."[179] Neither Hooker nor the school board issued a public statement warning citizens of the potential hazards of the chemical wastes in the dump.[180] The land was used eventually for residential housing; an elementary school was also built on the site.

In *Laying Waste*, Michael Brown writes, "Love Canal was simply unfit to be a container for hazardous substances, even by the standards of the day," particularly since it held not only seriously harmful solvents and pesticides but also dioxin, the "most toxic substance ever synthesized by man."[181] Over the years, the wastes seeped gradually into the surrounding earth and its waters, with predictably devastating consequences. To an astonishing degree the community suffered from miscarriages, birth defects, cancer, chromosome damage, skin rashes, headaches, ear infections, nervous disorders, and other ailments. Brown's account of his first visit to the area is disquieting:

> I saw homes where dogs had lost their fur. I saw children with serious birth defects. I saw entire families in inexplicably poor health. When I walked on the Love Canal, I gasped for air as my lungs heaved in fits of wheezing. My eyes burned. There was a sour taste in my mouth.[182]

Indeed, the dangers proved so severe—one study reported that dioxin levels were "among the highest ever found in the human environment"—that hundreds of families were evacuated and their homes purchased by the government and then bulldozed under or closed off as uninhabitable.[183]

The Love Canal incident may be unique in the degree of contamination and the amount of publicity it attracted, but it is not an isolated case. "Each day," a story in *Time* notes, "more and more communities discover that they are living near dumps or atop ground that has been contaminated with chemicals whose once strange names and initials—dioxin, vinyl chloride, PBB and PCB, as well as familiar toxins such as lead, mercury and arsenic—have become household synonyms for mysterious and deadly poisons."[184] There may be as many as 10,000 of these dangerous waste dump sites.[185] Moreover, the physical costs suffered by the Love Canal residents have been experienced elsewhere. There is mounting evidence that exposure to toxic agents increases the risk of health problems, including cancer, reproductive complications, kidney failure, and neurological disorders.[186] One estimate warns that contact with dangerous chemicals may cause as many as 45,000 deaths a year.[187]

Corporations should not be blamed in all instances for polluting the environment deliberately. Much of the pollution took place while companies were in compliance with governmental regulations and before the dangers of the toxic agents were fully understood. In the case of Love Canal, for example, it is difficult to determine how culpability should be divided between the Hooker Chemical Company and the City of Niagara, which Hooker apparently warned of the dump site's hazards (though both the federal government and the State of New York have large civil suits—claiming $124.4 million and $635 in damages respectively—pending against the company).[188] Nonetheless, a number of social commentators argue that corporate lawlessness is responsible for a significant amount of the public's victimization. As Ralph Nader contends about the effects of air pollution:

> The pervasive environmental violence of air pollutants has imperiled health, safety, and property throughout the nation for many decades....The efflux from motor vehicles, plants, and incinerators of sulfur oxides, hydrocarbon, carbon monoxide, oxides of nitrogen, particulates, and many more contaminants amounts to compulsory consumption of violence by most Americans. There is no full escape from such violent ingestions, for breathing is required. This damage, perpetuated increasingly in direct violation of local, state, and federal law, shatters people's health and safety but still escapes inclusion in the crime statistics. "Smogging" a city or town has taken on the proportions of a massive crime wave, yet federal and state statistical compilations of crime pay attention to "muggers" and ignore "smoggers"....Violators are openly flouting the laws and an administration allegedly dedicated to law and order sits on its duties.[189]

Although the data are somewhat limited, they lend credence to Nader's view. One study concludes that the violation of environmental protection standards is among the most frequent of all corporate offenses.[190] In a *Wall Street Journal* article, Barry Meier reports on another study indicating "that one out of every seven companies producing toxic wastes may have dumped illegally in recent years."[191] Meier notes that the wastes are dumped into places—streams and vacant lots, for example—where the risk of contamination is high but the likelihood of detection is slight. Further, since it was formed in 1983, the Environmental Protection Agency's 35-person Criminal Enforcement Unit has found no shortage of offenders. The unit has produced 126 indictments, and in the last two years has "helped convict 60 individuals and companies of criminally violating EPA statutes."[192]

Conclusion

The crime problem in America has a dual quality that is not always recognized or understood. Images embedded deeply in our cultural heritage, combined with frequent political rhetoric and constant attention by the media, sensitize us to the ravages of conventional illegal behavior. Certainly conventional criminality is individually and socially devastating, but the natural inclination to equate the "crime problem" with street crime can blind us to a second, seemingly more consequential, aspect of the problem: corporate lawlessness is pervasive and its effects are immense. "Suite crime" disrupts the social and institutional order, and its financial toll outweighs substantially the amounts stolen by street offenders. Most significantly, there is every indication that the physical costs of corporate crime surpass the bodily harm inflicted by those who prey more intimately on their victims. Each day, executives must make life-and-death decisions, and through negligence or intent they sometimes place profits above the safety and well-being of workers, consumers, and the general public. Contrary to what many citizens continue to believe, corporate crime is violent.

The seriousness of illegal corporate activities focuses attention on the question "How has this problem been attacked in the past and in more recent times?" In the next chapter, we will attempt to show how changes in several areas, including the prevailing socioeconomic context and our understanding of the concept of "person," have shaped the legal responses made in different eras to corporations engaging in socially injurious practices. In particular we will learn why our legal system is now prepared—in an unprecedented if still rudimentary fashion—to bring corporate illegalities, especially violent illegalities, within the reach of the criminal law.

Notes

[1] Irwin Ross, "How Lawless Are Big Companies?" *Fortune* 102 (December 1, 1980), pp. 56-64.

[2] Edwin H. Sutherland, "White-Collar Criminality," *American Sociological Review* 5 (February 1940), pp. 1-12; *White Collar Crime*. New York: Holt, Rinehart and Winston, 1949; "Crime of Corporations," in Karl Schuessler (ed.), *On Analyzing Crime*. Chicago: University of Chicago Press, 1973 (paper originally presented in 1948), pp. 78-96; and in the same volume, "Is 'White-Collar Crime' Crime?" (originally published in 1945), pp. 62-77.

[3] Gilbert Geis and Colin Goff, "Introduction," in Edwin H. Sutherland, *White Collar Crime: The Uncut Version*. New Haven: Yale University Press, 1983, p. xxx.

[4] Sutherland, *White Collar Crime*, p. 9.

[5] In order to avoid conceptual confusion, authors have begun to evolve separate terms, such as "business crime" or "organizational crime," to refer to distinct modes of illegality that fall under the more general heading of white-collar crime. See, for example, John E. Conklin, *"Illegal But Not Criminal": Business Crime in America*. Englewood Cliffs, New Jersey: Prentice-Hall, 1977.

[6] For an overview of this controversy, see George Vold, *Theoretical Criminology*. New York: Oxford University Press, 1958, pp.243-261, and Donald J. Newman, "pp. 78-96; White-Collar Crime: An Overview and Analysis," in Gilbert Geis and Robert F. Meier (eds.), *White-Collar Crime*. New York: The Free Press, 1977, pp. 50-64. Compare with Leonard Orland, "Reflections on Corporate Crime: Law in Search of Theory and Scholarship," *American Criminal Law Review* 17 (1980). pp. 501-520.

[7] Paul Tappan, "Who Is the Criminal?" in Gilbert Geis and Robert F. Meier (eds.), *White-Collar Crime*. New York: The Free Press, 1977, pp. 272-282.

[8] *Ibid.*, p. 275.

[9] *Ibid.*, p. 277.

[10] Sutherland, "White-Collar Criminality," p. 7.

[11] "Is 'White-Collar Crime' Crime?" p. 66

[12] *Ibid.*, p. 66. See also Sutherland, "White-Collar Criminality," p. 6.

[13] Marshall B. Clinard and Peter C. Yeager, *Corporate Crime.* New York: The Free Press, 1980, pp. 17-19, 43. See Neal Shover, "Defining Organizational Crime," in M. David Ermann and Richard J. Lundman (eds.), *Corporate and Governmental Deviance.* New York: Oxford University Press, 1978, pp. 37-40; Laura Shill Schrager and James F. Short, Jr., "Toward a Sociology of Organizational Crime," *Social Problems* 25 (April 1978), pp. 407-419.

[14] A number of scholars have rejected a narrow legalistic definition of corporate crime. Marshall B. Clinard remarks, for example, that "corporate crime, like white-collar crime (of which it is a part), is defined here as any act punishable by the state, regardless of whether it is punished by administrative or civil law." Similarly, John Braithwaite defines corporate crime "as conduct of a corporation, or individuals acting on behalf of a corporation, that is proscribed and punishable by law." He comments, "I take the view that to exclude civil violations from a consideration of corporate crime is an arbitrary obfuscation because of the frequent provision in law for both civil and criminal prosecution of the same corporate conduct. In considerable measure, the power of corporations is manifested in the fact that their wrongs are so frequently punished only civilly." See Marshall B. Clinard, *Corporate Ethics and Crime: The Role of Middle Management.* Beverly Hills: Sage, 1983, p. 10; John Braithwaite, "Enforced Self-Regulation: A New Strategy for Corporate Crime Control," *Michigan Law Review* 80 (June 1982), p. 1466, footnote 1. See also Sheila Balkan, Ronald J. Berger, and Janet Schmidt, *Crime and Deviance in America: A Critical Approach.* Belmont, Ca.: Wadsworth Publishing Company, 1980, pp. 165-167, and Jeffrey H. Reiman, *The Rich Get Richer and the Poor Get Prison: Ideology, Class, and Criminal Justice.* New York: John Wiley and Sons, 1979, pp. 44-94.

[15] Colin H. Goff and Charles E. Reasons, *Corporate Crime in Canada: A Critical Analysis of Anti-Combines Legislation.* Scarborough, Ontario: Prentice-Hall of Canada, 1978, pp. 2-15. Frank Pearce, *Crimes of the Powerful: Marxism, Crime and Deviance.* London, England: Pluto Press, 1976, p. 77. See also Richard Quinney and John Wildeman, *The Problem of Crime: A Critical Introduction to Criminology.* New York: Harper and Row, 1977, pp. 96-116, and Michael E. Milakovich and Kurt Weis, "Politics and Measures

of Success in the War on Crime," *Crime and Delinquency* 21 (January 1975), pp. 1-10.

[16] Anthony Platt, *The Child Savers: The Invention of Delinquency*. Chicago: University of Chicago Press, 1969; Richard Hofstadter, *Social Darwinism in American Thought*. Boston: Beacon Press, 1955; Stephen Jay Gould, *The Mismeasure of Man*. New York: W.W. Norton and Company, 1981.

[17] Platt, *The Child Savers*, p. 41. See also David J. Rothman, *Conscience and Convenience: The Asylum and Its Alternatives in Progressive America*. Boston: Little, Brown, 1980.

[18] E.A. Ross, *Sin and Society: An Analysis of Latter-Day Iniquity*. New York: Harper and Row, 1907, p. viii.

[19] Sutherland, "White-Collar Criminality," p. 11.

[20] President's Commission on Law Enforcement and Administration of Justice, *The Challenge of Crime in a Free Society*. New York: Avon Books, 1968, p. 158.

[21] As John Conklin has noted, "there is widespread acceptance of the view that the public is 'condoning, indifferent, or ambivalent' toward business crime." See his *"Illegal But Not Criminal"*, p. 17   Compare with James Q. Wilson, *Thinking About Crime*. Revised Edition. New York: Vintage Books, 1985, pp. 5-6.

[22] Donald J. Newman, "Public Attitudes Toward a Form of White Collar Crime," *Social Problems* 4 (January 1957), pp. 228-232; "Changing Morality: The Two Americas—A Time-Louis Harris Poll," *Time* 93 (June 6, 1969), pp. 26-27; Don C. Gibbons, "Crime and Punishment: A Study in Social Attitudes," *Social Forces* 47 (June 1969), pp. 391-397; Robert F. Meier and James F. Short, Jr., "Crime as Hazard: Perceptions of Risk and Seriousness," *Criminology* 23 (August 1985), pp. 393-395; Adam Clymer, "Low Marks for Executive Honesty," *New York Times* (June 9, 1985), Section 3, pp. 1, 6.

[23] Laura Shill Schrager and James F. Short, Jr., "How Serious a Crime? Perceptions of Organizational and Common Crimes," in Gilbert Geis and Ezra Stotland (eds.), *White-Collar Crime: Theory and Research*. Beverly Hills, Sage, 1980, p. 27; Marvin E. Wolfgang, "Crime and Punishment," *New York Times* (March 2, 1980). p. E-21; Francis T. Cullen, Bruce G. Link, and

Craig W. Polanzi, "The Seriousness of Crime Revisited: Have Attitudes Toward White-Collar Crime Changed?" *Criminology* 20 (May 1982), pp. 96-97; Robert F. Meier and James F. Short, Jr., "The Consequences of White-Collar Crime," in Herbert Edelhertz and Thomas D. Overcast (eds.) *White-Collar Crime Crime: An Agenda for Research*. Lexington, Massachusetts: Lexington Books, 1982, pp. 28-32; John Braithwaite, "Challenging Just Deserts: Punishing White-Collar Criminals," *Journal of Criminal Law and Criminology* 73 (Summer 1982), pp. 732-738.

[24] Francis T. Cullen, Gregory A. Clark, Bruce G. Link, Richard A. Mathers, Jennifer Lee Niedospial, and Michael Sheahan, "Dissecting White-Collar Crime: Offense Type and Punitiveness," *International Journal of Comparative and Applied Criminal Justice* 9 (Spring 1985), p. 22; James Frank, Francis T. Cullen, Lawrence F. Travis, III, and John Borntrager, "Sanctioning Corporate Crime: How Do Business Executives and the Public Compare?" Paper presented at the 1984 meeting of the Midwestern Criminal Justice Association; Peter G. Sinden, "Perceptions of Crime in Capitalist America: The Question of Consciousness Manipulation," *Sociological Focus* 13 (January 1980), p. 80. See also Francis T. Cullen, Richard A. Mathers, Gregory A. Clark, and John B, Cullen, "Public Support for Punishing White-Collar Crime: Blaming the Victim Revisited?" *Journal of Criminal Justice* 11 (No. 6, 1983), pp. 481-493.

[25] Cullen et al., "The Seriousness of Crime Revisited: Have Attitudes Toward White-Collar Crime Changed?"

[26] Orr Kelly, "Corporate Crime: The Untold Story," *U.S. News and World Report* (September 6, 1982), p. 29. See also Seymour Martin Lipset and William Schneider, *The Confidence Gap: Business, Labor, and Government in the Public Mind*. New York: The Free Press, 1983.

[27] Clymer, "Low Marks for Executive Honesty," Section 3, p. 1.

[28] Kathleen A. Schumacher, *Corporate Crime as a Social Problem: Public Perceptions of Costs and Control*. Unpublished M.S. Thesis, University of Cincinnati, 1986; Cullen et al., "Public Support for Punishing White-Collar Crime," pp. 487-488. One qualification must be added. Although citizens do not consider corporate crime to be as violent as street crime, they do not ignore the costs of corporate crime. The data in the Schumacher and Cullen et al. surveys indicate the opposite: the public views as extensive the economic costs of white-collar and corporate illegalities. In this regard, Robert F. Meier and James F. Short, Jr. have provided evidence to suggest

that citizens perceive the risk of being victimized by "white-collar hazards."
A 1980-1981 survey in eastern Washington state found that residents gave
high-risk ratings to economic white-collar hazards such as "being overcharged by a physician," "being sold a worthless or badly defective product,"
and "being illegally overcharged by manufacturers of products." Further,
the mean scores for these items were generally as high or higher than the
mean scores accorded to a list of "ordinary crimes." The risk ratings of violent white-collar hazards were lower, but this was also true for violent
street crimes. Unfortunately, the survey does not allow us to assess systematically the extent to which the Washington respondents perceived the rela-
tive violent risks associated with white-collar and ordinary crimes. First, as
Meier and Short noted, cross-category comparisons are problematic, "since
the inventory of offenses in each category is restricted." Second, the respondents were asked how likely it was that a hazard would "happen to you
within the next five years." Although this methodological approach measures perceived individual risk, it does not evaluate perceptions of the overall cost of a hazard or category of hazards to the larger society. Third, unlike the Schumacher and Cullen et al. studies, the Washington survey did
not include items that asked respondents directly to state which category of
crime they believed to have the highest economic and/or violent costs. See
Meier and Short, "Crime as Hazard: Perceptions of Risk and Seriousness,"
pp. 393-395.

[29] *Peoria Journal Star* (February 18, 1980), p. A-4.

[30] Empirical support for this conclusion can be drawn from Doris A.
Graber, *Crime News and the Public*. New York: Praeger, 1980. Graber
found that although her respondents "perceived white-collar crime as common and serious, albeit generally less serious than street crime," white-collar crime "assumed a secondary role to street crime in the audience's comments." The public "perceives both criminals and victims as largely flawed
in character, nonwhite, and lower class." See pp. 63, 64, 68.

[31] Gresham M. Sykes, *Criminology*. New York: Harcourt, Brace, Jovanovich, 1978, p. 96

[32] Charles R. Tittle, Wayne J. Villemez, and Douglas A. Smith, "The Myth
of Social Class and Criminality: An Empirical Assessment of the Empirical
Evidence," *American Sociological Review* 43 (October 1978), pp. 643-656.
See also Charles R. Tittle and Wayne J. Villemez, "Social Class and Criminality," *Social Forces* 56 (December 1977), pp. 474-502; Charles R. Tittle,

"Social Class and Criminal Behavior: A Critique of the Theoretical Foundation," *Social Forces* 62 (December 1983), pp. 334-358.

[33] John Braithwaite, "The Myth of Social Class and Criminality Reconsidered," *American Sociological Review* 46 (February 1981), pp. 36-57; Michael J. Hindelang, Travis Hirschi, and Joseph G. Weis, "Correlates of Delinquency: The Illusion of Discrepancy Between Self-Report and Official Measures," *American Sociological Review* 44 (December 1979), pp. 1002-1009; Marvin E. Wolfgang, Robert M. Figlio, and Thorsten Sellin, *Delinquency in a Birth Cohort.* Chicago: University of Chicago Press, 1972, pp. 244-255.

[34] Vernon L. Parrington, "The Progressive Era: A Liberal Renaissance," in Arthur Mann (ed.), *The Progressive Era: Liberal Renaissance or Liberal Failure?* New York: Holt, Rinehart and Winston, 1963, p. 8. See also, Gilbert Geis and Robert F. Meier, "Introduction," in their edited volume *White-Collar Crime.* New York: The Free Press, 1977, p. 6.

[35] Rothman, *Conscience and Convenience*, pp. 48-49.

[36] Quoted in Conklin, *"Illegal But Not Criminal"*, pp. 8-9.

[37] Ross, *Sin and Society*, pp. 8, 10-11.

[38] *Ibid.*, p. 47.

[39] *Ibid.*, p.126.

[40] Sutherland, "White-Collar Criminality," p. 1.

[41] *Ibid.*, p.1.

[42] Geis and Meier, "Introduction," p. 24; Sykes, *Criminology*, p. 97.

[43] Sutherland, "White-Collar Criminality," p. 1.

[44] *Ibid.*, p. 2.

[45] *Ibid.*, p. 2.

[46] Sutherland, "Crime of Corporations," pp. 79-80 (citations to the version contained in *On Analyzing Crime*). Presented one year before the publica-

tion of *White Collar Crime*, this essay contained the results of Sutherland's investigation of corporate illegality.

[47] *Ibid.*, p. 81.

[48] *Ibid.*, p. 94. For a more extended discussion of why "the enumeration of decisions as reported in these sources is certainly far short of the total number of decisions against these 70 corporations," see Sutherland, *White Collar Crime: The Uncut Version*, New Haven: Yale University Press, 1983, pp. 14-15.

[49] Sutherland, "Crime of Corporations," p. 80.

[50] *Ibid.*, p. 80.

[51] *Ibid.*, p. 80.

[52] Sutherland, *White Collar Crime: The Uncut Version*, p. 23. For a summary of the statistical findings of Sutherland's research, see pp. 13-25.

[53] Geis and Goff, "Introduction," p. xxviii. See also Stanton Wheeler, "Trends and Problems in the Sociological Study of Crime," *Social Problems* 23 (June 1976), p.528.

[54] Geis and Goff, "Introduction," p. xxx; Sykes, *Criminology*, p. 100.

[55] See also Marshall B. Clinard and Peter C. Yeager, "Corporate Crime: Issues in Research," *Criminology* 16 (August 1978), pp. 258-262; Sykes, *Criminology*, pp. 100-103.

[56] Kelly, "Corporate Crime: The Untold Story," p. 25.

[57] Clinard and Yeager, *Corporate Crime*, p. 116. The results of this research were originally reported in Marshall B. Clinard, Peter C. Yeager, Jeanne Brissette, David Petrashek, and Elizabeth Harries, *Illegal Corporate Behavior*. Washington, D.C.: U.S. Government Printing Office, 1979.

[58] Clinard and Yeager, *Corporate Crime*, p. 118.

[59] *Ibid.*, p. 116.

[60] *Ibid.*, p. 127. Clinard and Yeager reported that 210 of the 477 corporations in their sample had "two or more legal actions completed against them." Thus, as noted in the text, 44 percent of corporations were repeat offenders.

[61] *Ibid.*, p. 111; see pp. 112-113.

[62] Orland, "Reflections on Corporate Crime," p. 508. Orland believes that researchers should focus on "recorded criminal accusations and convictions against America's largest corporations" because of a "significant body of criminology that teaches that tabulation of recorded crime should be the starting point for determining the actual extent of the crime." That is, once the official crime rate is established, an "informed estimate" becomes possible of how much corporate crime goes unreported and unsolved. Notably, Orland observes that the "gap between recorded and actual corporate crime may be even greater than for other forms of crime." See pp. 508-509.

[63] *Ibid.*, pp. 501-502 (see footnote 4).

[64] *Ibid.*, pp. 509-510.

[65] Idalene F. Kesner, Bart Victor, and Bruce T. Lamont, "Board Composition and the Commission of Illegal Acts: An Investigation of Fortune 500 Companies," *Academy of Management Journal*, 29 (December 1986), p. 794. This research was a partial replication of an earlier study. See Barry M. Staw and Eugene Szwajkowski, "The Scarcity-Munificence Component of Organizational Environments and the Commission of Illegal Acts," *Administrative Science Quarterly* 20 (September 1975), pp. 345-354.

[66] Charles P. Alexander, "Crime in the Suites," *Time* (June 10, 1985), p. 56; Stephen Koepp, "The Year of the Big Splashes," *Time* (January 6, 1986), p. 79.

[67] Winston Williams, "White-Collar Crime: Booming Again," *New York Times* (June 9, 1985), Section 3, p. 1; Steven P. Rosenfield, "Corporate Crime Was Big Business in 1985," *Peoria Journal Star* (December 15, 1985), p. A-14.

[68] Given the changing social context and the emergent social movement against white-collar and corporate crime, we would anticipate that this ostensible rise in corporate crime has less to do with the changing incidence of corporate conduct and more to do with increases in both corporate prose-

cutions and the attention paid to these prosecutions by the media. Of course, this proposition awaits empirical verification. On the creation of crime waves, see more generally, Mark Fishman, "Crime Waves as Ideology," *Social Problems* 25 (June 1978), pp. 531-543.

[69] Carol J. Loomis, "White-Collar Crime," *Fortune* (July 22, 1985), p. 91.

[70] See, for instance, Jerry L. Wall and Bong-Gon Shin, "A Situational Examination of Industrial Espionage." Paper presented at the 1977 Meeting of the Academy of Management. More generally, see Marshall B. Clinard, *Corporate Ethics and Crime: The Role of Middle Management.* Beverly Hills: Sage, 1983.

[71] As Thomas I. Emerson commented in his review of Sutherland's *White Collar Crime*, "The 70 largest corporations are gigantic, rambling enterprises. They are subject to hundreds of statutes and thousands of administrative regulations. They have tens of thousands of employees, not all of whom can be kept under perfect control. Consequently, it would not be surprising if these large corporations ran afoul of the law with a fair degree of frequency." However, he also later remarked that based on his own experience with federal regulatory agencies, "I would conclude that the problem of white collar crime is, generally speaking, of the order of magnitude that Professor Sutherland depicts." See *Yale Law Journal* 59 (February 1950), pp. 581-585. See also Andrew Hopkins, "Controlling Corporate Deviance," *Criminology* 18 (August 1978), p. 200.

[72] John Braithwaite, *Corporate Crime in the Pharmaceutical Industry.* London: Routledge and Kegan Paul, 1984, pp. vii-viii. See also Clinard and Yeager, *Corporate Crime*, p. 21.

[73] FBI, *Uniform Crime Reports: Crime in the United States, 1984.* Washington, D.C.: U.S. Government Printing Office, 1985, p. 6; Bureau of Justice Statistics, *Households Touched by Crime, 1984.* Washington, D.C.: U.S. Government Printing Office, 1985.

[74] Bureau of Justice Statistics, *The Economic Cost of Crime to Victims.* Washington, D.C.: U.S. Government Printing Office, 1984, p. 3.

[75] For an excellent discussion of the fear of crime, see Charles Silberman, *Criminal Violence, Criminal Justice.* New York: Random House, 1978, Chapter 1, "Fear." More generally, see John E. Conklin, *The Impact of Crime.* New York: Macmillan Publishing Company, 1975. One caveat

should be added here. While fear of crime is a salient problem that diminishes the quality of life in America and is felt intensely by too many citizens, it would be wrong to exaggerate its prevalence or to ignore the fact that fear of victimization burdens certain groups (e.g., the elderly, women) more than others. See Francis T. Cullen, Gregory A. Clark, and John F. Wozniak, "Explaining the Get Tough Movement: Can the Public Be Blamed?" *Federal Probation* 49 (June 1985): 16-24; Stuart A. Scheingold, *The Politics of Law and Order: Street Crime and Public Policy.* New York: Longman, 1984.

[76] Sutherland, "White-Collar Criminality," pp. 4-5. For examples of those asserting that corporate and, more generally, white-collar crimes are more costly than conventional criminality, see Balkan et al., *Crime and Deviance in America*, pp. 167-168; Pearce, *Crimes of the Powerful*, pp. 77-79; Conklin, *"Illegal But Not Criminal"*, pp. 2-7; Goff and Reasons, *Corporate Crime in Canada*, pp. 11-13; Charles H. McCaghy, *Deviant Behavior: Crime, Conflict, and Interest Groups.* New York: Macmillan, 1976, pp. 204-213; Stuart L. Hills, *Crime, Power, and Morality: The Criminal Law Process in the United States.* Scranton, Pennsylvania: Chandler, 1971, pp. 167-168; Chamber of Commerce, *White-Collar Crime: Everyone's Problem, Everyone's Loss*, 1974, pp. 4-6; Richard Quinney, *Criminology.* Boston: Little, Brown, 1979, pp. 197-203.

[77] Stanton Wheeler and Mitchell Lewis Rothman, "The Organization as Weapon in White-Collar Crime," *Michigan Law Review* 80 (June 1982), p. 1414. It should be noted that Wheeler and Rothman's organizational crimes "need not be the result of corporate misadventure (though most of the organizational illegality...was committed by, or on behalf of, for-profit business organizations)." See p. 1409.

[78] FBI, *Uniform Crime Reports*, 1984, p. 151.

[79] Wheeler and Rothman, "The Organization as Weapon in White-Collar Crime," pp. 1424, 1426.

[80] For accounts of the Equity Funding Company of America scandal, see Lee J. Seidler, Frederick Andrews, and Marc J. Epstein (eds.), *The Equity Funding Papers: The Anatomy of a Fraud.* New York: John Wiley and Sons, 1977; Donn B. Parker, *Crime by Computer.* New York: Charles Scribner's Sons, 1976, pp. 118-174; Conklin, *"Illegal But Not Criminal"*, p. 46; and Edward Gross, "Organizational Structure and Organizational Crime," in G. Geis and E. Stotland, *White-Collar Crime.* Beverly Hills: Sage, 1980, pp. 71-73.

81 Alexander, "Crime in the Suites," p. 57; Merrill Hartson, "E.F. Hutton Pleads Guilty to Fraud," *Cincinnati Enquirer* (May 3, 1985), p. C-8; Barbara Rudolph, "E.F. Hutton's Simmering Scandal," *Time* (July 22, 1985), p. 53; "Capitalist Punishment," *The New Republic* (May 27, 1985), pp. 5-6.

82 Alexander, "Crime in the Suites," p. 56; John S. DeMott, "Dirty Money in the Spotlight: A Proposal to Get Tough on Banks That Launder Cash," *Time* (November 12, 1984), p. 85; "Capital Punishment," p. 5.

83 Susan P. Shapiro, *Wayward Capitalists: Target of the Securities and Exchange Commission.* New Haven: Yale University Press, 1984, p. 2.

84 *Ibid.*, pp. 31-32.

85 Wheeler and Rothman, "The Organization as Weapon in White-Collar Crime," pp. 1414-1415.

86 Alexander, "Crime in the Suites," p. 56; Ben L. Kaufman, "Seven Plead Guilty in ESM Collapse," *Cincinnati Enquirer* (April 18, 1986), pp. A-1, A-22; Karen Garloch, "ESM Officer to Take Cruise Before Sentence," *Cincinnati Enquirer* (April 26, 1986), pp. C-1, C-2; Karen Garloch, "Lines Gone, But Home State Story Isn't Over Yet," *Cincinnati Enquirer* (December 29, 1985), p. A-5; John J. Byczkowski, "Home State Bank Loss May Pass $100 Million," *Cincinnati Enquirer* (March 14, 1985), p. B-9.

87 Robert P. Gandossy, *Bad Business: The OPM Scandal and the Seduction of the Establishment.* New York: Basic Books, 1985, pp. 5-6; "OPM Leasing's 2 Former Top Executives Plead Guilty in a $200 Million Fraud Case," *Wall Street Journal* (March 15, 1982), p. 6.

88 Mark J. Green with Beverly C. Moore, Jr. and Bruce Wasserstein, *The Closed Enterprise System.* New York: Grossman, 1972.

89 Clinard and Yeager, *Corporate Crime*, pp. 134-136. See also Suzanne Weaver, "Antitrust Division of the Department of Justice" and Robert A. Klatzmann, "Federal Trade Commission," both contained in James Q. Wilson (ed.), *The Politics of Regulation.* New York: Basic Books, 1980.

90 Ross, "How Lawless Are Big Companies?" p. 57.

91 Clinard and Yeager, *Corporate Crime*, p. 142.

[92] Mark Green and John F. Berry, "White-Collar Crime is Big Business: Corporate Crime—I," *The Nation* 240 (June 8, 1985), p. 705.

[93] Ralph Nader and Mark Green, "Crime in the Suites: Coddling the Corporations," *The New Republic* 166 (April 20, 1972), p. 18.

[94] *Ibid.*, p. 18.

[95] Clinard and Yeager, *Corporate Crime*, p. 141.

[96] Green and Berry, "White-Collar Crime Is Big Business," p. 705; Green et al., *The Closed Enterprise System*, pp. 3-4; Nader and Green,"Crime in the Suites," p. 18; "Highway Robbery: The War on Bid Riggers," *U.S. News and World Report* (February 16, 1981), pp. 49-50; Clinard and Yeager, *Corporate Crime*, pp. 8, 133-154.

[97] For accounts, see Richard A. Smith, "The Incredible Electrical Conspiracy," in Donald R. Cressey and David A. Ward (eds.), *Delinquency, Crime and Social Process*. New York: Harper and Row, 1969, pp. 884-912; John G. Fuller, *The Gentlemen Conspirators: The Story of Price-Fixers in the Electrical Industry*. New York: Grove Press, 1962; Myron Watkins, "The Electrical Equipment Antitrust Cases: Their Implications for Government and For Business," *University of Chicago Law Review* 29 (Autumn 1961), pp. 97-110.

[98] Fuller, *The Gentlemen Conspirators*, pp. 57, 67.

[99] Gilbert Geis, "Deterring Corporate Crime," in M. David Ermann and Richard J. Lundman (eds.), *Corporate and Governmental Deviance*. New York: Oxford University Press, 1978, p. 281.

[100] Ralph Nader and Aileen Cowan, "Claims Without Substance," in Ralph Nader (ed.), *The Consumer and Corporate Accountability*. New York: Harcourt, Brace, Jovanovich, 1973, p. 97.

[101] Clinard and Yeager, *Corporate Crime*, pp. 254-256.

[102] Geis, "Deterring Corporate Crime," p. 282.

[103] Marshall B. Clinard and Richard Quinney, *Criminal Behavior Systems: A Typology*. New York: Holt, Rinehart and Winston, 1973, p. 217.

[104] Balkan et al., *Crime and Deviance in America*, p. 168. More generally, see Braithwaite, *Corporate Crime in the Pharmaceutical Industry*.

[105] Quoted in Clinard and Yeager, *Corporate Crime*, p. 11.

[106] Harold C. Barnett, "Corporate Capitalism, Corporate Crime," *Crime and Delinquency* 27 (January 1981), p. 9.

[107] Green and Berry, "White-Collar Crime Is Big Business," p. 706.

[108] Schrager and Short, "Toward a Sociology of Organizational Crime," p. 413.

[109] Clinard and Yeager, *Corporate Crime*, p. 8.

[110] Alexander, "Crime in the Suites," p. 56; "GE Pleads Guilty to Fraud: Company Agrees to Pay $1.04 Million Fine," *Cincinnati Enquirer* (May 14, 1985), pp. A-1, A-8; Randy Whitestone, "Three More GE Managers Charged in Fraud Case," *Cincinnati Enquirer* (July 17, 1985), p. F-4.

[111] Tom Morgenthau, "Waste, Fraud, and Abuse?" *Newsweek* (June 3, 1985), p. 22. See also Alexander, "Crime in the Suites," p. 56.

[112] Barbara Rudolph, "An Unexpected Fall from Grace: NASA's Chief Is Indicted in a General Dynamics Case," *Time* (December 16, 1985), p. 46.

[113] Alexander, "Crime in the Suites," p. 56.

[114] Diane Vaughan, *Controlling Unlawful Organizational Behavior: Social Structure and Corporate Misconduct*. Chicago: University of Chicago Press, 1983, pp. 1-19.

[115] Brent Fisse, "Community Service as a Sanction Against Corporations," *Wisconsin Law Review* (No. 5, 1981), p. 990. The $13.24 million fine was reduced to $5 million when Allied Chemical allocated $8 million to establish the Virginia Environmental Corporation, a non-profit corporation that would "fund scientific research projects and implement remedial projects and other programs to help alleviate the problem that Kepone has created...and...enhance and improve the overall quality of the environment in Virginia." See Brent Fisse and John Braithwaite, *The Impact of Publicity on Corporate Offenders*. Albany: State University of New York Press, 1983, p. 64.

[116] Green and Berry, "White-Collar Crime Is Big Business," p. 705; David Zwick and Marcy Bonstock, *Water Wasteland*. New York: Grossman, 1971, p. 33.

[117] Ralph Nader, "Compulsory Consumption," in Nader (ed.), *The Consumer and Corporate Accountability*. New York: Harcourt, Brace, Jovanovich, 1973, p. 179.

[118] *U.S. Budget in Brief: FY 1982*. The nine regulatory agencies include the FDA, OSHA, NHTSA, EPA, CPSC, FTC, SEC, ICC, and Antitrust Division of the Department of Justice.

[119] Sutherland, "White-Collar Criminality," p. 5.

[120] Quoted in Gilbert Geis, "Upperworld Crime," in Abraham Blumberg (ed.), *Current Perspectives on Criminal Behavior: Essays on Criminology*. New York: Alfred A. Knopf, 1981, p. 192.

[121] Clinard and Yeager, *Corporate Crime*, p. 8; Chamber of Commerce, *White-Collar Crime*, p. 7; Conklin, *"Illegal But Not Criminal"*, p. 7.

[122] Quoted in Christopher D. Stone, *Where the Law Ends: The Social Control of Corporate Behavior*. New York: Harper and Row, 1975, p. xi. See also, among others, Hills, *Crime, Power, and Morality*, p. 170, and Conklin, *Criminology*, p. 60.

[123] In this regard, see Michael Flannery, "76 Percent View Graft Here as Extensive, Poll Finds," *Chicago Sun Times* (January 29, 1978), pp. 1, 6; Lipset and Schneider, *The Confidence* Gap, p. 6.

[124] This tragic description became the title of a thorough analysis of this disaster and its impact on the lives of those who experienced it. See Kai T. Erikson, *Everything In Its Path: Destruction of Community in the Buffalo Creek Flood*. New York: Simon and Schuster, 1976.

[125] Quoted in Gerald M. Stern, *The Buffalo Creek Disaster*. New York: Vintage Books, 1976, p. 12. Stern furnishes a comprehensive account of the disaster and the attempts of its victims to win compensation from Pittston.

[126] Quoted in Erikson, *Everything In Its Path*, p. 183.

127 Stern, *The Buffalo Creek Disaster*, p. 70.

128 *Ibid.*, p. 299; "Pittston Settles Claims from '72 Dam Collapse Totaling $4,880,000," *Wall Street Journal* (January 25, 1978), p. 17. Note that a Special Grand Jury was convened to consider the possibility of criminal charges following the tragedy, but no indictments were handed down. According to Stern, although members of the Grand Jury apparently held strong sentiments against the company, a prosecutor had instructed them that it would be "legally and particularly practically difficult to sustain an indictment against Pittston." See pp. 73-74.

129 Stern, *The Buffalo Creek Disaster*, pp. 148, 151-153.

130 Erikson, *Everything In Its Path*, pp. 183-184.

131 *Ibid.*, p. 154.

132 *Ibid.*, p. 196.

133 Clinard and Yeager, *Corporate Crime*, p. 9; Ronald C. Kramer, "A Prolegomenon to the Study of Corporate Violence," *Humanity and Society* 7 (May 1983), pp. 149-178 and "Is Corporate Crime Serious? Criminal Justice and Corporate Crime Control," *Journal of Contemporary Criminal Justice* 2 (June 1984), p. 7-10; Braithwaite, "Challenging Just Deserts," p. 744; Reiman, *The Rich Get Richer and The Poor Get Prison*, p. 82 and, more generally, pp. 44-94; Hills, *Crime, Power, and Morality*, pp. 168-169; Ralph Nader, "Business Crime," *New Republic* 157 (July 1, 1967), p. 8 and "Corporate Disregard for Life," in his edited volume, *The Consumer and Corporate Accountability*. New York: Harcourt, Brace, Jovanovich, 1973, pp. 151-153.

134 Ralph Nader, Introduction," in Joseph A. Page and Mary-Win O'Brien, *Bitter Wages*. New York: Grossman, 1973, p. xiii.

135 National Institute for Occupational Safety and Health (NIOSH), *Prevention of Leading Work-Related Diseases and Injuries*. Washington, D.C.: U.S. Government Printing Office, 1985. See section titled "Severe Occupational Traumatic Injuries." This document is composed of articles reprinted from *Morbidity and Mortality Weekly Report*. A recent report places the number of workplace fatalities in 1984 at 3,740, and observes that this represents an increase of 21 percent over 1983. See Robert L. Simison, "Safety Last: Job Deaths and Injuries Seem to Be Increasing After Years of De-

cline," *Wall Street Journal* (March 18, 1986), p.1. More generally, see Daniel M. Berman, *Death on the Job: Occupational Health and Safety Struggles in the United States*. New York: Monthly Review Press, 1978; Joseph A. Page and Mary-Win O'Brien, *Bitter Wages*. New York: Grossman, 1973; Carl Gersuny, *Work Hazards and Industrial Conflict*. Hanover, New Hampshire: University Press of New England, 1981.

[136] Green and Berry, "White-Collar Crime Is Big Business," p. 706.

[137] Schrager and Short, "Toward a Sociology of Organizational Crime," p. 413.

[138] Balkan et al., *Crime and Deviance in America*, p. 171. See also John Braithwaite, *To Punish or Persuade: Enforcement of Coal Mine Safety*. Albany: State University of New York Press, 1985, p. 102.

[139] NIOSH, *Prevention of Leading Work-Related Diseases and Injuries*. See Table 2 in article titled "Severe Occupational Traumatic Injuries."

[140] Harry M. Caudill, "Manslaughter in a Coal Mine," *The Nation* 224 (April 23, 1977), p. 497. See also Reiman, *The Rich Get Richer and the Poor Get Prison*, pp. 45-46. Note that fifteen miners died in an initial explosion; a second explosion claimed the lives of eleven members of a rescue team.

[141] Joel Swartz, "Silent Killers at Work," in M. David Ermann and Richard J. Lundman (eds.), *Corporate and Governmental Deviance*. New York: Oxford University Press, 1978, pp. 114-128.

[142] Paul Brodeur, *Outrageous Misconduct: The Asbestos Industry on Trial*. New York: Pantheon Books, 1985, p. 355. See also Dorothy Nelkin and Michael S. Brown, *Workers at Risk: Voices from the Workplace*. Chicago: University of Chicago Press, 1984.

[143] NIOSH, *Prevention of Leading Work-Related Diseases and Injuries*. See article titled "Occupational Lung Diseases."

[144] *Ibid.*

[145] *Ibid.*

[146] *Ibid.* See articles titled "Occupational Lung Diseases" and "Occupational Cancers (Other Than Lung)."

[147] *Ibid.* See article titled "Occupational Cancers (Other Than Lung)."

[148] *Ibid.* See articles titled "Disorders of Reproduction," "Cardiovascular Diseases," and "Occupational Lung Diseases."

[149] Swartz, "Silent Killers at Work," p. 124.

[150] Brodeur, *Outrageous Misconduct*, p. 283.

[151] Details on the Film Recovery System's case were drawn from the following sources: Nancy Frank, *Crimes Against Health and Safety.* New York: Harrow and Heston, 1985, pp. 21-25; Rena Wish Cohen and Debbe Nelson, "Stefan Golab's Job Was a Death Sentence," *The Daily Herald* (October 30, 1983), pp. 1, 9; John Burnett, "Corporate Murder Verdict May Not Become Trend, Say Legal Experts," *Occupational Health and Safety* (October 1985), pp. 22-26, 58-59; Rick Kendall, "Criminal Charges on the Rise for Workplace Injuries, Deaths," *Occupational Hazards* (December 1985), pp. 49-53; "Murder in the Front Office," *Newsweek* (July 8, 1985), p. 58; Tim Padgett and Leslie Baldacci, "Execs Get 25 Years," *Chicago Sun-Times* (July 2, 1985), pp. 1-2; Bill Richards and Alex Kotlowitz, "Judge Finds 3 Corporate Officials Guilty of Murder in Cyanide Death of Worker," *Wall Street Journal* (June 17, 1985); Steven Greenhouse, "3 Executives Convicted of Murder for Unsafe Workplace Conditions," *New York Times* (June 15, 1985), pp. 1, 9; "Convictions May Jolt Corporate World," *Lexington Herald-Leader*, (June 16, 1985); Ray Gibson and William Presecky, "Indictments Cite Officials, 3 Firms," *Chicago Tribune* (October 20, 1983), pp. 1, 8; Barry Siegel, "Murder Case a Corporate Landmark," *Los Angeles Times* (September 15, 1985), pp. 1, 8-9.

[152] Burnett, "Corporate Murder Verdict May Not Become Trend, Say Legal Experts," p. 22.

[153] *Ibid.*, p. 22.

[154] Kendall, "Criminal Charges on the Rise for Workplace Injuries, Deaths," p. 49.

[155] Padgett and Baldacci, "Execs Get 25 Years," pp. 1-2.

[156]   Joan Claybrook and the Staff of Public Citizen, *Retreat From Safety: Reagan's Attack on America's Safety.* New York: Pantheon Books, 1984, p. 60.

[157]   Gilbert Geis, "Victimization Patterns in White-Collar Crime," in I. Drapkin and E. Viano (eds.), *Victimology: A New Focus, Volume V., Exploiters and Exploited.* Lexington, Massachusetts, 1973, p. 93; Braithwaite, "Challenging Just Deserts," p. 745.

[158]   Schrager and Short, "Toward a Sociology of Organizational Crime," p. 415.

[159]   Harrison Wellford, *Sowing the Wind.* New York: Grossman, 1972, pp. 17, 29, 130.

[160]   David R. Simon and D. Stanley Eitzen, *Elite Deviance.* Second Edition. Boston: Allyn and Bacon, 1986, p. 102. See also Neal Karlen with Jeff B. Copeland, "A 'Mystery Meat' Scandal," *Newsweek* (September 24, 1984), p. 31.

[161]   Clinard and Yeager, *Corporate Crime*, p. 266.

[162]   Claybrook et al., *Retreat From Safety*, p. 59.

[163]   Ralph Nader, *Unsafe At Any Speed: The Designed-In Dangers of the American Automobiles.* New York: Grossman, 1965. Nader's book and its impact will be discussed in Chapter 4.

[164]   J. Patrick Wright, *On a Clear Day You Can See General Motors: John Z. DeLorean's Look Inside the Automotive Giant.* New York: Avon, 1979, p. 65.

[165]   *Ibid.*, p. 67. Notably, Lee Iacocca shares the view that the Corvair was an unsafe vehicle. Thus, he commented that "GM had its fiascos, too, like the Corvair. Here I find myself in rare agreement with Ralph Nader: the Corvair really was unsafe." See Lee Iacocca, *Iacocca: An Autobiography.* New York: Bantam Books, 1984, p. 161. On the other hand, GM lost only one Corvair-related civil case that reached trial; other suits, however, were settled out of court. See Fisse and Braithwaite, *The Impact of Publicity on Corporate Offenders*, p. 28.

[166] Kermit Vandiver, "The Aircraft Brake Scandal," *Harper's Magazine* 244 (April 1972), pp. 45-52.

[167] Clinard and Yeager, *Corporate Crime*, p. 120.

[168] For case studies focusing on the physical costs of corporate illegality, see Braithwaite, *Corporate Crime in the Pharmaceutical Industry*, Chapters 3 and 4.

[169] *Ibid.*, p. 64. See also Paul D. Rheingold, "The MER/29 Story—An Instance of Successful Mass Disaster Litigation," *California Law Review* 56 (January 1968), 116-148.

[170] Morton Mintz, *At Any Cost: Corporate Greed, Women, and the Dalkon Shield*. New York: Pantheon Books, 1985.

[171] *Ibid.*, p. 4.

[172] *Ibid.*, pp. 3, 242.

[173] *Ibid.*, p. 7.

[174] *Ibid.*, p. 245. See also p. 242.

[175] *Ibid.*, p. 247.

[176] "Living, Dangerously, with Toxic Wastes," *Time* (October 14, 1985), p. 86. More generally, see the October 14, 1985 issue of *Time*, bearing the cover titled, "Toxic Wastes: The Poisoning of America."

[177] Clayborn et. al., *Retreat From Safety*, p. 118.

[178] Roger Rosenblatt, "All the World Gasped," *Time* (December 17, 1984), p. 20. More generally, see the December 17, 1984 issue of *Time*, bearing the cover titled, "India's Disaster: The Night of Death—A Global Worry."

[179] Quoted in Jay S. Albanese, "Love Canal Six Years Later: The Legal Legacy," *Federal Probation* 48 (June 1984), p. 54.

[180] Alan A. Bloch and Frank R. Scarpitti, *Poisoning For Profit: The Mafia and Toxic Waste in America*. New York: William Morrow and Company, 1985, p. 40.

[181]   Michael Brown, *Laying Waste: The Poisoning of America by Toxic Chemicals.* New York: Pantheon Books, 1979, pp. 10-11, 52. It should be noted that we have drawn a number of specific details about the Love Canal case from Brown's account. See pp. 3-59.

[182]   *Ibid.*, p. xii.

[183]   Albanese, "Love Canal Six Years Later," p. 53.

[184]   Ed Magnuson, "A Problem That Cannot Be Buried," Time (October 14, 1985), p. 76.

[185]   *Ibid.*, p. 76.

[186]   Bloch and Scarpitti, *Poisoning For Profit*, pp. 50-51.

[187]   Green and Berry, "White-Collar Crime Is Big Business," p. 706.

[188]   Jay Albanese has noted that the federal suit was filed on December 20, 1979 and charged Hooker "with dumping chemical wastes at four different sites in Niagara Falls." The New York State suit was filed on April 28, 1980 and named as the defendant both Hooker and its parent company, Occidental Petroleum Corporation. See his article, "Love Canal Six Years Later," p. 53. On the faculty of Niagara University and a close observer of the Love Canal case, Professor Albanese has informed us that as of this writing (May 1986), the suits against Hooker and Occidental Petroleum Corporation are still awaiting trial, with few ostensible signs that a settlement is likely.

[189]   Ralph Nader, "Introduction," in John C. Esposito, *Vanishing Air.* New York: Grossman, 1970, pp. vii-viii. See also Ralph Nader, "The Profits of Pollution," *The Progressive* 34 (april 1970), pp. 19-22.

[190]   Clinard and Yeager, *Corporate Crime*, pp. 116-117. More generally, see Jonathan Lash, Katherine Gillman, and David Sheridan, *A Season of Spoils: The Story of the Reagan Administration's Attack on the Environment.* New York: Pantheon Books, 1984.

[191]   Barry Meier, "Dirty Job: Against Heavy Odds, EPA Tries to Convict Polluters and Dumpers," *Wall Street Journal* (January 7, 1985), p. 1.

192 *Ibid.*, p. 1; "Prosecutions Increase in Environmental Cases," *Cincinnati Enquirer* (March 2, 1986), p. E-14.

Chapter 3
Corporate Criminal Liability: An Historical Overview

The preceding chapter developed the idea that corporate crime is a pervasive phenomenon, harmful to our society. Those who study the phenomenon, investigators as diverse as journalists and academic researchers, agree that a substantial number of United States corporations have been or are involved in criminal activity, often on a continuing basis. They also concur that corporate crime, like criminal behavior in general, is costly to us.

We all suffer when corporate crime causes us to doubt, for good reason, the effectiveness and fairness of our institutions, particularly our economic and legal institutions. In recent years we have been besieged by reports of dangerous products that were marketed knowingly, by embarrassing examples of unethical business practices, and by disclosures of corporate decision making that flagrantly disregarded our quality of life or violated the basic values that we espouse as a society. Too often, however, corporations and, sometimes, government have evaded rather than responded to these concerns. Such unresponsiveness tends to erode confidence in our institutions, producing cynicism and the crisis in legitimation that we discussed in the first chapter. As we noted, this loss of confidence is especially troublesome with respect to the law because faith in the legal order is essential to the legitimacy of government and its exercise of political power.[1] But despite the gravity of the deeds and the costs to all of us, the law, especially the criminal law, has often provided insufficient redress for the socially harmful behavior of corporations.

In the pages to follow, we will trace the development of the corporation from its beginnings as a rather limited collective entity to its present state as the dominant form of business enterprise. We will consider why and how the corporation has historically enjoyed a degree of immunity from the provisions of the criminal law. Finally, we will see that this immunity has gradually been eroded so that today corporations are increasingly held responsible, even by the criminal law, for their socially harmful behaviors.

Law and the Social Order

Law is a social institution that regulates human behavior. Along with other mechanisms of social regulation, such as custom and religion, law is characterized by norms and sanctions—that is, by expectations of behavior and a reward-punishment scheme that encourages compliance with these expectations. Notions of social harm tend to pervade discussions of law; it is commonly assumed, for example, that strongly held social values, those that are basic to the very existence of society and proscribe the most harmful behavior, fall within the ambit of the criminal law.[2] What we mean by "crime" is the contravention of these values, and the penal sanction is the societal response to their violation.

Of course, the content of law varies from time to time, as does the specific form of the penal sanction. In addition, the purpose or justification for the sanction has changed over the years. Punishment has existed in a variety of forms, such as imprisonment, all sorts of torture, and death. Rationales for the penal sanction have included (1) retribution in its various forms, such as deserved punishment, punishment as an expression of social reprobation, and punishment for expiation; (2) incapacitation or the isolation of offenders from society; (3) deterrence of either a specific offender or of the general population; and (4) reformative and later rehabilitative programs designed to effect changes in the behavior and values of offenders. Each rationale has predominated at some time in history. Rehabilitation, for example, has been the official justification for the penal sanction during the past one hundred years in the United States. To some extent, however, all these rationales have coexisted and exerted a combination of influences, although inconsistent, on the administration of penal sanctions.

Until recently these rationales for the penal sanction—punishment in its many forms and the normative component of the criminal law—have been applicable to conventional or street crime but not to corporate criminality. For years it was perhaps paradoxical to speak of corporate crime at all, in light of the legal convention that "at common law" a corporation could not commit a crime. According to the strict legalistic definition, crime presumes a prohibited act and a penal sanction—that is, an act prohibited by the criminal law and for which the criminal law specifies a punishment. But for reasons that will be discussed in this chapter, the actions of corporations were neither considered within the purview nor subject to the usual sanctions of the criminal law in the strict legalistic sense. For this reason, among others, the trial of the Ford Motor Company for reckless homicide is a landmark case.

Not surprisingly, the legalistic definition of crime guides the operation of the legal apparatus and probably enjoys popular support among the general population as well. But despite its widespread acceptance, the legalistic definition has not foreclosed academic debate on the question of what constitutes crime. It has been criticized as an exercise in circular reasoning: crime is whatever the criminal law says it is. In reaction, scholars have offered alternative definitions. The notion of social harm is typically incorporated into these definitions, although they vary as to its importance in the reformulation. For some scholars social harm is an element of equal importance with a prohibited act and a penal sanction, while for others it assumes a greater importance or even becomes the primary concern in defining crime.

The academic debate over the definition of crime has special relevance to corporate criminality and was generated, in fact, by a concern about that phenomenon. As we mentioned in the previous chapter, the legalistic definition was articulated early in a compelling way by Paul Tappan. He offered it to counter the definition suggested by Edwin Sutherland and other sociologists who were interested in corporate and white-collar criminality. Their formulations were designed to expand the concept of crime to include the actions of corporations that were socially injurious but not illegal. Those proposals reflected the belief that many business practices were harmful to society and should be considered criminal, but traditionally were excluded from the scope of criminal law because of the power and influence of the business community. They reasoned that a consideration of the notion of social harm might help to overcome that definitional bias. Tappan responded with the legalistic signification because he feared that the more sociological approach would result in a vacuous definition that would impede criminological analysis.[3]

The legalistic definition is the one applied by the legal apparatus, but the academic debate over the definition of crime remains lively today.[4] More important, this continuing controversy is still instructive because it forces us to consider the notion of social harm, a fundamentally important issue, when we ask, "What *is* the definition of crime? What *should* it be?"

The somewhat philosophical "is-versus-ought" issue is addressed only partially, or perhaps evaded, by the assumption noted earlier that the criminal law reflects those values believed most basic to the continuation of society. By implication, the criminal law proscribes those acts that are most detrimental or harmful to society, but this implication poses a dilemma. If it is true, it apparently fails to explain why many actions of corporations are not considered criminal even though their conduct has obviously been socially harmful over the years.

One of two responses is usually given to this problem. First, it is sometimes suggested that the social harm produced by corporations and their responsibility for this harm are difficult to perceive. The point is not simply that corporate crime is complex, which it often is, but rather that a kind of Parkinson's Law describes our understanding of crime; our comprehension is greatest when the phenomenon is simplest.[5] While crime is easily defined as a violation of *social* norms and (arguably) as *socially* harmful, our understanding of unlawful conduct tends to be fixated at the *individual* level. In fact, the entire crime-punishment nexus is highly individualistic. In the traditional model one person harms another and receives punishment. Criminal activity at a more complex level—such as a collective entity harming great numbers of scattered victims and receiving punishment—simply does not suggest itself and was inconceivable at common law. The early law was designed to regulate the behavior of individuals as natural persons, not a juristic person like the corporation. In a strict legalistic sense, the corporation had no mind to form the requisite intent to commit a prohibited act and no body to punish.[6] Therefore, no matter how grave the social harm, the corporation could not commit a crime.

The second answer reflects the assumption that the criminal law reflects and protects the most strongly held social values. Criminal behavior, according to this view, is an official pronouncement of society's moral boundaries. If an act is not a crime, either it does not transcend the boundaries or the law has temporarily lagged behind the moral sentiments. But boundaries are not permanent, and they change, though often with some lag, as society changes. Thus a behavior may be considered within society's moral boundaries at one time but outside at another. Therefore certain actions of corporations may not have been considered harmful enough to violate the moral boundaries at common law, but were viewed later as sufficiently serious to deserve the label "criminal."[7]

These two responses are usually given to the question of why corporate misbehavior was not considered a violation of criminal law. Crime, according to the traditional view, is highly individualistic, and/or the moral boundaries—that is, what is regarded as seriously wrong or harmful—have shifted only recently so that corporate malfeasance now provokes widespread disapproval. We use the "and/or" conjunction because these answers need not be mutually exclusive and because each is probably correct as far as it goes. But these answers still beg the question and generate yet another set of inquiries. Why is our perception of crime individualistic? Why did the moral boundaries shift?

To answer these questions and to address the more fundamental issue of the corporation's exclusion for years from the purview of the criminal law, we must analyze the development of the corporate form. This analysis must be sensitive to the historical context of law.

The Historical Context of Law

We suggest the need for an analysis of law that is historically specific and applicable to the development of the corporation. Historical periods are characterized by different perceptions of behavior, including crime, by different perceptions of responsibility for that behavior, and by particular conceptualizations of justice, the ultimate aim of the law.[8] Within historical periods we can comprehend specific connections and perhaps discover more general interrelationships among law and other social phenomena.

These interrelationships have been the subject of intellectual discourse, and a number of prominent scholars paid special attention to the importance of these interrelationships during the formative years of the social sciences, such as sociology. On several occasions, for example, we have alluded to the assumption that the criminal law reflects the most strongly held social values and that a relationship exists between law and the moral sentiments of society's members. Our statement, however, was rather attenuated; many who endorse this view develop a far more elaborate framework for the interaction. The French sociologist Emile Durkheim is frequently cited as support for this connection. Writing during the late 1800s and early 1900s, Durkheim addressed the degree to which law reflected the values that were common to the average member of society. In his analysis, however, legal norms were much more than a mere reflection of social values, especially in more complex societies. Changes in legal norms and in penal sanctions were not simply the mirror image of changing social values in Durkheim's scheme, but instead were attributed to increasing societal complexity, a decreasing role for religion in the regulation of behavior, and the degree of centralization of political authority.[9]

Of course, scholars differ as to which factors they consider most important for an understanding of legal norms or the transformations in the norms. Some writers minimize the impact of values in favor of other social factors. For Karl Marx, a German social scientist and a contemporary of Durkheim, the key factor was the mode of production, that complex set of relations that surrounds the economic base of society. Law and other social institutions constitute the superstructure that is built upon the economic base. According to Marx,

> The sum total of these relations of production constitutes the economic structure of society—the real foundation on which rise legal and political superstructures and to which correspond definite forms of social consciousness.[10]

Similarly, the economy was an important consideration for Max Weber, a German scholar who made his intellectual contributions at about the same time as Marx and Durkheim. Weber was especially concerned with the autonomy of law, the development of the legal profession, and their relationship to the rise of the bureaucratic state. He believed that the modern political organization, legitimated by the legal order, provided the rationality or predictability necessary for the emergence of capitalism as a sophisticated economic system.[11]

Clearly, Durkheim, Marx, and Weber offer different views, but they also show important points of agreement. Despite substantive debates, all three see law as a social institution that is intertwined with other institutions; law is sensitive to alterations in those institutions, and facilitates and contributes to the changes. These three scholars established the intellectual framework for theoretical analyses that address the interrelationship of law and other social institutions.

We are interested in a related, though more specific, issue: the emergence and the law's treatment of the corporation. Accordingly, we are guided by the pioneering efforts of Durkheim, Marx, and Weber. Our review of the historical record prompts us to focus on three factors that are of primary importance to an analysis of the corporation's development: the centralization of political authority in the state, the shift in the economic structure from feudalism through mercantilism to capitalism, and changes in "person" as a legal concept. Two of these factors obviously draw on those earlier scholars; the centralization of political authority is a significant issue for both Durkheim and Weber, and the economic structure is a central theme for Weber and Marx. In addition, we find the concept of person especially relevant because new dimensions of the meaning of person and the meaning of personal responsibility accompanied the acceptance of the corporation as a legal entity. Thus we suggest that we can best understand the emergence of the corporate form and its relationship to the criminal law through an historical analysis that is keyed to three factors: the state, the economy, and person as a legal concept. The remainder of this chapter will be devoted to such an analysis.

The Development of the Corporation

Corporations are the dominant business form in our society today; they are both pervasive and wield tremendous economic power. Their prevalence is reflected in the sheer number of corporations and in a diversity of size and organization that ranges from the individual entrepreneur to the transnational conglomerate. Their economic power is evidenced by wealth and productivity that in some of the larger corporations exceeds the gross national product of entire nations.

Yet, ironically, the pervasiveness of corporations in our society causes us to view them somewhat myopically. For, despite its considerable impact on our lives for good and bad, the corporate form is a relatively recent development. The dominance of the corporate form and the explosive growth that produced it date to just over one hundred years ago. As recently as the early 1800s, the corporation was a rarity in the United States; before then the corporate form evolved at what we must regard as a plodding pace.

The development of the corporation followed a complex and circuitous route, accompanying significant and interrelated transformations in the economic structure of society, the nature of political authority, and the concept of person. The emergence of the corporation is best understood within the context of the large-scale social changes that occurred through the Middle Ages and into the Industrial Revolution.

Early History

The history of the corporation begins in Europe early in the Middle Ages, when feudalism was the dominant institutional feature of society. Feudalism was characterized by a way of life that differed greatly from the conditions that had prevailed in earlier centuries. During more primitive times, society was comprised of small groups of people, often kinship groups, who banded together to insure survival. These groups were a homogeneous population with little economic or political division of labor.

This pattern changed with the feudal period. Economically, feudalism entailed an agrarian existence linked to the ownership of land parceled into feudal estates. Even social and legal interactions—that is, the rights and responsibilities that people owed one another—were informed by this arrangement. The relationships that revolved around feudalism were hierarchical, and included definite superiors (the feudal lords) and subordinates (the serfs). Sir Henry Maine, a nineteenth century expert on the history of legal development, described this arrangement as a "status relationship"—that is, one's place in the hierarchy was determined at birth and was rarely transcended.[12] Rights and responsibilities existed as a set of reciprocal obligations and expectations between the serfs, who owed their basic existence and fealty to the feudal lord (as had their parents to the previous lord), and the lord, who inherited the fidelity and labor of the serfs along with the duty of providing for their subsistence.

Feudalism was characterized by a decentralized pattern of political authority; the power resided for the most part in the feudal estates rather than in the collective population, as in earlier days. There was no powerful state as yet, and the most significant development of centralized authority took place not in the state but in the church. At this stage the regulation or maintenance of social order that accompanies political power was in the hands of the feudal lords and the church. The authorities enjoyed different spheres of influence—the secular and the sacred—although there was considerable overlap and occasional conflict.

In primitive times, long before the feudal period, the focus of social regulation was to restore the social order or equilibrium that was disturbed when someone violated a norm. Accordingly, sanctions tended to be collective both in purpose and administration. For example, violations that threatened the entire group, such as breaking a taboo, were sanctioned to appease the supernatural, and the punishment might be administered by the group. Even disputes that were relatively individualistic often produced something of a collective response. Acts of retaliation were likely to come from a victim's kin and were directed against the offender or the offender's close relatives. But whether a violation threatened the group as a whole or only a few members, responsibility for a wrongdoing was a matter of strict liability. According to one source, "liability was founded on the act of doing damage rather than on any subjective state of, or degree of care exercised by, the defendant."[13] The major issue was the injury, and liability was imputed through a variety of vicarious and indirect methods; someone might be held responsible for an injury because he or she was nearby when it occurred. Oracles and other supernatural signs were also important in assigning liability.[14]

During the feudal period, by contrast, responsibility was perhaps less collective, at least in the sense of kinship groups. Even so, it was still a far cry from the internal, individual matter that it would later become. Because criminality as embodied in the legal concept of *mens rea* remained undeveloped, internal volition and subjective intent were less important than the external, objective relationship between a violation and the person punished as accountable. The maintenance of social order persisted as the basis of sanctions, although that sense of equilibrium now referred to stability on the feudal estate. Of course, that order was defined by the lord who administered the sanction as the superior in the hierarchial arrangement that characterized feudalism. Feudalism thus shaped not only the view of social harm that was now defined as a disturbance of the feudal order but also the administration and purpose for the imposition of sanctions.

The concept of person was simple and limited during the feudal period. It denoted the rights and responsibilities of an individual as a natural person, and was rarely applicable to a collective entity. Partnerships existed, but merely as assemblages of individuals, each with his or her own rights and responsibilities, not as juristic persons. Corporations thus did not exist.

In summary, wealth during the feudal period consisted primarily of land separated into feudal estates and owned by individuals. Rights and responsibilities and the political authority that governed them were largely a function of the feudal arrangement. The concept of person was limited and individualistic, and there was little place for forms of collective ownership. This pattern began to change, however, amid the societal upheavals of the Middle Ages.

The Middle Ages

The economic structure of European Society was shaped by feudalism early in the Middle Ages. Wealth meant land, but the right to own land was available only to those few with the good fortune to be born to it. During the fourteenth and fifteenth centuries, however, feudalism gave way to mercantilism and an economy based on trade. Commerce within and between nations appeared, and with it came the merchants who displaced the feudal lords as the primary economic actors in society. Merchants, too, owned property, but that ownership included commercial interests, not just land.

Shipping, the heart of the trading economy, flourished with continual advances in shipping technology. Ships became larger and faster and more profitable. But they also became more expensive to outfit, and trading ventures were more costly to undertake. For a variety of reasons (e.g. pirates, losses at sea), such ventures became riskier as well. Merchants were forced to pool their investments, and more complex and increasingly collective business forms were developed to accommodate these ventures. The trading company was probably the most important collective entity for the shipping economy.

Technological advances were not limited to shipping, of course; they occurred in other modes of transportation and in other sectors of business as well. Manufacturing eventually became as important as shipping, and European economies prospered with the transition to capitalism during the seventeenth and eighteenth centuries. With the dawning of the Industrial Revolution, the capitalists became the significant economic actors in society. The capitalists, like the merchants and traders before them, combined their resources or capital to achieve maximum economic growth. The collective business enterprise, in this case the joint stock company, facilitated the necessary concentration of capital. (Later in this section we will discuss more fully the trading company and the joint stock company, not only as business forms but also in terms of their relationship to the centralization of political authority and their ramifications for the legal concept of person). With the transition to capitalism, property took on yet another meaning: it changed from physical possession for one's own use to a source of value in exchange.[15]

Thus, in only a few centuries, the economic structure of European society was transformed from feudalism through mercantilism to capitalism. The transformation was massive and, not surprisingly, paradoxical as well. Amid unprecedented economic growth and prosperity, the old social order was disrupted and ultimately broke down. Accordingly, the upheavals that occurred in the Middle Ages included a transition in the nature of political authority and the establishment of a new social order.

A relocation of political authority accompanied the transformation in the economic structure of society. We will avoid the potentially reductionistic argument about which was the more significant change (with the implication that one caused the other) by simply suggesting that the political and the economic transformations each contributed to and were influenced by the other.

The political power of the feudal lords was by no means unchecked, even during the height of feudalism. As we mentioned previously, the church was also a powerful force during that period, and an uneasy truce existed between the two. And, of course, the church facilitated the decline of the feudal lords' authority. More important, however, as the economic dominance of the feudal lords waned, political power shifted from their hands to the state. The shift occurred with the strong support of the bourgeoisie, the increasingly powerful merchants of the emerging middle class. They supported the interests of the monarchy—the centralized state—against those of both the feudal lords and the church. Their growing economic power made their political support significant. Moreover, the Middle Ages witnessed the emergence of political doctrines such as the social contract, which justified both the ownership of property by the bourgeoisie and the concentration of political power in the state.

The shift of political power was a complex phenomenon, and to suggest that power simply vested in the state misses much of that complexity. The notion of state, for example, included both the monarchy and local authorities. During the mercantile period in England, the political authority of the feudal lords dissipated but remained somewhat local, residing for a time in the boroughs and counties, primarily in the hands of justices of the peace. Of course, the crown could tax the localities and grant or withhold business privileges, so even then the centralization of political authority was under way.[16]

That pattern was to continue throughout the Middle Ages. As the centralized state became stronger, its willingness and ability to regulate the entire population grew more pronounced. The expansion of state control occurred throughout Europe and England in both civil and criminal law. In civil matters, for example, the English Crown extended its control over local authorities and business interests via the royal charter, an official grant that conferred legal existence. With respect to the criminal law, the consolidation of power in the state proceeded through several stages. Initially, the Crown merely sought to limit blood feuds by encouraging victims or their kin to accept a compensatory payment rather than engage in retaliatory acts against an offender. Later the Crown became a public prosecutor for violations that disturbed the "King's Peace," thereby displacing local criminal jurisdiction. Eventually the Crown prosecuted and sanctioned criminals for offenses against the monarchy; the state had become the definer of legal norms.[17]

In both the civil and criminal spheres, the centralization of political authority culminated in the codification of laws and ultimately in lawmaking by legislation. For Sir Henry Maine, legislation represents the highest stage of legal development, and it exists only in modern, dynamic societies.[18] The modern legal system with its formally rational laws is also central to Max Weber's analysis; such a legal apparatus is an essential element of the modern bureaucratic state. Indeed, it is a condition precedent to the development of capitalism.[19]

The changes in the economic structure of society and in the nature of political authority were interrelated with the third transformation that occurred during the Middle Ages—the meaning of person as a legal concept. The meaning of the concept changed in two respects: first, it expanded beyond the limited definition of a natural person to include collective entities that were recognized as juristic persons; second, the nature of personal responsibility changed.

One of the earliest cases of legal recognition of a collective entity was occasioned by a dilemma that concerned the ownership of churches in the waning days of feudalism. Traditionally, the feudal lord erected a church on his estate and consequently enjoyed property rights in it. He also had the authority to select the priest, and the religious rites and activities incidental to the feudal, agrarian existence were performed in his church. But by the thirteenth century, the decline of feudalism was under way and the power of the feudal lord had begun to diminish on a number of fronts, including ownership of churches and associated property. The law was then confronted with a question for which there was no ready answer: if the feudal lord no longer owned the church and related property as an individual, who did? A number of legal fictions served as temporary solutions to the problem, but eventually it was concluded that the church owned itself, namely, the building, the property, and any income it generated from whatever source. Those who managed the church's affairs could transact business in its name, essentially as guardians. Of course the church was not a natural person but rather enjoyed a special status, that of a juristic person. The law recognized the church and also protected it, almost as a legal infant, from those who managed it as guardians.[20] In a sense that status was the best of both worlds.

The concept of a juristic person was extended still further during the thirteenth and fourteenth centuries to include English boroughs or townships. The boroughs incurred both financial rights and responsibilities as they gained the political authority that we mentioned earlier. The responsibilities included debts, usually rents and fines that were owed to the Crown. The rights included levying tolls and selling franchises. Further, such revenue-producing assets were transferable. The status of a juristic person facilitated these financial transactions by creating a collective entity that could conduct business as if it were a natural person.

The recognition of that special status reflected the increasing centralization of political authority. In the first place, the Crown was really a creditor with respect to the monies collected from boroughs; accordingly, when the boroughs enhanced their business prospects they added to the Crown's revenue. In addition, the Crown was involved in the financial rights of the boroughs in an even more important way. The rights to tolls and franchises and the ability to sell those rights were available only through the status of a juristic person, and that special status was conferred by the Crown through royal charters. In other words, the capacity to generate revenue depended on being recognized as a collective entity, and that recognition was the state's prerogative.[21]

This point is significant for two reasons. First, the collective entities that were recognized as juristic persons, including the corporation, developed largely at the pleasure of the state. Second, during much of its historical development, the corporation acted in a quasi-governmental capacity, in this case collecting tolls. As we shall see later, the first corporations that existed in the United States operated under strict charters from the states, and their activities were often quasi-governmental. These facts may partially explain the frequently preferential treatment enjoyed by corporations; they were a child of the state and in many instances performed the duties of the state.

One of the best examples of the complex interaction of business interests, political authority, and the development of a collective entity is the English trading company. The trading company emerged in the sixteenth century as one of the business forms that allowed merchants to pool investments and conduct business on a larger scale. At first the companies resembled partnerships wherein members engaged in business as individuals even though they had combined their resources. As trading ventures became even more elaborate, however, the companies developed into collective entities trading on joint stock. For a time, companies existed only for a single trading venture, but eventually they became permanent enterprises for investment.

Although business was the primary purpose of the trading companies, they shared with other phases of corporate development a secondary, quasigovernmental role. A significant share of the English economy was devoted to trade with other nations and to the colonization of new lands. The companies facilitated trade and, in new territories, often served in a political capacity until England could formally establish a colonial government.[22] The trading companies were actually viewed as an arm of the state. They owed their existence to the royal charter, whose antecedent may be found in the earlier entitlements to English boroughs that were also granted for the performance of business and governmental activities. The royal charter granted legal existence to the trading companies while further consolidating power in the centralized state as the grantor of that existence.

This symbiotic relationship was evidenced by the passage of the Bubble Act in 1719, in which the operation of unchartered joint stock companies was declared unlawful. The unchartered joint stock company was a rather accommodating, if informal, type of enterprise that owed its composition to prevailing business practices. (Ironically, it became more widespread after the passage of the prohibitory legislation.) The Bubble Act produced a financial panic that caused the collapse of some chartered companies; as a result, the demand for charters declined drastically. Following the loss of confidence in chartered companies, the legal community devised a number of ingenious methods that circumvented the restrictions of the Bubble Act and made the unchartered joint stock company even more popular. Typically, lawyers created the companies through contractual agreements, essentially using a deed of settlement that was adopted from the fourteenth-century trust. Once created, the company was virtually immune from suit, and the members enjoyed an unofficial limited liability. To an increasing extent, the joint stock company resembled the modern corporation, and a specialized corporate bar was created as an indirect result.[23]

Other kinds of collective entities were developed between the fourteenth and sixteenth centuries. Some had less to do with the increasing centralization than either the boroughs or the trading companies, but nonetheless contributed to an extension of the concept of person that included juristic persons. One such collective entity was the trust, a legal device that became popular in the fourteenth century. Mentioned earlier in connection with joint stock companies, the trust was initially a vehicle for passing land or the profits from land to one's heirs while avoiding the severe legal and financial restraints that otherwise attached to an inheritance. The owner conveyed to trustees the legal title to land by deed of settlement; these trustees held it for the owner's benefit during life and, upon his or her death, for the benefit of the designated beneficiary/*cestui que* trust. The trustees were akin to a juristic person because they held legal title not as individuals, but as an ongoing collective entity.[24]

The willingness to recognize a juristic as distinguished from a natural person was further evidenced in the sixteenth century. Again the issue was a legal dilemma, but in this case, one that had definite political overtones. The dilemma concerned the conveyance of land by the King who, as a minor, lacked the legal capacity to engage in such a transaction. As a resolution, English law recognized the Crown as two persons: one, the current King as a natural person; the other, the Crown as a political role, an entity with legal standing that transcended the King as an individual.[25] With this solution, English law in effect recognized the "corporation sole," in which an individual and the individual's successors became more than a natural person, guaranteeing a legal entity's existence in perpetuity through incorporation.

A third example, the rather old concept of *universitas*, was uncovered as part of a revival of interest in Roman law among legal scholars. A *universitas* was an association that was treated as an entity rather than as a group of individuals. It was not related directly to business, but instead gave a collective status to guilds and professional organizations. Even these groups, however, could not be created under Roman law except by action of the sovereign. Thus even those ancient assemblages evidenced the link between a collective entity and the state.[26]

The revival of interest in Roman law resurrected other concepts that were far more significant than the *universitas*. In doing so, it contributed to the second change in the legal concept of person that we identified earlier—a change in the nature of personal responsibility. In particular, English and European legal scholars rediscovered and were greatly influenced by the concepts *culpa* and *dolus*. These concepts addressed the notion of intent, an internal and subjective state: *culpa* connoted fault or negligence and *dolus*, connoting more intent, implied guile or deceit. *Culpa* and *dolus* were part of a new legal doctrine that appeared during the Middle Ages, a doctrine that included the emergence of *mens rea*—a guilty mind or criminal intent—and a theory of criminal negligence.[27] As a result, the legal focus for criminal responsibility shifted to the individual.

Of course, the church had long advocated the idea of moral guilt for individual sin, a concept of culpability that entailed a mental element. But during primitive times a sort of strict liability prevailed, and neither intent nor individual responsibility were especially important considerations with respect to wrongdoing. Similarly, during the feudal period, the imputation of accountability for a wrong was an external, objective concern. In both periods, the restoration of order was the primary issue. The secondary issue of who should be sanctioned was a matter of kinship, whim, physical proximity to a wrong, or a variety of other means whereby the determination was made.

That state of affairs, however, changed with the massive upheavals of the Middle Ages. The transition to mercantilism and then to capitalism signaled an end to the agrarian life and the social order based on the reciprocal obligations between lord and serf. A substantial portion of the population moved from the countryside to towns and eventually to the cities, and wage labor became an important element of economic life. The nature of political authority also changed as the feudal lords lost their privileged positions to the increasingly powerful centralized state. In short, an old order ended and a new order appeared. And as the importance of kinship groups or of position within the feudal hierarchy faded into the past, the individual became the focal point of society.   Sir Henry Maine has described the change as a shift from "status to contract." A person was no longer locked at birth into the rigid feudal structure, where relationships were based on status, but instead experienced the mobility and freedom of legal relationships based on contract.[28] The person became a citizen, not a subject. The rights and responsibilities of citizens *vis-a-vis* other citizens and the centralized state were ultimately expressed in a new theory of political obligation—the social contract. The social-contract theory explained the derivation and legitimacy of the state and the obligation to obey its laws. It further provided a philosophical justification for the equality and freedoms of citizens and for their expanding rights, including a right to own property that was not limited to the feudal lords.[29] Thus the legitimacy of the centralized state was enhanced by the modern legal apparatus with its formally rational laws that applied equally to all citizens as individuals.   Of course, the individualization of a citizen's responsibility under the social contract also prevailed with respect to criminal liability. For most crimes, *mens rea* became a necessary condition for conviction and punishment. As the legal scholar Blackstone noted, "to constitute a crime against human laws, there must first be a vicious will."[30] The issue of who would be sanctioned was now internal and subjective.

Corporate Development: A Summary

The corporation emerged as the transition from feudalism to capitalism generated demands for new business forms, collective entities that could accommodate the combined resources of individuals and facilitate business on a grand scale. The state, a collective entity itself, responded to these demands by creating such forms, which it then recognized as juristic persons; thus it gained political support from these entities while maintaining control over them.

With respect to the general population, the state maintained both support and control through political authority that was premised on the tenets of social-contract doctrine. Individuals enjoyed the rights of citizenship, but these benefits carried a reciprocal obligation: obedience to the law as defined by the state. The theory of political obligation legitimated the centralized state's exercise of political power, and, at the same time, reflected the individualization of responsibility that occurred with the transition to capitalism. The trend toward individualization, sometimes characterized as the development of a bourgeois morality,[31] entailed a focus on *mens rea* in the criminal law and, in the civil sphere, the sanctity of the wage labor contract.

In our analysis of corporate development, we have emphasized the transformations that occurred during the Middle Ages with respect to economic structure, the nature of political authority, and the legal concept of person. This is not to suggest the complete absence of other contributing factors. We note that religion, for example, a factor stressed by both Durkheim and Weber, fostered the demise of the feudal lord's political authority and the development of an individualized moral culpability that informed *mens rea* in the criminal law. And with Weber, we recognize the importance of an autonomous legal apparatus, especially the legal profession. (Recall the Bubble Act and the role of the "corporate bar" in perpetuating and expanding the joint stock company, a forerunner of the corporate form.) Despite such influences, however, the continual interaction of the three more encompassing factors had the most salient impact on the corporation's development.

By the eighteenth century, the corporation was an established fact, a juristic person that derived its existence from the state and was recognized in law as more than the sum of its individual members. As with the earlier trading company and joint stock company, the corporation could transact business in its name, own assets, and transfer shares, and by the nineteenth century its members officially enjoyed a limited liability for collective debts.[32] Always a child of the state, and often a functionary as well, the corporation benefited throughout its development from the preferential treatment that characterized its status as a special person. The corporation was not only a juristic person for business purposes, with many of the rights of citizenship, but it also enjoyed such protections as limited liability. On the other hand, with respect to the criminal law, the corporation was not defined as a natural person and was incapable of the individualized intent that was the essence of *mens rea*. Thus the behavior of the corporation was not within the regulatory scope of the criminal law.

Corporations in the United States

In many respects, the history of the corporate form in the United States parallels the developments in England and in the rest of Europe. This parallelism is not surprising for two reasons. First, much of what would become the United States was initially claimed and governed as territories or colonies by England and other European nations. Many of the juristic persons that were, in a sense, forerunners of the corporation were already recognized in civil or common law, and their usage was extended to this country as a part of the law of those governing nations. Even after the colonial period and independence from England, the common law continued to exert a strong influence on legal development in the United States.

Second, the United States also experienced aspects of the transformations that we described above, and their impact on the development of the corporate form was as significant here as in Europe. Of course, the United States entered the historical picture after those transformations were under way, so situational differences also existed. There was, for example, no true feudal period in this country, but the economic structure of the United States did undergo transitions from an agrarian existence in colonial days through an era of commerce and trade to capitalism and, ultimately, to the Industrial Revolution. Moreover, these economic changes were accompanied by major battles over the nature of political authority in the new nation, battles that inevitably ended with more power centralized in the state.

By the time this country gained its independence, the individualization of responsibility that characterized the shift from "status to contract" was virtually completed and *mens rea* was an established element of the criminal law. These features were incorporated into our legal system along with the notion of citizenship that formed the basis of political obligation in social-contract doctrine. The concept of person would undergo an even more important change in the late 1800s, when the provisions of due process were extended to include the corporation. Thus, as we shall see in this section, the interaction of economic and political factors, as well as the interrelated

concept of "person," shaped the development of the corporation throughout the nineteenth century.

The Early 1800s

In the seventeenth century, England and other European nations expanded their economies and their political influence by colonizing "the New
World." Trading companies such as the Virginia Company and the Massachusetts Bay Company were the vehicles through which England extended
its influence. The trading companies contributed to the development of
both England and the colonies, and they also reflected the stage of legal development of collective entities. They existed at the pleasure of the state,
they performed governmental and business activities, and, at the outset,
they were a mixture of individual and collective enterprise.

Most collective entities operated under charter during the colonial period; churches and boroughs were among the most frequent examples.
Those chartered collective entities were rare, however, and the law that
regulated the civil sphere applied for the most part to individuals rather
than to collectives. Although the Bubble Act was eventually made applicable to the colonies, it had even less regulatory impact here than in England.
The few corporations that existed were relatively small and often operated
in a quasi-governmental capacity.[33]

The corporation became increasingly popular in the decades following
independence, and an increasing number of companies were chartered with
private business as their sole purpose. Here, as in England, the corporate
form accommodated the combination of capital that was essential for the
complex enterprises of the late eighteenth and early nineteenth centuries.
But again, the significance of those economic issues is best appreciated if we
also focus on the concept of a legal person and on the interrelated changes
in the nature of political authority—an especially important consideration in
the early years of the nation.

The decades following the American Revolution were a unique historical
period in which the United States began its existence as a nation, although
the slate was not blank, to be sure. Even after the political authority of
England was thrown off, the common-law heritage remained. Social-contract doctrine, for example, which altered the nature of political obligation
in England, supplied the philosophical rationale for the revolution and the
break with England, and continued to inform the concept of citizenship that
was a basic tenet of the new nation.[34] Still, much remained to be decided;
thus, although the new government was to reflect social contractarian principles, the specific form was a matter for intense debate. That debate exem-
plified social-contract thinking in a practical sense because there were ac-

tual, not hypothetical, discussions about the form of government that would be created.

The central issue in the debate was the disagreement between the Democrats and the Federalists regarding the degree of centralization of political authority. Democrats such as Benjamin Franklin and Thomas Jefferson remembered the mischief caused by the English monarchy and opposed a strong central government. Instead, they trusted the common sense of the common people. The Federalists, including George Washington and Alexander Hamilton, favored a powerful national government. They were less trustful of the common people, preferring a system wherein the elites would have more influence. As one Federalist put it, "Those who own the country ought to govern it."[35]

The Democratic position carried the day at the first Constitutional Convention. Although the Articles of Confederation (1777) created a national government, the powers of the executive were made weak, there was no federal judiciary, and the government was clearly subordinate to the sovereign states. But this situation was to change shortly. Limited trade with England and restrictive trade barriers between states produced a serious economic depression, which caused a crisis in the Confederation. In response, a second Constitutional Convention was convened, in which the issue of centralization of political authority reopened. By blaming decentralized government for the existing economic troubles of the nation, the Federalists fared better.

Alexander Hamilton, perhaps the chief architect of federalism, argued that the nation's survival and prosperity depended on its political economy. He envisioned an alliance between a strong national government and a powerful national economy.[36] The second Constitutional Convention produced the Constitution (1787) and a form of government that met Hamilton's conditions for a successful nation.

The United States government had a strong executive, an independent judiciary, and a national law-making power. It enjoyed the exclusive right to establish tariffs, coin money, and maintain a military force—a power that would prove useful again and again in the alliance between government and business. And although the philosophical foundations of the government were steeped in social-contract doctrine and the attendant rights of citizens, many of the important political institutions were, in a sense, "protected" from the common people. The input of citizens was limited through the selection of a president by the Electoral College, the appointment of a federal judiciary, and a Senate that gave a disproportionate voice to a small Eastern aristocracy.[37] Suffrage also reflected that elitism.

The government's commitment to and support of business was the key to Hamilton's dream of a national economy. The support included direct subsidies of money, grants of land, and the construction of canals. But it was the United States Supreme Court that contributed most to the development of the corporate form and the alliance of government and business.

Approximately 200 new corporations were chartered in the decade following the ratification of the Constitution. The incorporation of so many new businesses foretold the coming era of large-scale collective enterprises, although at that time certain constraints tended to limit the potential --influence of the corporate form. The Federalists had twice proposed a federal incorporation provision at the second Constitutional Convention, but their proposal was rejected in favor of incorporation at the state level. Incorporation, then, was a state matter. This condition allowed legislatures to scrutinize carefully each charter request so as to insure that the prospective corporation complied with the rather severe restrictions on corporate purpose, size, and duration.[38]

That situation might have undermined corporate growth had the Federalists not found another means for shaping the political economy—the Supreme Court. Under the leadership of Chief Justice John Marshall, a staunch Federalist, the Supreme Court rendered decisions throughout the formative early 1800s that strengthened the federal government and the national economy.

The relevant opinions began with *Marbury v. Madison*,[39] wherein Marshall courageously, and with little or no legal basis, created the power of judicial review: the Supreme Court would be the final arbiter when legislative action was suspected of contradicting the Constitution. During Marshall's term as Chief Justice, the Court's interpretation of the Constitution in such cases always resulted in "the enlargement of the powers of the central government and diminution of state power to control economic activity."[40] Marshall accomplished those Federalist objectives through his interpretation of two Constitutional provisions: the contract clause and the commerce clause (in the Constitution, see Article I, Sections 8 and 10).

Although the contracts clause was written into the Constitution to protect the existing property rights that were threatened by the demise of the Articles of Confederation, its inclusion bordered on a moral imperative with respect to property and contract.[41] The new government accepted the sanctity of contracts, a view inherent in the shift that Sir Henry Maine described as "status to contract." Marshall invoked the contract clause in two notable cases. In *Fletcher v. Peck*,[42] the Court prevented the Georgia legislature from annulling a land transaction of the previous legislature; the contract stood even though the earlier legislature had transferred the land fraudulently. In *Dartmouth College v. Woodward*,[43] the Court held that a royal charter to Dartmouth College was a contract and, as such, could not be altered by the New Hampshire legislature. Both cases preserved the sanctity of contracts but, more important, they elevated the federal government above the popularly elected state legislatures in legal matters that affected business. Similarly, Marshall relied on the commerce clause in *Gibbons v. Ogden*[44] and *Brown v. Maryland*[45] to strike down state regulation of interstate commerce. He interpreted the commerce clause broadly to restrict economic protectionism by individual states and to empower only the federal Congress to regulate interstate business activity. mean that the federal Congress alone could regulate such business. Since there was little federal regulation at the time, this meant that corporations were virtually unfettered in their development.

Along with the absence of constraining legislation, other dynamic forces then in operation also contributed to success in the economic sector. Business historian Alfred Chandler has argued that the first westward expansion of the population was an especially significant stimulant in the early 1800s. He has suggested that such fundamental population shifts combined with governmental policy to facilitate the development of "big business" in the United States.[46]   As a result of all these factors, corporations flourished during the period of Marshall's tenure as Chief Justice. The Court eliminated many restrictive state regulations and Congress, through subsidies and other indirect contributions, provided an environment that was supportive of business. Thus the interaction among economic interests, the centralization of political authority, and the helpful view of the concept of person under the social-contract doctrine all encouraged corporate growth during the first part of the nineteenth century.

The Mid-1800s

The corporation was an integral element of the political economy when Marshall left the bench in 1836. It became even more important during the mid-1800s, a period of continued economic growth. Of course, substantial changes on a variety of fronts accompanied economic prosperity in the United States, as they had in England. The population of the cities swelled considerably and the westward expansion of the country continued. Technological advances in communication and transportation, especially the railroads, facilitated that expansion and marked the development of the United States as an industrial nation.

The corporation contributed significantly to those developments and became an increasingly popular business form during that period of industrialization. Almost half the businesses incorporated between 1800 and 1860 were chartered in a single decade—the 1850s.[47]   As corporations grew in number they also grew in size, in many instances becoming the large-scale collective enterprises that would eventually dominate economic life in the

United States and abroad. Much of the organizational structure that would eventually characterize big business emerged during this period.

> The railroads, with their huge capital outlay, their fixed operating costs, the large size of their labor and management force, and the technical complexity of their operations, pioneered in the new ways of oligopolistic competition and large-scale, professionalized, bureaucraticized management.[48]

The federal government remained supportive of corporate development, acting chiefly through Supreme Court decisions that further centralized political authority with respect to economic matters, especially those affecting the corporation. The Court's protection of the corporation continued, even though Marshall's successor, Chief Justice Roger Taney, was less than enthusiastic about the growing economic power of corporations. A Jacksonian Democrat who advocated judicial restraint with regard to judicial review, Taney took the position that the commerce clause did not preclude all state laws regulating business; he held a limited view of the contract clause as well.[49] Nonetheless, the Court's rulings during the Taney era favored a national economy, with the corporate form as the principal vehicle for larger enterprises.

Three cases characterize the Taney Court on economic matters. In *Bank of Augusta v. Earle*,[50] the Court ruled that a corporation chartered in one state could do business in another, although states retained the authority to regulate the entry of such "foreign" corporations. By the time of the *Earle* decision, of course, states wanted new corporations and actually competed for them by facilitating incorporation requirements. In most states, incorporation became a matter of general law rather than the special charter that had been scrutinized so closely by legislatures in the early 1800s. In *Swift v. Tyson*,[51] the Taney Court attempted to create a body of national commercial law of. Previously, when no question of federal law was at issue in a case, federal courts had applied the law of the state in which they were located. But in *Swift*, the Court ruled that federal courts should apply national laws of commerce rather than applicable state laws, which were sometimes inconsistent with these general rules. The notion of a general or national rule arose again in *Cooley v. Board of Wardens*.[52] Although Taney had expressed the opinion that the commerce clause did not absolutely prohibit state regulation of business, the Court held in *Cooley* that certain types of business, to be determined by the Court, demanded uniform rules and hence could not be regulated by individual states.

Bolstered by the Supreme Court's protection and the fertile environment of an expanding economy, the corporate form flourished, facilitating the transition to business on a grand scale. Yet, ironically, a byproduct of that very success threatened the existence of the powerful corporations. As the industrial corporations grew, so did the number of serious accidents involving workers and others. Accordingly, the number of personal-injury suits filed against corporations for negligence increased markedly in the mid-1800s. Often the corporate defendants were clearly negligent, and the damages sought from them tended to be substantial because the injuries produced by industrial accidents were so grave or, in many instances, so widespread. Corporations frequently escaped liability, however, through several legal doctrines that protected them from the potentially devastating effects of personal-injury suits. Essentially tort defenses that emerged in England early in the 1800s, these doctrines reflected the continuing preferential treatment afforded corporations in their special status as juristic persons.

Plaintiffs in these cases alleged that corporate defendants were at fault; corporations had negligently failed to conduct their businesses as reasonable people would, accidents had consequently resulted, and hence the defendants were liable. One defense used by corporate defendants in such suits was assumption of risk: plaintiffs could not recover damages if injured after voluntarily placing themselves at risk. The standard interpretation was that employees had accepted the possibility of industrial accidents by agreeing to work for industrial employers. Contributory negligence was a second defense: since fault was the issue, plaintiffs could not recover damages if they contributed in any way to accidents through their own negligence. Similarly, plaintiffs were barred from recovery against corporate defendants if their injuries were due to the negligence of co-workers. Under the fellow-servant rule, liability was displaced from corporate defendants to co-workers who, of course, had few resources. Finally, some plaintiffs were denied recovery under the English common-law doctrine that tort actions were personal and died with the plaintiff. U.S. Courts had never favored this defense until the mid-1800s, when courts in several states invoked it to hold for railroads who were defendants.[53]

In numerous cases corporate defendants successfully interposed such defenses in state courts during the mid-1800s. Their success in escaping liability for personal-injury accidents evidenced their special status. On the one hand, there was the economic reality that courts were simply unwilling to burden business. And on the other, courts treated the corporate juristic person as just another individual, one whose responsibility or liability for accidents was no greater than that of any other individual, including its employees. That individualization would become even more advantageous to corporations in the coming decades.

The Late 1800s

Expanding markets, supportive government policies, and protection from tort liability continued throughout the mid-1800s. By the end of the Civil War, a healthy national economy was firmly in place and the corporation had reached full bloom as a permanent fixture. The oil companies and the railroads were especially prosperous during that period of industrialization, and there was a boom in consumer goods that were produced for an increasingly urban population. Despite a favorable business climate, the economic picture was not altogether perfect for corporations. They needed predictable prices and markets to facilitate long-range planning and maximize growth, but normal competition and frequent cutthroat practices undercut that predictability and threatened even the large companies. Yet this dilemma had an obvious resolution: to reduce the uncertainties of competition through greater control over the immediate business environment.[54] Many companies attempted that resolution through business combinations, such as holding companies and trusts. Large, already successful corporations, especially oil and railroad companies, grew even larger and were able to control every facet of their operations through horizontal combination and vertical integration. Chandler has described the emergence of these horizontal combinations, noting that small manufacturers in a number of industries merged into large companies for competitive reasons in what was becoming a truly national market. In other industries, vertical integration was the strategy. Companies stressed the ownership of raw materials and component parts to cut costs and to assure control over the sources of supply, and thus over the entire process. The Standard Oil Trust, for example, was involved in the production of crude oil, pipelines, and refineries.[55]

Not surprisingly, these business combinations made enemies as they neutralized competition and increased their economic power. Their enemies included smaller enterprises that now were at a competitive disadvantage, farming interests, and populists who feared the centralization of economic power in the trusts as well as in other combinations. As might be expected, the strength of opposition was often in direct proportion to the success of a business combination in dominating its arena. Thus the oil and railroad companies, which were among the most successful enterprises, attracted the most vocal critics and were the most frequent targets of calls for reform.

The history of corporate development in the United States had long been characterized by limitations on state regulations and few constraints from Congress. By the end of the 1800s, however, a growing sentiment against the oil and railroad companies prompted Congress to enact two pieces of regulatory legislation. First, the Interstate Commerce Act (1887) was aimed at railroad rates and business combinations among the railroads. Second, the Sherman Antitrust Act (1890), directed primarily at the oil companies, outlawed combinations, especially trusts, that restrained trade. With the passage of those laws, Congress *appeared* to be responsive to popular demands for reform. The reality proved to be far different, however, because state regulatory power was displaced again in favor of a national approach to economic matters, and those corporations that were the targets of the regulatory legislation grew even more powerful.

The Interstate Commerce Act, for example, was designed to regulate the railroads. The Act created the Interstate Commerce Commission, a federal agency empowered to exercise control over many aspects of interstate transportation. Thus the Act further centralized economic policy in the federal government. As Hamilton and the Federalists had envisioned, such national policy fostered continuing economic development and the ascendancy of big business. Once control was centralized, the Interstate Commerce Commission would tend to act as a protector rather than a regulator of the railroads.

The historical record has turned up a supportive sidelight on this point. During a debate over the constitutionality of the Interstate Commerce Commission, the president of a railroad sought advice from a friend, the Attorney General of the United States, about the posture railroads should adopt with respect to the Commission. The Attorney General advised his friend against opposition from the railroads, noting that the creation of the Commission had satisfied public demands for reform, that the agency would actually protect the railroads from hostile legislation, and that the courts would limit power of the Commission.[56] Within only a few years, the Supreme Court, applying a "rule of reasonableness," limited the Commission's power to regulate railroad rates.[57]

In many respects, the history of the Sherman Antitrust Act is similar to that of the Interstate Commerce Act. Proffered as a reform that was directed at a specific industry, oil companies in this case, the Sherman Act outlawed all business combinations that restrained trade. But like the Interstate Commerce Act, the Sherman Act was a popular reform that regulated very little. Some commentators have suggested that the Act represented a political compromise; at a time when the increasing power of corporations was a concern to the government and the public, the Act was designed to regulate corporations without hampering the productive efficiency of big business.[58] The oil companies grew larger and more powerful in spite of the Act, and mergers continued unabated as corporate lawyers used the holding company in lieu of the trust. Initially, there were few prosecutions under Sherman; as one source has noted, when the Act was invoked, it was more frequently against unions than against business combinations.[59] Questions arose about the interpretation of the legislation, but eventually the Supreme Court applied its "rule of reason" to prosecutions under the Sherman Act. The Court retained the final authority to determine whether a particular business combination was an *unreasonable* restraint of trade.[60] Indeed, because the Court's involvement in these matters was so extensive, economist John Commons concluded that the Supreme Court could be seen, somewhat ironically, as "the first authoritative faculty of political economy in the world's history."[61] The Court continued to breathe life into Hamilton's dream.

One of the more important cases of the period, and one that demonstrates the Court's interventionist role in the political economy, was *Santa Clara County v. Southern Pacific Railroad.*[62] For the first time, the Court held that corporations were persons within the meaning of the due-process clause of the Fourteenth Amendment. With this recognition, the evolution of the concept of person with respect to the corporate form was completed. In a sense, the corporation became an individual and thus enjoyed the constitutional protections of a natural person. Throughout the late 1800s, the Court employed the concept of an individualized corporate person in a blatantly probusiness fashion, erecting upon it a new constitutional protection—liberty of contract. Liberty of contract, as expounded through the opinions of Justice Stephen Field, was a creation of the Court that literally read into the Constitution the economic doctrine of *laissez faire*. This constitutional protection lacked a proper legal foundation and was absurd in its application. Powerful corporations and giant business combinations were depicted as individuals in need of protection from their own employees as well as from governmental health and safety legislation. And the Supreme Court, via the newly found freedom of contract, was the vehicle of that protection.

The Court's probusiness decisions were justified through its own legal ratiocinations, and in addition, by the popular ideology of rugged individualism. According to Thurman Arnold, a law professor and former the head of the Justice Department's Antitrust Division, the personification of the corporation existed in the public eye as well as in the legal mind and explained why *laissez faire* was tolerated, at least for a time.

> The origin of this way of thinking about organization is the result of a pioneer civilization in which the prevailing ideal was that of the freedom and dignity of the individual engaged in the accumulation of wealth. The independence of the free man from central authority was the slogan for which men fought and died ... Since individuals are supposed to do better if left alone, this symbolism freed industrial enterprise from regulation in the interest of furthering any current morality.[63]

Ironically, the individualization of corporations and the benefits that resulted from such a characterization occurred when these very business combinations were the most powerful force in the national economy. Even when popular sentiment turned against them and the myth of rugged individualism in the small entrepreneuer was rejected, corporations continued to thrive, overwhelming such reform efforts as the Interstate Commerce Act and the Sherman Antitrust Act.

The corporation was an indomitable presence during the late 1800s, essentially for the same reasons that it had prevailed throughout the century. The interaction of economic factors, continued centralization of the political economy, and a favorable construction of the concept of person made the corporation even more powerful and rendered it virtually immune to regulation. Many companies were able to take control of their economic environment, thereby reducing the market uncertainties and increasing the success of their operation through holding companies, trusts, and other means, such as horizontal and vertical integration. These successes spawned serious opposition, but the attempts to control the large corporations ultimately strengthened them. Reform legislation tended to displace the regulatory power of the states, thus further centralizing economic policy in the newly created federal administrative agencies. These agencies often took a probusiness stance; when they did attempt to control corporate excesses, the Supreme Court stepped in with its "rule of reason" and limited not the corporations but the regulatory endeavor. Equally important, the Supreme Court finally recognized the corporation as a person with the constitutional protections that the Fourteenth Amendment guarantees to citizens. This recognition, combined with the economic doctrine of *laissez faire*, propelled the corporation into the twentieth century.

The Twentieth Century

Many of the trends that had begun during the middle and later 1800s had reached their zenith by the turn of the century. By this time the United States was an industrial giant. The economy had become a truly national marketplace, linked by communication and transportation—initially the railroads and later the automobile. Moreover, there was an ever-present demand for consumer goods from an increasingly urban population.[64]

If the marketplace had become national, so had the corporation. The corporation was firmly established as a large-scale enterprise characterized by vertical integration and, in many instances, by a widely diversified line of products. These enterprises were highly bureaucraticized organizations with centralized management, which coordinated the activities of interdependent departments and divisions. Perhaps one of the most important aspects of the management hierarchy was the sophisticated accounting system. The comptroller's office in these firms generated the data that were indispensable to the operation of such complex organizations; these data were the information base for cost control and centralized planning. Authorities such as Max Weber and Alfred Chandler have identified the accounting function as a distinguishing feature of the modern business form.[65] Chandler has noted that, by the early 1900s, cost cutting was more important to business than interfirm competition, and this was certainly the case in oligopolistic industries.[66] The competition that existed, especially among the producers of consumer goods, was directed at creating new customers. The advertising and marketing divisions had become a major dimension of the business picture and would continue as such throughout the coming years.[67]

The corporation was the dominant form of business enterprise, and many of its organizational and managerial characteristics were already in place. Corporations had attained the size and structure that was necessary for national operations, and the era of mergers and combinations ended during the first decade of the 1900s. The most significant innovation yet to come was the application of emerging technologies to business purposes, and the attendant appearance of research and development components in many companies.[68] Thus, as the United States moved into the twentieth century, it had a viable national economy driven by large-scale corporations.

Similarly, the state had become a powerful force by the turn of the century. The unique historical relationship whereby the state both regulated and protected business had produced, as Alexander Hamilton had predicted in the early days of the republic, a strong central government that would become even stronger in the years ahead. Indeed, many authorities have used such appellations as the "positive state," the "welfare state,"and the "therapeutic state" to describe the growing involvement of government in our lives.[69]

During the twentieth century, the state penetrated deeper than ever into all facets of social existence. In some respects, this intensified involvement was prompted by public demand. In the economic sphere, for example, people remained concerned about the power of big business and its impact on us.

> The socially uncontrolled entrepreneurial initiative that led to America's leap into world predominance as an industrial power in the last third of the nineteenth century was accomplished by a ruthless spirit of competition that left little room for concern

about the welfare or working conditions for those at the bottom.[70]

Although the heyday of mergers was past, resentment against big business, notably the oil and railroad trusts, continued. Legislation such as the Sherman Antitrust Act admittedly had been rather ineffectual, but public demand for regulatory reform persisted, and even became an important political theme in several presidential campaigns in the early 1900s. Furthermore, concern about the negative impact of business extended to related issues, such as unsafe conditions in the workplace. As an ironic byproduct of the burgeoning industrial economy, serious industrial accidents were becoming more prevalent, but little compensation was granted when workers or others were injured. Accordingly, demands were made for reform, primarily by organized labor.

In addition to matters of industrial safety, there were calls for state action in other areas; for example, the state also addressed health and safety concerns in consumer-goods industries and regulated the sale of food and drugs. The state began to provide financial assistance to the needy, became more involved in education, and intervened in a number of social issues. In short, citizens were more dependent on government, which necessitated its intrusion on a variety of fronts.

This expanded role for the state reflected more than the simple response to public demand. The state, especially at the federal level, had become a highly bureaucratized and autonomous entity. Scholars from Emile Durkheim to Max Weber have analyzed this historical trend toward centralized government and its impact on the social order. More recently, Jurgen Habermas, a contemporary authority on Western capitalism, has observed the tendency of the modern state to penetrate more deeply into the economic and the sociocultural realms (see Chapter 1). As Habermas has noted, however, this tendency is not without irony. As the state intrudes deeper into these spheres and extends its authority, it generates a need for greater legitimation to justify the use of this authority. In many instances the state cannot meet this demand; hence, modern society has a tendency toward crises of legitimation.[71]

Nevertheless, the state played a stronger regulatory role during the early 1900s with respect to the economic sector in general and the corporation in particular. The U.S. Supreme Court, however, was far less important in this regard than it had been in earlier years, possibly in part because of the ascendancy of the presidency. In this century the executive branch has grown in power, often at the expense of the federal judiciary (witness the constitutional controversy between the U.S. Supreme Court and President Franklin Roosevelt's "New Deal" package). The Court also yielded much of its influence in economic matters to Congress, even as it continued to favor business interests. In *Standard Oil Co. of New Jersey v. U.S.*,[72] the Court applied its "rule of reason" to protect a corporation from the provisions of the Sherman Act, but as a matter of statutory rather than constitutional interpretation. In a sense, the Court deferred to and could be overruled by Congress.[73] Thus the focus of attention on matters of economic policy shifted from the U.S. Supreme Court to the executive and legislative branches of the federal government.

In some respects this trend had begun in the late 1800s, especially in federal economic legislation. The Interstate Commerce Act (1887) and the Sherman Antitrust Act (1890) were certainly examples of Congressional economic policy, and this sort of regulatory endeavor continued into the 1900s. Both the Federal Trade Commission Act (1914) and the Clayton Act (1914), for example, represented a further effort by Congress to prohibit business activities that restrained trade. The Clayton Act was intended to resolve some of the ambiguities that had plagued the Sherman Act by proscribing specific types of practices that impeded competition. The Federal Trade Commission Act created a federal agency that would monitor and maintain information on business practices, and could sanction anticompetitive behavior via fines.[74]

As in the past, these federal regulatory efforts were prompted in part by public demands that something be done about the giant corporations. At the same time, however, deeper Congressional involvement in economic policy reflected that complex interaction whereby the state both regulated and protected business, and, incidentally, bolstered its legitimacy. Congress prohibited conduct that restrained trade while guaranteeing the stability and predictability that was essential for rational planning and continued corporate growth in a national economy.

> The provisions of new laws attacking unfair competitors and price discrimination meant that the government would now make it possible for many trade associations to stabilize, for the first, time prices within their industries, and to make effective oligopoly a new phase of the economy.[75]

These legislative enactments quieted the clamor for reform by making the government appear to be responsive to the public interest, and thereby contributed to the state's legitimacy. But these laws also favored big business by stabilizing the business environment; they were frequently endorsed by the leaders of major corporations and by professional business organizations.

The history of workers' compensation legislation illustrates the complexities that surrounded efforts to effect reforms in the economic sector. As mentioned earlier, the industrial workplace of the early 1900s was characterized by hazards, and accidents occurred because of these conditions. Organized labor was concerned about the frequency and seriousness of industrial injuries and about the lack of corporate liability based on the prohibitory tort defenses that we discussed above. Labor challenged these defenses as suits were filed again and again in state courts for personal-injury compensation because of industrial accidents. Corporate defendants evaded liability in many cases, but plaintiffs sometimes recovered damages, and the pressure for reform continued.

In this environment, the National Civic Federation (NCF), a national organization that spoke for the business community, mounted a campaign that was designed to secure passage of workers' compensation laws in various state legislatures. The NCF drafted model legislation and lobbied extensively among state governments for these laws. Encouraged by their professional organization, many prominent corporate leaders joined the campaign and endorsed the concept. The NCF also acquired the public support of President Theodore Roosevelt, and later of President William Howard Taft. Congress passed a limited workers' compensation law in 1908, a number of state legislatures soon followed suit, and by 1920 most states had enacted such legislation.

These laws benefited a number of interests, including accident victims, the business community, and government. Workers and others enjoyed a statutory remedy that overrode tort defenses, and they could now receive compensation for personal injuries arising out of industrial accidents. Corporations could project an image as responsible citizens who were concerned about accident victims. Moreover, they avoided the uncertain outcome of litigation because the amount of recovery was fixed by statute—the legislation made for predictability. Federal and state legislatures addressed a serious social and political issue and thus appeared to be responsive to the public interest. Finally, state courts, which had been favorably disposed to corporate defendants in these cases, escaped the criticism of labor and of political leaders such as President Roosevelt.[76]

The campaign for workers' compensation legislation provides an excellent case history of social and economic reform during the first two decades of the twentieth century. In addition, it provides two other important insights that are perhaps even more relevant to our analysis of the emergence of corporate criminal responsibility. First, early in the 1900s, the nature of government involvement in matters of economic policy changed somewhat. The passage of workers' compensation triggered a substantial upsurge of activity in such matters at the state level. Second, this legislation evidenced a trend in the law with respect to corporate responsibility for socially harmful behavior. Corporations were increasingly held accountable for their actions.

Edging Toward Criminal Culpability

Throughout much of its evolution, the corporation enjoyed virtual immunity from civil and criminal liability. An indisputable boon to corporate growth, this preferential treatment was the historical legacy of several interrelated factors, including the special relationship wherein the corporation was created by and existed at the pleasure of the state and frequently performed quasi-governmental functions. As a result of this status, the early corporation experienced many of the benefits and suffered few of the burdens of citizenship.

The broad idea of citizenship, as it developed historically, also benefited the corporation. Citizenship was a distinctly individualistic idea, as manifested in laws that addressed the behavior of individuals as natural persons, not of juristic entities such as the corporation. This idea is most apparent in the criminal law with the development of *mens rea*, a legal concept that focused attention on individual culpability. The appearance of *mens rea* marked an important change in the issue of personal responsibility, and it eventually became an essential element in the definition of crime. This legal concept, however, served as an exculpatory mechanism because the corporation, as a juristic person, was considered incapable of forming the requisite intent for the imputation of criminal responsibility under the strictures of *mens rea*.[77]

Thus the corporate form flourished because of this special status, which included many of the benefits of law, such as due-process guarantees, but few of the obligations, such as liability. As we have seen, however, this advantageous situation had begun to change during the late 1800s and early 1900s. In tort law, for example, the likelihood that a plaintiff would recover damages increased significantly. This change was due to judicial activity and statutory enactments that negated some tort defenses, eased the burden of proving negligence, and raised the standard of care for certain groups of tortfeasors. In the case law of the 1800s two doctrines emerged that favored plaintiffs in tort actions. The doctrine of *res ipsa loquitur* created a rebuttable presumption that the defendant was negligent in certain accidental-injury cases. The "last clear chance" doctrine offset prohibitory tort defenses, permitting even a negligent plaintiff to recover damages if the defendant could have prevented an injury after discovering the risk of an accident.[78] In addition, a number of states passed laws that were equally important in personal-injury cases. Of course, workers' compensation legislation meant that prohibitory tort defenses no longer barred recovery of damages for many accident victims. Moreover, several states enacted legislation that raised the standard of care required for those who were frequent parties in tort litigation, especially chronic corporate defendants such as the railroads.[79] Thus corporate immunity in the civil sphere dissipated, and corporations were increasingly held liable when their conduct caused accidents and injuries.

Corporate criminal responsibility emerged in a similar pattern. For years, corporations had enjoyed an immunity from the criminal law, largely because of the provisions of *mens rea*. Corporate employees and executives might be prosecuted successfully as individuals, but corporations as organizations were incapable of forming the intent that was an essential element in most crimes. This immunity was eroded, however, initially through the imposition of liability that was related to civil law and later by an expansion of the legal concept of person with respect to corporations and the criminal law.

As we have noted, a number of states statutorily raised the standard of care imposed on selected populations during the later 1800s. Typically, the statutes specified both the duties that were required in areas that greatly affected the public (e.g., the operation of railroads, the sale of food and liquor) and the appropriate sanctions if a member of the targeted population should neglect any of these duties and fail to exercise the prescribed standard of care. In a sense, these laws created a new category of crime—the public-welfare offense—that was specifically applicable to certain kinds of corporate wrongdoing.[80] Corporations were now accountable in criminal law for such offenses as selling adulterated food and failing to maintain safety precautions and equipment. While these were criminal offenses, judges tended to treat them essentially as civil matters akin to a public nuisance, arising from nonfeasance or from the failure to perform a required duty. Public-welfare offenses were a special category of crime, penalties were usually fines, and intent was not a necessary element that had to be proven. Yet because *mens rea* remained an element of and had to be proven for such crimes as homicide, a corporation lacked the requisite intent for them.[81]

Notably, even the corporation's immunity from charges of the crime of homicide began to disappear early in the 1900s, and in a manner that was consistent with the development of the public-welfare offenses described above. In some instances, corporate responsibility for homicide grew out of regulatory legislation. In *U.S. v. Van Schaick*,[82] a 1904 case, a court held that a steamship corporation could be guilty of manslaughter when deaths resulted from the failure to provide life preservers as required by statute. In other cases, criminal responsibility reflected a further extension of civil liability, primarily through principles of negligence. In *People v. Rochester*

Railway and Light Co. (1909),[83] a New York court applied the doctrine of *respondeat superior* in a manslaughter case that resulted when the corporate defendant's agent improperly installed a gas device. Under this doctrine, the liability of the agent would have been imputed to the corporation.

In these cases, *mens rea* was not so important an issue as was the meaning of "person" in the applicable statutes. Statutes varied, but a standard definition of homicide was the "killing of one person by another." The question was whether a corporation was encompassed within the definition of a person. The indictment in the *Rochester Railway* case[84] was dismissed because the relevant statute defined homicide as "the killing of one human being by the act, procurement or omission of another." The court construed "another" to mean a human being, not a corporation. *Commonwealth v. Illinois Central Railroad Co.*[85] had a similar result. In *State v. Lehigh Valley Railroad Co.*,[86] however, the court refused to follow the limiting definition of person and upheld an indictment for criminal homicide against a corporate defendant. Using language couched in terms of negligence and nonfeasance, the *Lehigh Valley* court endorsed the notion of corporate criminal responsibility unless something in the nature of the offense or the sanction simply made such liability impossible. In the more recent case of *People v. Ebasco Services, Inc.* (1974),[87] a New York court was willing to uphold an indictment for negligent homicide, emphasizing the importance of the state legislature's intent to include corporations within the purview of criminal statutes. However, the indictment was dismissed on other technical grounds.

By the second decade of the twentieth century, then, legislation and judicial opinion recognized the responsibility of corporations in the criminal law for socially harmful behavior. This situation—the dissipation of corporate immunity from criminal conduct—confirms the analysis that we have proffered throughout this chapter. The corporation had become the dominant form of business enterprise and affected many aspects of life in the United States. We were a nation of consumers, and corporations supplied the consumer goods. We were a nation of industry, and corporations provided the raw materials and the production processes that fueled industrialization. Ironically, however, the same business activities that produced corporate growth and economic prosperity often endangered lives and caused accidents, injuries, and even death. Accordingly, the state, at various levels, increased the standard of care that was required of corporations as well as their accountability when the standard was not met. This change occurred in the civil and criminal spheres and was accomplished through both statutory and case law.

The willingness to impose greater liability and, in a sense, "take on the corporation," reflects the maturity of the state and the autonomy of the legal order. We discussed the significance of autonomy in Chapter 1 when we presented Max Weber's ideas about law and legitimacy. Weber has suggested that the legitimacy of the law, and ultimately of the state as well, is due partially to the autonomy of the legal order, which operates independently of either the political or the economic system.[88] From the late 1800s onward, state court judges manifested such independence by holding corporations to ever greater accountability, especially in criminal matters. Often their decisions were based on the interpretation of statutes or on legal precedent; public-welfare offenses, for example, were grounded in the application of liability in nuisance to quasi-public entities such as municipal corporations. Again and again, however, the judges in these cases addressed issues of broad social policy and predicated their decisions on such issues. Corporations had a significant impact on life in this country—often an undeniably adverse impact—and they would be brought within the scope of criminal regulations, regardless of legal precedent or statutory language. The court's opinion in the *Lehigh Valley Railroad* case, mentioned earlier, illustrates the predominance of policy considerations over legal precedent:

> We need not consider whether the modification of the common law by our decisions is to be justified by logical argument: it is confessedly a departure at least from the broad language in which the earlier definitions were stated, and a departure made necessary by changed conditions if the criminal law was not to be set at naught in many cases, by contriving that the criminal act should be in law the act of a corporation.[89]

Similarly, a federal district court in the *Van Schaick* case focused on matters of social policy rather than on specific statutory language. The court held that the absence of any punishment appropriate to a corporation, traditionally a bar to corporate criminal liability, was simply an inadvertent omission and not an indication of legislative intent to grant corporate defendants an immunity from prosecution.[90]

Several commentators have discussed the expansion of corporate criminal responsibility in terms of social-policy considerations.[91] They have suggested that the law changed to meet the growing complexities of modern life and the changing social conditions of the twentieth century. As one authority has described it, the legal pendulum swung from the protection of individual interests, defined as freedom from government interference, to the protection of social interests through increased regulation.[92]

The decisions in these cases and the language in which the opinions were written demonstrate a genuine effort by the judges as representatives of the legal order to be responsive to changing conditions in society. In light of the circumstances, this responsiveness probably contributed to the legitimacy of the legal order and law. As we noted in Chapter 1, a fundamental criterion for legitimacy, and hence for effectiveness, is that the law must sometimes fulfill its promise. The law must regulate socially harmful behavior and do so in an equitable manner.[93] The imposition of greater corporate responsibility, especially in criminal matters, moved the law toward the fulfillment of its promise. Some of the opinions suggest that the judges realized the importance of corporate criminal liability to the legitimacy of the law. The court in the *Lehigh Valley Railroad* case, for example, explained its decision to vary from legal precedent and uphold an indictment against a corporation for criminal homicide as "a departure made necessary by changed conditions if the criminal law was not to be set at naught."[94]

Of course the corporation has remained the dominant form of business enterprise in the United States and has become an even more powerful economic force in the latter half of this century. We have identified and discussed several interrelated factors that have facilitated this success throughout its evolution. More recently, however, these same factors have weakened the immunity from prosecution that had traditionally characterized and benefited corporate development, and have fostered the current situation wherein a corporation may be held legally liable for its criminal behavior. The law, however, is a dynamic social institution, and the development of corporate criminal responsibility that we have presented is not the end of the story. Social conditions continue to change, and the issue of corporate criminality is once again on the public agenda.

Conclusion

The industrial corporation provided a vehicle for the concentration of risk capital as well as the organizational structure for economic coordination and bureaucratic rationalization. Corporations provided an investment outlet for small as well as large investors, with limited personal liability dispersing the risks and transferable ownership increasing their speculative attractiveness.[95]

The giant corporations that dominate business today worldwide are descended from those small and initially rare collective forms that we described in this chapter. Over the years, however, the collective enterprise has become increasingly popular and successful. Facilitated by interrelated changes in the economy, the centralization of political authority, and the concept of person, the corporation has developed as an essential vehicle for complex business endeavors.

Throughout that development, the corporation has consistently enjoyed a special status in the law. As a juristic person, the corporation has always drawn its very existence from the state, and has been a creation and a protectorate of the state. For much of its history, the corporation has contributed to the economic vitality of the state and, in many instances, performed quasi-governmental functions as well. Thus the special status is not surprising, although the quasi-governmental duties have given way largely to purely business functions. Nonetheless, the corporation has benefited from its preferential treatment in the law.

For some time the corporation was recognized as and enjoyed the constitutional protections of a person, but without many of the responsibilities and obligations that represent the "cost" of the social contract. That individualization of the corporate person, however, did not extend to criminal law. In spite of occasional exceptions, conventional wisdom held that a corporation could not commit a crime. It had neither a mind to fulfill the *mens rea* requirement nor a body to take punishment. That limited view of criminal responsibility may now be more understandable in view of the history of the corporate form.

During the twentieth century, however, the corporation lost some of its immunity from criminal responsibility, initially for nonfeasance or regulatory violations and eventually for other crimes as well. The law now recognizes the criminal culpability of corporations, and the legal stage is set for further extensions of corporate liability.

Moreover, as we noted earlier, public awareness and concern about the socially harmful behavior of corporations seems to have increased with the recent disclosures of business practices that threaten us economically and physically. The trial of the Ford Motor Company for reckless homicide emerged from this setting. In the chapters to follow we will discuss this trial, its background, and its implications.

Notes

1 See Max Weber, *Economy and Society*. Edited by Guenther Roth and Claus Wittich. New York: Bedminister Press, 1968, pp. 941-954; David Trubeck, "Complexity and Contradiction in the Legal Order: Balbus and The Challenge of Critical Social Thought About Law," *Law and Society Review* 11 (1977), p. 540; Jurgen Habermas, *Legitimation Crisis*. Boston: Beacon Press, 1975; and David Friedrichs, "The Law and the Legitimacy Crisis: A Critical Issue for Criminal Justice," in R. G. Iacovetta and Dae H. Chang (eds.), *Critical Issues in Criminal Justice*. Durham: Carolina Academic Press, 1979, pp. 290-311.

2 Emile Durkheim, *The Division of Labor*. New York: The Free Press, 1964.

3 For an overview of the debate, see Paul W. Tappan, "Who Is the Criminal?" in Gilbert Geis and Robert F. Meier (eds.), *White Collar Crime*. Revised edition. New York: The Free Press, 1977, pp. 272-282 (originally published in 1947); Edwin H. Sutherland, "Is 'White-Collar Crime' Crime?" in Karl Schuessler (ed.), *On Analyzing Crime*. Chicago: University of Chicago Press, 1973, pp. 62-77 (originally published in 1945); Marshall B. Clinard, "Criminological Theories of Violations of Wartime Regulations," American *Sociological Review* 11 (June 1946), pp. 258-270; and Thorsten Sellin, *Culture Conflict and Crime*. New York: Social Science Research Council, 1938.

4 See Marshall B. Clinard and Peter C. Yeager, *Corporate Crime*. New York: The Free Press, p. 281, and Leonard Orland, "Reflections on Corporate Crime: Law in Search of Theory and Scholarship," *American Criminal Law Review* 17 (1980), pp. 506-510.

5 Jeffrey H. Reiman, *The Rich Get Richer and the Poor Get Prison: Ideology, Class, and Criminal Justice*. New York: John Wiley and Sons, 1979, pp. 143-151; Cyril Northcote Parkinson, *Parkinson's Law*. New York: Ballantine Books, 1957, pp. 39-49.

6 Glenn A. Clark, "Corporate Homicide: A New Assault on Corporate Decision-Making," *Notre Dame Lawyer* 54 (June 1979), pp. 911-913.

7 For an interesting application of the "shifting boundaries" argument with respect to the Ford Pinto situation, see Victoria Lynn Swigert and Ronald A. Farrell, "Corporate Homicide: Definitional Processes in the Creation of Deviance," *Law and Society Review* (No. 1, 1980-1981), pp. 161-182.

[8] Iredell Jenkins, *Social Order and the Limits of Law*. Princeton: Princeton University Press, 1980, pp. 334-336.

[9] Emile Durkheim, "Two Laws of Penal Evolution," *Economy and Society* 2 (1973).

[10] Karl Marx, Contributions to a *Critique of Political Economy*. Translated by N. I. Stone. Chicago: Charles H. Kerr, 1904 (originally published in 1859), p. 11. See also Maureen Cain and Alan Hunt (eds.), *Marx and Engels on Law*. London: Academic Press, 1979.

[11] Trubeck, "Complexity and Contradiction in the Legal Order," p. 538.

[12] Henry Sumner Maine, *Ancient Law*. Edited by Fredrick Pollock. London: John Murray, 1930 (originally published in 1861), pp. 180-182.

[13] John Davis, "The Development of Negligence as a Basis for Liability in Criminal Homicide Cases," *Kentucky Law Journal* 26 (1937-1938), p. 209.

[14] J. Robert Lilly and Richard A. Ball, "A Critical Analysis of the Changing Concept of Criminal Responsibility," *Criminology* 20 (August 1982), p. 171.

[15] John Commons, *Legal Foundations of Capitalism*. Madison: University of Wisconsin Press, 1959 (originally published in 1924), pp. 25-54.

[16] Russell Hogg, "Imprisonment and Society Under Early British Capitalism," *Crime and Social Justice* 12 (Winter 1979), pp. 4-17.

[17] Egon Bittner and Anthony Platt, "The Meaning of Punishment," *Issues in Criminology* 2 (1966), pp. 87-89; Davis, "The Development of Negligence as a Basis for Liability in Criminal Homicide Cases," p. 210.

[18] Maine, *Ancient Law*, pp. 180-182.

[19] David Trubek, "Max Weber on Law and the Rise of Capitalism," *Wisconsin Law Review* (1972).

[20] James S. Coleman, "Power and the Structure of Society," in M. David Ermann and Richard J. Lundman (eds.), *Corporate and Governmental Deviance*. New York: Oxford University Press, 1982, pp. 39-40.

21 James Willard Hurst, *The Legitimacy of the Business Community in the Law of the United States, 1780-1970*. Charlottesville: University of Virginia Press, 1970, pp. 3-4.

22 Harry Henn, *Corporations*. St. Paul: West Publishing Company, 1961, pp. 13-14.

23 *Ibid.*, pp. 14-15.

24 Coleman, "Power and the Structure of Society," pp. 42-44.

25 *Ibid.*, pp. 41-42.

26 Henn, *Corporations*, p. 10.

27 Emilio Binavince, "The Ethical Foundation of Criminal Liability," *Fordham Law Review* 33 (1964), p. 16; Louis Westerfield, "Negligence in the Criminal Law: A Historical and Ethical Refutation of Jerome Hall's Arguments," *Southern University Law Review* 5 (1979), pp. 183-184.

28 Maine, *Ancient Law*, pp. 180-182.

29 Wolfgang Friedman, *Legal Theory*. Fifth edition. New York: Columbia University Press, 1967, p. 137.

30 William Blackstone, *Commentaries on the Laws of England, IV*. London: Dawsons of Pall Mall, 1966 (originally published in 1803), p. 21.

31 Habermas, *Legitimation Crisis*; Lilly and Ball, "A Critical Analysis of the Changing Concept of Criminal Responsibility," pp. 173-174.

32 Coleman, "Power and the Structure of Society," p. 50.

33 Lawrence Friedman, *A History of American Law*. New York: Simon and Schuster, 1973, pp. 166-169.

34 W. Friedman, *Legal Theory*, p. 127.

35 Quoted in Wallace Mendelson, *Capitalism, Democracy, and the Supreme Court*. New York: Appleton-Century-Crofts, 1960, p. 7.

36 *Ibid.*, pp. 6-18.

37 Francis Fox Piven and Richard A. Cloward, *The New Class War: Reagan's Attack on the Welfare State and Its Consequences.* New York: Pantheon Books, 1982, pp. 66-80.

38 Henn, *Corporations*, p. 16.

39 1 Cranch 137 (1803).

40 Arthur Selwyn Miller, *The Supreme Court and American Capitalism.* New York: The Free Press, 1968, p. 21.

41 *Ibid.*, pp. 19 and 36.

42 10 U.S. 87 (1810).

43 4 Wheaton 518 (1819).

44 9 Wheaton 1 (1824).

45 12 Wheaton 419 (1827).

46 Alfred Chandler, Jr., "The Beginnings of 'Big Business' in American Industry," *Business History Review* 33 (Spring 1959), pp. 2-3.

47 Miller, *The Supreme Court and American Capitalism*, p. 44.

48 Chandler, "The Beginnings of 'Big Business' in American Industry," p. 5.

49 Mendelson, *Capitalism, Democracy, and The Supreme Court.* pp. 36-38.

50 13 Peters 519 (1839).

51 16 Peters 1 (1842).

52 53 U.S. 299 (1851).

53 For a more detailed discussion of these tort defenses, see L. Friedman, *A History of American Law*, pp. 409-415.

54 Gabriel Kolko, *The Triumph of Conservatism.* New York: The Free Press, 1963, p. 3; Lawrence Friedman and Jack Ladinsky, "Social Change

and the Law of Industrial Accidents," *Columbia Law Review* 67 (January 1967).

[55] Chandler, "The Beginnings of 'Big Business' in American Industry," pp. 11, 17, 26.

[56] Miller, *The Supreme Court and American Capitalism*. pp. 65-66.

[57] *Smyth v. Ames*, 169 U.S. 466 (1898).

[58] Harry V. Ball and Lawrence M. Friedman, "The Use of Criminal Sanctions in the Enforcement of Economic Legislation: A Sociological View," *Stanford Law Review* 17 (January 1965), p. 200.

[59] James Inverarity, Pat Lauderdale, and Barry Feld, *Law and Society: Sociological Perspectives on Criminal Law*. Boston: Little, Brown, 1983, p. 231.

[60] *Standard Oil Co. of N.J. vs. U.S.*, 221 U.S. 1 (1911).

[61] Commons, *Legal Foundations of Capitalism*, p. 7.

[62] 118 U.S. 394 (1886).

[63] Thurman Arnold, *The Folklore of Capitalism*. Garden City, N.J.: Blue Ribbon Books, 1941 (originally published in 1937), pp. 185-186 and 189.

[64] Chandler, "The Beginnings of 'Big Business' in American Industry," p. 2.

[65] *Ibid.*, p. 16; Randall Collins, "Weber's Last Theory of Capitalism: A Systematization," *American Sociological Review* 45 (December 1980), p. 926.

[66] Chandler, "The Beginnings of 'Big Business' in American Industry," pp. 27-28.

[67] Alfred Chandler, Jr., *The Visible Hand: The Managerial Revolution in American Business*. Cambridge: Harvard University Press, 1977, pp. 290-299.

[68] *Ibid.*, pp. 240-244.

[69] See Miller, *The Supreme Court and American Capitalism*, Chapter 3; Nicholas Kittrie, *The Right To Be Different: Deviance and Enforced Therapy*. Baltimore: Johns Hopkins University Press, 1971.

[70] James Weinstein, *The Corporate Ideal in the Liberal State: 1900-1918*. Boston: Beacon Press, 1968, p. 40.

[71] Jurgen Habermas, *Legitimation Crisis*. pp. 69-72.

[72] 221 U.S. 1 (1911).

[73] Miller, *The Supreme Court and American Capitalism*, p. 63.

[74] Inverarity, Lauderdale, and Feld, *Law and Society: Sociological Perspectives on Criminal Law*, pp. 235-237.

[75] Kolko, *The Triumph of Conservatism: A Reinterpretation of American History*, p. 268.

[76] Friedman and Ladinsky, "Social Change and the Law of Industrial Accidents," pp. 60-65; Weinstein, *The Corporate Ideal in the Liberal State: 1900-1918*, pp. 40-61.

[77] Henry Edgerton, "Corporate Criminal Responsibility," *Yale Law Journal* 36 (1926-1927), pp. 827-828.

[78] L. Friedman, *A History of American Law*, p. 418.

[79] *Ibid.*, p. 419.

[80] Francis Bowes Sayre, "Public Welfare Offenses," *Columbia Law Review* 33 (January 1933), pp. 55-88.

[81] *Ibid.*, pp. 70-73.

[82] 134 F. 592 (2d Cir. 1904).

[83] 195 N.Y. 102, 88 N.E. 22 (1909).

[84] *Ibid.*

[85] 152 Ky. 320, 153 S.W. 459 (1913).

[86] 90 N.J.L. 372, 103 A. 685 (1917).

[87] 77 Misc. 2d 784, 354 N.Y.S. 2d 807 (1974).

[88] Trubek, "Complexity and Contradiction in the Legal Order," p. 540.

[89] 90 N.J.L. 373, 103 A. 685 (1917).

[90] 134 F. 592 (1904).

[91] Sayre, "Public Welfare Offenses"; Clark, "Corporate Homicide: A New Assault on Corporate Decision-Making"; James Elkins, "Corporations and the Criminal Law: An Uneasy Alliance," *Kentucky Law Journal* 65 (1976), pp. 73-129.

[92] Sayre, "Public Welfare Offenses," p. 68.

[93] E. P. Thompson, *Whigs and Hunters: The Origin of the Black Act.* New York: Pantheon Books, 1975, p. 263.

[94] 90 N.J.L. 373, 103 A. 685 (1917).

[95] Inverarity, Lauderdale, and Feld, *Law and Society: Sociological Perspectives on Criminal Law*, p. 221.

PART II

THE FORD PINTO CASE
AND BEYOND

Chapter 4
Assessing Blame

"Watch out! There's going to be an accident!" yelled Albert Clark as he glanced at the oncoming traffic on Highway 33. A moment later, his anticipation turned to horror. "It was like a large napalm bomb. It was nothing but flames. I couldn't see anyone in the vehicle. It was nothing but a big ball of flames."

Hurriedly he pulled his mini motorhome to the side of the road and sprinted across the highway. His wife, Pauline, followed close behind.

First they saw Robert Duggar, one of the drivers involved in the collision. Fearing that his Chevy van would also be engulfed in flames and wanting to help, Duggar had jumped from his seat and run toward the burning vehicle ahead. At the sight of the inferno he dropped to his knees and began to pound the ground with his fists. "Take care of him. Get him out of here," instructed Clark. Pauline grabbed Duggar by the arm and made him sit by the side of the road. When asked if he was hurt, the sobbing Duggar could only reply, "No. Help them. Help them."

As he approached the fiery car, Clark was joined by a local farmer, Levi Hochstetler. They were shocked at the sight of the driver, Judy Ulrich. Badly burned, her foot was still caught in the car door, which had jammed with the force of the collision. Now she was pleading for help.

The searing heat from inside the auto drove them back as they tried to pry the door loose. Finally, on the third attempt, they were able to pull her free. As she lay on the ground, waiting for the ambulance to arrive, Judy suddenly called out, "Girls, the girls, are they okay?" A bystander answered comfortingly, "Yes, they're okay. We got them out of the car." Soon after that Judy was rushed to the hospital with third-degree burns over 95 percent of her body. She died approximately eight hours later. She was eighteen years old.

"The girls," however, did not escape the car. Judy's sixteen-year-old sister Lyn and her cousin Donna Ulrich, visiting from Illinois and born just a day apart from Judy, were trapped inside the burning vehicle. With the temperature of the fire over a thousand degrees, Albert Clark, Levi Hochstetler, and the others at the scene could only watch in horror. The two girls perished seconds after their car had burst into flames.[1]

The Ulrichs crashed and died on August 10, 1978. Although their ages and the manner of their deaths make this a particularly tragic event, they were part of a larger phenomenon: the carnage that occurs each year on the nation's highways. Judy, Lyn, and Donna were three of the 50,145 Americans killed in automobile wrecks during 1978.[2]

Yet in another sense the girls' crash proved unique. For the first time in the nation's history, the legal arm of the state did not attribute a highway death either to a mistake or to outright recklessness on the part of a driver. Instead, a little more than a month after the fiery collision, a local county prosecutor secured an indictment suggesting that a major American corporation, Ford Motor Company, should be held criminally liable for the Ulrichs' deaths.

Why did the state seek to blame Ford for robbing three teenagers of their lives? The state could have concluded that the collision was an accident—case in which inattention, sloppy driving, and perhaps bad luck combined to produce tragic consequences on Indiana's Highway 33. The conservative prosecutor, Michael Cosentino, might have singled out Robert Duggar and argued that he was responsible for the crash. After all, Duggar would have made a good candidate to take the rap; only recently this twenty-one-year-old man had reacquired his driver's license, which had been suspended after he received tickets for speeding (twice), failing to yield, and running a stop sign. Not only had Duggar's Chevy van, with "Peace Train" emblazoned on its front hood, rammed the Ulrichs' car from behind, but investigations also revealed that his vehicle contained two half-empty beer bottles, five grams of pot, rolling papers under the seat, and pills in the ashtray.

In assessing blame, however, Cosentino and his staff decided that the collision was not merely an accident and that Duggar was not the real culprit; instead, they saw it as a case of reckless homicide on the part of Ford. To some extent, their interpretation of the accident and the action it demanded were idiosyncratic. In a different locale and with different personalities involved, thoughts of corporate criminality might not have emerged. However, to understand why the prosecutor officially blamed Ford for the Ulrichs' deaths, we must consider more than personalities and unique circumstances. We must also consider the context in which the crash occurred.

Two circumstances form the background to Ford's indictment on charges of reckless homicide. First, the automobile in which the Ulrich girls were incinerated was a 1973 Pinto. As will be seen below, questions about dangers in the Pinto's design had arisen by the time of the collision, and many people across the nation—including members of the legal profession—were prepared to believe that Ford had sacrificed safety in pursuit of profits. Second, and more broadly, the events of the decade preceding the crash had transformed both Americans' view of corporations and the government's possible reactions to the conduct of big business. Had the Ulrichs perished just a few years earlier, it is unlikely that an attempt at a criminal sanction of Ford would have been made. Had they died a decade earlier, it is doubtful that even the prospect of a prosecution would have been entertained.

Thus, while Ford's indictment was a special event—indeed, so unusual that its announcement drew considerable national attention—it is best seen as a product of the times. Described differently, the "Pinto case" signified the social and legal changes that had placed corporations under attack and made them vulnerable to criminal intervention in an unprecedented way.

In the pages to follow, this theme will furnish the framework for our analysis of why Michael Cosentino blamed Ford for the three deaths on Highway 33—a tragedy that took place miles away from Ford's headquarters in Dearborn, Michigan and from the New Jersey plant that had manufactured the Ulrichs' Pinto five years before.

A Sign of the Times

For much of its history, as we have seen in previous chapters, the American corporation enjoyed near-immunity from legal intervention by the state. Yet, in more recent times, this protected status has been threatened as repeated assaults have edged the corporation toward increasing criminal culpability. Though variations exist in different jurisdictions, the opportunity to fight wayward business with criminal sanctions is now clearly present.

This opportunity is important in two respects. On the one hand, it means that prosecuting a corporation is not legally impossible; thus the idea of initiating a criminal action is not dismissed immediately as unfeasible. On the other hand, this growing opportunity can motivate prosecutions by showing the possibility of success in an action that formerly would have promised few, if any, rewards.[3] Thus, as the law evolves so as to suggest that corporations are not immune from criminal penalties—as more and more business enterprises and their executives are brought before the court—the practical outcome of prosecuting a corporation appears more favorable. Taking on a corporation no longer seems a fruitless effort, but an important, possibly intriguing, challenge with a reasonable chance for a payoff. Further, as this perception spreads, interest may increase, and a "movement" against "corporate crime" may take shape. As discussed in Chapter 1, we believe this movement has begun.

These observations become significant when we consider the timing of the indictment of Ford on charges of reckless homicide. After reviewing the evidence surrounding the Ulrichs' deaths, Michael Cosentino was convinced that Ford made a conscious decision "to sacrifice human life for private profit."[4] Yet aside from his moral outrage, this question remains: what allowed Cosentino to jump from this insight to the conclusion that it was *legally* possible for him to prosecute a major corporation on charges of reckless homicide?

In part, he based this judgment on his knowledge that the recently revised Indiana criminal code contained a provision for "reckless homicide," which *might* be used to indict and try Ford for manufacturing the Pinto in which the Ulrichs were incinerated. He instructed his staff to research this possibility and consulted with William Conour of the Indiana Prosecuting Attorney's Office, who had been involved in drafting the "reckless homicide" statute.[5] Both Cosentino's staff and Conour agreed that a prosecution under the statute was legally permissible.

But these facts, taken by themselves, fail to explain why Cosentino even began his search for an applicable statute and entertained the idea that as prosecutor he might bring Ford within the reach of the criminal law. As we will see presently, moral outrage, the history of the Pinto, and the lack of civil redress all entered into Cosentino's thinking at some point.[6] Something else was present as well: a changing legal context. Granted, he would break new legal ground by being the first to prosecute a corporation for violence stemming from the reckless design of a consumer product, but he also confronted the Ulrichs' deaths at a time when the law had clearly edged toward corporate criminal culpability. Pragmatically, this meant that the law was sufficiently developed to make conceivable the innovative step of taking on Ford—it would no longer be dismissed out of hand as legally impossible. Additionally, corporations were now appearing regularly in civil courts in product liability cases and, increasingly, in criminal courts on charges such as price fixing and dumping hazardous wastes. On a professional level, Cosentino would not only be joining a movement within his occupation but also embarking on an adventure. Some of his colleagues might consider him a bit misguided, but the times were such that others would consider him a celebrity (indeed, his profession would eventually honor him).[7]

Thus the changing legal environment removed the constraints that traditionally would have precluded the prosecution of Ford. Cosentino had sufficient legal precedent on his side, and was operating at a historical juncture when members of his profession were not only applying criminal sanctions to corporations but also writing in law journals about the pressing need to make "the punishment fit the corporation."[8] In this light it is not surprising that he considered the possibility of prosecuting Ford.

Another issue remained, however: could he anticipate that people outside his staff would support the idea of hauling a corporation into court? Could he reasonably expect that in conservative Elkhart County, he would be able to win an indictment and then a conviction? Was it politically feasible for him, an elected official, to devote time and resources to taking on Ford? At first, Cosentino was uncertain what the public reaction would be. Therefore he decided not to try to sway the members of the grand jury toward indicting Ford when he brought the circumstances of the case before them; they would be his barometer of community sentiment. After the announcement of the grand jury's decision to charge Ford with three counts of reckless homicide, Cosentino felt that the local residents were divided evenly about the wisdom of his pursuing the case. Later, as the facts surrounding the Ulrichs' deaths were publicized, he believed that the vast majority of citizens backed his actions.[9]

What if the collision on Highway 33 had occurred a decade, or perhaps two decades, earlier? Apart from recent legal developments that had made corporations more vulnerable, would Cosentino (or any similar prosecutor) have risked accusing Ford (or any similar major company) of homicide? Would he have had any confidence that a grand jury would return an indictment and that the electorate would support his calling a corporation a reckless killer? To be sure, Cosentino's righteous anger at the girls' deaths may have prompted him to pursue a case against Ford, regardless of how foolhardy it seemed. But we believe that his initial uncertainty about the public's reaction would have been much greater, and would have constrained him from stepping outside his "normal" role as a local prosecutor to become a corporate crime fighter. A decade or two before the Ulrichs' Pinto crash, the idea of criminally sanctioning corporations was only beginning to take hold.

By contrast, the social context of the late seventies had become increasingly conducive to the prosecution of questionable corporate conduct. Indeed, as one commentator wrote in 1977, "the corporation, which touches us all, is under attack as never before."[10] Of course, it would be unrealistic to assert that the "corporation" as a business form was on the brink of collapse or even of fundamental transformation; however, this commentator's remark makes us aware that the reputation of corporations and their executives had been sullied. People had come to mistrust big businesses and to suspect that they were willing to step outside the law in the pursuit of profit. This context made the prosecution of Ford possible; it increased the likelihood that citizens in Elkhart would believe that Ford, like other companies, was capable of doing wrong. For Michael Cosentino, this trend meant that his prosecution would express rather than violate the public will.

Why was the public ready to doubt the trustworthiness of corporations? In particular, why was it ready to blame a company like Ford for killing three teenagers? As Peter Berger has observed, what people see as plausible largely depends on their social experiences.[11] An explanation or interpretation of a situation only "makes sense" to the extent that it confirms the "reality" of a person's everyday life. When an explanation does not resonate with this reality—or, to use Alvin Gouldner's terms, when it violates a person's "background assumptions" about the nature of society—it simply does not "ring true" or seem believable.[12]

These considerations help to provide a framework for understanding why corporations such as Ford were vulnerable to attack. As noted briefly above and in more detail in earlier chapters, the events of the decade before the Ulrichs' Pinto crash upset the social order and challenged the legitimacy of America's central institutions. Living through this period changed many people's "reality" and led them to revise their basic assumptions about America. Seymour Martin Lipset and William Schneider have argued that for many citizens these new "assumptions" were rooted in an unprecedented "confidence gap" or "cynicism toward all major institutions in American society," which emerged in response to the events of the day. On the basis of voluminous data drawn from opinion polls, they concluded that

> ...the decline of confidence after 1965 was a response to events, or to the perception of events. Beginning in the mid-1960s, the country experienced an unremitting barrage of bad news. In the initial period—roughly 1965 to 1974—most of this bad news flowed from disastrous events in the political system rather than the economy—the Vietnam War, protest movements, Watergate, exposés of corruption in high places, and urban violence. Beginning with the oil embargo at the end of 1973, bad news about the economy tended to command the country's attention, albeit accompanied by a regular smattering of social conflicts, foreign policy disasters, and political scandals....In order for confidence in institutions to be restored to a significantly higher level, we will need a sustained period of good news....A durable restoration of trust in institutions will require something more than a shift in the ideological posture of government; it will require an improved level of performance.[13]

Big business did not escape the influence of this general erosion of confidence. To be sure, the legitimacy crisis had not grown so far as to support the sentiment that America's capitalist system should be scrapped in favor of a socialist economy. Faith in the ideal of a free-enterprise system still remained high.[14] Yet as Lipset and Schneider discovered, "the period from 1965 to 1975...was one of enormous growth in anti-business feeling."[15] Echoing this theme, a more recent column in the *Wall Street Journal* reported that "a huge share of Americans have adopted a cynical view of the ethics practiced by the country's leaders in the professions as well as in business....[The] public gives executives low marks for honesty and ethical standards."[16]

Empirical indicators of the declining confidence in corporate America are readily available:

—In 1965, an average of 68 percent of citizens polled on their attitudes toward eight major industries stated that they had "very" or "mostly" favorable feelings. By 1977, that figure had dropped to 35.5 percent.

—On the basis of studies conducted every second year between 1975 and 1981, only 15.5 percent of the respondents answered that they possessed a "high" amount of "trust and confidence in large companies." Similarly, a mean of only 33 percent rated the "ethical and moral practices of corporate executives" as "excellent or good."

—Asked how much "confidence" they had in the "people running major companies," less than one-third of a national sample contacted in 1973 and 1974 answered "a great deal." By the early 1980s, this had slipped even further to 26 percent.

—Roper surveys in the late 1970s indicated that two-thirds of the public agreed with the statement, "American industry has lost sight of human values in the interest of profits."

—Asked to assess the occupational prestige of business executives, less than one-fifth of a 1981 national sample gave the rating "very great." Executives were ranked ninth out of fifteen occupations behind scientist, doctor, minister, lawyer, engineer, teacher, athlete, and artist. Moreover, fully 78 percent of a 1979 sample felt that the "presidents of major business corporations" are "generally overpaid."[17]

The pervasive cynicism and antibusiness feelings suggested by these findings were fertile ground for a movement against corporate crime. Lacking confidence in the integrity of business leaders, many citizens believed that neither law nor morality would prevent companies, particularly large and powerful companies, from engaging in socially injurious conduct when profits were at stake. As Lipset and Schneider observed, the public had come to associate "bigness with badness" and to assume that "businesspeople...will act in a socially responsible way only when the public interest coincides with their self-interest, that is, when there is something in it for them."[18] Considering this climate of opinion, we can understand why even a conservative prosecutor like Michael Cosentino could expect jurors and voters in Elkhart County to back the bold idea of accusing a corporation of reckless homicide. In addition, when we consider that the prevailing climate had helped to quicken legal developments that moved the corporation toward increased criminal culpability, it is equally apparent why Cosentino's prosecution of Ford can be seen as a sign of the times.

Changing circumstances made a case against Ford socially and legally possible, but one other fact must be added to explain why Cosentino decided to seek an indictment: the Ulrichs were driving in a Pinto. Had they perished in any other automobile, it is doubtful that thoughts of reckless homicide would have emerged, even in 1978. By that time, however, Ford's Pinto had been investigated by the national media and, for many, symbolized the worst side of corporate America. Indeed, as we will see below, a crusade against the Ford Pinto was well under way by the time Cosentino first learned of the deaths of three teenage girls and began to assess the blame for this tragic event.

The Pinto Crusade

Profits Versus Safety

In 1965 Ralph Nader published his penetrating and widely discussed book, *Unsafe at Any Speed*. As noted in Chapter 2, this book called attention to structural defects in GM's Corvair, which caused the vehicle to become uncontrollable and to overturn at high speeds. This would have been an important revelation in itself, but Nader's exposé accomplished much more. Apart from showing the Corvair's defects, Nader challenged his readers to think beyond the dangers inherent in one automobile to the dangers inherent in the nature of corporate decision making. People needed to understand, he argued, that strong, unfettered forces prevailed within big business—including the automobile industry—and led executives to sacrifice human well-being for profits.

This message came at a time when the "confidence gap" was beginning to grow and when mistrust of corporate executives was spreading. Thus it fell upon increasingly receptive ears and helped to shape the thinking of citizens and of many elected officials regarding corporate misconduct. A decade after the appearance of *Unsafe at Any Speed*, Nader's message that companies traded lives for profits clearly affected what people would believe about Ford's handling of the Pinto.

Nader began his critique of the motor-vehicle industry by noting that "the automobile has brought death, injury, and the most inestimable sorrow and deprivation to millions of people."[19] This observation raises the question of who is responsible for the "gigantic costs of the highway carnage." According to Nader, the major car manufacturers have invariably had a ready answer: "If only people would take driver education and were not so careless when behind the wheel, then the highway death toll would be minimal." But Nader offered a different interpretation. Attributing accidents to "driver fault," he warned, was merely a case of blaming the victim.[20] As long as the victims of the crashes—the drivers—are held responsible for their own fates, he stated, attention is diverted away from the industry's role in producing cars that are "unsafe at any speed." Such ideology protects corporate interests, but only at the cost of continuing to jeopardize human lives:

> The prevailing view of traffic safety [blaming drivers] is much more a political strategy to defend special interests than it is an empirical program to save lives and prevent injuries....[U]nder existing business values potential safety advances are subordinated to other investments, priorities, preferences, and themes designed to maximize profit.[21]

Nader contended that the push for profits, not poor driving, explains why people are perishing in cars like the Corvair. In offering this explanation Nader was not so naive or dogmatic as to accuse executives of consciously setting out to make dangerous vehicles. Rather, he was asserting that the blind pursuit of profits creates conditions within corporations that are conducive to the production of defective cars. Specifically, he understood that companies place a high priority on two factors that they see as essential to high sales and profit: style and cost. Although nobody wants an unsafe product, conflict inevitably arises when a design feature that would increase safety, such as a rear-end stabilizer or a larger windshield for better vision, makes a car look less attractive or increases its purchase price.[22] As Nader observed, the rewards within companies are given ultimately to those who are prepared to advance corporate sales, not to those who are excessively bothersome about safety. Clearly, then, the organizational context encourages decent, if ambitious, executives to risk cutting corners on safety in hopes of boosting sales and advancing their careers. Nader concluded:

> In the making of the Corvair, there was a breakdown in this flow of both authority and initiative. Initiative would have meant an appeal by the Corvair design engineers to top management to overrule the cost-cutters and stylists whose incursions had placed unsafe constraints on engineering choice. There are, however, deterrents to such action that regularly prompt the design engineer to shirk his professional duty. It is to the keepers of those most sacred totems—cost reduction and style—that corporate status and authority accrue.[23]

These realities made it clear to Nader that the automakers could not be trusted to protect consumer interests. The failure of the industry to police itself demanded that outside regulation be imposed:

> A great problem of contemporary life is how to control the power of economic interests which ignore the harmful effects of their applied science and technology. The automobile tragedy is one of the most serious of these man-made assaults on the human body....The accumulated power of decades of effort by the automobile industry to strengthen its control over car design is reflected today in the difficulty of even beginning to bring it to justice. The time has not come to discipline the automobile for safety; that time came four decades ago.[24]

Again, Nader's words were not without consequence. Fearing that his book might threaten Corvair sales, GM hired detectives to investigate Nader in hopes of discrediting him. Snooping into his background not only failed to reveal any damaging evidence, but when GM's probe became public, it stained the company's reputation. (GM eventually issued a public apology to Nader and paid $425,000 to settle a civil action he had brought on grounds of invasion of privacy.)[25] Ironically, the investigation seemed to confirm Nader's indictment of the auto industry's attenuated morality, and the whole affair helped to turn him into a national figure.

As we know, Nader did not decline this opportunity to promote his agenda and to launch a consumer movement that flourished and that continues today.[26] His influence was felt across corporate America,[27] but he had a special impact on car makers. "Largely as a result of exposés by Ralph Nader," comment Clinard and Yeager, "the auto industry has been the subject of increasing criticism for its lack of ethics, violations of law, and general disregard for the safety of the consumer."[28]

In this light, it is not coincidental that in 1966, the year after the publication of Nader's best-selling book, the U.S. Congress passed the Highway Safety Act, which mandated federal regulation of the automotive industry and led to the creation of an enforcement agency, the National Highway Traffic Safety Administration (NHTSA). Indeed, Brent Fisse and John Braithwaite have observed that "this Act is largely a legacy of *Unsafe at Any Speed*" and of Senate hearings to consider industry regulation, during which GM executives were grilled about prying into Nader's background.[29] As one writer commented in 1966:

> The hearings were a sensation, and did as much as anything to bring on federal safety standards. "It was the Nader thing," said one senator whom I asked how it had all come about. "Everyone was so outraged that a great corporation was out to clobber a guy because he wrote critically about them. At that point, everybody said the hell with them." "When they started looking in Ralph's bedroom," said another Hill man, "we all figured they must really be nervous. We began to believe that Nader was right."[30]

As evidenced by GM's reaction to Nader, consumerism and federal safety regulations were not greeted kindly by the major automotive corporations. Their initial grumblings grew more intense as the industry's control of the market was threatened by a combination of escalating gasoline prices and an influx of inexpensive, fuel-efficient foreign imports. By the beginning of the 1970s, the costs of meeting NHTSA regulatory standards were perceived as a serious danger to the profitability of the American auto industry, and thus had to be resisted. "Safety" had become a dirty word in the headquarters of the big auto manufacturers.

This attitude about safety is illustrated well by conversations drawn from the Watergate tapes. On April 27, 1971, between 11:08 and 11:43 a.m., Henry Ford II and Lee Iacocca (then president of Ford Motor Company) talked with Richard Nixon and John Ehrlichman in the Oval Office. The purpose of this visit was to ask the President to help Ford Motor Company obtain relief from the pressing problems created by the safety standards imposed by the Department of Transportation (which housed NHTSA).[31]

In the first moments of the meeting, President Nixon quickly set the tone, commenting:

But we can't have a completely safe society or safe highways or safe cars and pollution-free and so forth. Or we could have, go back and live like a bunch of damned animals. Uh, that won't be too good, either. But I also know that using this issue, and, boy this is true. It's true in, in the environmentalists and it's true of the consumerism people. They're a group of people that aren't really one damn bit interested in safety or clean air. What they're interested in is destroying the system. They're enemies of the system. So what I'm trying to say is this: that you can speak to me in terms that I am for the system.

He then continued:

I try to fight the demagogues, uh, to the extent we can. Uh, I would say this: that I think we have to know that, uh, the tides run very strongly. I mean, you know, the, it's the kick now. You know, the environment kick is in your ads, of course. You're reflecting it. Kids are for it and all the rest, they say. Uh, the safety thing is the kick, 'cause Nader's running around, squealing around about this and that and the other thing....

Now, tell me the problems you've got with, uh, the industry, with the Department of Transportation, and all these things and let me listen.

Soon after these remarks Henry Ford II began to outline his concerns:

I think the thing that concerns us more than anything else is this total safety problem. And, uh, what we're worried about really, basically, is—this isn't an industry problem—is really the economy of the United States, if you want to get into the broad picture because, uh, we represent the total automotive [unintelligible] supply, industry supplies, dealers, dealer [unintelligible] the whole bit, about one-sixth of G.N.P. Now, if the price of cars goes up because emission requirements is gonna be in there, even though we, though we've talked about this morning, safety requirements are in there, bumpers are in there. And these things are, and that's leaving out inflation and material costs increases, which are also there.

Nixon responded:

In other words, it'll, it'll kick up the prices of cars and of all of them, the inexpensive ones and the others too.

Henry Ford:

We see the price of a Pinto...going something like fifty percent in the next three years with inflation part of it, but that's not the big part of it. It's the safety requirements, the emission requirements, the bumper requirements...

If these prices get so high that people stop buying cars...they're gonna buy more foreign cars; you're going to have balance-of-payment problems.

Nixon:

Right. I'm convinced.

Lee Iacocca now entered the conversation, focusing on the problems that attended the implementation of safety regulations by the Department of Transportation:

I'm worried about the, the fact the Department of Transportation, not willfully, but maybe unknowingly, is really getting to us...

And I keep saying, "The clock is running and we are wasting money." It, it just kills me to see it starting with Ford. We are becoming a great inefficient producer, and what they're doing to us.

But I think for the basic safety standards, now, the key officials over there—I've talked to 'em now, for two years constantly...and they're dedicated—and they say, "Well, we're gonna get on to this, but we've had problems." And they talk about Naderism, and, uh, you know, the...the great pressure on them and so forth.

He then focused on the incursions of foreign competitors into American markets:

And, and, and ya say, "Well, what has this to do with safety?" Well it has one big thing to do with it. They [foreign competitors] are gonna put whatever is demanded by law in this country on at a buck fifty an hour, and we're, we just cracked seven dollars an hour.

Returning to the regulatory issue, Iacocca remarked:

We are in a downhill slide, the likes of which we have never seen in our business. And the Japs are in the wings ready to eat us up alive. So I'm in a position to be saying to Toms and Volpe [DOT officials], "Would you guys cool it a little bit? You're gonna break us." And they say, "Hold it. People want safety." I say, "Well, they, what do you mean they want safety? We get letters...We get about thousands on customer service. You can't get your car fixed. We don't get anything on safety! So again, give us a priority." We cannot carry the load of inflation in wages and safety in a four-year period without breaking our back. It's that simple, and, and that's what we've tried to convey to these people.

Later, Nixon promised to review Ford's situation:

...let me take a look at the whole, uh, John, what I can do here. But the other thing is I want to see what the hell the Department [of Transportation] is doing in the future.

Echoing the Ford officials' reasoning, Nixon then stated:

I'll have a look at the situation, and I will on the air bag thing and the rest. And, uh, and uh, but, but I think this is an element that had, you see, goes beyond the DOT because it involves America's competitive position, it involves the health of the economy, uh, it involves a lot of things...

I want to find out, I want to find out what the situation is, if cost-effectiveness is the word.

Nixon continued:

...a lot of, what, what it really gets down to is that uh,...it, it is uh,...progress,... industrialization, ipso facto, is bad. The great life is to have it like when the Indians were here. You know how the Indians lived? Dirty, filthy, horrible. [Followed by laughs in the room].

At the end of the meeting, Nixon gave Ford the name of a "contact person," but reserved final judgment on matters brought before him:

Now, John [Ehrlichman] is your contact here...

...and, uh, particularly with regard to this, uh, this air bag thing. I, I don't know, I, I may be wrong.

I will not judge it until I hear the other side.

When juxtaposed with the themes in *Unsafe at Any Speed*, these conversations illuminate the conflict over the appropriate balance of safety and profits that raged as America moved into the seventies. In Nader's view, big companies were callously and recklessly endangering human life in their efforts to maximize profits. Cost-effectiveness, not the Golden Rule, was their governing morality. Corporate leaders dismissed such talk as naively or maliciously undermining the nation's economy. Safety was now the fad of those on the political left; if not resisted, it had the potential to cripple industries that were already struggling to fight off foreign competitors.

It was in this context that the Ford Pinto was conceived and produced. Under Lee Iacocca's direction, Ford moved quickly to market the Pinto before Volkswagen and the Japanese manufacturers monopolized small-car sales. Iacocca's formula for success was simple but rigid: the vehicle must weigh under 2,000 pounds and cost under $2,000. "Lee's car," as the Pinto was known at Ford, was rushed through production, taking only twenty-five months as opposed to the normal forty-three.[32] The 1971 model rolled off the production line and into showrooms in September 1970. It cost only $1,919 and weighed in under the 2,000-pound limit.[33]

Though pleased by this success, Ford executives were still concerned about the price of safety. The Pinto had won the initial battle with cost, but faced a war against rising expenditures and vigorous competition. As we have seen, this is one reason why Henry Ford II and Lee Iacocca traveled to Washington to meet with President Nixon. During this time, too, Ford executives made the decision not to guard against potential fuel-leakage problems caused by the placement of the Pinto's gas tank, which made it vulnerable to puncture in rear-end collisions. In an internal company memo dated April 22, it was recommended that Ford "defer adoption of the flak suit or bladder on all affected cars until 1976 to realize a design cost savings of $20.9 million compared to incorporation in 1974."[34] Whether Ford was reckless in its calculation that improved safety precautions were not worth a substantial reduction in profit would be questioned increasingly in the years ahead.

Pinto Problems

After six years of sales, there were over 1.5 million Pintos on the nation's roads. Although "Lee's car" was the most popular American make, all was not right with the Pinto. Concern about the Pinto's safety had grown, beginning modestly but then escalating in intensity. By August 10, 1978—the day the Ulrichs died in the burning wreck of their 1973 Pinto—the car's problems had received exposure in the national media, and NHTSA had pressured Ford to issue a recall notice to Pinto owners. A crusade against Ford's Pinto was under way.

Jack Anderson and Les Whitten were perhaps the first to claim that Ford, despite having the technology to do so, had consciously refused to fix the potentially lethal hazard posed by the placement of the Pinto's gas tank. They began their December 30, 1976 column in the *Washington Post* by claiming, "Buried in secret files of the Ford Motor Co. lies evidence that big auto makers have put profits ahead of lives." This "lack of concern," they lamented, "has caused thousands of people to die or be horribly disfigured in fiery crashes." And all this, they said, was preventable: "Secret tests by Ford have shown that minor adjustments in the location of the fuel tank could greatly reduce the fiery danger." Moreover, "repositioning of the tank would cost only a few dollars more per car"—not much of a price when human lives are at stake. "In the long run," they warned, "the auto makers are saving little with this 'cost cutting.'"[35]

Nine months later, these criticisms were elaborated in Mark Dowie's scathing condemnation of Ford, called "Pinto Madness." This award-winning report, which appeared in the September-October issue of *Mother Jones*, detailed Ford's allegedly cold and calculating decision to market a "firetrap." Again the message was clear: in the name of profits, "Ford Motor Company sold cars in which it knew hundreds of people would needlessly burn to death".[36] To make certain that this message would not remain buried in the pages of *Mother Jones*, Dowie announced the publication of "Pinto Madness" at a Washington, D.C. press conference attended by Ralph Nader. The gathering was held on August 10, 1977—ironically, exactly one year before the three Ulrich girls were incinerated in their Pinto.

"Are you driving the deadliest car in America?" To this rhetorical question, Dowie supplied a frightening answer: "By conservative estimates, Pinto crashes have caused 500 burn deaths to people who would not have been seriously injured if the car had not burst into flames. The figure could be as high as 900."[37]   But what made the Pinto "burst into flames" even when the impact of a collision was not great enough to inflict severe bodily harm on its occupants?   According to Dowie, the lethal defect in the Pinto was the placement of the car's gas tank only six inches from the rear bumper.   When hit from behind--even at speeds as low as 30 mph--the bumper was pushed forward into the tank, creating two potential hazards. First, the tube leading from the tank to the gas cap often was ripped away, thus causing fuel to gush out.   Second, the bumper could propel the tank forward into the car's differential housing (the bulge in the middle of the rear axle).   If that happened, four bolts on the housing would puncture the gas tank, again allowing fuel to spill.   At that point, all that was needed to ignite the fuel and to create an inferno was a spark—from steel against steel or from steel against pavement.

In Dowie's opinion this was not merely an unfortunate or unavoidable engineering mistake.   Ford, he claimed, knew about the defect and knew how to fix it.   In fact, as "internal company documents" revealed, "Ford has crash-tested the Pinto at a top-secret site more than 40 times and...every test made over 25 mph without special structural alteration of the car has resulted in a ruptured fuel tank."[38]   Eight of these tests, moreover, were made before the vehicle was delivered to dealerships across the nation. Other tests conducted before marketing showed that it was possible to eliminate fuel leakage in one of four ways: by placing a piece of steel between the gas tank and the bumper; by inserting a plastic protective device between the tank and the bolts on the differential housing; by lining the tank with a rubber bladder; or, as with Ford's Capri, by positioning the gas tank over the rear axle.   Although Ford had the technology to minimize the Pinto's hazards, they chose, Dowie observed, not to do so.

Why would Ford consciously endanger the lives of their customers? Dowie offered a simple but damning answer: cost-effectiveness.   Inside Ford, Dowie's sources told him, it was well understood that profit was the guiding principle and that safety didn't sell.   When asked whether anyone had gone to Lee Iacocca and informed him of the Pinto's problems, a high-ranking company engineer responded, "Hell no.   That person would have been fired.   Safety wasn't a popular subject around Ford in those days. With Lee it was taboo."[39]   To exacerbate matters, the Pinto was being produced under rigid price and weight restrictions ($2,000 and 2,000 pounds), and under a time schedule that made delays intolerable and changes costly. The pressure was on.   "Whenever a problem was raised that meant a delay on the Pinto," Dowie's engineer informant said, "Lee would chomp on his cigar, look out the window and say, 'Read the product objectives and get back to work.'"[40]

Even so, Dowie noted that the Pinto could have been made safe at relatively little expense. Lining the gas tank with a rubber bladder would have only cost $5.08 per car and Ford knew this as early as January 15, 1971. Ford's concern, however, was not with saving lives but with cost-effectiveness. In the end, Dowie contended, they determined that it would be cheaper to fight or to settle any civil suits stemming from fiery Pinto crashes than to fix the car.

To back this assertion, Dowie published a chart developed by Ford that related to leakage in fuel systems when a car rolled over in a crash. The company used this chart in lobbying against proposed federal regulations that would have mandated more stringent fuel-leakage standards. Placing the value of a human life at $200,000 and the cost to preventing leakage at $11 a vehicle, they concluded that the cost-benefit ratio was not favorable to dictating improved safety.[41] The exact calculations, as reported by Dowie, were as follows:

$11 VS. A BURN DEATH

Benefits and Costs Relating to Fuel Leakage
Associated with the Static Rollover
Test Portion of FMVSS 208

BENEFITS

Savings: 180 Burn deaths, 180 serious burn injuries, 2,100 burned vehicles.
Unit Cost: $200,000 per death, $67,000 per injury, $700 per vehicle.
Total Benefits: 180 X ($200,000) + 180 X ($67,000) + 2,100 X ($700) = $49.5 million.

COSTS

Sales: 11 million cars, 1.5 million light trucks.
Unit Cost: $11 per car, $11 per truck.
Total Cost: 11,000,000 x ($11) + 1,500,000 X ($11) = $137 million.

In Dowie's view , Ford used this kind of analysis to reach the conclusion that it was impractical initially to fix or later to recall the Pinto. Instead, they adopted a strategy of sustained resistance against any safety regulations that threatened profits. "Ford succeeded beyond its wildest expectations," Dowie observed, for it was not until 1977 that NHTSA imposed a rear-end collision standard that would minimize the potential of fuel leakage. Yet Dowie remained troubled, remarking that the new standard would "never force the company to test or recall the more than two million pre-1977 Pintos still on the highway. Seventy or more people will burn in those cars for many years to come. If the past is any indication, Ford will continue to accept the deaths." Dowie concluded by wondering "how long the Ford Motor Company would continue to market lethal cars were Henry Ford II and Lee Iacocca serving 20 year terms in Leavenworth for consumer homicide."[42]

Dowie's exposé was the most important factor in triggering a crusade against Ford's "Pinto madness." In reflecting on the Pinto affair, Ford executives told Brent Fisse and John Braithwaite that the article was "the real watershed." Fisse and Braithwaite agree that "the adverse publicity began in earnest" at this point.[43] The most immediate effect, however, was on NHTSA. In the prevailing social climate, they could not ignore the claim that profits were being placed above human lives. The day after the Washington, D.C. press conference announcing Dowie's charges against Ford, NHTSA undertook a preliminary evaluation of the Pinto's dangers. As a result, a month later (September 13) they initiated "a formal defect investigation...to determine whether the alleged problem constitutes a safety-related defect within the meaning of the National and Motor Vehicle Safety Act of 1966."[44]

Soon the Pinto was capturing media headlines again. In mid-February 1978 came the astonishing report that a jury had awarded Richard Grimshaw, a Pinto burn victim, $125 million in punitive damages, "the largest award ever made by a jury in a personal injury case."[45] This amount was added to $2.8 million in compensatory damages awarded to Grimshaw; another $666,280 was allocated to the family of Lily Gray, who had died in the accident. *Time* magazine called the total judgment "Ford's $128.5 Million Headache."[46]

On May 28, 1972, Grimshaw was riding with his fifty-two-year-old neighbor, Lily Gray, when her Pinto stalled on Interstate 15 near San Bernardino, California. They were hit from behind by a vehicle traveling approximately 35 mph. Within moments their car was engulfed in flames. Mrs. Gray died two days later. Grimshaw, then thirteen, survived the crash although he suffered burns over 90 percent of his body and lost his nose, his left ear, and much of his left hand.[47]

At the civil trial, Mark Robinson, Grimshaw's lawyer, presented the jury with evidence that Ford had conducted five crash tests before marketing the Pinto, which showed that the car was susceptible to fuel leakage. Then he exhibited a Ford memo stating that the company would delay fixing the Pinto's gas tank in order to save $20.9 million. He also used company records to prove that the gas-tank defect could have been remedied for merely $10 a car. "We were charging," he said at the end of the case, "that Ford Motor Company had consciously, knowing that those tests had failed, put out that model to save 10 bucks a car at the risks of hundreds of human lives and hundreds more injuries like Grimshaw's."[48] For "willfully neglecting" his client's safety, he asked for $100 million in punitive damages—the amount of money he estimated Ford had saved from not fixing the defective Pintos manufactured before 1977.

The jury agreed with Robinson's logic and went one step further. They did not think that $100 million was enough; this amount would allow Ford to break even. Therefore they raised the punitive damages to $125 million. The foreman of the jury justified this action by asserting, "We wanted Ford to take notice. I think they've noticed."[49]

As a footnote, a judge later reduced Grimshaw's total award, including punitive damages, to $6.6 million. In May 1981 the California Court of Appeal upheld this award, declaring that "Ford's institutional mentality was shown to be one of callous indifference to public safety. There was substantial evidence that Ford's conduct constituted 'conscious disregard' of the probability of injury to members of the consuming public."[50] Ford's subsequent appeal to the state's Supreme Court was set aside. While contemplating a further appeal to the U.S. Supreme Court, the company settled with Grimshaw for $7.5 million (the $6.6 million plus interest). Grimshaw, who had endured nearly seventy operations to remedy his fire-related injuries, made this response to the outcome of the case:

> It could have been more just. Not that I'm greedy. But there was no punishment. It was no sweat to Ford. You always wish you could be that way you were in the beginning. And someone dying in the accident. You can never replace that.[51]

After the initial *Grimshaw* decision, the crusade against the Pinto continued to mount. The American Trial Lawyers appealed to Ford to recall all defective Pintos still on the highways. In Alabama, a class-action suit on behalf of the owners of 1971-1978 models asked for $10,000 in damages for each plaintiff because the cars "were negligently designed and engineered so that they are dangerously vulnerable." Pinto owners in California filed a similar suit; meanwhile, individual victims across the nation continued to bring Ford into court, seeking large punitive awards. Fearing possible civil actions, employers in Oregon began to take Pintos out of service. The State of Oregon withdrew over three hundred of the cars, while Multnomah County, in which Portland is located, took sixty-five off the road. Salem sought to solve its Pinto problem by instructing employees who drove the car to avoid highways and to stay under 35 mph. Northwest Bell Telephone, unwilling to take any chances, impounded and sold its six Pintos.[52]

The pressure against Ford did not abate. In May 1978, NHTSA sent a letter to Lee Iacocca, informing him of the agency's evaluation of the Pinto's safety. For Ford, the news was not good. "Based on our investigations," NHTSA wrote, "it has been initially determined that a defect which relates to motor vehicle safety exists in these 1971-1976 Ford Pintos and 1975-1976 Mercury Bobcats." Specifically, NHTSA stated that the fuel tanks and filler necks (leading from the tank to the gas cap) "are subject to failure when the vehicles are struck from the rear. Such failure can result in fuel leakage, which in the presence of external ignition sources can result in fire." The "fire threshold" in a rear-end collision was placed "at closing speeds between 30 and 35 miles per hour." Further, since the fuel tank design was similar on the 1975-1976 Mercury Bobcat, that car was also subject to possible recall. NHTSA then told Ford that a public hearing on the safety defect would be held on June 14, at which time the company could "present data, views, and arguments respecting this initial determination."[53]

To justify their conclusions, NHTSA attached an "Investigation Report" which contained, among other things, the results of crash tests conducted by Dynamic Science, Inc. of Phoenix. These "fuel tank integrity collision tests" left few doubts of the Pinto's hazardous design. When hit from behind at 35 mph by a Chevrolet Impala, the first two Pintos tested (a 1971 and a 1972 model) exploded into flames. Eight other Pintos in the evaluation leaked, averaging a fuel loss of two gallons per minute. NHTSA called this a "significant leakage." By contrast, six crash tests conducted on 1971 Chevrolet Vegas—a vehicle comparable to the Pinto—produced "no fires" and minimal gasoline loss when compared with that sustained by the Pintos.[54]

In the face of this evidence and the impending public hearing scheduled by NHTSA, Ford announced that it was recalling 1.5 million 1971-1976 Pintos and 1975-1976 Bobcats. Although they denied any wrongdoing in their press release, Ford promised to equip each vehicle with both a polyethylene shield to prevent the bolts on the differential housing from puncturing the gas tank and with a longer filler pipe and a seal to reduce the chance that the pipe would be dislodged in an accident.[55] They said it would take them three months—until September—to send official recall notices to owners.[56]

This date was too late for the Ulrich girls; the letter from Ford did not reach their household until February 1979, months after their deaths.

Two days after Ford declared its recall, the Pinto received national exposure again. [Permission for the following excerpt comes from © CBS Inc. 1978 All rights reserved. Originally broadcast June 11, 1978 over the CBS Television Network on 60 MINUTES: IS YOUR CAR SAFE?] On Sunday evening, June 11, viewers of *60 Minutes* were greeted with Mike Wallace's question, "Is your car safe?" He answered, "Well, if you're driving a Ford Pinto, vintage 1971 to '76, the answer seems to be: Not as safe as it could be." Wallace then proceeded to tell the Pinto story.

Richard Grimshaw was the first to be interviewed. The audience learned that he had been in the hospital for four months following his Pinto burn accident, and had returned for "about 65 major surgeries." Reading from the brief for Grimshaw's case, Wallace noted that Grimshaw's lawyers were claiming that Ford "deliberately and intentionally...made a high-level corporate decision which they knew would kill or maim a known and finite number of people." He added, "Now that is one extraordinary allegation." The lawyer replied, "Well, we had a lot of proof."

Soon afterward this view was corroborated by Harley Copp, a former $150,000-a-year executive engineer who had worked at Ford for 30 years. Copp observed that style, not safety, was the dominant consideration in making cars at Ford and elsewhere in the industry. Engineers who spoke out about safety didn't "get that promotion" or "salary increase." This observation was not surprising, given the attitudes of those in charge of the company. As Henry Ford II told Copp, "this safety business is all a bunch of politics; it's going to go away, and we're going to handle it in Detroit." The Pinto, Copp asserted, was a product of this thinking. Mike Wallace commented, "I find it difficult to believe that top management of the Ford Motor Company is going to sit there and say, 'Oh, we'll buy 2,000 deaths, 10,000 injuries, because we want to make some money or we want to bring in a cheaper car.'" Copp replied, "You can't buy that?"

Herbert Misch, a twenty-three-year veteran and vice-president of environmental and safety engineering at Ford, was quick to take issue with this view. "I have never known a decision to be made to build an unsafe product or an unsafe characteristic of a product because of cost, or for any other reason, for that matter." Wallace immediately challenged this contention by noting the cost-benefit chart published in Dowie's "Pinto Madness." Misch countered by saying that the value placed on human lives was set by the government, not by Ford, and that the memo has "been taken totally out of context, and people led to believe that the Ford Motor Company is so callous that we wouldn't spend eleven dollars to save that many lives, and it's an untruth."

But Wallace would not let go. Did not a Ford document state that the company would save $20.9 million by deferring the repair of the Pinto? Were not Ford engineers told not to locate the gas tank over the rear axle because it would cost $10 more? Had not Ford trumpeted its Fiesta in Europe as safer because the tank was "located forward of the rear axle to avoid spillage in the event of a collision"? And had not the Company omitted this information from the American Fiesta advertisements and then taken the trouble to delete all references to gas-tank placement from the car's European brochure? At the end of this interrogation, Misch could only answer: "Well, I— and I— I don't know that. And I don't— the reasons why it was taken out."[57]

Like Mike Wallace, other reporters found the Pinto matter a fascinating and eminently newsworthy upperworld scandal. Indeed, as Victoria Swigert and Ronald Farrell have observed, the case gained growing notoriety. Based on a content analysis of newspaper reports, their data show that the attention given to the Pinto's problems escalated markedly after Dowie's article and the announcement of the Grimshaw decision. Other changes took place as well during the Pinto crusade; the stories not only increased in quantity but also changed in quality. Early reports tended to focus on the defect in the Pinto's gas tank; later columns described the crash victims who were incinerated or horribly burned. In Swigert and Farrell's terms, harm was now being "personalized." These later accounts also stressed that this harm was being done "willfully" in an effort to maximize corporate profits, and that Ford, in denying any culpability, was "unrepentant" for having manufactured a dangerous automobile. Ford was portrayed much like a conventional sociopathic criminal: hurting people in the pursuit of money and feeling no guilt. As described by Swigert and Farrell,

> The emerging public imagery of the manufacturer was confirmed in media accounts of its production policies. Newspapers reported that the company was aware of the defectively constructed fuel tank and of the death and injury that it produced. Based on a cost-benefit analysis, however, Ford chose to continue production and sale of the vehicle. This depiction of the corporation, along with the application of a vocabulary of deviance and the personalization of harm, had the effect of transforming a consumer problem into a crime. At issue was no longer bad-faith sales to unwitting consumers, but reckless violence against individuals in exchange for corporate profit.[58]

The Pinto in the Media

In summary, by the time of the Ulrichs' crash in August 1978, Ford was under attack from Pinto victims, wary owners, a federal regulatory agency, consumer leaders such as Ralph Nader, and members of the magazine, newspaper, and television media. This many-sided "crusade" against the Pinto publicized the view that Ford had willingly moved far beyond the moral boundaries that ought to constrain corporate conduct.[59]   As Swigert and Farrell noted, a "vocabulary of deviance"[60] had been introduced. Ford was not called careless, but ruthless. Even the prospect of people tragically and terribly burned to death could not stop their quest for profit. Something had to be done. Perhaps, as Mark Dowie suggested, the only solution was to do what we do with other killers: lock them up.[61]

A new way of describing Ford's moral character was not the only byproduct of the Pinto crusade. Both the civil cases and the NHTSA investigation had unearthed damning evidence, ranging from internal company documents to crash tests. This information was now in the public domain and being publicized by reporters who were anxious to show that crime occurred in corporate suites, not just in city streets. Further, all of the anti-Pinto activity helped to create a pool of experts, such as Harley Copp, who were willing to testify against Ford.

It was at this point that Michael Cosentino faced the task of assessing blame for the Ulrichs' deaths. Though initially he did not know much about the Pinto, he quickly learned the whole story. And this knowledge, along with the specifics of the accident and the existence of a larger social and legal context increasingly conducive to holding corporations accountable for their misbehavior, led Cosentino to two conclusions. As a man of good conscience, he thought that Ford had gone too far and was to blame for the fiery crash on Highway 33. As a pragmatic elected official, he was beginning to realize that it was indeed feasible for him to bring Ford Motor Company into court and to make them pay for their "crime."

Blaming Ford

The Accident

It was a happy time, full of promise, for the Ulrich family. Judy had just recently graduated from high school and was waiting to study interior design at a commercial college in the fall. Her sister, Lyn, was looking forward to her junior year at Penn High School, where she had been a straight-A student. And it was always a special occassion when cousin Donna visited from Illinois. The visits offered the chance to have fun and to share their excitement about and commitment to Christianity.[62]

It was past 5:30 when the three teenagers hurried out the door of the Ulrichs' brick ranchhouse. They were leaving to play volleyball at a Baptist church located in Goshen, some twenty miles away. The temperature hovered over 80 degrees, but was accompanied by a slight breeze and few clouds. It seemed an ideal evening to ride through the Indiana countryside.

Perhaps out of courtesy to her cousin, but more likely because she knew what was expected of the youngest, Lyn hopped into the back seat of her sister's yellow Pinto. The auto was a used 1973 model, but Judy was happy to have her first car and happy that her parents were helping her with the payments as a graduation present. Once Donna had settled into her seat, Judy was ready to drive off. The trip to Goshen would take the girls from the small town of Osceolo (where the Ulrichs lived) toward Elkhart by way of Highway 33.

As later accounts would reveal, they made a fateful stop on their brief journey. The gas was running low, and Judy pulled into a self-service Checker station. When they drove away, they apparently left the gas cap on the roof of the car.

About a mile and a half down the road, the cap flew off the roof and landed on the other side of the five-lane highway. Judy cautiously made a U-turn and flipped on her four-way emergency flashers. Then she drove back westward, slowing as the Pinto approached the lost gas cap. It was impossible to pull completely off the road to avoid the traffic because Highway 33 was bordered by an eight-inch-high curb.

Meanwhile, Robert Duggar was approaching from behind in his Chevy van. He had just passed a police car coming in the opposite direction and equipped with radar. Quickly checking his speedometer, he was relieved to see that he was going 50 mph, well within the posted limit of 55 mph. Feeling the urge for a cigarette, he glanced down and reached for his pack, which had fallen on the floor of the van. When he looked up, he was shocked to see the Ulrichs' Pinto only ten feet in front of him.

There was no time to avoid a collision. The van's front bumper, a thick pine board, rammed into the Pinto's rear. Duggar immediately smelled gasoline; an instant later the Pinto burst into flames.

Interpreting the Accident

Shortly before 6:30, state trooper Neil Graves received a call from the dispatcher. The news was not good; there was an accident on Highway 33, just north of Goshen. As a six-and-a-half year veteran of the force, investigating crashes was nothing new for Graves. He had already witnessed the aftermath of 987 accidents.

As sociologist David Sudnow has observed, the experience of participants in the criminal justice system leads them to gain "knowledge of the typical manner in which offenses of given classes are committed, the social characteristics of the persons who regularly commit them, the features of the settings in which they occur, the types of victims often involved, and the like."[63] Offenses that coincide with this knowledge are viewed as "normal crimes," and the participants know how to react when they confront such cases. The procedure is less clear, however, when the conduct in question violates the expected parameters—for example, when one confronts an elderly criminal.

Neil Graves's experiences on the road had taught him that there was a "normal" accident that resulted in loss of life, involving high speeds, alcohol or other substance abuse, broken bodies, and substantial damage to all vehicles involved in the crash. As he drove up Highway 33, he expected to find these circumstances.

The Accident Scene

From the beginning, however, Graves was troubled by the oddness of this accident; certain things did not fit the normal pattern. As he pulled onto the scene at 6:39, the firefighters had just finished extinguishing the Pinto's fire. It struck Graves that this was only the third fire he had seen in nearly a thousand collisions, and all of those had involved extremely high speeds. He had the difficult job of being the first to look inside the Ulrichs' vehicle, and found that what the bystanders suspected was tragically true: two charred bodies were inside. For Neil Graves it was a heart-wrenching picture, which would give him nightmares in the coming months. As he commented later, "that's a sight indelibly burned on my mind. I'll never forget it for the rest of my life."

Recovering from this initial shock, he proceeded to check the interior of the car. The water used to douse the fire had accumulated in the front floor, but Graves noticed that it was mixed with something else. He dipped his fingers in the liquid and took a small sample to sniff. Then it dawned on him: he was smelling gasoline. Somewhat bewildered, Graves could not understand how this could have happened. As lab tests would reveal later, the passenger compartment had been splashed with gasoline before the fire had ignited.

This was not the only unusual aspect of the accident. All the witnesses of the crash told Graves that both vehicles were moving when they collided and that the speed difference was at most 30 mph. They felt that this would only be a fender-bender, but then, suddenly, the Pinto exploded into flames.

Graves was also puzzled by the difference in the damage to each vehicle. Duggar's van sustained only minor dents, a pushed-in front grill, and one cracked headlight. By contrast, the back of the Pinto had collapsed like an accordion, and only the burned-out shell of the car remained. Graves, a veteran investigator of highway wrecks, found it hard to believe that the two vehicles had been in the same accident.

"Consciously or subconsciously," as Graves would later put it, another factor was at work. Six months before that evening he had picked up a copy of *Mother Jones* magazine from a newsstand. That issue had featured Dowie's "Pinto Madness." Even today Graves cannot say how much that article shaped his investigation of the accident. In any event, his memory would be jogged by the next day and the odd aspects of the accident scene would begin to make sense.

Meanwhile, Terry Shewmaker, Cosentino's thirty-year-old assistant prosecutor, had just returned home. He was greeted with a call from a local television station asking him about the accident. This was the first he had heard of the tragedy, and he called the Elkhart County sheriff's office to learn more. The details were disturbing: two dead, one burned critically. Shewmaker hung up and immediately dialed his boss at home. Because of the gravity of the case, Cosentino instructed him to treat the accident as a potential homicide.

Struck by the horrible deaths of the three teenage girls, the local citizens and media searched to assess blame. Some felt that Highway 33, with its treacherous eight-inch curbs, was at least partially at fault. However, when it was learned that pills, suspected to be amphetamines (though they proved to be caffeine), were found in his Chevy van, the local consensus was that Robert Duggar was to blame. By 4:00 on Friday, the day after the accident, Duggar had been arrested on charges of possessing an illegal drug.

On the national level, word of the Pinto burn deaths received a very different interpretation. On Friday, while working at a part-time job that helped make ends meet, Neil Graves repeatedly received calls. As expected, the local media tracked him down. But this was not all; he was also contacted by such national media sources as UPI, AP, and CBS's Dan Rather. These callers did not ask about the possibility of a drugged-up driver but about the defects in an automobile. Combined with the oddities of the accident and Dowie's article, these questions made Graves begin to think that the Pinto, and not Duggar, might be to blame for the Ulrichs' deaths the night before.

Graves's next step was to get in touch with Mark Dowie. Dowie retold the particulars of the "Pinto Madness" story and offered to forward a reprint. He also gave Graves the names of Harley Copp, the ex-Ford engineering executive, and Byron Bloch, a safety expert. Both Copp and Bloch had worked against Ford in Pinto civil cases (such as the Grimshaw trial), and Copp had appeared on the *60 Minutes* segment on the Pinto. In effect, Graves, and thus Cosentino, now belonged to the network of people who were crusading against the Pinto.

Over the weekend, the evidence gathered at the accident site was processed and prepared for examination. Cosentino sat down with Graves, Shewmaker, and the rest of his staff to consider what, if anything, the prosecutor's office should act upon. The others quickly came to share Graves's gut feeling—formed the night of the crash—that this was not a normal case. When he viewed photographs of the vehicles, Cosentino could not believe the disparity in the damages to the Pinto and to the van. He was also bothered by the eyewitness testimony indicating that this should have been just a minor crash. Most troubling were the pictures of the dead girls; they were, as Terry Shewmaker remarked, "incredible." Those at the meeting could not help feeling that no one should have to die in this way. It was clear that the case deserved further investigation.

In the days that followed, calls and information continued to flow into the prosecutor's office. Lawyers with civil cases pending against Ford for its handling of the Pinto contacted Cosentino and offered to furnish him with damaging corporate documents. Some may have acted out of altruism, but there was also a pragmatic motive: a criminal decision against Ford would hurt the company's chances in civil trials and thus would bolster the lawyers' bargaining power in out-of-court settlements. As Cosentino noted later, his office became a "clearinghouse" for Pinto documents.

This information would be valuable, of course. Yet while Cosentino was considering where to proceed, the repeated offers to share "inside" tests and memoranda had other, perhaps more significant, effects. For one thing, they revealed that Ford's corporate shield had been pierced. Cosentino would not have to start from scratch; he would have some documents, a good idea of where to look for others within Ford, and some confidence that the corporate giant could be forced to relinquish secret materials. Building a case against the company was not out of the question; if civil lawyers could do it, then so could he.

In addition, each outside contact—whether from lawyers or from the media—sensitized Cosentino to a way of thinking about the accident: Ford knew that the Pinto was dangerously defective, consciously chose to place profits over safety, resisted all attempts to make the company fix the car, and showed no signs of remorse over what it had done.[64] In short, it was said, the company had gone too far. Disregarding normal moral boundaries, it had placed its own needs above the welfare of innocent citizens. For a "law and order" prosecutor, this idea had a familiar ring and suggested a well-conditioned response: immoral offenders should pay for their crimes.[65]

Thus Consentino became increasingly convinced that Ford was to blame for the Ulrichs' deaths. The abnormal aspects of the crash, Dowie's article, input from safety experts, internal Ford documents, and media interest—when taken together—firmly reinforced this conclusion. One issue remained, however: was it possible under Indiana law to prosecute a corporation for the violence that resulted when it knowingly produced and failed to repair a hazardous consumer product? Recently the state had revised its criminal code, which now included an enabling statute providing for corporate criminal liabilty and a statute for reckless homicide (in fact, this had become effective forty-one days before the Ulrichs' deaths on August 10, 1978). Cosentino knew the law and felt certain that Ford could be taken to criminal court under these statutes. To test his view, he asked his staff to research the question. He also requested an opinion from William Conour of the Indiana Prosecuting Attorney's office, who had been involved in drafting the reckless homicide provision. The response was unanimous: Ford could be held criminally liable under Indiana law.

"Reckless homicide" is one of several general categories of homicide that have been established by legal tradition and written into modern criminal statutes to address the wrongful taking of human life. Unlike the charge of murder, which is considered the most serious category of homicide and thus deserving of the harshest punishment, the charge of reckless homicide does not require the prosecutor to prove that the accused intended to kill anyone. It is enough to show that a death—even if unintended—resulted from the reckless behavior of the accused, and that a reasonable person would have known that the behavior was life-threatening. Because Cosentino would be trying to prove essentially that the Ulrich girls' deaths were caused by Ford's reckless choice of profits over safety—the company's management obviously did not *intend* to kill any of its customers—reckless homicide was the most logical offense category for the prosecution to consider using against Ford.

Scarcely two weeks after the accident, then, Cosentino was prepared to seek a path-breaking indictment against a major American corporation and to join the crusade against the Pinto. He was now convinced that Ford had acted immorally, and he was fully capable of explaining its conduct with a term—"reckless homicide"—previously reserved for conventional criminals. With evidence and expert witnesses (such as Bloch and Copp) available, he also knew that it was feasible to develop a case against Ford. Finally, as mentioned above, Indiana law seemed to offer the option of bringing the company within the reach of the criminal sanction.

Yet Cosentino was, after all, a prosecutor in a conservative county. On the brink of making legal history, he was reluctant to move too hastily. He would put his feelings to one final test before taking on the fourth largest corporation in the world.

The Grand Jury

Elkhart County is located in northern Indiana just east of South Bend and a few miles south of Interstate 80. Its population of over 125,000, including the city of Elkhart with about 45,000, is composed of typical "middle Americans." Conservatives outnumber liberals by over two to one, and secular influences have yet to erode the deep spiritual commitment of many citizens. Indeed, because of the strong Mennonite and Amish heritage in the region, religion continues to flourish, often with a fundamentalist flavor. Elkhart residents are proud that the county is the "mobile-home capital of the world" and that a number of other industries are also doing well. More than a few self-made millionaires were born, raised, and live in Elkhart, and this fact is evidence enough to the local people that in America hard work and smart entrepreneurship can still be parlayed into success.

This context surrounded Mike Cosentino as he considered the prospect of prosecuting Ford. As an elected official, he had to be sensitive to what the public would think about this bold action. To be sure, he was running unopposed in the upcoming November election, and thus any political liability would not be immediate. Also, under Indiana law, he had the power to file charges against a defendant without grand jury approval. But Cosentino, a conservative man, was not comfortable about embarking on a case that would not be supported by his community both inside and outside the courtroom.

Would conservative citizens with a firm faith in capitalism believe that Ford could be a criminal? Cosentino thought they might, but some doubts remained. One possible solution suggested itself: to bring the case before a grand jury. As a small sample of the community, a grand jury could be a "sounding board," Cosentino believed. He could present the evidence but not try to sway the jury—as prosecutors often do—to return an indictment. In this way the jurors would provide a good indication of the average citizen's feelings about criminalizing corporate conduct.

Yet other considerations remained. On a general ideological level, Cosentino was not anti-big business; he "had no burning desire to prosecute Ford." He was motivated by his belief that people in the system have a moral obligation to play by the rules of the game. There was also an economic element: Cosentino, then a forty-one-year-old father of two, was a part-time prosecuting attorney with a salary of $23,000. The balance of his income came from a lucrative civil practice in which he often represented corporate clients (his law partners included his retired predecessor as prosecutor, C. Whitney Slabaugh, and assistant prosecutor Terry Shewmaker). He was concerned that a time-consuming trial might hurt his and the firm's income, and that attacking a corporation might cause some accounts to seek counsel elsewhere. His partners, however, promised to carry the load at the firm, and Cosentino was confident that his civil clients would understand his actions against Ford once he explained his reasoning. After all, he felt that in "99.9 percent" of all cases, the criminal law should not be invoked to control business enterprises. It was only when giant corporations— like Ford, not like those he typically represented—had shown that they were immune to normal regulatory and civil actions that criminal penalties should be considered.

Perhaps the deciding factor in Cosentino's thinking was the sentiment expressed by Mattie and Earl Ulrich, the parents of Judy and Lyn. Had they opposed any further action, Cosentino says, he would have ended the case. The Ulrichs, however, supported the idea of prosecuting Ford and offered to help in any way possible. As deeply religious people they were motivated less by retributive feelings than by a sense that there must have been some higher purpose for their daughters' fate. Maybe the case against Ford would give meaning to their tragic loss.

With all barriers finally swept aside, Cosentino convened a six-member grand jury to consider what action, if any, the state should take. Word of his decision spread quickly to Ford headquarters in Dearborn, Michigan. Three in-house lawyers were sent to inform Cosentino of the wisdom of abandoning the course he was about to follow. Visiting him in his Elkhart office, they allegedly threatened to halt the case through a federal restraining order and arrogantly (in Cosentino's opinion) dismissed his case as a joke that had already proceeded too far. After all, didn't he know who he was dealing with?

The meeting was brief, and the Ford lawyers, with their condescending approach, miscalculated the situation. Mike Cosentino had a strong will and was not about to back down from a fight. Difficult circumstances were not new to him. Raised in a broken home by a mother who supported the family by working as a waitress, Cosentino worked hard to become a high school football standout. His athletic prowess earned him a scholarship to Beloit College, where he majored in philosophy. After a stint in the military service, he tended bar in the evenings to help put himself through law school at the University of Wisconsin. In 1967 he joined the law firm and prosecutorial staff of C. Whitney Slabaugh. When Slabaugh retired, Cosentino ran for the county prosecutor's office on a "law and order" platform. He captured the Republican primary by less than one hundred votes; in conservative Elkhart, this victory was tantamount to winning office.

By the time the Ford lawyers came to dissuade him from pursuing a grand-jury investigation, Mike Cosentino, the epitome of the "American dream," had become a successful man. His civil practice was flourishing; he was a popular elected official. He was also known for his intense, flamboyant courtroom manner. Competitive by nature, he was proud that he had tried twenty-five homicide cases and had won a conviction in every instance. He was not pleased to be told by "slick" corporate lawyers that he didn't know what he was doing. After all, who the hell did Ford and its lawyers think *they* were dealing with?[66]

Undaunted by Ford's attempt to block his efforts, Cosentino pressed on with the grand jury hearings. Again, from a desire not to depart too radically from community norms, he tried consciously not to manipulate the jury into indicting Ford; he would let the evidence speak for itself. Further, any action would be directed against the corporation as a whole. Establishing the culpability of individual executives seemed too complex a task, especially because he considered it unlikely that Michigan would extradite top Ford officials to Indiana.

Behind closed doors, the six jury members were shown physical evidence from the crash site and internal Ford documents. Byron Bloch, the automotive safety expert, was brought in to analyze the particulars of the Ulrichs' accident and to comment on the Ford memos and reports. The jurors learned about Ford's crash-testing policies from Harley Copp, the former Ford engineering executive who was forced to retire from the company at age fifty-five. The company said the action was necessary because of Copp's excessive absenteeism; others, however, believed he was forced out because he was too outspoken about safety issues.

On September 6 the grand jury issued summonses to Henry Ford II and Lee Iacocca. They wanted to hear Ford Motor Company's side of the story. At first the automaker hinted that it would refuse to obey any such dictates, but through a compromise achieved a satisfactory arrangement: Ford would send two of its engineers to explain why the company was not culpable in its handling of the Pinto.

The grand jury did not accept Ford's interpretation and decided that there was enough evidence to suggest that the company was to blame for the Ulrichs' burn deaths. On September 13, 1978, they voted unanimously to hand down three felony indictments against Ford for reckless homicide.[67] They decided, however, *not* to take any criminal action against Robert Duggar, the driver of the Chevy van. Though he may have been careless, eyewitness testimony confirmed that he was not speeding and blood tests revealed no trace of alcohol or drugs. Finally, the grand jury recommended that the eight-inch curbs on Highway 33 be removed; this was done some ten months later.

The indictment, which William Conour helped Cosentino and his staff draft, asserted that "Ford Motor Company, a corporation," had caused the Ulrichs' deaths "through the acts and omissions of its agents acting within the scope of their authority with said corporation." It charged that Ford "did recklessly design and manufacture a certain 1973 Pinto...in such a manner as would likely cause said automobile to flame and burn upon rear-end impact," permitted the Pinto "to remain upon the highways and roadways of Elkhart County, State of Indiana," and "did fail to repair and modify said Pinto." This "reckless disregard for the safety of other persons," the indictment concluded, led the Ulrichs to "languish and die by incineration."[68] With these words, legal history had been made. For the first time a major corporation in the United States had been indicted (and, ultimately, prosecuted) on the charge of reckless homicide for making and failing to recall an allegedly defective product that resulted in a consumer's death.[69]

Local reaction to this news was mixed. Some Elkhart citizens supported the action; others were cynical about Cosentino's motives. It was suspected that indicting Ford was a publicity ploy to gain the fame he needed to run for a higher office.

Perhaps the most common response was one of confusion. As David "Scoop" Schreiber, a reporter for the *Elkhart Truth*, observed, many people were genuinely puzzled by the action of their "law and order" prosecutor and wondered "why Mike would do this." Schreiber also suggested that community outrage was diminished somewhat by the fact that the Ulrichs lived in Osceola, which is located just over the Elkhart line in St. Joseph's County. The Ulrichs did not attend Elkhart schools, were not known well by many residents, and thus in a sense were outsiders.

Cosentino believed that public opinion was divided evenly. Neil Graves, however, conducted an informal poll in a South Bend mall; his numbers were seventy percent against prosecuting Ford, thirty in favor. Graves also found some opposition among other state troopers, and his superiors initially opposed the idea of assigning him to the case full time. Nonetheless, Cosentino and Graves were fairly confident. Both were respected professionals, and both felt that sentiments would change as soon as people—like the grand jury—learned the facts about Ford's handling of the Pinto. By their accounts, public opinion had indeed shifted markedly in favor of the prosecution by the time the Pinto case had ended.

On the national level, the response was quite different. Cosentino received some hate mail decrying his action, but generally the feedback was encouraging. The news media, recognizing that historical firsts make good copy, flooded his office with calls and highlighted his attack on Ford in prominently displayed stories. Those who were already familiar with the Pinto's problems took advantage of the situation to celebrate Cosentino's wisdom and courage. A delighted Ralph Nader remarked that Ford's indictment "is going to send tremors through the highest levels of the executive suites throughout the country."[70] Similarly, *Mother Jones*, the magazine that published Dowie's "Pinto Madness" story, issued a press release stating that it "salutes the Elkhart Grand Jury for this indictment." The magazine's editors, however, added this caveat:

> We...respectfully suggest that criminal investigations be commenced immediately on the roles played in this [Pinto marketing] decision [by three Ford vice-presidents,] Ford President Lee Iacocca, and Chairman of the Board Henry Ford II.[71]

Meanwhile, Ford Motor Company, stung by the news of the indictments, was mobilizing its immense resources to put a stop to Cosentino's game plan. To be sure, Ford stood to suffer only a minimal penalty from a conviction: a maximum fine of $30,000—$10,000 for each count of reckless homicide. Since Ford was a corporation, it could not, as in the case of an individual offender, be incarcerated. And a $30,000 fine was insignificant to the fourth largest corporation in the world. The case had other possible ramifications, however, and Ford had reason to fear these: the use of a criminal conviction against Ford in Pinto-related civil cases where enormous punitive damages were at stake; the loss of consumer confidence resulting in declining sales; the specter of a trial precipitating more stringent federal safety regulations (see Chapter 5 for an extended review of these issues). Although these points were only a matter of speculation, the automaker did not wish to take this kind of risk. Cosentino may have had some success in his own backyard, but now Ford intended to hire the best legal minds available to see that this Pinto matter was quickly put to rest.

Conclusion

In his best-seller *Megatrends*, John Naisbitt observed that "most of the social invention occurs in just five states." These "bellwether" states, "again and again the places where new trends begin," are California, Florida, Washington, Colorado, and Connecticut.[72] It is not surprising that Indiana does not appear on this list; the state and its people may have many admirable qualities, but Hoosiers are not generally thought to be social trendsetters.

Yet even if Indiana is not one of the five "bellwether states" that signal what is to come, it may be a place that tells us what has arrived—what changes have taken hold sufficiently to penetrate deeply into the American social fabric. Thus it seems significant that Ford was indicted not in a jurisdiction that experimented constantly with new social policy but in a community—Elkhart—that takes pride in traditional values and practices. This fact suggests that the movement against white-collar crime and, more specifically, the attack on questionable corporate conduct have reached the heart of middle America. Social, political, and legal circumstances have combined to create the possibility that even a Republican "law and order" prosecutor in a conservative county will seek—and win—an indictment against a giant corporation. Seen in this light, the Ford Pinto case is important not merely for the legal precedent it would set, but also because it is fundamentally a sign of the times.

Notes

[1] This account of the accident was drawn from Lee Patrick Strobel, *Reckless Homicide? Ford's Pinto Trial.* South Bend, Indiana: And Books, 1985, pp. 7-16; Dennis Byrne, "The Pinto, the Girls, the Anger," *Chicago Sun-Times* (September 17, 1978). pp. 5, 50; and the following articles by local reporter David Schreiber that were published in the Elkhart Truth: "Eyewitnesses Tell of Pinto Crash" (January 17, 1980), "Witness saw Pinto Become Ball of Flame" (January 18, 1980), "Duggar Describes Tragic Pinto Scene" (January 22, 1982).

[2] Hugh McCann, "The Pinto Trial," *Detroit News Magazine* (January 6, 1980), p. 23.

[3] This point was taken from Cynthia Fuchs Epstein's observation that female interest in law and in legal specialties previously reserved for males was not merely the result of changing sex roles but also of the emergence of opportunities that prompted women to pursue nontraditional career paths. As Epstein has commented, "The opening up of opportunities proved immediately effective in creating interest. And, contrary to popular myths, it was not necessary for women to go through long years of 'resocialization,' retraining, or reorientation to prepare for their new roles." See *Women in Law.* Garden City, N.Y.: Anchor Books, 1984, p. 380.

[4] David Schreiber, "Cosentino Defends Charges," *Elkhart Truth* (October 25, 1978).

[5] Interview with Michael Cosentino, June 1983.

[6] *Ibid.*

[7] Cosentino was a keynote speaker at the 1980 meeting of the American Bar Association. He was also featured prominently in a series of articles on the case that appeared in the *National Law Journal.*

[8] See, for example, John C. Coffee, Jr., "Making the Punishment Fit the Corporation: The Problems of Finding an Optimal Corporation Criminal Sanction," *Northern Illinois University Law Review* 1 (1980), pp. 3-36. The legal literature debating the wisdom of criminally sanctioning corporations has grown remarkably since the mid-1970s and is now voluminous. Since

many of these sources and the central points of this debate will be reviewed in Chapter 7, further citations are not listed here.

[9] Interview with Michael Cosentino, June 1983.

[10] John L. Paluszek, *Will the Corporation Survive?* Reston, Va.: Reston Publishing Company, 1977, p. 3.

[11] Peter L. Berger, *The Heretical Imperative: Contemporary Possibilities of Religious Affirmation.* Garden City, N.Y.: Anchor Books, 1966.

[12] Alvin W. Gouldner, *The Coming Crisis of Western Sociology.* New York: Avon Books, 1970, p. 29.

[13] Seymour Martin Lipset and William Schneider, "Confidence in Confidence Measures," *Public Opinion* 6 (August-September 1983), p. 44.

[14] Seymour Martin Lipset and William Schneider, *The Confidence Gap: Business, Labor, and Government in the Public Mind.* New York: Free Press, 1983, p. 72. See also Kathy Bloomgarden, "Managing the Environment: The Public's View," *Public Opinion* 6 (February-March 1983), pp. 47-51; "Opinion Roundup: the Balance Sheet on Business," *Public Opinion* 5 (October-November 1982), p. 21.

[15] Lipset and Schneider, *The Confidence Gap*, p. 31.

[16] Roger Ricklefs, "Public Gives Executives Low Marks for Honesty and Ethical Standards," *Wall Street Journal* 64 (November 2, 1983), p. 31.

[17] Lipset and Schneider, *The Confidence Gap*, pp. 35, 78, 171; "Opinion Roundup: No Reduction in Pop Cynicism," *Public Opinion* 6 (December-January 1984), p. 32; "Opinion Roundup: Occupational Prestige," *Public Opinion* 4 (August-September 1981), p. 33.

[18] Lipset and Schneider, *The Confidence Gap*, pp. 380, 382.

[19] Ralph Nader, *Unsafe at Any Speed: The Designed-In Dangers of the American Automobile.* New York: Grossman Publishers, 1965, p. vii.

[20] For a discussion of the concept of "blaming the victim," see William Ryan, *Blaming the Victim.* New York: Random House, 1971.

[21] Nader, *Unsafe at Any Speed*, p. 236.

[22] The question of whether "safety sells" has remained controversial since Nader's initial writings. For contrasting, though not entirely contrary views, see Marshall B. Clinard and Peter C. Yeager, Corporate Crime. New York: The Free Press, 1980, p. 259 and Lee Iacocca with William Novak, *Iacocca: An Autobiography*. New York: Bantam Books, 1984, p. 297.

[23] Nader, *Unsafe at Any Speed*, p. 40.

[24] *Ibid.*, pp. ix, xi.

[25] After his settlement with GM, Nader decided to use the proceeds (minus legal expenses) for the "continuous legal monitoring of General Motor's activities in the safety, pollution and consumer relations area." See "GM and Nader Settle His Suit Over Snooping," *Wall Street Journal* (August 14, 1970), p. 4. For accounts of GM's reaction to Nader, see J. Patrick Wright, *On a Clear Day You Can See General Motors: John Z. De-Lorean's Look Inside the Automotive Giant*. New York: Avon Books, 1979, p. 64, and Brent Fisse and John Braithwaite, *The Impact of Publicity on Corporate Offenders*. Albany: SUNY Press, 1983, pp. 30-33.

[26] Thus, in a review of opinion studies, Joseph Nolan concluded that "by 1990, if not before, the notion that companies are responsible for their products in perpetuity will be firmly embedded in the public consciousness—and to an increasing extent, in our laws." See "Business Beware: Early Warning Signs in the Eighties," *Public Opinion* 4 (April-May 1981), p. 57. See also "Opinion Roundup: Taxes and Regulation," *Public Opinion* 5 (October-November 1982), p. 23; *The Chronicle of Higher Education* (February 1, 1984), p. 14; and Timothy Harper, "Environmental Issues Gaining Importance," *Cincinnati Enquirer* (August 29, 1984), p. A-10.

[27] In two samples, for example, large proportions (89 and 62.8 percent) of business executives disagreed with the statement that "consumerism or the consumer crusade has not been an important factor in changing business practices and procedures." See Thomas J. Stanley and Larry M. Robinson, "Opinions on Consumer Issues: A Review of Recent Studies of Executives and Consumers," *Journal of Consumer Affairs* 14 (No. 1, 1980), p. 215.

[28] Clinard and Yeager, *Corporate Crime*, p. 254.

[29] Fisse and Braithwaite, *The Impact of Publicity on Corporate Offenders*, p. 35.

[30] Quoted in Fisse and Braithwaite, *The Impact of Publicity on Corporate Offenders*, pp. 35-36.

[31] All quotes cited below are taken from "Watergate transcripts" prepared by The National Archives and titled "Part of a Conversation among President Nixon, Lide Anthony Iacocca, Henry Ford II, and John D. Ehrlichman in the Oval Office on April 27, 1971, between 11:08 and 11:43." This information was acquired initially by lawyer Foy Devine for use in a civil suit against Ford conducted in Georgia *(Stubblefield v. Ford Motor Company)*.

[32] Mark Dowie, "Pinto Madness," *Mother Jones* 2 (September-October, 1977), p. 21.

[33] Strobel, *Reckless Homicide?* p. 82. Some accounts have placed the actual weight of the Pinto at 2,030 pounds. See Robert Lacey, *Ford: The Men and the Machine.* Boston: Little, Brown, 1986, p. 575.

[34] *Ibid.*, p. 88.

[35] Jack Anderson and Les Whitten, "Auto Maker Shuns Safer Gas Tank," *Washington Post* (December 30, 1976), p. B-7.

[36] Dowie, "Pinto Madness," p. 18.

[37] *Ibid.*, p. 18.

[38] *Ibid.*, p. 20.

[39] *Ibid.*, p. 21.

[40] *Ibid.*, p. 21. Dowie also noted another major obstacle in fixing the safety defects of the Pinto: to reduce the time required to get the Pinto on the market, Ford had begun to tool the machines that would produce the car's parts while product development was yet to be completed. Thus any design changes would be more costly than usual because of the investment already made in the tooling process. Also, for Lee Iacocca's view of the Pinto, see *Iacocca: An Autobiography*, pp. 161-162.

[41]   *Ibid.*, p. 24.   For the original Ford memorandum and chart, see E.S. Grush and C.S. Saunby, "Fatalities Associated with Crash Induced Fuel Leakage and Fires." Significantly, this document assessed fuel leakage in a rollover test and not in rear-end collisions.   Although the problems that arose during rear-end impacts caused the controversy surrounding the Pinto, Dowie did not highlight this distinction.   Even so, the most damning aspect of the Ford document was its suggestion that the company would willfully sacrifice human life in the effort to maximize profits.

[42]   *Ibid.*, p. 32.

[43]   Fisse and Braithwaite, *The Impact of Publicity on Corporate Offenders*, p. 43.

[44]   Office of Defects Investigation Enforcement (NHTSA), *Investigation Report, Phase I, C7-38: Alleged Fuel Tank and Filler Neck Damage in Rear-End Collision of Subcompact Passenger Cars (1971-1976 Ford Pinto, 1975-1976 Mercury Bobcat)*, (May 1978), pp. 1-2.

[45]   Roy Harris, Jr., "Jury in Pinto Crash Case: 'We Wanted Ford to Take Notice,'" *Washington Post* (February 15, 1978), p. A-2.

[46]   "Ford's $128 Million Headache," *Time* (February 20, 1978), p. 65.

[47]   Harris, "Jury in Pinto Crash Case," p. A-2.

[48]   "Award $128 Million Damage Suit," *AP News Release* (February 14, 1978).

[49]   Harris, "Jury in Pinto Crash Case," p. A-2.

[50]   "Award Upheld in Pinto Fire Suit," *Los Angeles Times Wire Service* (May 30, 1981).

[51]   "Pinto Crash Victim Picks Up the Pieces," *Beacon-News* (January 24, 1983), p. A-5.

[52]   Victoria Lynn Swigert and Ronald A. Farrell, "Corporate Homicide: Definitional Processes in the Creation of Deviance," *Law and Society Review* 15 (No. 1, 1980-1981), p. 172; Reginald Stuart, "Pintos Withdrawn in Oregon Dispute Over Tank Safety," *New York Times* (April 21, 1978), pp. D-1, D-13.

[53]   Letter to L.A. Iacocca from Howard Dugoff, Deputy Administrator, NHTSA, U.S. Department of Transportation (May 8, 1978).

[54]   Office of Defect Investigation Enforcement (NHTSA), *Investigatory Report, Phase I*, pp. 11-12, Figure 1. See also Strobel, *Reckless Homicide?* pp. 22-23.

[55]   Strobel, *Reckless Homicide?* pp. 23-24.

[56]   Larry Kramer and Charles S. Rowe, Jr., "Nader Hits Ford on Recall," *Washington Post* (August 2, 1978), p. B-3.

[57]   All quotes taken from the transcript of "Is Your Car Safe?" *60 Minutes* 10 (No. 40, June 11, 1978), CBS Television Network. It should be noted, however, that Misch later charged that his interview was "cut and spliced," and thus did not accurately present his responses or views of the Pinto's safety. See Strobel, *Reckless Homicide?* p. 222.

[58]   Swigert and Farrell, "Corporate Homicide," p. 181.

[59]   More generally, see Chapter 1. See also Joseph R. Gusfield, "Moral Passage: The Symbolic Process in Public Designations of Deviance," *Social Problems* 15 (Fall 1967), pp. 178-188.

[60]   Swigert and Farrell, "Corporate Homicide," pp. 170-172.

[61]   Dowie, "Pinto Madness," p. 32.

[62]   The account of the accident and the response to the accident were based largely on June 1983 interviews with Michael Cosentino, his assistant Terry Shewmaker, State Trooper Neil Graves, and newspaper reporter David Schreiber. One of the Authors, William J. Maakestad, had acquired much first-hand information from his involvement with the prosecution during the subsequent case against Ford. We also relied on Schreiber's news reports and on excellent descriptions contained in Strobel's *Reckless Homicide?* Finally, although reconstructing a social situation several years after its occurrence is not without risks, we have made every effort to insure that our account contains no misstatement of any major fact and as few inaccuracies as our method of analysis allows.

[63]   David Sudnow, "Normal Crimes: Sociological Features of the Penal Code in a Public Defender Office," *Social Problems* 12 (Winter 1965), p. 259.

[64]   Swigert and Farrell, "Corporate Homicide," pp. 174-176. Also instructive is Lee Iacocca's statement on the Pinto: "We resisted making any changes, and that hurt us badly." See *Iacocca: An Autobiography* , p. 162.

[65]   For a discussion of the nature of conservative "law and order" criminal justice ideology, see Francis T. Cullen and Karen Gilbert, *Reaffirming Rehabilitation*. Cincinnati: Anderson Publishing Co., 1982, pp. 36-42, 91-104. See also Francis T. Cullen, Gregory A. Clark, John B. Cullen, and Richard A. Mathers, "Attribution, Salience, and Attitudes Toward Criminal Sanctioning," *Criminal Justice and Behavior* 12 (September 1985), pp. 305-331.

[66]   This interpretation of Cosentino's encounter with Ford's lawyers was drawn from our June 1983 interview with him in his Elkhart office. It was our impression that Cosentino resented the condescending attitude of the lawyers as manifested in their implication that he did not really know what he was embarking upon. See also Strobel, *Reckless Homicide?* pp. 33-34.

[67]   The grand jury also indicted Ford on one misdemeanor charge of "criminal recklessness." Cosentino later dropped this charge, however, so that it would not be possible for a trial jury to compromise and convict Ford of this lesser offense.

[68]   Quotes taken from the indictments returned by the Elkhart Superior Court Grand Jury on September 13, 1978, *State of Indiana v. Ford Motor Company.*

[69]   As noted in Chapter 3, other corporations had previously been indicted on charges of murder and negligent homicide. The Ford indictment, however, was unique because it was recent, it involved the fourth largest corporation in the world, and it was fundamentally a product liability case. Thus, in *Corporate Crime*, p. 261, Clinard and Yeager observed that "the case was the first ever in which an American corporation had been criminally prosecuted in a product liability matter." Similarly, according to Strobel in *Reckless Homicide?* p. 29, "And yet the idea was without precedent. No American manufacturer or individual executive had ever been criminally charged in connection with the marketing of an allegedly unsafe product." See also Malcolm E. Wheeler, "In Pinto's Wake, Criminal Trials Loom for More Manufacturers," *National Law Journal* (October 6, 1980), p. 27.

70   Quoted in Byrne, "The Pinto, the Girls, the Anger," p. 50.

71   Press release titled "Indiana Grand Jury Brings 3 Counts of Reckless Homicide Against Ford Motor Co./*Mother Jones* Responds."

72   John Naisbitt, *Megatrends: Ten New Directions Transforming Our Lives*. New York: Warner Books, 1984, pp. xxvii-xxviii.

Chapter 5
Getting To Trial:
The Obstacle Course Begins

> Many persons told us they believed the prosecution to be
> 'silly'—and that was their word for it—since the maximum poten-
> tial penalty to Ford under the criminal statute was a fine of
> $30,000, $10,000 per count. The Ford Motor Company, as
> might be expected, disagreed with the prosecution too. It vari-
> ously labeled the prosecution bizarre, novel, destructive, sinister,
> and (borrowing the criminal defendant's old trick of accusing
> the accuser) reckless. Ford never once, however, contended
> that the prosecution was silly because only $30,000 was at stake.
> —Michael Cosentino[1]

A strategic response to the landmark indictment was not long in coming
from Ford headquarters: avert a jury trial at all costs. To this end, Ford
spared no expense; the company immediately retained Mayer, Brown and
Platt—a 185-member law firm with its principal offices in Chicago—to develop a legal strategy by which to quash the indictment. Roger Barrett
headed a team of about ten attorneys charged with primary responsibility
for the case. Soon afterward, Ford added the prestigious national law firm
of Hughes, Hubbard and Reed to its legal stable. Philip Lacovara, who had
served as a Watergate prosecutor while based in the firm's Washington office, was among the lawyers from that firm who worked on the Pinto indictment. It is not unusual for a corporate giant to employ outside counsel,
often called "hired guns," for such specialized cases. As we shall see, this
was only the first of many displays of the tremendous resources at Ford's
disposal. The pretrial legal obstacle course, which would take the prosecution almost a year to complete, had begun.

Fears at Ford

As noted, Ford management was not concerned with the less-than-haunting prospect of a $30,000 fine. The comment by Cosentino which introduces this chapter makes a point that has been substantiated by Brent Fisse and John Braithwaite in their book, *The Impact of Publicity on Corporate Offenders*. In their chapter on the Pinto prosecution, the authors note that Ford management was concerned with both the short-term and long-term effects of standing trial in criminal court before the entire country.

Regarding *short-term* financial effects, several observers have noted that at the time of the indictment, the Pinto had just begun to recover from a 40 percent drop in sales following the June recall.[2] In an article that appeared, ironically, just two days before the indictment, the *Wall Street Journal* stated flatly that the Pinto "still threaten[ed] to become the company's biggest albatross since the ill-fated Edsel of two decades ago.[3]

In addition, as reporter Lee Strobel remarked, the company was troubled by other Pinto concerns:

> With the number of Pinto and Bobcat lawsuits continuing to rise toward 50, and total damages of more than one billion dollars being sought, Ford lawyers feared a conviction could cause plaintiffs' lawyers to hold out for higher civil court settlements and even encourage new lawsuits. The evidence disclosed during a criminal trial also might be used by lawyers in civil lawsuits to strengthen their cases if they wound up in front of a jury.[4]

Fisse and Braithwaite discuss in greater depth four major *long-term* effects that Ford feared with regard to a criminal trial: tarnishing the corporate image, lowering the personal reputations of executives, creating worry about longer-term effects on sales, and arousing concern about legislative implications. Let us examine these in order.

First, Ford executives were clearly concerned that extended media coverage of a homicide trial in which Ford was the defendant would tarnish the corporate image, affecting investors' funds and the public trust. Considering the cumulative effect of recurrent newspaper, magazine, radio, and television accounts of Pinto investigations, recalls, and civil lawsuits (such as *Grimshaw*), the company regarded the coverage of such a landmark criminal trial as potentially devastating, regardless of the ultimate legal verdict. Ford knew that the coverage of a corporate homicide trial would be extensive, not only because of the legal issues and implications but also because a "morality play" scenario—an evil corporate giant pitted against grief-stricken parents and an outraged prosecutor—was being established. In addition, the fire of public debate was stoked at this time by Henry Ford II's highly publicized quote: "The lawyers would shoot me for saying this, but I think there's some cause for the concern about the car. I don't even listen to the cost-figures—we've got to fix it."[5]

Second, although the Elkhart County grand jury did not return individual indictments against any executives who were involved with the development of the Pinto, as the company had feared, the fact remained that corporate officers would be forced to testify at trial and to explain internal decisions and operations under cross-examination by a criminal prosecutor. One view of this scenario was expressed as follows:

> Even though no executives were formally charged, prosecutors had to present evidence that the car had been defectively designed and that the corporation had been reckless in failing to warn consumers. A corporation acts through its executives, and so the prosecutors, in effect, would be trying individual members of Ford management for their decisions regarding the Pinto. Ford executives, accustomed to receiving community respect commensurate with their high social status and lucrative salaries, cringed at such a degrading possibility. Even if they felt they had done nothing wrong, the idea of undergoing public interrogation and insinuations was a humiliating thought.[6]

It also has been argued, however, that Ford executives actually welcomed the opportunity to "set the record straight" on the Pinto and that the existence of a "one big family" attitude among those within the Detroit auto industry made the prospect of industrywide condemnation unlikely; perhaps this attitude even led to a kind of "hometown support" for Ford employees.[7] One must conclude, however, that if Ford management had been given the choice of defending its product and honor with the aid of attorneys in a highly publicized criminal trial or using the skill of public relations personnel in a creative advertising campaign, they surely would have chosen the latter.

Third, the long-term effect on sales feared by Ford was twofold: (1) the questions raised publicly about the safety of the Pinto would rub off on other Ford models, thus calling their safety into question, and (2) another substantial downturn in Pinto sales would raise the company's fleet fuel economy average above the level required by federal law, forcing Ford to restrict sales of its highly profitable full-size autos. According to Fisse and

Braithwaite, "Ford's sensitivity on [the safety] issue was particularly acute since its executives worried that adverse publicity from the Pinto trial could trigger resistance to the new Escort, a car essential to the company's recovery in the 1980s."[8] As for fuel economy, the Energy Policy and Conservation Act of 1975 had influenced the number of larger cars that could be sold by requiring that the average fuel economy figure for all cars sold fall within certain guidelines. As a result, if sales of more fuel-efficient cars like the Pinto decreased, the company would be forced to restrict the marketing and sales of cars from its larger—and, at that time, more profitable—lines.[9]

Finally, company executives feared a federal legislative response. As one possible consequence, NHTSA might promulgate more rigorous safety standards regarding rear-end collisions, which would affect not only Ford but also its competitors. Another possibility might be action by Congress to designate certain corporate activities influencing consumer safety as criminal violations of federal law; thus they would transfer the responsibility for future corporate prosecutions of this type to federal prosecutors, who had access to much greater resources. The implications, of course, would reach far beyond the automotive industry to affect manufacturers throughout the country.

In sum, Ford was ready, willing, and able to commit its massive corporate resources to the Pinto case *not* because of any threat posed by the criminal penalties of the State of Indiana, but because of the number and variety of longer-term countervailing forces that could be unleashed against the company as a result of the trial. With this possibility in mind, the officers and directors of Ford were determined neither to take any chances nor to cut any corners.

Building a Local Team

In Elkhart, the celebration over the indictment did not last long. Although the first hurdle had been negotiated successfully, Cosentino knew that many more obstacles would have to be overcome. Grand jury proceedings clearly favor the prosecutor, but once the trial process begins the criminal rules of procedure and evidence shift in favor of the defendant.[10] In addition, Ford's tremendous resources would certainly be brought to bear against the tight budget and small staff of the prosecution team. Up to this point essentially two men, a part-time prosecutor and his chief deputy, had furthered the prosecution against the multinational corporate defendant.

Once the glow of the landmark indictment and the subsequent headlines had faded, Cosentino and Shewmaker soberly assessed the obstacles created by the disparity between the economic and human resources available to each side. This was an unfamiliar position for a prosecutor, especially because many of the criminal trials in state courts involve an indigent defendant.[11] Normally the prosecutor's office not only has the economic advantage in budget, staff, and support services, but it also has a head start on investigations, witness interviews, laboratory analyses, and other pretrial preparations.[12] In this case, however, the prosecution had far fewer resources than its corporate opponent. As Shewmaker remarked, "Somehow we've got to find a way to imitate a 100-man law firm; otherwise, we won't stand a chance."[13] Knowing that Ford had retained at least two large firms to help the company prepare for battle, the prosecutors spent several days gathering whatever economic and human resources they could.

On the economic side, Cosentino requested and received a $20,000 stipend from the Elkhart County Council to supplement the normal operating budget of this office. He was pleased with the Council's decision, especially in light of the fact that the county's renowned mobile-home industry had been devastated by the recession and the escalating gas prices of the late 1970s. Yet he also knew that he would probably have to forego an experimental crash test on a 1973 Pinto, because it would cost approximately $10,000 and consume half his budget, and forego certain expert witnesses, who were demanding their normal fees of at least $750 per day. In addition to the $20,000 stipend, the prosecution received a commitment from the Indiana State Police to provide the use of planes, helicopters, and crime lab facilities at no expense. As a further means of cutting costs, Cosentino learned that the federal government would turn over, without charge, its cache of internal Ford documents, NHTSA films, and investigatory reports regarding the Pinto.[14]

With respect to human resources, Cosentino and Shewmaker obtained commitments from each of the following individuals within days of the indictment:

> *Neil Graves.* As the Indiana State trooper who was the first investigator on the scene of the accident and a prime influence on the decision to prosecute, Graves was assigned full time to the case by his state police supervisor. Throughout the case, he worked closely with Cosentino and the prosecutor's chief investigator, *Billie Campbell.*
>
> *William Conour.* After providing early assistance in drafting the indictment from his Prosecuting Attorney's office in Indianapolis, Conour offered further help by interpreting the statutory language that was to be applied to a corporate rather than a

living person. As noted, Conour had been one of the drafters of the newly revised Indiana Criminal Code.

Bruce Berner. A highly regarded criminal law professor at nearby Valparaiso University, Berner was recommended to Cosentino by a student law clerk working in his office. After a series of consultations with the prosecutors, he was appointed Special Deputy Prosecuting Attorney and given primary responsibility for the legal theories that would be applied in the case. To assist him in this task, Berner received a large amount of research support from a small but dedicated group of law students at Valparaiso.

Terry Kiely. A former law professor of Shewmaker's at DePaul University, Kiely was a logical choice because of his expertise in product liability and corporate governance. Like Berner, he made a commitment to serve pro bono publico as a Special Deputy Prosecuting Attorney. In the division of labor that was established, Kiely handled evidentiary issues, including the crucial Ford documents. A core group of law students from DePaul also volunteered a significant amount of time in assisting Kiely with this task.

John Ulmer. A trial attorney and close friend of Cosentino from nearby Goshen, the hometown of two of the Ulrich girls, Ulmer took a leave of absence from his civil practice to volunteer his assistance with trial preparation. Ulmer was also appointed Special Prosecuting Attorney.

A few observations may be made about this unpaid staff that came to Elkhart to join Shewmaker's "imitation 100-man law firm." First, at the time they committed themselves, these volunteers could not have known that they would ultimately dedicate nearly fourteen months of their lives to the prosecution. (Of course, there was no possibility of sharing in any contingency fee, because this was a criminal case.)[15]

Second, although the law professors and their students initially became interested in the case because of its theoretical issues and national implications, their academic involvement was eventually transformed into a kind of moral commitment. According to Berner, he and Kiely "got religion" after seeing the photographs of the deceased girls and then reviewing the content of Ford's own internal documents. In Berner's words:

Originally, of course, I got involved because of the novel legal questions presented by the indictment. It was only after I became involved that I saw the photographs and met the families of the girls. It is nonetheless hard for me to separate the motivating force of the legal issues from that of the personal aspect of the tragedy. They were at all times during the prosecution mutually reinforcing. Part of what we were saying is that a corporation like all other persons must be forced at times to look at the very personal tragedies it causes....All I can say about the photos [of the girls at the accident scene] was that they immediately made me ill and that I cannot, to this day, get them out of my head.[16]

As a result, the volunteer prosecutors grew stronger in their resolve. This feeling became especially important when Ford's relentless legal machinery and massive economic resources threatened to overwhelm them.

Third, Cosentino made a conscious decision to keep the prosecution primarily a matter of "local talent." Although a handful of law professors from various parts of the country had begun to call and offer their assistance on a part-time, long-distance basis, Cosentino decided to limit the decision-making staff to those who had joined forces early.[17] The reasons for this decision were not provincial but practical. The smaller-scale coordination and communication to which Cosentino was accustomed as Elkhart County Prosecutor could not be maintained with a rotating advisory counsel which constantly needed orientation and updating. In addition, the case was being tried in the state court system under the new Indiana Criminal Code, and only limited legal information or knowledge could be gained from those unfamiliar with Indiana law and practice. Finally, additional transportation and telecommunication costs could have bankrupted the already strained budget of $20,000, which had to pay for expert witnesses, preparation of evidence, and other costs attending the trial preparation of such a large and complex case.

A final observation concerns the diversity of backgrounds among the individual prosecutors. As already noted, Cosentino was a conservative, law-and-order Republican prosecutor who counted several corporations among his civil practice clients—hardly the type of character one would expect to be heading a case that was often associated with liberal, "Nader-like" causes and reforms.[18] On the other hand, Berner and Kiely were law professors with liberal political and social views and virtually no criminal trial experience. After a period of adjustment, during which the three men struggled to overcome personal differences, they developed a deep mutual respect and a strong working relationship while striving toward the same goal: a conviction of Ford on all three counts of reckless homicide.

Although the volunteer attorneys, law professors, and students who became such an integral part of the prosecution team may have initially viewed their involvement as a unique opportunity to influence the course of a landmark criminal case, the moral content of the prosecution soon served as a binding force for everyone involved. Cosentino and Shewmaker, who had previously attempted to express the moral outrage of an entire community by themselves, were now joined by a diverse group of committed individuals. Each contributed something different to the Herculean effort of negotiating the obstacles set up by Ford, and each was bound to the effort by the strong sense that a moral crusade was unfolding.

Automakers and Liability for Defective Products: Edging Toward Criminal Culpability?

The [prosecution] seeks to transform an incident that traditionally is judged under the civil law into a basis for criminal prosecution....There is neither a need nor a proper basis for this court to strain to entertain these criminal charges which...are a novel and unprecedented effort to stretch the criminal process to fit the allegations of a product liability case.

—from a Ford memorandum
in support of its motion to
dismiss the indictment.[19]

As we indicated in Chapter 3, a criminal prosecution, whether viewed from a utilitarian or a moral perspective, represents only one means of controlling corporations outside the framework of regulatory agencies. Indeed, private civil suits have been used far more extensively than criminal prosecution in response to the individual and social harm caused by business. The law of product liability deserves special attention in this regard; the development of the law in this area has led to an explosion of litigation between consumers and business and to a plethora of debates concerning the social costs and benefits of safety in modern industrial society.[20]

The following survey of leading civil cases in this field reveals the role of the auto industry in the development of product liability theory. This review also shows the relationship of automaker-related cases to two goals or functions of law: the "distributive" function, in which the law is used to remedy harm already caused by making wrongdoers pay restitution to private citizens and/or to society in general, and the "reductive" function, in

which the law is used to reduce harmful behavior by deterring its from occurrence in the first place. Implicit in our discussion is the proposition that
it was consistent, both historically and symbolically, for Ford to be the defendant in a landmark *criminal* case that extended traditional notions of
corporate illegality because American automakers have frequently appeared
as defendants in landmark *civil* cases that applied new product liability theory. This discussion sets the context for understanding the significance of
this legacy of product liability as applied to the Pinto prosecution.

The problems related to product liability in the early twentieth century
are rooted in *Winterbottom v. Wright*,[21] an English case decided in 1842. In
that case, the defendant contracted with a Postmaster General to supply
what might be considered a precursor to the automobile, a coach, and to
maintain it in good condition. The plaintiff, a hired coachman, was injured
when a defective wheel collapsed while he was making his mail deliveries.
The English court held that the seller was not liable to the coachman, for
the duty to maintain the coach was owed only to the party with whom the
seller had contracted—even though it was foreseeable that someone other
than the buyer would drive the coach. In a sense, the court extended the
concept of *caveat emptor* ("let the buyer beware"), substituting "employee"
for "buyer" and restricting rights of action to those with whom the defen-
dant/manufacturer had a direct contractual relationship.

As the industrialization of society and the distribution of mass-produced
goods made remoteness of manufacturers from consumers the rule rather
than the exception, the result was virtually a "liability insulation" for manufacturers. However, this refuge from legal responsibility, which reflected the
widespread nineteenth-century policy of promoting industrial expansion and
innovation at the expense of human life and limb, was relatively short-lived
in the United States. The history of product liability law in the twentieth
century records the insistent efforts of American courts to displace the policy of *Winterbottom* and the early cases in the U.S. that followed its lead.

MacPherson v. Buick Motor Company,[22] decided in 1916, remains perhaps the most influential decision ever rendered on product liability. In
MacPherson, the plaintiff was thrown from his new Buick and injured when
a wooden wheel crumbled. The feisty Scotsman promptly sued Buick for
negligent inspection, even though he had purchased the auto from a dealer
and thus had no privity of contract with the manufacturer. In allowing the
plaintiff to recover damages from Buick, New York Superior Court Judge
Benjamin Cardozo's opinion imposed upon industry the legal duty not to
place negligently any product with an "*imminently* dangerous defect" into
the stream of commerce. Before *MacPherson*, the general rule of nonliability had been limited by only a narrow exception, which applied only when
"*inherently* dangerous products" like mislabeled drugs, adulterated foods,

and faulty explosives caused an injury.[23] *MacPherson* opened the door to a much broader judicial interpretation and application of negligence theory; by 1946 every state had adopted the New York court's reasoning and applied it not only to automobiles but to a great variety of consumer and industrial goods.[24]

In practice, however, the negligence theory had its limitations. Foremost among them was the practical difficulty of proving the *specific* acts or omissions that constituted negligence on the part of the manufacturer. This procedure frequently required the plaintiff to enter the manufacturer's plant, examine the production process, and pinpoint the carelessness that led to the defect in the product.[25] Considering the time and expense involved in such a discovery process, plaintiffs' attorneys more often than not determined that the costs and risks of such a negligence suit outweighed the potential benefits. Thus, even though the automotive industry's tremendous growth led to a sharp rise in injuries and deaths related to auto defects, a large number of potential claims went uncontested. It became clear that further development of the law of personal injury was necessary and could be justified on the basis of welfare economics and utilitarian morality.[26] As a result, the courts and legislatures gradually recognized two alternative theories which made it possible for a plaintiff to win his or her case without the requirement of proving negligence: implied warranty and strict liability in tort.

Implied warranty, the first of these "no fault" theories to be recognized, was grounded in contract rather than tort law. Stated simply, this theory protected the ultimate buyer by imposing, *as a matter of law*, a guarantee by the manufacturer and the seller that the product would be reasonably suitable and safe for the general purpose for which it was manufactured and sold.[27] As a part of the codified commercial law that was replacing the common law of contracts in the field of sales, this protection extended a manufacturer's liability for many kinds of injuries and deaths caused by defective products. Under prevailing freedom of contract principles, however, these broad legal protections were initially subject to disclaimer; as a result, it was common for manufacturers simply to waive them and/or substitute far more restrictive warranties in their preprinted sales contract. A typical example was the limited "90 day or 4000 mile" warranty offered by American automakers in the late 1950s. The effect of this "protection," the concept and language of which were developed by the Automobile Manufacturers Association, was to waive any and all warranties implied by law and to substitute a promise only to replace any defective parts returned by the consumer. The "90 day or 4000 mile" warranty, then, protected the car and its parts—but not the driver and the passengers—from the consequences of a defect. However, in the 1960 landmark *Henningsen v. Bloomfield Motors,*[28] which involved a defective steering column, the Supreme Court of New Jersey held that such attempts by an automaker to eliminate virtually all protections and obligations other than the replacement of defective parts were contrary to recent developments in the law, violative of public policy, and legally void. Other states soon followed New Jersey's lead, and the broader protections intended by the courts and legislatures to be embodied in implied warranty theory were eventually restored.

The second response to the limitations of negligence theory—and to those of implied warranty as well—was strict liability in tort.[29] The theory was first sanctioned judicially for use in product liability in *Greenman v. Yuba Power Products*,[30] a 1963 California case involving a defective power tool. The California Supreme Court held that a manufacturer could be held strictly liable for any physical injuries that were caused by "*unreasonably* dangerous" product defects. The court made it clear, however, that strict liability was not the same thing as absolute liability; that is, the fact that a defective product caused an injury would not in itself result in an automatic judgment. A plaintiff was required to prove that the injury-causing defect (1) existed at the time it left the control of the manufacturer and (2) caused the product to be not merely dangerous but *unreasonably* dangerous.[31] Although this theory was eventually used in product liability suits against manufacturers of a wide range of consumer and industrial goods, it was used perhaps most consistently and most successfully against automakers, whose products were associated with the most frequent and most visible cause of deaths and injuries to the public at large: highway accidents.

Although for several years the concept of "unreasonably dangerous" was restricted generally to mechanical or design defects that actually caused an automobile to become involved in an accident, a federal court in the 1968 case of *Larsen v. General Motors*[32] set a new course for product liability law: it imposed a duty upon automakers to design their vehicles in such a way as to prevent the *aggravation* of injuries. While noting that an automaker is certainly under no duty to design a "crash-proof" vehicle, the court held that the unfortunate realities of accident statistics meant that collisions, though not preventable by automakers, are foreseeable; therefore, a duty existed to provide not only a means of transportation but a reasonably safe means. The rule in this decision, often referred to as the "crashworthiness" or "enhancement" doctrine, broadened the concept of "unreasonably dangerous" and has since been applied in about two-thirds of the states, including Indiana.[33]

The three product liability theories just sketched—negligence, implied warranty, and strict liability in tort—require automakers to provide a remedy in the form of *compensatory* damages in the case of injury or loss of life caused by dangerously defective products. Thus the three theories have provided the means by which the distributive function of law is served in the field of product liability. The last decade, however, has recorded a new phenomenon in product liability law: the widespread imposition of additional, *punitive* damages designed to punish and deter (or reduce) market behavior that reflects a flagrant indifference to public safety and welfare. In cases where plaintiffs' claims for punitive damages have been successful, it has generally been shown that manufacturers, including automakers, abused their responsibility concerning product safety in at least three ways:

1. Failing to take even the most basic steps to acquire efficient safety information through tests, inspections, or postmarketing monitoring;

2. Neglecting to remedy dangerous conditions known to exist in the product and refusing to adopt feasible and inexpensive corrective measures plainly needed in light of the substantial risk of harm presented;

3. Misleading the public by concealing known, substantial dangers in order to enhance the marketability of the product.[34]

While the criminal law—at least before the Pinto prosecution—had left these kinds of marketing misconduct virtually untouched, punitive damages have been used in a quasi-criminal manner on an increasing number of occasions to serve the reductive or deterrent function of law. Once again we can point to a case involving an automaker, *Grimshaw v. Ford Motor Company* (see our discussion in Chapter 4), to demonstrate the effect of new developments in product liability theory. Although the record $125 million punitive damage award was eventually reduced on appeal, the jury's message to corporate boardrooms was clear: punitive damages could and would be used to make a powerful statement that would deter corporations from designing, manufacturing, and marketing potentially dangerous products.

The movement in American law away from the insulating effect of early contract law theory and toward the distributive and reductive effects of strict liability theory (and, increasingly, punitive damages) did not occur in neat, linear stages. In addition, many gray areas have emerged in the complex field of product liability. Nonetheless, to borrow a concept introduced in Chapter 3, the application of new liability theories to dangerously defective products reflects social and legal developments that have *edged corporations closer and closer to criminal culpability in a nonregulatory context.* As the first homicide prosecution of a manufacturer for its business decisions regarding the design and marketing of a product, the Pinto case might thus be seen as a logical and even foreseeable consequence of this historical and theoretical movement.

Although a prosecution like the Pinto case may have been foreseeable on the American legal horizon, it hardly guaranteed that the first actual case would meet with unqualified success. It should be remembered, however, that in landmark cases success is often judged by different standards. In the context of a "normal" criminal trial, for example, one in which well-established statutory provisions are applied within a familiar factual context, a conviction is the only acceptable measure of success.[35] On the other hand, in a case that explores uncharted legal waters, the real success is often the *legitimation* of the breakthrough effort, which occurs when a court decides to recognize and apply new legal theory, regardless of the trial verdict.[36]

Of course, the legitimation of new theory can be sought by either the prosecution, the defense, or both in any particular case, and history ultimately becomes the judge of its legal significance. In the Pinto case, it was the prosecution that sought to legitimate its theory of corporate homicide in what would normally be the context of a product liability suit and thus to write a new page in the history of corporate criminality. The final section of this chapter analyzes the many pretrial obstacles that faced Cosentino and his staff faced in their efforts to gain such legitimacy through the Indiana judicial system.

The Indictment of an American Corporation: Facing the Obstacles

A decision to apply the criminal process to manufacturers whose products may be involved in an accident which results in injury presents so major a policy question that it must, in the first instance, be addressed by the legislature. Such an application of the criminal law would drastically expand common conceptions of criminal responsibility and would wipe out the basic distinctions between civil wrongs and criminal offenses.

The present indictment is not authorized by anything the Indiana legislature has intended to criminalize, and the prosecution of this case as a "groundbreaking" experiment violates several basic constitutional provisions.

—from a Ford memorandum
in support of its motion to
dismiss the indictment[37]

For months after the grand jury had handed down the indictment, Ford's hired legal staffs spent considerable time and effort in attempting to avert a jury trial. Ford's primary attack on the indictment took the form of a comprehensive motion to dismiss which drew upon statutes, cases, administrative regulations, and constitutional principles at both state and federal levels. The legal obstacles created through this motion, prepared and submitted by the giant Mayer, Brown and Platt law firm, generally followed two premises: first, that the indictment was *conceptually* unsound because corporations have neither the legal nor the physical capability of committing the crime of reckless homicide; second, that the indictment was *constitutionally* flawed because several fundamental rights afforded to corporations as persons under the law had been denied. Either premise, if proven to the satisfaction of the Indiana court, would have sounded the death knell for the indictment. Like any good team of defense attorneys, Ford's lawyers were simply making use of every means at their disposal to get the case thrown out of court and, even more important, out of the public eye.

For Cosentino, Ford's attack presented the most challenging task of the case: to research and develop a broad base of legal support for his corporate homicide theory that would overcome each of the pretrial objections raised by Ford. It was time to organize the volunteer staff of professors and their students and put them to the test. Valparaiso's Berner and DePaul's Kiely were assigned to respond to different aspects of the conceptual and constitutional attacks on the indictment. In the manner of any law firm with associates, they would delegate in turn certain research responsibilities to the students who had volunteered their time and effort. This task often caused everyone involved to work late into the night and to travel long distances on weekends. With DePaul in downtown Chicago, Valparaiso in rural northwest Indiana, and Elkhart in north central Indiana, Cosentino's coordination of efforts and meetings became a major undertaking. Not all the students who initially volunteered stayed on through the many months of research, but the few who did remain received once-in-a-lifetime experience and the highest of commendations from their professors:

> The students were absolutely fantastic. They were highly motivated and were highly competent. I think an impartial observer of the research would conclude we had the better of it even though knowing the massive research resources Ford had. It is hard now to know why this is so. It's fun to talk about people who are pure of heart having the strength of ten, but it doesn't help. If [our students] had been on the Ford team, we probably would have been out-researched. It just happens that we were lucky enough to have top-flight people at the time.[38]

The ensuing "battle of the legal memos" produced a mountain of research that explored Ford's conceptual and constitutional challenges. Although these lengthy legal briefs were being prepared for the benefit of a single trial court judge at the local level in Elkhart County, the adversaries conducted a prodigious amount of research: the numerous memoranda submitted by the parties averaged nearly fifty pages per document. In addition, the scholarship reflected in the briefs is frequently outstanding. Indeed, many sections of the briefs read more like scholarly articles than trial court memoranda. One of the advantages often cited for our adversary system of justice is that a judge cannot really know the strength of an argument until he or she has heard it from lawyers who have dedicated all the powers at their disposal to its formulation. It is clear that the adversary system was serving its purpose in this sense; Ford's and Cosentino's staffs exchanged no fewer than four major volleys of pretrial motions, and in the process they created an impressive legacy of research and argumentation pertaining to corporate criminality.

We will examine this legacy in three parts. The first section addresses the *conceptual* issues attendant to corporate homicide by (1) reviewing general common-law principles of corporate criminal liability; (2) surveying the few cases in United States history before the Pinto case that considered criminal indictments of corporations for homicide; and (3) analyzing specific arguments made by Ford and the prosecution pertaining to the conceptual difficulties of applying corporate homicide theory under Indiana law. The second section examines the *constitutional* dimensions of the case by (1) noting the corporation's status within the general context of constitutional protections and (2) detailing specific arguments made by the adversaries regarding key constitutional issues. The third section concludes the chapter by discussing the Indiana court's final resolution of these conceptual and constitutional challenges.

Conceptual Obstacles

Common Law Development of Corporate Criminal Liability: Another View

As seen in Chapter 3, English common law stood clearly for the proposition that a corporation could not commit a crime.[39] This policy was based on both theoretical and practical premises. First, the fact that a corporation had no mind meant that it could not entertain the appropriate criminal intent (*mens rea*) required for all common-law crimes. Second, the absence of

a physical being precluded imprisonment, the primary punishment available under common law.

This blanket rule of nonliability for corporations, however, was abolished relatively early in the United States. Units of local government were among the first collective entities considered to be juristic persons (recall Chapter 3); they also were the first juristic persons to be held criminally responsible. The master/servant analogy was applied to this situation: just as a master was responsible for the actions of a servant, municipal corporations were adjudged criminally liable when the actions of their officials (their "servants") created a public nuisance—as when, for example, they failed to maintain public roads. A subsequent and similar development was the attachment of criminal liability to business corporations Early in the nineteenth century, private corporations were typically chartered to fulfill public functions, such as building or maintaining roads. They, too, were held criminally liable for creating public nuisances if they failed to perform their duties adequately.[40]

Principles that alter traditional common-law doctrine are normally assimilated quite slowly and in piecemeal fashion by state courts, and recognition of corporate criminal liability was no exception. Even so, the final vestiges of *de jure* (legally sanctioned) immunity for corporations from liability for common-law crimes eventually disappeared after the corporation grew to become a dominant force in American business and society. Virtually all prosecutions of corporations before 1900 occurred in response to nonfeasance and regulatory offenses. The modern view that a corporation could be held accountable for crimes of intent committed by its agents was adopted in the 1909 landmark case of *New York Central Railroad v. United States*.[41] In upholding a conviction under federal laws, the U.S. Supreme Court dismissed the broad claim of corporate criminal immunity advanced by the railroad:

> It is true that there are some crimes which in their nature cannot be committed by corporations. But there is a large class of offenses...wherein the crime consists in purposely doing the things prohibited by statute. In that class of crimes we see no good reason why corporations may not be held responsible for and charged with the knowledge and purposes of their agents, acting within the authority conferred upon them.[42]

When the Supreme Court finally discredited any lingering doubts cast by the common-law rule of nonliability, the foundation had been laid for a wider range of corporate criminal prosecutions under both state and federal law. Even though strict liability regulatory statutes continued to be the primary source of prosecutions, the *New York Central* decision led to a more intense examination of the relationship between corporations and the criminal law during a period marked by populism and a distrust of "big business," and may have served as a precedent for many of the corporate criminal provisions written into later health and safety legislation.[43]

Even today, however, questions remain about the applicability of certain criminal statutes—especially those requiring proof of criminal intent—to corporations. Generally, whether a corporation is subject to criminal liability under a given statute is determined by the nature of the offense and the perceived legislative intent for promulgating the law.[44] The following section provides an historical survey of different courts' responses when confronted with the issue of corporate culpability for homicide, the most serious of all common-law crimes.

Corporate Homicide in American Courts

One writer has observed that corporate criminal liability for homicide is an enigmatic concept. The ambiguity stems from two factors: the definition of homicide and the infrequency of criminal prosecutions against corporations for this offense.[45] As we noted briefly in Chapter 3, literal readings of statutory definitions of manslaughter and reckless homicide have occasionally created conceptual difficulties for judges faced with applying homicide statutes to corporate defendants.[46] Even so, an historical survey of corporate homicide cases indicates that most of the courts that have considered the issue have demonstrated a willingness to overcome such difficulties.

Before we review these cases, one comment is necessary. As may be apparent, we presented several of the cases in our discussion of the historical development of corporations (see Chapter 3). We have chosen to reexamine them in greater detail in this chapter because of their special significance as legal precedents cited by the prosecution and by Ford during their crucial pretrial arguments.

Surprisingly, it appears that the first American case to recognize corporate homicide was decided by a New Hampshire court 125 years before the Ford Pinto prosecution. In *B., C. and M. Railroad v. State*[47] an indictment was returned in 1855 against a public carrier for causing the death of a citizen through the "negligence and misconduct" of its agents. In rejecting the defendant corporation's argument that "additional and onerous" liabilities would flow from such an interpretation of the law, the court emphasized a corporation's unique ability to create hazards to the very public that had granted its existence. *B., C. and M.* is an early and isolated case that could hardly be said to characterize a general recognition of the corporate homicide concept in the mid-nineteenth century. The decision deserves special attention, however, for at least two reasons. First, it represents an early example of judicial recognition of a social imperative justifying the application of strong legal sanctions against corporations that created serious and unnecessary risks to the public safety. Second, it provides a representative example of the important historical role that railroads played in the development of corporate criminal liability. Indeed, the railroad industry's "contributions" to this area of the criminal law might be seen to parallel those which helped define and expand concepts of tort law during the mid-to-late 1800s.[48]

Nearly fifty years passed before another corporate homicide case was reported in the United States. In *United States v. Van Schaick*,[49] decided in 1904, a U.S. District Court addressed one of the oldest obstacles to corporate criminal liability: the absence of an appropriate statutory punishment. In upholding an indictment for the death of 900 passengers caused by the defendant corporation's failure to make its vessel seaworthy, the court skirted the issue of the inappropriateness of imprisonment (the only statutorily prescribed punishment) by suggesting that the social utility of corporate homicide outweighed a legislative oversight.

> A corporation can be guilty of causing death by its wrongful act. It can with equal propriety be punished in a civil or criminal action. It seems a more reasonable alternative that Congress inadvertently omitted to provide a suitable punishment for the offense, when committed by a corporation, than that it intended to give the owner impunity simply because it happened to be a corporation....[50]

In 1917, New Jersey became the next state to consider the conceptual issues surrounding corporate homicide. In *State v. Lehigh Valley R.R. Co.*,[51] while the court admitted that difficulties might arise occasionally regarding a corporation's liability for such specific intent crimes as treason or murder, it distinguished the offense of negligent homicide and upheld the indictment by stating:

> A corporate aggregate may be held criminally for criminal acts of misfeasance or nonfeasance unless there is something in the nature of the crime, the character of the punishment prescribed therefor, or the essential ingredients of the crime, which makes it impossible for a corporation to be held. Involuntary manslaughter does not come within any of these exceptions....[W]e can think of no reason why it cannot be held for the criminal consequences or its negligence or its nonfeasance....[52]

B., C. and M., Van Schaick, and *Lehigh Valley* all involved privately run corporations that provided public transportation for profit. This fact may have been a consideration in each court's determination that social welfare mandated the application of common-law criminal concepts—not merely regulatory statutes—to these corporations. As we noted in Chapter 3, however, not every prosecutor's attempt to obtain a corporate homicide indictment has withstood similar scrutiny by the appellate courts. In the following two cases, indictments returned by grand juries were quashed because of strict judicial construction of statutory language. (As we shall see, Ford relied heavily on each of these cases.)

People v. Rochester Ry. and Light Co.,[53] a New York case dating from 1909, concerned a manslaughter indictment obtained after the "grossly improper" installation of gas devices in a home resulted in the occupant's death. Although the court dismissed the indictment, it did so only because the statute defined homicide as "the killing of one human being...by another," thus manifesting legislative intent to exclude corporate entities. While emphasizing that its decision rested on definitional rather than policy grounds, the New York court's dicta indicated that there would be no inherent problems in the application of a revised homicide statute that prohibited corporate recklessness:

> We have no doubt that a definition of certain forms of manslaughter might have been formulated which would be applicable to a corporation, and make it criminally liable for various acts of misfeasance and nonfeasance...similar to that here charged against the respondent....[54]

In *State v. Pacific Power Co.,*[55] the explosion of an unattended load of dynamite on a parked company truck caused a pedestrian's death. In this 1961 case, an Oregon court held similarly that a proper reading of its criminal code led to the conclusion that a corporation simply could not commit manslaughter as it was then defined. The legislative intent reflected in the wording of the statute made it clear that only *human* deviations from acceptable behavior were anticipated. Furthermore, because the penalty for manslaughter was both a fine and imprisonment, the court concluded that an appropriate administration of the sanctions was impossible. As in *Rochester,* however, the court's dicta expressed a sympathetic attitude toward the increased use of corporate criminal sanctions and noted the historical trend away from the broad immunities of the common law.

Before the Pinto case, the most recent appellate decision addressing the issue of corporate homicide was rendered by a New York court in 1974, sixty-five years after the *Rochester* decision had been handed down in the same state. In *People v. Ebasco Services, Inc.*,[56] two men were killed when a cofferdam collapsed. The corporation responsible for its installation was indicted for negligent homicide. Recalling the court's earlier decision in *Rochester*, the defendant argued that the same reasoning should apply, preventing indictments for corporate homicide. The *Ebasco* court, however, recognized the linchpin of the *Rochester* decision as that court's determination of the legislative intent behind the homicide statute. After carefully reviewing the relevant provisions of the revised New York Penal Code, the court distinguished *Rochester* by pointing out three important statutory changes contained in the updated Code. First, the definitional section for homicide stated: "A person is guilty of criminally negligent homicide when, with criminal negligence, he causes the death of another person."[57] Second, a related explanatory provision noted: "'Person,' when referring to the victim of a homicide, means a human being who has been born and is alive."[58] Third, a general definitional section added: "'Person' means a human being, and where appropriate, a public or private corporation."[59]

Placing the indictment within this context, the court held that the explanatory provision's more limited definition of a "person" as a living human being (which excluded corporations) was clearly intended by the legislature to apply only to the victim of a homicide, and not to the offender. Futhermore, the court observed that the only purpose of the limitation was to exclude abortions from the definition of homicide. The opinion also cited the language in *Rochester* which seemed to be "inviting" the legislature to bring corporations within the statutory purview of corporate homicide. Even though the indictment was ultimately dismissed on other grounds, the *Ebasco* court concluded that the broader definition of "person" applied and that the revised New York Penal Code manifested a legislative intent to include corporations among those persons having the capability to commit homicide.[60]

The preceding survey of cases does not provide a single operative principle regarding the application of homicide statutes to corporations. As one commentator has observed:

> Given the ubiquitous nature of corporations in our society, economic and social considerations have preempted the importance of anachronistic theories and conceptual consistency. This does not, however, resolve the issue completely since a definitive rule has yet to be produced. The absence of both judicial consideration and legislative guidance in many states suggests that uniform treatment regarding the compatibility of criminal homicide and the corporate entity must await further development.[61]

Notably, the pretrial battles waged in the Pinto case, accompanied by their broad economic and social implications, revived many of the conceptual and definitinal issues just discussed. The following section analyzes the adversaries' arguments and the Indiana court's resolution of these issues.

The Interpretation of Reckless Homicide in the Pinto Case

As the preceding survey indicates, the success of previous corporate homicide indictments has turned largely upon judicial interpretation of relevant statutory language. The court's approach to the conceptual questions raised by Ford was no exception. Significantly, the fact that Indiana's Penal Code had been rewritten completely and had become effective less than a year before Ford's indictment meant that almost no case law existed which interpreted anything about the new reckless homicide statute, much less anything about its application to corporations. Indeed, Ford's attorneys had used adjectives like "novel" and "bizarre" in their briefs to describe Cosentino's indictment for corporate homicide. Not surprisingly, the prosecution in a reply brief reacted strongly to the choice of labels attached to the prosecution: "It is not the prosecutor's legal theory which is 'novel' or 'bizarre.' The novel element instead is Ford's alleged conduct of deliberately placing on the nation's highways over one million vehicles, known by it to possess an intolerably unsafe design, which would predictably and unnecessarily take human life."[62] In any event it was, as lawyers say, clearly a case of first impression; the stage had been set for a lengthy battle over the interpretation of Indiana's new law.

Building upon conceptual arguments that were similar to those made by corporate defendants in *Rochester* and *Pacific Power*, Ford's motion to dismiss attacked vigorously the prosecution's interpretation of Indiana's reckless homicide statute and concluded that corporations simply were not covered under the law. This contention elicited an equally vigorous response from the prosecution. Cosentino and the law professors were well aware of American judges' predilection for weighing questions concerning any new or unusual application of criminal statutes in favor of the accused, a tendency that reflects our society's deep distrust of discretionary power in the hands of law enforcement officials. Accordingly, Berner, Kiely, and their students increased their already hectic pace (because the fall term was in session, the students and professors had regular class schedules) to prepare what they hoped would be a clear and convincing line of argument showing the applicability of the reckless homicide statute to Ford. The following discussion presents summaries of the conceptual challenge made by Ford in its memoranda supporting the motion to dismiss. (The Indiana court's resolution of the conceptual issue will be analyzed in the final section of this chapter.)

Ford's first argument was grounded in its construction of Indiana's definition of reckless homicide, which reads: "A *person* who recklessly kills another *human being* commits reckless homicide."[63] Asserting that any uncertainties or ambiguities must be construed in favor of the defendant, Ford contended that the plain meaning of "another" in the statutory context was "one of the same kind." Hence, since the victim was referred to as "another human being," it followed that the perpetrator of the crime must also be human.[64]

'You have the right to remain silent . . .'

Is the Pinto a Criminal? The Corporation as a Legal Person

Ford's second argument employed analogy in an attempt to persuade the court that a corporation could not conceptually be a "homicidal person" under Indiana law. Conceding for the sake of argument that "person" as defined in the Penal Code might include corporations for some purposes, Ford argued that certain uses of the term within the Code led to a logical exclusion of corporations by virtue of physical—and thus legal—impossibility:

> There are numerous examples in the Criminal Code where the legislature has used the word "person" to refer exclusively to a human being. See, e.g., the section prohibiting rape....("A person who knowingly or intentionally has sexual intercourse...") Thus, although corporations may generally be covered by the definition of "persons," there are clearly crimes—essentially crimes of violence against other human beings—where it is irrational to read the statutes as applying to corporations.[65]

Ford's attorneys thus concluded that just as it would be impossible for a corporation to commit rape, neither could it commit the violent physical crime of homicide.

Knowing that the conceptual obstacle set before them was central to their adversary's pretrial attack, the professors quickly assigned their best students to work with them to validate Cosentino's application of the reckless homicide statute against a corporate being. Personal conferences led to assignments of preliminary research, the completion of which led to more brainstorming and further research. After several weeks and numerous drafts, the finished product was finally turned over to Cosentino for review.

In the resulting memorandum filed in opposition to the motion to dismiss, which Cosentino called "the finest body of legal research I have ever been associated with," the professors-turned-prosecutors responded to Ford's initial line of argument by citing two relevant sections of the Penal Code. First, they pointed out that "person" and "human being" were distinguished clearly in the Penal Code definitional section:

> 'person' means a human being, corporation, partnership, unincorporated association or governmental entity.

> 'human being' means an individual who is born and is alive.[66]

Second, in perhaps its clearest statement on the matter, a separate section of the Indiana Penal Code provided that:

A corporation, partnership, or unincorporated association may be prosecuted for any offense; it may be convicted of any offense only if it is proved that the offense was committed by its agent acting within the scope of his authority.[67]

The memorandum then explained that the use of "another" reflected a lesiglative intent to negate liability for suicide or its attempt, and it was noted that previous judicial interpretations supported this contention.[68] The prosecution thus concluded that Ford's argument was unfounded and that a corporation could be convicted of any crime in Indiana, providing that (1) the crime was committed by a corporate agent and (2) the agent was, at the time, acting within the scope of his or her authority.

The prosecutors then proceeded to dismiss summarily Ford's second line of argument, based on its rape analogy, by recalling the basic characteristics of the corporation as legal fiction. Labeling as "simply incorrect" the defendant's premise that "person," in the context of the rape statute, could not include a corporation, the memorandum began by reciting the elementary notion that a corporation was merely a legal fiction created by law. Then, in one of the most memorable passages contained in any of the numerous pretrial briefs, Berner and Kiely demonstrated succinctly how Ford's rape analogy distorted and exploited the "fictional person" concept of the corporation as actor:

Of course, a corporation cannot itself engage in sexual intercourse; a corporation cannot itself *do* anything. As it is a fictional person, it can act *only* through its natural-person agents. A corporation has no genitals, to be sure, but neither does it have a trigger finger, a hand to forge a check, an arm to extend a bribe nor mind to form an intent or to "consciously disregard" the safety of others. Nevertheless, a corporation is liable for all crimes of its agents acting within their authority. The unlikelihood of corporate rape liability is because sexual intercourse by its agents will almost always be outside the scope of their authority—not because the crime is definitionally ridiculous (emphasis added by prosecution).[69]

Constitutional Obstacles

That a large corporation may have more substantial financial resources is no more valid ground for depriving it of its constitutional rights than is possession of greater wealth by an individual.

—Excerpt from *United States
v. Security National Bank*[70]

* * *

One thing very interesting about the Pinto case, which was also very frustrating, is that the criminal process is designed on the assumption that the comparative economic advantage is with the prosecution. When this is untrue in a given case, the prosecution is twice cursed—once for having fewer resources and once for playing by rules that assume it has more. In connection with one of their motions, Ford attorneys were citing *Gideon v. Wainwright* and other Warren court decisions extending rights to defendants, and I was struck by the irony of it.

—Bruce Berner, Special
Deputy Prosecutor[71]

Henry Ford II, who personally reviewed many of the legal documents before the lawyers submitted them to the court, reportedly preferred the development of constitutionally based challenges over the kind of conceptual argument discussed above. Certainly he held this preference because a dismissal based on well-recognized constitutional principles might appear more legitimate in the public eye than one based on mere "legal technicalities."[72] As a result, Ford attorneys put forward several constitutional arguments in their motion to dismiss. Any one of them, if not counteracted by Cosentino and his staff, would have been sufficient to stop the prosecution in its tracks and allow Ford to avoid being brought to trial. Of these arguments, two merit special attention:[73]

1. Indiana's reckless homicide statute, as applied against automakers, was preempted by the National Traffic and Motor Vehicle Safety Act of 1966, and thus the prosecution violated the supremacy clause of the U.S. Constitution.

2. Indiana's reckless homicide statute, which did not become effective until 1977-78, was being applied to conduct that predated it (the design, manufacture, and marketing of the 1973 Pinto), and thus the prosecution violated the *ex post facto* clauses of the Indiana and U.S. Constitutions.

We have chosen to examine these arguments in detail for two reasons. First, they were considered by most observers to represent the strongest of all the pretrial arguments made by Ford and thus were subjected to comprehensive and rigorous analyses by the adversaries (and, in time, by the Indiana court). Second, even though the court ultimately dismissed each of Ford's pretrial objections, these two particular arguments resurfaced during the trial and presented Cosentino again with serious legal obstacles, as we shall see in Chapter 6. The following two sections present summaries of these constitutional challenges and the prosecution's rebuttal arguments.[74] (The Indiana court's resolution of the constitutional issues will be analyzed in the final section of this chapter.)

The Supremacy Clause: The Power to Regulate

The first argument developed by Ford's legal counsel was grounded in the supremacy clause of the U.S. Constitution, Article VI, clause 2, which provides:

> This Constitution, and the Laws of the United States which shall be made in pursuance thereof...shall be the supreme law of the Land; and the Judges in every State shall be bound thereby, anything in the Constitution or Laws of any State to the Contrary notwithstanding.

Ford argued that by passing the National Traffic and Motor Vehicle Safety Act (referred to hereinafter as The Safety Act), which established a federal system to regulate safety in automative design, manufacture, and modification, Congress intended to preempt any application of state criminal laws in the same field.[75] Ford asserted that the principles of preemption under the supremacy clause prevailed not only when there was an express conflict between a federal statute and a state law but whenever Congress had chosen to regulate any field comprehensively. U.S. Supreme Court cases old and new (a landmark 1824 decision, *Gibbons v. Ogden*,[76] and an influential 1977 case, *Jones v. Rath Packing Co.*[77]) were cited to support the conclusion that even when state law shares a common policy with a federal statute, prohibits conduct similar to that ehjoined by federal law, or is not preempted completely by federal legislation, it must give way "whenever Congress has comprehensively occupied a field, as it has in the area of safety-related regulation of automotive design and manufacture."[78]

After reviewing several provisions of the Safety Act, Ford contended that "Congress not only devised a network of mechanisms to develop, implement, and enforce safety standards, but it also specified the appropriate penalties if the provisions are violated: *civil* penalties only."[79]   An extensive review of the legislative history behind the Safety Act, Ford continued, indicated that Congress had intended to preserve only state civil actions based on product liability theory and not state criminal actions.[80]   Under our system of federalism, Ford seemed to be saying, the buck must stop somewhere; Congress, under the authority of the supremacy clause, had decided that the responsibility for regulating auto safety must both begin and end at the federal level.

Ford concluded its preemption argument by warning of the potentially dire consequences should a state criminal jury be allowed to judge the safety of an automobile:

> An automobile manufacturer cannot, as a practical matter, produce an automobile according to two sets of standards, one established by the federal agency, and the other constructed by a state criminal jury. Even more clearly, any automobile manufacturer cannot be forced to confront 51 different sets of standards—since Indiana has no greater power in this field than any of the other 49 states.[81]

This first constitutional obstacle initially caused significant concern among the prosecution staff. Had the balance of power under our system of federalism shifted so as to eliminate the possibility that an individual state might use its criminal justice resources to prosecute a wayward corporation? After conducting their own research, however, Berner and Kiely were convinced that Ford's preemption arguments were not nearly as problematic as they had appeared initially. The prosecution's first response to Ford was that the indictment represented a constitutionally sound example of a state's broad police powers to enact criminal laws protecting the health, safety, and welfare of its citizens. While asserting that such authority vested by the police powers is reserved to the states under the Tenth Amendment and is fundamental to our system of federalism, the prosecution emphasized that the reckless homicide statute was *not* a regulatory measure but simply a traditional part of Indiana's criminal statutory scheme. No conflict existed between the statute and the Safety Act because no precedent could be found for the proposition that Congress had *ever* intended to preempt a state's prerogative under its police powers to enact and enforce a general statutory system of criminal law.

Like Ford's attorneys, Berner and Kiely drew upon old and new precedents to support their propositions. Citing, as Ford had, *Gibbons v. Ogden*, the prosecution argued that the 1824 landmark could be read to suggest that the preemption doctrine applies *only* when the federal regulatory scheme is so pervasive that it is reasonable to assume that Congress intended to leave no room for state regulation. A more recent case, which confirmed this interpretation for the prosecution, was *Raymond Motors v. Rice*,[82] a 1978 Supreme Court decision that considered a preemption challenge to a state highway regulation. A particularly salient part of this decision, quoted by the prosecution, stated that:

> the Court has been most reluctant to invalidate...'"state legislation in the field of safety where the propriety of local regulation has been long recognized."'...In no field has this deference to state regulation been greater than that of highway safety regulation....Thus, those who would challenge state regulations said to promote highway safety must overcome a "strong presumption of validity."[83]

The prosecution's memorandum then noted that Ford had been unable to cite even a single case in which a traditional, general criminal statute was found to have been preempted by a federal regulatory scheme.[84] After several cases were cited to support the view that the courts have long been reluctant to preempt a state's general criminal law, this line of reasoning concluded with an analogy based on federal labor laws:

> If the State of Indiana enacted a criminal law which made it an offense for employees to engage in violence on a strike site so as to interfere with the right to picket, such a statute may be considered to be in direct conflict with federal labor laws and be deemed preempted. However, if the State chose to prosecute such individuals under State assault and battery provisions, clearly there would be authority to do so without reference to the federal regulatory scheme. The State's right to prosecute the Ford Motor Company for its reckless behavior resulting in the death of three persons within its borders is equally obvious, regardless of the provisions of the federal regulatory scheme created by the Traffic Safety Act.[85]

The prosecution responded to Ford's other argument, the undesirability of the "multiple standards" that might result from allowing criminal juries to consider automotive safety, by noting how that issue had been addressed in civil product liability cases. After observing that the federal guidelines in the Safety Act were intended to establish *minimum* standards only, the prosecution tersely cited the following passage from *Turner v. General Mo-*

tors,[86] a 1974 civil case that rejected essentially the same argument when raised by another automaker:

> The danger that juries will arrive at conflicting conclusions is a hazard every manufacturer who distributes nationally runs. The complex, technical questions facing juries, aided by expert testimony, cannot be more difficult than the question in such fields as medical malpractice. *Finally, the argument that a single jury verdict may have profound consequences disrupting an essential industry has been characterized as contending that the desirability of immunity from liability is directly proportional to the magnitude of the risk created.* (emphasis added by prosecution)[87]

In a subsequent brief, which perhaps showed the "battle-readiness" they had developed, the prosecution chided Ford for what they termed its "Chicken-Little" arguments pertaining to the potential negative consequences of a corporate homicide trial to manufacturers generally:

> If this prosecution proceeds, the national economy will not crumble, international trade will not collapse, and the sky will not fall. What will happen—and Ford knows it—is that a jury may find it guilty of the reckless homicide of Judy, Donna and Lyn Ulrich.[88]

The Ex Post Facto Clause: A Question of Timing

In what Cosentino and his legal team considered the strongest challenge to the indictment, Ford's motion to dismiss charged that the reckless homicide statute as applied to the facts of this case violated the *ex post facto* clauses of the Indiana and United States Constitutions.[89] In the words of the U.S. Supreme Court, this Fifth Amendment provision was designed to protect against "imposed punishment for past conduct [which was] lawful at the time it was engaged in."[90] Similarly, Ford noted, in a 1931 case the Indiana Supreme Court had given clear expression to this prohibition when it wrote:

> An ex post facto law is a legislative act relating to criminal matters retroactive in its operation, which alters the situation of an accused to his disadvantage, or deprives him of some lawful protection to which he is entitled, as a law which imposes a punishment for an act which was not punishable when it was committed....[91]

In contrast to Ford's preemption argument, which was based on the supremacy clause's limitation of "states' rights" under our federalist system, the second challenge was rooted in the Bill of Rights, which protects against potential abuses of state and federal criminal laws. Ford's factual basis for this argument centered on a comparison of two crucial dates: first, the date when the reckless homicide statute became effective and second, the date when the alleged criminal conduct actually occurred. Regarding the first date, it should be recalled that Indiana's Criminal Code had been rewritten recently. As a result, liability for homicide caused by reckless *acts* did not take effect under the new Code until October 1, 1977. Not until ten months later, on July 1, 1978, was the statute amended to impose liability for homicides caused by reckless *omissions* as well. Ford directed the court's attention to language in the indictment which charged that the defendant had recklessly designed and manufactured the 1973 Pinto in which the girls died on August 10, 1978; the company pointed out that its conduct concerning these business operations must have occurred before late 1972, when the car was first marketed. Hence, more than four years had elapsed between Ford's designing and manufacturing of the 1973 Pinto and the Indiana legislature's passage of the reckless homicide statute. Ford concluded that even if the prosecution *could* prove recklessness on the part of the company, the retroactive application of the reckless homicide statute was barred by *ex post facto* principles. For this reason, Ford concluded confidently, "the entire indictment must be dismissed."

Again, for Cosentino and his research staff of professors and students, no other pretrial obstacle created as much concern as Ford's *ex post facto* challenge. There was certainly no question that the design, manufacture, and marketing of 1973 Pintos had occurred years before 1977, when the revised reckless homicide statute had taken effect. Yet the accident and the deaths had not occurred until *after* the effective date of the law: Might this fact be taken into account in order to resolve the *ex post facto* dilemma?

After spending considerable time on this crucial issue, Professor Berner devised two lines of attack for the prosecution. The first concerned establishing the date of the offense. The prosecution disagreed with the premise that the criminal conduct occurred before 1973. Berner contended that the date of the *completion* of the offense—*not* the date of the initial steps in the commission of a crime—determine whether *ex post facto* provisions have been violated.[92] Maintaining that homicide in Indiana is committed as of the date of the victim's death, the prosecution cited passages from two Indiana cases to illustrate this point:

A homicide consists not only of striking the final blow which produced the death, but is not complete until the victim has died [sic].[93]

* * *

The crime we are talking about [homicide] is a composite one. The stroke does not make the crime. The death does not make the crime. It is the composition of the two.[94]

To lend further support to this proposition, it was noted that the statute of limitations for homicides in Indiana begins to run on the date of death, *not* at the time the causative act was committed. Hence, because Ford could not possibly have been prosecuted for homicide until after the girls died, the prosecution concluded that no *ex post facto* violation had occurred.[95]

Berner introduced his second line of attack by drawing attention to the language used in the indictment. As noted previously, Ford had been charged specifically in the indictment with both reckless acts *and omissions*. Whereas Ford in its argument had emphasized the affirmative acts of designing and manufacturing the 1973 Pinto, the prosecution reminded the court that the defendant's omissions—regarding its duty either to repair the vehicle or to warn its owners—constituted important elements of the offense. Although the reckless homicide statute was amended later to include omissions as well as acts, the deaths of the Ulrich girls occurred even after the amended statute took effect—albeit by only 41 days (July 1 to August 10). The prosecution then followed the citation of numerous cases with the statement, "It is universally recognized that when a defendant acts over a period of time, a relevant criminal statute enacted or amended to the defendant's detriment presents no *ex post facto* problem."[96]   (To provide further support, it was noted that Indiana courts had followed this same line of reasoning only recently in rejecting *ex post facto* challenges to its new habitual offender law.) The prosecution thus concluded that once any actionable act or omission was shown to have postdated a criminal statute, all of the defendant's prior acts and omissions could be considered by the court without offending either the Indiana or the United States Constitution.

Before presenting how the Indiana court resolved the conceptual and Constitutional issues discussed above, we examine in the following section another, somewhat broader, issue that was debated during the pretrial stage by lawyers and non-lawyers alike: Were there any other features of Indiana law that encouraged Ford's prosecution?

Corporate Homicide and the Distributive
and Reductive Functions of Law

Traditionally, the social control of corporations has been primarily a function of civil cases and administrative action, not of the criminal law. According to Christopher Stone, although the first question asked about measures to control operations is often "How well do the measures work?", a more functional inquiry would be "What are the measures trying to accomplish?" As Stone has observed (and as noted earlier in this chapter), the law generally seeks to accomplish one or both of two divergent but not mutually exclusive goals:

> One goal is fundamentally *distributive*. When losses occur in society, the law aims to distribute them fairly and reasonably....[I]f a car does not perform as adequately as the purchaser was given fair reason to believe it would, the law, as an ideal, aims to place the unanticipated repair bills on the company's doorstep, rather than the purchaser's.

> But while making a corporation pay damages to persons it has injured is an important goal of the law, it is, in one sense, a secondary goal. A person who has received a cash settlement for the loss of his vision or his limbs has not really been, as the law is fond of saying, "made whole."

> Thus, what we should expect of law, as a more primary goal, is that it reduce...the incidence of harmful behavior in the first place. This is what we might call its *reductive goal.*(emphasis in original)[97]

What Stone terms the distributive goal is furthered through the application of civil law and its remedies, particularly compensatory damages. Except in states that are beginning to provide for compensation to victims of crime in narrowly defined circumstances, the criminal justice system is simply not designed to accomplish the distributive goal of law.[98] The reductive goal, on the other hand, may be promoted by either criminal or civil sanctions. In the criminal justice system this goal is furthered through the deterrent effect of criminal penalties. On the civil side, a primary means by which to reduce or deter egregiously harmful corporate behavior in the future is through court-awarded punitive damages.[99] Although punitive damages are imposed far less frequently than compensatory damages, the past twenty years have seen a marked increase in the use of punitive damages to serve the quasi-criminal function of deterrence.[100] Indeed, before the Indiana prosecution, many of the numerous Pinto civil cases brought in various states involved claims for both compensatory and punitive damages. As observed previously in this chapter and in Chapter 4, *Grimshaw* remains the most notable of these cases.[101]

Criminal penalties, which normally take the form of monetary fines when applied to corporations,[102] and punitive damages, imposed in civil cases only when a defendant's behavior is alleged to have been "reckless" or "willful and wanton," serve a similar function in furthering the reductive goal. What then is the essential difference between civil and criminal law in terms of application? An increasing number of legal scholars perceive the distinction as primarily economic.[103] An important aspect of this school of thought has recently been summarized as follows:

> The cost of criminal litigation is borne by the state; that of civil litigation by the private citizen. Thus, the "morality or immorality of proscribed conduct has little to do with whether the law labels the conduct criminal or leaves enforcement in private hands...." In some instances, the potential award to the litigant is assumed incentive enough to motivate civil action against an offender; in others, the benefits of private litigation are outweighed by the cost of such proceedings. In order to ensure punitive action against rule violators, these latter instances have been "socialized" through the use of criminal law. From this perspective, then, the application of criminal codes to corporate misconduct is largely a matter of administrative efficiency.[104]

This viewpoint is presented here because it relates directly to one of the most critical and most common questions that was raised in the aftermath of the indictment: Would corporate criminal prosecutions of this type, funded by tax dollars, contribute anything to the public interest when better-developed and less burdensome theories are available on the civil side in the form of product liability suits? Putting aside for the moment all consideration of the moral nature of the case, the economic pragmatists must answer "yes." The reasoning is as follows. Normally, when a person dies or is injured as a result of a defective product, the civil law provides incentive for private litigation, and the law is set in motion toward its distributive goals (via compensatory damages) or, if flagrant misbehavior is involved, toward its distributive and reductive goals (via compensatory and punitive damages). These results, however, assume that legally recognized causes of action and appropriate remedies are readily available to facilitate each goal. But, what happens if the law effectively denies the plaintiff access to an appropriate civil remedy? This is exactly what occurred in the Pinto case. Because a just and adequate legal remedy was unavailable under state law, the criminal prosecution represented the only meaningful legal response. For reasons that will be discussed below, Indiana law essentially foreclosed the civil alternatives that one would expect to be available to product liability plaintiffs: namely, compensatory and punitive damages.

As a result, the burden of "seeking justice" shifted to state authorities because there was no practical way for the surviving parents to pursue either the distributive or the reductive goals through civil remedies.[105] The absence of civil remedies, then, along with the willingness of a resolute state prosecutor to take on the case, distinguish the legal response to the accident in Indiana from the preceding responses to Pinto cases elsewhere, including *Grimshaw*.[106] Paradoxically, the fact that the three girls were killed rather than injured created the barrier to civil remedies. Under Indiana's wrongful death statutes,[107] surviving parents may recover damages only for the pecuniary interest in their child's life, which is measured by "the value of the child's services from the time of [death] until he would have attained his majority, less his support and maintenance."[108] Because the Ulrich girls were eighteen or nearly eighteen (the age of majority in Indiana), any compensatory damages awarded would have been speculative and nominal. In addition, a long line of Indiana cases has held that neither the pain and suffering of the deceased nor the mental anguish, grief and sorrow, or loss of happiness suffered by the next of kin are recoverable.[109]

Finally, and most important, a 1978 Indiana decision had reaffirmed an early policy decision by the Indiana Supreme Court and made it clear that Ford could not have been subjected to punitive damages for the wrongful deaths of the girls.[110] This is a crucial point, because it is through the imposition of punitive damages that reckless business behavior has been increasingly sanctioned and deterred.[111] In the light of such firmly entrenched limitations on civil remedies, Cosentino remarked that "the criminal prosecution truly serve[d] as the sole opportunity for the people of Indiana to express their outrage, to punish the defendant for the death[s] of these girls and to deter this defendant and others from like recklessness in the future."[112] Notably, this gap in Indiana's civil remedies was used by the prosecutors in their legal brief to develop a powerful justification—based on sound social policy principles—for taking Ford to trial.

Thus the legal gap afforded virtual civil immunity to defendants who may have recklessly caused the death of persons who were young, unmarried, and without careers. This situation recalls the period in nineteenth-century America when tort actions were considered "personal"; any right to file suit died along with the victim. Because the damages caused by a wrongful death were difficult to measure and because courts were reluctant to impose a "pensioner role" upon businesses, especially railroads, during their growth years, it practically became "more profitable for the defendant to kill the plaintiff than to scratch him."[113]   Although the law has progressed far enough to eliminate this type of injustice in most instances, exceptions remain in which private civil actions are rendered virtually impotent, as in the Pinto case. If the severe restrictions discussed above were limited to the State of Indiana, perhaps because of quirks or loopholes in its statutory and case law, the mobilization of the Elkhart County prosecutor's forces might be viewed simply as an isolated attempt to fill an unusual void left by one state's legal legacy. Yet a recent review of the law at the state and federal levels indicated that at the present time there are no meaningful legal alternatives to the kind of response elicited from Indiana authorities by the perceived recklessness of Ford's behavior: the application of the state's general criminal laws to a corporate entity.

A majority of states appear to be in accordance with Indiana's nine-teenth-century method of limiting compensatory damages in cases involving the wrongful death of a dependent child.[114] More important in terms of the potential role of the criminal law, however, is the fact that *as many as thirty-one states do not allow recovery of punitive damages in any wrongful death cases, notwithstanding the fact that the defendant's reckless, malicious, or willful and wanton state of mind can be proven.*[115] Furthermore, although the issue is far from settled, a majority of courts that have decided the issue have held that general insurance provisions in business liability policies imply coverage of punitive damages. Thus, because the effect of such indemnification agreements is to shift the punishment to a third party, it also shifts the retributive effect and at least partially weakens the deterrent function.[116] The end result is that civil remedies in a majority of states do not sufficiently address the culpability of a business for recklessly conducting its affairs in ways that endanger the lives of the public. Viewed in this light, the corporate homicide prosecution led by Cosentino served to provide a striking example of one state's response to the conflict created by the law's desire to achieve its reductive goal and the inability of the existing civil process to carry it out.[117] Cosentino once said that a criminal prosecution would probably be appropriate in "no more than one percent" of all cases where corporations caused harm and only when other sanctions proved ineffective. It was clear, however, that he and his staff could not have been any more convinced of its appropriateness than they were in the Pinto case.

One final observation: In the context of this dichotomy between the civil and the criminal law, the reactions and motivations of the Ulrich girls' families were not overlooked. According to Berner, "The Ulrichs immediately and unreservedly supported Mike Cosentino's effort to bring the criminal prosecution. One could make all sorts of guesses as to what would lead them to do that; my own personal feeling is that they were extremely decent people with a very powerful sense of right and wrong and were persuaded Ford was wrong."[118] With this comment in mind, as the Indiana court continued to examine the legal arguments for and against holding the trial and as a final decision drew near, it is clear that the status of insurance, punitive damages, and other economic legislation in Indiana did not tell the whole story. Cosentino knew that he was not only responding to the systemic limitations of civil law in Indiana; he was also representing the moral conscience of the Ulrich families and their communities.

Conclusion: Closing the Debate

Nearly five months had passed since the tragedy on U.S. Highway 33; nearly four months since the grand jury's indictment of Ford. In the meantime, amid the flurry of research and the proliferation of memoranda, 1978 had passed into history. With the new year came the retirement of Judge Charles E. Hughes, the nearly seventy-year-old Elkhart Superior Court judge who had had the responsibility for handling the Pinto case from the beginning. After having convened the grand jury, issued the warrant, and allowed the parties a generous period in which to prepare their pretrial arguments, Hughes was due to retire on January 1, a date that had been set before his involvement in the case. Slated to succeed the highly respected Hughes was Donald W. Jones, a former Elkhart Court judge who had been elected to the Superior Court judgeship in November 1978. The youthful Jones, who had launched his legal career as a public defender, took over with a reputation as a thorough researcher and an excellent communicator. Since the adversaries' final memoranda in support of their positions had just been filed in the Superior Court, Jones would have no grace period in which to cut his new judicial teeth on less exceptional and lower-profile legal disputes. Instead he would be faced immediately with making a pretrial decision which would be reported across the country by the reporters who were now standing vigil at the Elkhart County courthouse.

Judge Jones heard two hours of oral arguments, during which Ford (represented primarily by Roger Barrett of Mayer, Brown and Platt) and the prosecution (represented by Cosentino, Berner, and Kiely) summarized the legal positions stated in their briefs. The judge spent the remainder of January 1979 studying the many issues that had been raised by the motion to dismiss. Meanwhile, the adversaries waited eagerly for some sign that a decision had been reached. The members of the prosecution team felt highly vulnerable because they knew that Judge Jones could throw the case out of court at any time if he was persuaded by any one of Ford's numerous arguments.[119] Considering the thousands of hours that had been donated to the cause over the past four months, the lawyers, professors, and students found this possibility too painful even to consider.

On the other hand,the Ford staff was disconcerted by the idea that the multinational company might actually be forced to stand trial for three counts of reckless homicide. The possibility of a trial must have appeared significantly more real than it had several months earlier. Before the indictment, according to both Cosentino and Berner, Ford representatives privately seemed "amused" by the prosecution's corporate homicide theory, although they were by no means unconcerned that it had been brought to bear against their company.[120] Nonetheless, the legal staff that the company had amassed in preparing its full-scale attack on the indictment made it perfectly clear that the case was no longer "amusing" to Ford management, if indeed it ever had been.

On Friday afternoon, February 2, 1979, the main courtroom in the Elkhart County courthouse was alive with nervous, speculative conversation from the standing-room-only crowd of lawyers, reporters, students, business people, and other spectators. When Judge Jones made his entrance at one p.m., the conversational din was replaced by a tense, anticipatory silence. Almost six months had passed since the Ulrich girls' deaths, and the fate of Ford's motion to dismiss and Cosentino's prosecutorial response would be revealed at last by the newly elected Superior Court judge.

Jones did not prolong the tension. "There are substantial factors in this case for which there are no precedents in law," he began, giving no clue as to how he planned to rule. Shortly after, with an abruptness that surprised those in attendance, Jones looked up from his prepared text and tersely announced his decision: "The indictment is sufficient; I therefore deny the motion to dismiss."

The sense of relief could be both seen and heard throughout the courtroom as Cosentino and his staff congratulated one another, reporters raced toward the prosecution's table or the lobby telephones, and spectators renewed their animated conversations. Only the attorneys for Ford and the company representatives from Detroit failed to exhibit signs of any relief as they picked up copies of Jones's twenty-page written opinion, packed their briefcases, and prepared to leave.

Just outside the courtroom doors, television reporters were prepared to obtain statements from the principals. Cosentino, glowing in the aftermath of the decision, was brief but enthusiastic: "The court has justified our position. As far as the law is concerned, a corporation can be indicted for homicide....We're over our major hurdle."

Earl and Mattie Ulrich, whose privacy prosecution staff members had guarded closely at their request, agreed reluctantly to give the press a short statement. "There comes a day of reckoning," the father of Judy and Lyn told the hushed crowd quietly but dramatically, "and I think that day of reckoning is here."

Roger Barrett, showing obvious concern and frustration at his failure to thwart the prosecution's case before trial, would only state the obvious—"I'm disappointed, naturally"—before he hurried to lead the phalanx of lawyers from Ford and from Mayer, Brown and Platt out of the building.[121]

In light of his written opinion, Judge Jones had little difficulty in disposing of Ford's contention that conceptually it was impossible for a corporation to commit reckless homicide under Indiana law. In rejecting this argument, Jones paid particular attention to three factors. First, he acknowledged that in Indiana the traditional doctrine of corporate criminal immunity had eroded gradually; this legal development, the prosecution had argued, was consistent with the historical trend nationwide. Second, the judge relied on the New York court's reasoning in *People v. Ebasco Services*,[122] the country's most recent precedent on corporate homicide. After reviewing the similarities between New York's and Indiana's reckless homicide statutes, Jones drew support from the *Ebasco* court's opinion for his own conclusion that a business corporation could be considered capable of committing homicide: "In construing whether the corporation could be charged with criminal liability the [New York] Court, by way of dicta, stated that while a corporation could not be a victim of a homicide, there was no manifest impropriety in applying the broader definition of person to a corporation with regard to the commission of a homicide...."[123] Third, and most important, Jones was persuaded by the clear expression of legislative intent in the Indiana Criminal Code section that stated, "A corporation, partnership or unincorporated association may be prosecuted for *any* offense" (emphasis added).[124] Although he reminded the parties that a corporate conviction could be obtained "only if it is proved that the offense was committed by its agents acting within the scope of [their] authority," Jones concluded that the Indiana legislature had never intended to grant corporations blanket immunity from criminal prosecution, even for reckless homicide.[125] As a result, the conceptual foundation of the prosecution—that a corporation could be punished for the violent crime of reckless homicide—had received new life after a long burial in a handful of all-but-forgotten cases.

By contrast, the constitutional challenges raised by Ford were not as easily dismissed by Jones. No fewer than sixteen of the twenty pages in his opinion were dedicated to the consitutional matters so thoroughly researched and argued by the adversaries. In the following discussion of Judge Jones's resolution of Ford's preemption and *ex post facto* challenges, it is clear that although Cosentino had been given the right to proceed to trial, his victory was not absolute. Although Jones concluded unequivocally that the prosecution was standing on firm theoretical ground, his opinion also showed that a handful of obstacles remained, which Ford could use to restrict Cosentino's options at trial.

In ruling that the application of Indiana's reckless homicide law was not preempted by federal auto safety laws, Jones relied on guidelines established in *Perez v. Campbell*,[126] a 1971 U.S. Supreme Court decision. In that case, the Court indicated that questions concerning potentially overlapping state and federal laws were to be resolved through the use of a two-tier inquiry: Did a review of the construction and operation of the two statutes indicate that they served substantially common purposes? If so, did there appear in the federal law a "clear and manifest" intent by Congress to supersede the state's police powers?[127] Only if the answer to both inquiries was "yes" could a state law be considered to have been preempted by federal law and thus declared unconstitutional.

In reviewing the purposes of the two laws alleged by Ford to be conflict, Jones followed the guidelines laid out in *Perez*. After noting that the law places the burden of proving any constitutional conflicts on the party that makes the challenge (Ford), Jones described the essential purpose of the National Highway Traffic and Motor Vehicle Safety Act by citing a concise statement from *Chrysler Corporation v. Tofany*,[128] an influential 1969 precedent that had considered another preemption challenge involving the Safety Act: "The express purpose of the [Safety Act]...is the reduction of traffic accidents."[129] Jones then agreed with the prosecution that the case was preceeding under the general criminal code of Indiana and *not* under any automobile regulatory scheme. In contrast to the purpose of the Safety Act, which was to reduce the number and seriousness of traffic accidents by regulating auto safety standards (as well as other traffic-related factors), Indiana's reckless homicide laws were designed to serve the traditional goals of virtually any homicide statute: deterrence and retribution. The fact that the alleged criminal behavior in this case happened to involve auto safety, Jones concluded, did not prevent the State of Indiana from enforcing its criminal laws in order to achieve these ends.

The negative answer to the first inquiry in *Perez's* two-tier test made the second inquiry moot. Jones's opinion, however, went on to note that historically the courts have given a strong presumption of constitutional validity to the exercise of a state's police power (the authority that is granted to each state under our system of federalism to protect the general health, safety, and welfare of its citizens). Without proof of a "clear and manifest" supercession of this authority by Congress—something that appeared to be absent from the Safety Act—Jones concluded that in this case the application of the reckless homicide statute represented a valid exercise of Indiana's police powers and thus had not been preempted by federal law.

Even so, certain aspects of the federal regulatory issues raised by Ford remained unresolved. For the prosecution, perhaps the most crucial issue concerned the possible impact of federal auto safety standards on the trial itself. If Ford could introduce evidence, for example, that its Pinto complied with or even surpassed any federal rear-end crash standards, what effect would this evidence have? Would such evidence establish that Ford, by meeting government-established standards, could not possibly have been guilty of recklessness? Might Ford divert the jury's attention from the moral issues at hand by making what already promised to be a lengthy, complex trial even more so through the introduction of a maze of federal regulatory laws? As Ford's attorneys considered their strategy for the upcoming trial, Cosentino and his staff had a strong feeling that this was not their last encounter with obstacles related to the federal regulation of automobiles.

In another section of his opinion, Jones cited his reasons for ruling in addition that Indiana's newly revised reckless homicide statute was not being applied retroactively and thus did not violate *ex post facto* principles. Jones was apparently persuaded by the "continuation theory" advanced by the prosecution: although Ford's design and marketing of the 1973 Pinto preceded Indiana's adoption of its revised criminal code in 1977 and 1978, both the company's continuing refusal to recall and repair its Pintos and the Ulrich girls' deaths postdated the adoption. Several precedents were cited to lend support to this interpretation, but Jones appeared to be influenced especially by *U.S. v. Reed*,[130] a federal prosecution in which the defendant was convicted of violating a statute that prohibited possession of instruments used for wiretapping. Jones explained its relevance to the Pinto prosecution as follows:

> The defendant in [*U.S. v. Reed*] purchased the equipment before the statute was effective. In affirming the conviction, the court noted that there were many cases which had dealt with and rejected an *ex post facto* argument of some element of a crime where the element "but not the prohibited act" had come into being or taken place prior to the passage of the criminal statute.

> An examination of the [Pinto] indictment shows an allegation of the continuation of acts and essentially alleges that the reckless design and manufacture was simply an antecedent fact to the defendant's alleged reckless act of failure to repair after the new code took effect...Since the alleged reckless act of failing to re-

pair occurred after the passage of the present penal code, no *ex post facto* consideration is applicable and the statements referring to the design and manufacture were just to show the factual basis for the duty to repair.

Since it appears that at least part of the indictment is based entirely upon alleged reckless conduct occurring entirely after the passage of the reckless homicide statute [the failure to repair], the dismissal of the indictment on *ex post facto* grounds is not justified.[131]

This interpretation would have profound consequences for the forthcoming trial. Although he had ruled that the indictment was not constitutionally defective, Jones's approach meant that the prosecution's allegation of recklessness in the design, manufacture, and marketing of the 1973 Pinto could not remain the central issue of the case against Ford. Instead, because each of these business functions preceded the implementation of the new criminal code by several years, proof of Ford's recklessness at any of these stages could be offered *solely* for the purpose of demonstrating that the company had created for itself the duty to recall and repair any defective Pintos. In other words, proving beyond a reasonable doubt that Ford recklessly disregarded human safety in its design, manufacture, and/or marketing of the 1973 Pinto would *not* be enough to sustain a conviction: the prosecution would be forced to go one step further and also prove that the company's primary recklessness lay in its *failure to recall and repair* the Ulrich family's Pinto before August 10, 1978, the day of the accident.

For the forthcoming trial, then, the critical issue of recklessness had split into two parts: (1) Did Ford even have a legal duty to warn Pinto owners and repair any defects in the fuel tank system? (2) If so, was Ford's failure to warn the Ulrich family before the accident in reckless disregard of this duty? Consentino now understood that the success of the prosecution's case would depend upon his ability to convince a jury beyond any reasonable doubt that the answer to both questions was "yes."

Yet another issue, potentially even more serious, troubled the prosecution. The amended provision of the reckless homicide statute, which permits prosecution of any person who caused a death by failing to perform a required duty (in addition to affirmatively acting in opposition to one), had gone into effect on July 1, 1978—*only forty-one days before the Ulrich accident*. Jones's opinion made it clear that this forty-one day period, or "window," would have a significant effect on the requirements of proof at the trial. In essence, the *ex post facto* considerations required the prosecution to show that during the forty-one days between the implementation of the law and the Ulrichs' deaths on August 10, Ford had been reckless in its failure to recall and repair the Ulrich family's Pinto. As a result, Cosentino would need to determine exactly what Ford management's policies and operations were during this period and to prove that they constituted reckless disregard for the safety of Pinto owners. The practical problems related to the task of investigating and presenting these internal corporate matters loomed large.

Thus Cosentino was troubled by the fact that in two recent appellate court decisions, Ford had been severely chastised for "misrepresenting" and "withholding" important information regarding internal safety records and reports.[132] His concern was not that Ford would be uncooperative—what criminal defendant ever willingly assists the prosecution?—but that even if other information relevant to the Pinto existed, it would never see the light of day. Facing problems such as this, Cosentino realized—as he had months before, after the grand jury's return of Ford's indictment—that he and his staff would have little time to savor their victory in advancing their case past the pretrial obstacles presented by Ford.

Although certain aspects of Judge Jones's decision posed practical problems for the prosecution at trial, it represented a major triumph for Cosentino's volunteer staff over the forces of Ford and its cadre of lawyers. There can be no doubt that it also served to legitimate the prosecution's corporate homicide theory in the eyes of the American public (not to mention the legal and business communities) in at least two ways. First, it demonstrated that it was indeed possible for a county prosecutor, to proceed against a powerful and resourceful corporate defendant within the criminal justice system of at least one state. Second, it showed that a fundamental redefinition of corporate misbehavior—from a "bad business decision" to a "violent criminal act"—could be justified under the right circumstances. Although this was only one case, it had clear implications for American business. As Ralph Nader observed after the indictment was upheld, Ford's board of directors was not the only one that followed the case closely. Corporate boardrooms across the country, he asserted, were watching and thinking, "We could be next..."[133]

Each side began its preparations for the upcoming trial with certain concerns. Realistically, Cosentino knew that the obstacles would continue. He wondered whether his small budget and staff would be able to hold out as the case shifted from a battle of legal memos, in which each side had more or less equal access to law libraries, to a battle in the courtroom, where, in Berner's words, the rules "twice curse the prosecution when the economic advantage is with the defendant."[134] Ford, on the other hand, finally had to face the fact that the final confrontation would take place where the company least wanted to do battle: inside an Indiana county courthouse, before a local jury and the national media.

Notes

[1] Excerpt from a keynote speech given by Cosentino in Honolulu at the 1980 American Bar Association's annual convention (co-authored with Berner).

[2] Lee Patrick Strobel, *Reckless Homicide? Ford's Pinto Trial*. South Bend, Indiana: And Books, 1980, p. 39.

[3] Andy Pasztor, "Ford Tries Low Prices to Revive the Pinto as Consumer Fears Still Nag the Small Car," *Wall Street Journal* (September 12, 1978), p. 48; cited in Strobel, *Reckless Homicide?* p. 40.

[4] Strobel, *Reckless Homicide?* p. 41.

[5] Ford was quoted by Walter Guzzardi, Jr. in "Ford: The Road Ahead," *Fortune* (September 11, 1978), p. 42.

[6] Strobel, *Reckless Homicide?* p. 41. Some commentators have criticized this account as too harsh. See, for example, Brent Fisse and John Braithwaite, *The Impact of Publicity on Corporate Offenders*. Albany, N.Y.: State University of New York Press, 1983, pp. 50-51.

[7] Fisse and Braithwaite, *The Impact of Publicity on Corporate Offenders*, p. 51.

[8] *Ibid.*, p. 51.

[9] *Ibid.*, p. 51.

[10] In addition to gaining control of the first and often best information available in a case, a prosecutor generally possesses broad discretion and control over the indicting process, and many of the basic procedural protections available to the defendant at trial are not available at the grand jury hearing. Although the historical performance of the grand jury as a safeguard against unjust prosecution has been widely recognized, contemporary opponents have argued that "the grand jury usually degenerates into a rubber stamp wielded by the prosecuting officer according to the dictates of his own sense of property and justice." See Livingston Hall, Yale Kamisar, Wayne R. LaFave, and Jerold H. Israel, *Modern Criminal Procedure*. St. Paul: West, 1969, pp. 791-794.

[11] Virtually any study of criminology will include discussion of the relationship between crime and poverty and the reasons why indigents appear as defendants in such a high percentage of criminal prosecutions. See, for example, Sue Titus Reid, *Crime and Criminology*. Third edition. New York: Holt, Rinehart & Winston, 1982.

[12] It can be said that the prosecutorial advantage of a "head start" existed in the early stages of the Pinto case as well; Cosentino, Shewmaker, and Graves commenced investigations within hours of the accident. Indeed, Ford attorneys later complained on several occasions that they felt disadvantaged because they had to interview certain individuals in the Elkhart community after those individuals had been in contact with someone from the prosecution.

[13] Strobel, *Reckless Homicide?* p. 45.

[14] Cosentino did not gain the cooperation of federal agencies easily, however. After "running into a brick wall" in trying to obtain certified copies of crucial documents, for example, Cosentino said he was forced to contact a state senator, who in turn contacted Ralph Nader's office in Washington, D.C., before federal government employees would respond to his requests. Cosentino stated, however, that once the door was opened, agency cooperation was "excellent."

[15] The absence of pay for the long hours of work quickly became the focus of some good-natured gallows humor among the prosecutorial staff. Mock-strikes, for example, were sometimes staged by the student volunteers, who demanded that Cosentino provide "better pay, better hours."

[16] Taken from a letter written by Berner to W. J. Maakestad, dated July 16, 1981 (hereinafter cited as Berner's letter to author).

[17] Author William Maakestad became involved at this point in the case. Virtually the only other exception to the "local talent" commitment was an early consultation with Leonard Orland, a law professor at the University of Connecticut who had done some research in the field of corporate criminality.

[18] See our discussion in Chapter 4 pertaining to the background and character of Elkhart County State Prosecutor Cosentino.

[19] Defendant's Memorandum in Support of Motion to Dismiss (filed October 23, 1978), pp. 1-2, in *State v. Ford Motor Co.*, No. 5324 (Ind. Super. Ct.) (hereinafter cited as Ford's Memorandum).

[20] For a general introduction to the field of products liability see, for example, William Kimble and Robert Lesher, *Products Liability.* St. Paul: West, 1979.

[21] 10 M. & W. 109, 152 Eng.Rep. 402, 11 L.J.Ex. 415 (1842).

[22] 217 N.Y. 382, 11 N.E. 1050, 1916 L.R.A. 696, 1916C Ann.Cas. 440 (1916), affirming 160 App.Div. 35, 145 N.Y.S. 462 (1914).

[23] See generally Justice Cardozo's discussion of these precedents in the *MacPherson* case (see note 22).

[24] Cornelius W. Gillam, *Products Liability in the Automobile Industry: A Study in Strict Liability and Social Control.* Minneapolis: University of Minnesota Press, 1960, p. 47. See also C.A. Peairs, Jr., "The God in the Machine: A Study in Precedent," *Boston University Law Review* 29 (January 1949), pp. 37-78.

[25] Although in a few jurisdictions theories were developed judicially which eased the plaintiff's burden under certain circumstances, the fact remained that in most cases negligence theory required specific proof of fault before liability could attach—even if it could be proved easily that the product was both defective and unsafe.

[26] Gillam, *Products Liability in the Automobile Industry*, pp. 6-9.

[27] This approach became known generally as the implied warranty theory, which was imposed judicially under limited circumstances before it was written into the Uniform Commercial Code in 1962.

[28] 32 N.J. 358, 161 A.2d 69 (1960).

[29] According to William Prosser, three main points make up the rationale for the development and acceptance of the strict liability theory as a supplement (and in many cases a replacement) for the negligence and warranty theories: "First, the public interest in human life and safety demands the maximum possible protection that the law can give against which they are helpless to protect themselves; and it justifies the imposition, upon all sup-

pliers of such products, of full responsibility for the harm they cause, even though the supplier has done his best. Second, the maker, by placing the goods upon the market, represents to the public that they are safe and suitable for use; and by packaging, advertising or otherwise, he does everything that he can do to induce that belief. Third, it is already possible to enforce strict liability by resort to a series of actions, in which the retailer is first held liable on a warranty to his purchaser, and indemnity on a warranty is then sought successively from other suppliers, until the manufacturer finally pays the damages, with the added costs of repeated litigation. This is an expensive, time-consuming, and wasteful process, and it may be interrupted by insolvency, lack of jurisdiction, disclaimers, or the statute of limitations, anywhere along the line." See William Prosser, *Handbook of the Law of Torts*. Fourth edition. St. Paul: West, 1971, p. 6.

[30] 59 Cal.2d 57, 377 P.2d 897 (1963).

[31] Section 402A, Restatement, Torts 2d.

[32] 391 F.2d 495 (8th Cir. 1968).

[33] *Huff v. White Motor Co.*, 565 F.2d 104 (7th Cir. 1977), cited in State's Memorandum, p. 15.

[34] See generally David G. Owen, "Punitive Damages in Products Liability Litigation," *Michigan Law Review* 74 (June 1976), pp. 1258-1371.

[35] This statement obviously represents the viewpoint of prosecuting attorneys, and does not take into account the possibility that a plea-bargaining agreement may have been considered, at least initially, in the best interest of the State for administrative or other reasons. From the viewpoint of defense attorneys, an acquittal (or, under certain circumstances, a conviction of a lesser included offense) would be the corresponding measure of success.

[36] This observation, of course, does not mean that prosecutors are ever personally satisfied with less than a guilty verdict. Regardless of their pretrial successes, prosecutors, like athletic teams, are evaluated almost solely on the basis of "wins" and "losses."

[37] Defendant's Memorandum, pp. 1-2.

[38] Berner's letter to author. Law students from Valparaiso and DePaul who assisted Berner and Kiely included, among others, Don Seberger, Eugene Schoon, Cathy Schmidt, Donn Wray, Mary Lawton, Deidra Burgman, Dan Lane and Mike Meyer.

[39] See, for example, Wayne R. LaFave and Austin W. Scott, *Criminal Law*. St. Paul: West, 1971, pp. 229-230.

[40] Thomas J. Bernard, "The Historical Development of Corporate Criminal Liability," *Criminology* 22 (February 1984), p. 6.

[41] 212 U.S. 481 (1909).

[42] *Ibid.*, pp. 494-95.

[43] See generally Nancy Frank, "From Criminal to Civil Penalties in the History of Health and Safety Laws," *Social Problems* 30 (June 1983), pp. 532-544.

[44] LaFave and Scott, *Criminal Law*, pp. 229-230.

[45] Glenn A. Clark, "Corporate Homicide: A New Assault on Corporate Decision Making," *Notre Dame Lawyer* 54 (June 1979), pp. 911-951.

[46] For further discussion, see our analysis of this issue in Chapter 3. The reader should note that to date there have been no recorded indictments of corporations for either murder or voluntary manslaughter.

[47] 32 N.H. 215 (1855).

[48] For an excellent discussion of this issue, see Lawrence M. Friedman, *A History of American Law*. New York: Touchstone, 1973, pp. 409-427.

[49] 134 F. 592 (2d Cir. 1904).

[50] *Ibid.*, p. 374.

[51] 90 N.J.L. 372, 103 A. 685 (1917).

[52] *Ibid.*, p. 374.

[53] 195 N.Y. 102, 88 N.E. 22 (1909).

[54] *Ibid.*, p. 107, 88 N.E. at p. 24.

[55] 226 Ore. 502, 360 P.2d 530 (1961).

[56] 77 Misc.2d 784, 354 N.Y.S.2d 807 (1974).

[57] *Ibid.*, p. 786, 354 N.Y.S.2d at p. 810.

[58] *Ibid.* (emphasis by the court).

[59] *Ibid.*, p. 787, 354 N.Y.S.2d at p.811

[60] The *Ebasco* indictment was dismissed on due process grounds, the court stating that the indictment's language "was not sufficiently precise so as to apprise each defendant individually as to the conduct which was the subject of the accusation against him or it individually."

[61] Clark, "Corporate Homicide," p. 917. The failure of corporations to avoid prosecution for homicide on conceptual grounds since the Ford Pinto case (see our discussion of recent cases in Chapter 7) appears to indicate that the "further development" to which Clark refers has been favorable to prosecutors.

[62] State's Memorandum in Opposition to Motion to Dismiss (filed December 1, 1978), p. 2, in *State v. Ford Motor Co.*, No. 5324 (Ind. Super. Ct.) (hereinafter cited as State's Memorandum).

[63] Indiana Code Sec. 35-42-1-5.

[64] Ford's Memorandum, pp. 24-25.

[65] *Ibid.*, pp. 25-26.

[66] Indiana Code Sec. 35-41-1-2, cited in State's Memorandum, p. 8.

[67] Indiana Code Sec. 35-41-213(a), cited in State's Memorandum, p. 8.

[68] *State v. Lehigh Valley Railroad*, 90 N.J.L. 372, 103 A. 685 (1917); cited in State's Memorandum, p. 12.

[69] State's Memorandum, p. 10.

[70] 546 F.2d 492, 494 (2d Cir. 1976).

[71] Berner's letter to author.

[72] Sec Strobel, *Reckless Homicide?* pp. 41-42.

[73] The other two constitutional arguments presented by Ford in its memorandum were as follows: (1) The reckless homicide statute, applied in such a way as to attempt to regulate automobile safety, violated the commerce clause of the U.S. Constitution. (2) The same statute, through its vague and untimely application under the facts of this case, violated defendant's due process rights, which are afforded by the Indiana and U.S. Constitutions.

Note also that much of the substance of the constitutional arguments was developed by the Los Angeles law firm that Ford had also retained, Hughes Hubbard and Reed, and not by Mayer, Brown and Platt of Chicago. See Strobel, *Reckless Homicide?* p. 42.

[74] Note that our discussion of these issues is not intended as a treatise on the complicated interplay between constitutional law and corporate prosecutions, but merely as an analysis of the particular constitutional objections raised by Ford in the context of the Pinto case. For an excellent discussion of several constitutional issues that may arise when a corporation is a criminal defendant, see Howard Friedman, "Some Reflections on the Corporation as Criminal Defendant," *Notre Dame Lawyer* 55 (December 1979), pp. 173-202.

[75] Ford's Memorandum, p. 48.

[76] 22 U.S. 1 (1824).

[77] 430 U.S. 519 (1977).

[78] Ford's Memorandum, p. 43.

[79] *Ibid.*, p. 45.

[80] *Ibid.*, p. 48.

[81] *Ibid.*, pp. 48-49. Ford used essentially the same reasoning to support another one of its constitutional arguments: that the prosecution represented

an undue burden on interstate commerce and thus violated the commerce clause of the U.S. Constitution. See note 73.

[82] 434 U.S. 429 (1978).

[83] *Ibid.*, pp. 443-444 (citations omitted).

[84] State's Memorandum, p. 57.

[85] *Ibid.*, p. 58.

[86] 514 S.W.2d 497 (Tex. Civ. App. 1974).

[87] *Ibid.*, p. 506.

[88] State's Supplemental Memorandum in Opposition to Motion to Dismiss (filed December 20, 1978), pp. 1-2, in *State v. Ford Motor Co.*, No. 5324 (Ind. Super. Ct.).

[89] Indiana Constitution Art. I, Sec. 24; U.S. Constitution Art. I, Sec. 10.

[90] *Garner v. Los Angeles Board*, 341 U.S. 716, 721 (1951); cited in Ford's Memorandum, p. 32.

[91] *In re Petition to Transfer Appeals*, 202 Ind. 365, 174 N.E. 812 (1931).

[92] State's Memorandum, p. 46.

[93] *Alderson v. State*, 196 Ind. 22, 25, 145 N.E. 572, 573 (1924); cited in State's Memorandum, p. 47.

[94] *Carrier v. State*, 233 Ind. 456, 134 N.E.2d 688 (1956), quoting Brockway v. State, 192 Ind. 656, 138 N.E. 88 (1923); cited in State's Memorandum, p. 47.

[95] State's Memorandum, p. 48.

[96] State's Memorandum, p. 50. Fourteen cases were cited in support of this proposition.

[97] Christopher D. Stone, *Where the Law Ends: The Social Control of Corporations.* New York: Harper and Row, 1975, p. 30.

[98] Over half the states now provide for victim compensation under statutorily determined circumstances. See, for example, William E. Hoelzel, "A Survey of 27 Victim Compensation Programs," *Judicature* 63 (May 1980), pp. 485-496.

[99] The threat of statutorily prescribed civil penalties may also deter corporate misbehavior, but only in narrowly defined situations. Punitive damage awards are generally more widely available and have been used more frequently in civil cases involving reckless business decision making. See note 100 and accompanying text.

[100] See generally Vincent M. Igoe, "Punitive Damages: An Analytical Perspective," *Trial* (November 1978), pp. 48-53; Owen, "Punitive Damages in Products Liability Litigation," pp. 1258-1371; Comment, "Criminal Safeguards and the Punitive Damages Defendant," *University of Chicago Law Review* 34 (Winter 1967), pp. 408-435.

[101] *Grimshaw v. Ford Motor Co.*, No. 197761 (Orange Cty. Super. Ct. filed Nov. 22, 1972). According to studies by NHTSA, at least thirty civil cases in addition to Grimshaw had been filed against Ford by May 1978 in connection with the Pinto's fuel tank design. There are no reliable estimates of the total number of Pinto suits that have been filed to date.

[102] A wide range of articles is now available which discuss the legal problems attendant upon the application of criminal sanctions, including fines, against corporations. Examples include Comment, "Criminal Sanctions for Corporate Illegality," *Journal of Criminal Law & Criminology* 69 (Spring 1978), pp. 40-58, and Note, "Corporate Crime: Regulating Corporate Behavior Through Criminal Sanctions," *Harvard Law Review* 92 (April 1979), pp. 1227-1394.

[103] See, for example, Harry V. Ball and Lawrence M. Friedman, "The Use of Criminal Sanctions in the Enforcement of Economic Legislation: A Sociological View," *Stanford Law Review* 17 (January 1965), pp. 197-223, and Lawrence M. Friedman, "Two Faces of Law," *Wisconsin Law Review* 13 (No. 1 1984), pp. 13-35.

[104] Victoria Swigert and Ronald Farrell, "Corporate Homicide: Definitional Processes in the Creation of Deviance," *Law and Society Review* 15 (No. 1 1980-1981), pp. 161-182. See also Ball and Friedman, "The Use of

Criminal Sanctions in the Enforcement of Economic Legislation: A Socio-logical View," p. 214.

Ball and Friedman, proponents of the economic school of thought, make this interesting observation concerning the inefficiency of regulation through the criminal process: "The shift to administrative enforcement takes place partly because criminal sanctions drag with them all the tradi-tional safeguards surrounding the defendant. Proof beyond a reasonable doubt, trial by jury, and other forms of protection are required. The social-ization of remedies thus has the dysfunctional result of making large-scale enforcement difficult for reasons irrelevant to the purpose of making the proscribed acts illegal."

[105] Even if the legal restrictions concerning civil remedies were not present, the possibility exists that parents of children who suffered a premature, wrongful death would decline to pursue a monetary settlement on religious or moral grounds. In addition, certain families might suffer considerable psychological effects by accepting money from the individual or company re-sponsible for the death of their child.

[106] No. 197761 (Orange Cty. Super. Ct. filed Nov. 22, 1972). See footnote 101.

[107] Ind. Code Ann. Sec. 34-1-1-8 (Burns 1973 & Supp. 1982).

[108] *Pennsylvania Co. v. Lilly*, 73 Ind. 252,254 (1881). Although the Indiana civil code provides both a general wrongful death statute, Ind. Code. Ann. Sec. 34-1-1-2 (Burns 1973 and Supp. 1982), and a wrongful death statute for children (see note 107), the same result would have been produced under either alternative. Futhermore, the two statutory schemes are mutually ex-clusive and thus could not have been pursued simultaneously, according to *Vera Cruz v. Chesapeake & Ohio Ry. Co.*, 192 F. Supp. 958 (N.D. Ind. 1961).

[109] See *Ohio & Miss. R.R. v. Tindall*, 13 Ind. 366 (1859); *Estate of Pickens v. Pickens*, 264 N.E.2d 151 (Ind. 1970); *Hahn v. Moore*, 133 N.E.2d 900 (Ind. Ct. App. 1956). This line of cases reflects an early common-law tradition which, legally speaking, viewed the primary value of children as the amount of labor they contributed to the household.

[110] The early Indiana Supreme Court decision was *Taber v. Hutson*, Ind. 322 (1854), with *Glissman v. Rutt* 372 N.E.2d 1188 (Ind. Ct. App. 1978) in accord.

[111]   See footnote 100.

[112]   Statement made in Elkhart by Michael Cosentino, explaining the State Indiana's position against Ford's Motion to Dismiss (December 23,1978).

[113]   William Prosser, *Handbook of the Law of Torts*. Third edition. St. Paul: West, 1964, p. 924. For a fascinating historical discussion of this issue, see Friedman, *A History of American Law*, pp. 409-427.

[114]   See generally 25A C.J.S. Death Sec. 125 (1966) and 67A C.J.S. Parent & Child Sec. 137-52 (1966).

[115]   The following states appear to have statutes that specifically allow punitive damages in wrongful death cases: Kentucky, Massachusetts, Mississippi, Nevada, New Mexico, North Carolina, Oregon, South Carolina, Texas, and Wyoming. States permitting punitive damage awards by judicial interpretation include the following: Arizona, Arkansas, Florida, Missouri, Montana, Tennessee, and West Virginia. See Comment, "Corporate Homicide: The Stark Realities of Artificial Beings and Legal Fictions," *Pepperdine Law Review* 8 (No. 2 1981), pp. 393-394; see especially footnote 166. For further discussion, see also Arden C. McClelland and Harold J. Truett III, "Survival of Punitive Damages in Wrongful Death Cases," *University of San Francisco Law Review* 8 (Spring 1974), pp. 585-608.

[116]   See Comment, "Corporate Homicide," pp. 389-393.

[117]   The prosecution also argued that in this case the general criminal law was a more appropriate vehicle by which to accomplish the same goals as punitive damages because of the possibility of financial overkill: where punitive damages are assessed in multiple cases against a corporation, the total societal loss that could occur following the financial devastation of that company must be considered.   Ironically, by taking the position that it is necessary to balance the social costs and the benefits of repeated applications of punitive damages against corporations, the prosecution borrowed a line of reasoning normally employed by corporations seeking to avoid the burden of such damages. See State's Memorandum, pp. 25-27. For an extended discussion of this issue, see the opinion of Circuit Court Judge Friendly in *Roginsky v. Richardson-Merrell, Inc.*, 378 F.2d 832 (2d Cir. 1967).

[118]   Berner's letter to author.

[119]   Had Judge Jones decided, however, that the indictment was constitutionally or conceptually invalid, Cosentino could have appealed his decision.

[120]   From conversations with Cosentino and Berner, June 1983.

[121]   This account of Judge Jones's decision and its immediate aftermath was drawn partially from Strobel, *Reckless Homicide?* pp. 55-56.

[122]   See footnote 56.

[123]   *State v. Ford Motor Co.*, No. 5324, slip. op. at p. 8 (Ind. Super. Ct. Feb. 2, 1979).

[124]   Ind. Code Sec. 35-41-213(a); cited in State's Memorandum, p. 8.

[125]   See footnote 123, p. 9.

[126]   402 U.S. 637 (1971).

[127]   See footnote 123, p. 11.

[128]   419 F.2d 499 (2d Cir. 1969).

[129]   Ibid., p. 511.

[130]   489 F.2d 917 (6th Cir. 1974).

[131]   See footnote 123, p. 14.

[132]   The two cases, both civil, were *Rozier v. Ford Motor Co.*, 573 F.2d 1332 (5th Cir. 1978), and *Buehler v. Whalen*, 374 N.E.2d 460 (1977).
        Both cases are unusual in terms of the strong language used by appellate court justices to condemn Ford and its attorneys for unethical practices. "Through its misconduct in this case," the federal court hearing *Rozier* concluded, "Ford completely sabotaged the federal trial court machinery, precluding the 'fair contest' which the Federal Rules of Civil Procedure are intended to assure. Instead of serving as a vehicle for ascertainment of the truth, the trial in this case accomplished little more than the adjudication of a hypothetical fact situation imposed by Ford's selective disclosure of information."
        In its *Buehler* decision, the Supreme Court of Illinois stated: "We cannot condemn too severely the conduct of the Ford Motor Corporation in the

discovery procedures here. It gave false answers to interrogatories under oath. It secreted evidence damaging to its case. Under the circumstances, the trial court would have been justified in striking the answer of this defendant and submitting to the jury only the issue of damages."

[133] Statement by Ralph Nader during appearance at Western Illinois University after the Ford indictment, Spring 1979.

[134] Berner's letter to author; see especially text accompanying footnote 71.

Chapter 6
Trying Ford

Bringing Ford to trial had not been an easy task. Since the days immediately after the deaths of the Ulrich girls, Cosentino had been confronted with a series of obstacles that had to be overcome before Ford's culpability could be weighed in a courtroom.

The initial barriers were largely personal and perceptual. Was Ford Motor Company really to blame for the tragic consequences of the accident? Should Cosentino bring criminal charges against a corporation? Would his community, as represented by a grand jury, support a prosecution? Once these uncertainties were resolved and his course of action determined, Cosentino faced the more concrete problem of assembling a prosecutorial team with the expertise to handle the complex legal issues raised by Ford's attorneys in their attempt to quash the indictment for reckless homicide against the corporation.

In their showdown with Ford, Cosentino and his colleagues had sacrificed much of themselves. The case consumed many hours of work, and they also felt the constant anxiety of knowing that all their efforts would be wasted if Judge Jones barred them from continuing with the prosecution. Yet now that they had secured the court's permission to take Ford to trial, the time seemed well spent and the corporation seemed less formidable than it had originally. In the battle of legal briefs, Cosentino's group had more than held its own. They were optimistic that the corporate Goliath could be beaten.[1]

Even so, Cosentino retained a healthy sense of caution. From the inception of the case, he had wondered when Ford was going to use its considerable resources and bring out its "big guns." Now that the reputation of Ford Motor Company was hanging precariously in the balance, Cosentino was not left to wonder very long. Realizing that there was no room left for mistakes, Ford executives moved quickly to acquire the services of the best legal talent available. Their search led to James Foster Neal, one of the nation's foremost criminal defense attorneys.

Although short in stature at 5'7", the forty-nine-year-old Neal was long in experience. He had burst into the national spotlight in the early 1960s, when he was appointed as an assistant to Attorney General Robert Kennedy. Although still in his early thirties at the time, he was given the task of prosecuting former Teamsters boss Jimmy Hoffa. His initial attempt to convict Hoffa on charges of accepting $1 million in illegal payments ended in a hung jury. His second crack at Hoffa, however, succeeded in winning a guilty verdict on the charge of jury tampering. After several attempts by other government attorneys, Neal was the first lawyer to secure Hoffa's conviction.

A decade later, the Watergate scandal provided Neal with another opportunity to participate in a trial of historical importance. As the government's chief trial lawyer, he prosecuted the main Watergate case, which resulted in the convictions of John Ehrlichman, H. R. Haldeman, and John Mitchell. His performance led Watergate judge John Sirica to conclude, "He's the best lawyer I ever heard in a courtroom." Leon Jaworski praised Neal by adding, "I am as much impressed with him as any trial lawyer I have ever seen. And I have seen many in fifty years of practicing law."

In the period between the Hoffa and Watergate cases, Neal returned to his home state of Tennessee, where he served as U.S. Attorney. In 1971, he joined with Aubrey B. Harwell, Jr. to establish a profitable private practice in Nashville, with a branch office in Washington. The firm's clients included such celebrities as Dolly Parton, Johnny Cash, and Roy Orbison. Neal and Harwell also gained valuable experience by representing corporations like Volkswagen, GM, Subaru, and Union Carbide against product liability suits.

Much of Neal's effectiveness in the courtroom stemmed from his ability to mix a strong thirst for success with a genuine, folksy personal style. Since his boyhood days as the son of a tobacco and strawberry farmer, Neal's intense competitiveness had earned him a string of honors: a football scholarship to the University of Wyoming, the rank of captain in the Marine Corps during the Korean war, and the status of top student in his graduating class at Vanderbilt University School of Law. As a lawyer, he lost none of this desire to win. When he took a case, he would work endless hours preparing for trial; he would miss no detail and leave nothing to chance. As one Nashville prosecutor observed, "If there is a weakness in a case, he flat tears into it."

Yet Neal's country roots softened the hard-driving edge of his personality. Though he had rubbed shoulders with Washington's elite, he could still talk plainly with common folks. Neal's middle-Tennessee drawl has been characterized as "somewhere between Kentucky twang and Southern aristocrat."   During a trial, as another Nashville attorney noted, "he cultivates that country-boy image a little, but very effectively.   He'll have every juror thinking he's his long-lost friend before he's through."   As Judge Sirica concluded after the Watergate affair, Neal was "able to convince jurors that he is not trying to hoodwink them...[he is] a master of the art of jury psychology."

Why should Neal want to use his considerable talents to defend a giant company which was accused of such insensitivity that it allowed three teenagers to perish in a burning Pinto?   A monetary factor was present, of course.   Neal commanded high fees, and Ford was clearly ready to meet his asking price.   In this instance, no one, including company officials, disputed the strong rumor that Neal's firm received $1 million for taking on Ford's case and that the company spent another million on additional expenses related to the Pinto case.

Money, however, was not the whole story; indeed, it was probably not even the major part of the story.   The financially secure Neal did not have to take on all paying customers.   As he commented, "I pick and choose my cases pretty carefully these days."   If not for reasons of profit, then, why did he pick the makers of the Pinto?   It appears that two considerations influenced his decision.

First, the case involved fascinating and important legal issues.   National attention would surely surround the criminal prosecution of a major corporation for reckless homicide, and the trial potentially would occupy a prominent place in American legal history.   Such an opportunity was too good to pass up; it was Jim Neal's kind of case.   As Neal commented two years after the case had been decided, he saw Ford's prosecution as "one of the ten or fifteen most important trials in this century" and "one of the one or two most important trials" in his career.

The second consideration was ideological.   To be sure, Neal was no staunch conservative.   He had worked under Robert Kennedy, prosecuted top Republican officials in Watergate, and would later head Walter Mondale's presidential campaign in the State of Tennessee.   Jimmy Carter had considered him as a possible successor to Clarence M. Kelly as director of the FBI, and he is often mentioned as a possible Democratic gubernatorial candidate in his home state.   Yet Neal had also come to believe that corporations, which were responsible for much of the good in society, had become an easy and fashionable legal target.   "American industry," he noted, "is unable to keep up with all the federal regulations and restrictions.   It's so easy to attack big companies."   In Neal's view, the prevailing social context had put corporations like Ford on the defensive and turned them into underdogs.   As for the Pinto, he did not believe that Ford officials had consciously built a dangerous car, and he opposed the idea that Ford could satisfy all federal regulations and still be prosecuted under Indiana state law. Viewed together, these factors made Neal comfortable in taking on an "unpopular cause....I believe in what I am doing. I believe what I'm doing is right. I don't think that this case should have ever been brought."[2]

These sentiments were shared by his partner, Aubrey Harwell. In general, Harwell did not believe that the criminal law was appropriate in manufacturing cases like the Pinto. His reasons for this view were both practical and legal. Practically, he felt that the nation's criminal courts were already overburdened with crowded dockets and backlogs. In a society as litigation-minded as ours, it would be troublesome to create a whole new area of criminal law. Pragmatic considerations aside, Harwell's primary reservation regarding corporate criminal liability was the legal issue of intent. He believed that malicious intent typically was lacking in corporate cases, although he would not go so far as to dismiss criminal liability altogether. "Where intent can be demonstrated," he commented, "the corporation should be subjected to criminal prosecution like any other person. All of us are responsible for our actions."

Yet, was not Ford culpable of consciously allowing potentially lethal products to remain in the hands of unsuspecting customers? Harwell was adamant that Ford was innocent; again, intent was the significant issue. According to Harwell, the Ford people were honorable; they did not have the malicious intent to manufacture a death trap. He was convinced that Ford did not believe the Pinto was an unusually dangerous automobile. Even so, Harwell admitted that he would not want his family to drive a Pinto or any other small model and that motorcycles were "absolutely off limits" to his sons. Aside from fuel economy concerns, small cars simply were not as safe as larger cars. Harwell believed, however, along with Ford, that the Pinto was no more dangerous than other small automobiles on the market.[3]

This general perspective was shared, if not embraced, by Malcolm E. Wheeler, a third key member of the defense team. Once again, the paradoxical features of the Pinto case were apparent. If corporate crime fighter Michael Cosentino had all the trappings of a law-and-order conservative, then corporate defender Wheeler seemed to be the classic liberal. A 1969 graduate of Stanford Law School, he had devoted a great deal of time to performing free legal work in the Haight-Ashbury section of San Francisco. In 1971, he joined the law faculty at the University of Kansas, where he taught a course on prisoner rights and took on cases defending Native Americans.

Yet the thirty-five-year-old Wheeler had another side. Liberal causes aside, he was also an expert on antitrust legislation. In 1974, he was hired by the Los Angeles office of the prestigious Wall Street firm, Hughes, Hubbard and Reed, whose clients included the Ford Motor Company. After

Ford's devastating loss in the Grimshaw civil case, Wheeler was assigned the task of developing a new defense that would protect the company against similar defeats in future liability suits. As a graduate not only of Stanford Law School but also of the Massachusetts Institute of Technology, he had the expertise to grasp the technical complexities of the Pinto and to place them within a legal context. By the time of the Ulrichs' deaths, he understood well the many aspects of the Pinto controversy. He would prove to be a valuable addition to Ford's defense team.

As with Neal and Harwell, the appeal of the Pinto trial to Wheeler was twofold. First, he saw the legal significance of the case. It was, he admitted, "an opportunity I couldn't turn down. I think everyone agrees it's a real ground-breaking case." He also believed in a cause: the idea that the criminal law was an inappropriate sanction in product liability cases and that Ford was an inappropriate target of Cosentino's prosecution.[4]

Wheeler argued that it was easy to sensationalize the injuries suffered by consumers, to blame corporations for placing profits above safety, and to offer the criminal sanction as a panacea for the risks created by the manufacturing process. But these claims, he observed, were attractive precisely because they played on emotions and proposed simplistic solutions to complex problems. Indeed, Wheeler perceived real danger in campaigns against corporations—like the one being waged against Ford—that embraced the noble goal of protecting the public's interests but ulitimately were based on misinformed good intentions rather than on thoughtful analysis.

Wheeler had no shortage of reasons for opposing the extension of the criminal law into the realm of product liability and for issuing a warning that this would be an imprudent reform. First, he could find little evidence that the current regulatory system did not function adequately to control corporate conduct. After all, manufacturers already faced the prospect of administrative recalls of faulty products, pressures from consumer groups, expensive losses in civil suits, and unfavorable publicity that threatened sales and profits when lawsuits were filed. "Such a broad array of noncriminal deterrent forces," he asserted, "attends few other activities engaged in by members of our society."

Second, Wheeler felt that much of the impetus behind the call to apply criminal sanctions stemmed from the perception that corporations placed a dollar value on human life and crassly ignored safety considerations when they did not prove cost-effective. In Wheeler's eyes, however, cost-benefit analysis was at the core of the manufacturing process. Executives had to balance safety against factors such as a product's price, durability, comfort, efficiency, style, and overall marketability. The alternative to the systematic assessment of costs and benefits was decision-making based not on careful evaluation but on intuition and idiosyncratic standards—clearly not an attractive option.

Third, Wheeler questioned whether the threat of criminal sanctions would in fact serve the public's interests. There was a risk, he cautioned, of too much deterrence. If companies feared the constant threat of criminal prosecution, they would be forced to place excessive emphasis on product safety. As a consequence, quality and cost levels in other product areas might suffer, even though the public had not shown that it wished to place safety above all other concerns. In particular, prices would inevitably rise and have the socially regressive effect of excluding many poorer consumers from purchasing new products. Disadvantaged citizens would be priced out of the new-car market and compelled to buy used vehicles—which threatened, ironically, to be less safe than those to which they currently had access.

As a fourth consideration, Wheeler wondered whether the criminal justice system was equipped to handle intricate corporate cases. He was concerned that the criminal sanction carried such a heavy stigma that even corporations found innocent in a trial would suffer damaged reputations. This sullied image could diminish consumer faith in the firm, jeopardize profits, and potentially cost workers their jobs. What provisions could the criminal justice system make for rectifying this harm? Further, Wheeler observed that juries were ill prepared to weigh the complex factors involved in the production process. "Lay jurors," he asserted, "have neither common experience nor statutory guidance to assist them in judging the propriety of that conduct under general criminal statutes." Of course, this was also true in civil cases, where decisions often were made on "gut feelings" rather than on expert assessment of all relevant facts. Even so, much more was at stake in labeling a company criminal. "Subjecting manufacturers to that irrational antipathy in a civil suit for compensation is bad enough," lamented Wheeler, but "doing it in a criminal proceeding is much worse." Finally, Wheeler contended that gearing up the criminal justice system to attack corporations either would lessen the system's capacity to deal with common-law offenses or would require substantial budgetary increases so that the state could hire the personnel required to undertake the fight against corporate illegality. "It is far from clear," he concluded, "that it is socially desirable to devote already scarce police, prosecutorial, and judicial resources to the criminal prosecution of product manufacturers."[5]

In the end, Neal, Harwell, and Wheeler saw their defense of Ford as morally correct because of their conception of the appropriate relationship between business and the criminal law. Cynics could portray this view, as well as their interpretation of Ford's criminal culpability, as mere justifications for taking a case that promised to bring a healthy fee and professional prestige, just as cynics could claim that in prosecuting Ford, Cosentino was seeking publicity and political reward. Nonetheless, the members of the defense were ready to articulate an ideology that could compete with the popular vision of "Pinto madness." Ford Motor Company, they argued forcefully, was not a sociopath that randomly victimized its customers, but a responsible citizen that obeyed federal regulations and carefully weighed all factors in manufacturing a product that the public wanted: a small, afford-able American car.

Moreover, Ford had done well in hiring a talented legal team who would know how to use the many resources that the company placed at their dis-posal. Michael Cosentino had had to overcome a series of obstacles in bringing Ford to trial; this team would require him to negotiate a far more demanding obstacle course before he could convict Ford on charges of reckless homicide.

The Road to Winamac: A Change of Venue

Ford's opening gambit was an attempt to move Cosentino off his home turf by arguing that the bias against the Pinto in Elkhart was strong enough to warrant a change of venue. This strategy was important to the defense because of the real possibility that the local community would regard the company with suspicion. Something else was at stake as well: even if Elkhart citizens were not consciously prejudiced against Ford, they were likely to be familiar with their popular prosecutor. To potential jurors, Cosentino would not be an outsider undertaking an unusual case against a well-known corporation but an elected official pursuing his duty for his con-stituents. In addition, Cosentino would be trying the case before a judge who knew him and respected his work. The home-court advantage was likely to give him the edge in close calls.

There were also pragmatic considerations. Ford lawyers bristled at the media portrayal of the prosecuion as a David pitted in a battle with a cor-porate Goliath. After all, Cosentino not only drew upon the help of legal volunteers in his campaign against Ford, but also had the resources of the State of Indiana at his disposal: the highway patrol, the coroner's office, and criminal laboratories.[6] Yet, unlike the resources for a corporation-funded defense, the prosecution's resources were largely fixed, not liquid. Thus Cosentino's team could rely upon volunteer time and expertise and could use existing state facilities and personnel, but could not transform these resources into cash that could be allocated for other, unanticipated purposes. This lack of flexibility was not a critical disadvantage as long as the trial was held in Elkhart, close to the homes of those involved in the prosecution and Cosentino's office. Should the trial be transferred to another jurisdiction, however, the dearth of cash reserves would prove more serious. The prosecution would have to bear the added expenses of food, lodging, travel, office space, and local legal assistance. With a $20,000 budget, this change of venue would place an additional strain on Cosentino. His opponent, of course, would not have to practice frugality.

Donald W. Jones, the judge who had permitted the case to reach the trial stage, presided over the hearing in which Ford argued its request for a change of venue. The defense came well-prepared. To prove bias against the Pinto, they commissioned a telephone survey of 600 homes in Elkhart and the surrounding five counties; the price of the poll reportedly matched Cosentino's entire $20,000 budget. The investment was wise, however, for the survey's results gave empirical support to Ford's claims. In Elkhart County, 37.6 percent of the "potential juror population" answered, "Ford is guilty of the criminal charges of reckless homicide." Another 18.7 percent responded that Ford was "probably guilty as charged," and another 12.6 percent said that they "could not give the State and Ford a fair trial." Thus the total of "prejudiced jurors" in Elkhart was placed at 68.9 percent; for the five surrounding counties the figure was 50.8 percent.[7] The defense solidified its position further by calling Hans Zeisel, a nationally known legal scholar, to the stand. Zeisel, who would surface again as a Ford consultant during jury selection, testified that his content analysis of local news reports revealed that 86 percent of the stories were biased against the defense. A fair trial, he concluded, was not possible in the Elkhart area.

Cosentino countered by pointing out that there had been no change of venue in many highly publicized cases (e.g., the Watergate trials). He also observed that Ford's Pinto advertisements balanced any negativism that could have accumulated from pretrial media coverage, and he argued that according to Ford's data, nearly two-thirds of the Elkhart residents had yet to decide that the company was guilty. Perhaps the most convincing support for the prosecution's stance came from a letter sent to Ford by Joseph M. Webb, a professor of communications at the University of Evansville. The letter contained Webb's rationale for declining to testify on Ford's behalf: he did not believe that there was enough evidence to show that the corporation "has been prejudiced in the news media."[8]

On April 10, 1979, Judge Jones ended his deliberations and handed down his decision: the case would not be tried in Elkhart or in the five adjacent counties; Ford had won a change of venue. A critical question now emerged: where would the landmark trial be held? To resolve this matter, Judge Jones presented a list of five counties to which the case could be transferred. Ford was granted the right to make the first and third choices in eliminating a potential site; the prosecution would have the second veto and then make the final choice between the fourth and fifth counties. After alternating vetos had been exercised, Cosentino was left to choose between Grant and Pulaski Counties.

With so much at stake, the decision was difficult. The scouting report on Harold P. Staffeldt, the circuit court judge in Pulaski County, was mixed. Cosentino's sources noted that he was "unbiased and fair...is especially good on evidence and runs a tight ship." Yet, in words that would later prove prophetic, the report also warned that Staffeldt was usually "pro-state but because of the nature of our case it would be hard to determine....He is a strict construction of statute judge and does not care for 'screwball' arguments....The main thing that the Judge does not want is to be reversed on appeal and he would take the most conservative approach." The potential jurors, however, were characterized in uniformly positive terms: "The jury would be fair and impartial....[F]armers in this county do not like or trust big business."[9] The problem with Grant County was that many citizens were employed in the local Chrysler and Delco plants. Cosentino feared the risk of having a jury that was favorable, even if only unconsciously, to the automotive industry. This concern tipped the scales; the trial would be held in Pulaski County.

The Pulaski county seat was the small community of Winamac, located fifty-five miles southwest of Elkhart and described by one reporter as "a sleepy Tippecanoe River town in the soybean fields of central Indiana." The community had a population of 2,400, three luncheonettes, and one motel; penny parking meters lined its three-block business district. The trial would take place in the tallest structure in Winamac, a three-story limestone courthouse built in the late nineteenth century. The courtroom, located on the second floor, featured old woodwork lined with green and gold flocked wallpaper. The courtroom, refurbished with padded gold-colored seats, accommodated about seventy-five observers. The judge's bench rested below a picture of George Washington, flanked on one side by a copy, of the Bill of Rights and on the other by a copy of Lincoln's Gettysburg address.[10]

Harold P. Staffeldt had been hearing cases here since his appointment as circuit court judge in 1969. Sixty years of age, white-haired, thin, and fond of bold polka-dot bow ties, Staffeldt was a lifelong resident of Winamac. He received his legal training at Tulane University and returned to his hometown in 1947 to establish a local practice. Though he was not experienced in homicide cases ("we don't have any murderers around here"), he had presided over product liability cases. Most often in these cases, farmers sued feed companies "when their cattle don't grow plump."[11]

With the site of the trial determined, Ford quickly set up its defense operations. One of its first and shrewdest moves was to hire Lester Wilson as local counsel. For a number of years, Wilson had shared a law office and a secretary with Harold Staffeldt. In addition to Wilson, the defense team included over ten lawyers, a public relations executive from corporate headquarters, a professional jogger to rush materials from the courtroom to the defense's office, numerous typists and secretaries, and college students whose tasks included filling coffee cups and carting around boxes of files and evidence. Ford also imported word processors, copiers, a videotape recorder to monitor television network reports, and a machine to transmit paperwork between Winamac and the Ford offices in Dearborn, Michigan.

To accommodate the equipment and their small army, Ford rented a former restaurant and installed offices. Because Lester Wilson's law office was not large enough, they knocked down a wall and expanded into the barbershop next door. (The barber was amply compensated and was promised that the shop would be reconstructed once the trial had ended.) The Ford staff was housed in four rooms rented from the lone motel in town and in nine brand-new furnished apartments; the apartments reportedly cost $27,000 a month. Transportation did not prove problematic; the local Ford dealership supplied the cars.[12]

The defense also arranged to purchase one additional luxury: daily transcripts of the trial. This item was not inexpensive: nine dollars a page, for a total of more than $50,000 for the trial. The transcripts were a good investment, however; they gave Neal and his associates the opportunity to review testimony when preparing cross-examinations and challenges of previous prosecution contentions. In the face of his limited resources, Cosentino had to forego this advantage.[13]

Ford barely edged out Cosentino in the race for Lester Wilson's services. Cosentino called Wilson early one morning only to discover that Ford had hired him the previous evening. As a second choice for local counsel, the prosecutor selected David Tankersley, a young and capable Winamac attorney. Tankersley, however, did not have any special relationship with the judge.

The prosecution's team set up shop in Tankersley's office. The space was somewhat cramped, but adequate for their needs. Lodging proved to be more of a problem, since there was little local housing and Ford had rented most of the units available. On a tip from an FBI agent, Cosentino discovered two cottages next to Bass Lake, ten miles to the north of Winamac. Typically empty during the off-season, the cottages were not built to withstand the winter's cold. Still, the price was right: at $800 a month, they would do.

Despite this minimal cost, funds were short. To lessen the burden, Cosentino used his own money to pay most of the bills for rent, telephone, and utilities. Everyone else would chip in for groceries. No local dealership offered to supply free cars: Cosentino managed the daily trip to Winamac in his 1976 Chevrolet Blazer.[14]

The Art and Science of Selecting a Jury

Jury selection for the Pinto trial began on Monday morning, January 7, 1980. Almost a year and a half had passed since the Ulrich girls had perished; the time had come to choose the people who would assess whether Ford was to blame for the reckless endangerment and homicide of the three teenagers. The jurors would be drawn from a pool of nearly 250 Pulaski County citizens. Both the prosecution and the defense would have an opportunity to question each potential juror, and each side had ten "peremptory challenges," which they could use to exclude any person from the jury without cause. Other citizens could be excused from jury duty by Judge Staffeldt, either because they were too prejudiced to render a fair decision or because of personal exigencies.

Both Neal and Cosentino came fully prepared to pick a jury sympathetic to their cases, in part because of their past experiences. Their previous records of repeated success in the courtroom indicated that each had mastered the art of jury selection. Nonetheless, the Pinto trial was a different game. The ideology surrounding the case was anomalous and seemingly contradictory; a conservative was fighting a "liberal" cause and Ford was portraying itself as a victim of the overreach of the law. In such a context, it was riskier than usual to predict which way potential jurors would lean upon entering the case. The help of outside experts would be needed to minimize the possibility of misinterpretation and error.

James Neal used science to corroborate his "lawyer's sense" of what constitutes a good juror. Although he ultimately trusted his intuition in making jury selections, Neal valued empirical data because they furnished additional perspective and thus increased his confidence.[15] Once again, Ford settled for nothing less than the best consultant in the field: Hans Zeisel. The seventy-four-year-old Zeisel had worked in marketing research when he immigrated to the United States; later he joined the law faculty at the University of Chicago. He achieved prominence as one of the foremost experts on juries when he collaborated with Harry Klaven on their celebrated book, *The American Jury*. His consulting fee was reportedly one thousand dollars a day.

To develop a profile of a juror favorable to the defense, Zeisel conducted an extensive survey of registered voters in four states. His study revealed that women in general, and young women in particular, would be the worst jurors for Ford, while older men would be the best. The only exceptions to this trend were females who drove trucks. Such a respondent, Zeisel concluded from his data analysis, "became a man for purposes of jury selection; she was a good juror for Ford." Zeisel not only provided a juror model, but also attended each day of the selection process and consulted with Neal during breaks. In general, there was little disagreement between his advice and the assessments Neal made based on his questioning of the potential jurors.[16]

In this regard, Neal used the *voir dire* process to probe the underlying ideology of the jurors. Thus he did not confine his questions to eliciting only direct anti-Ford sentiments. Instead, he tried to learn the extent to which a prospective juror embraced liberal causes, supported government safety regulations, and mistrusted corporations. Those who felt positively about Ralph Nader and Common Cause (who thought that the government should mandate air bags, believed that a small car should be as safe as a luxury automobile, and were suspicious of corporate America) had little chance of surviving Neal's challenge.[17]

Unlike his opponent, Cosentino did not have the option of hiring an expensive consultant on jury selection. He did, however, hold valuable discussions with psychiatrist Dr. Otto Klassen, director of a community mental health center in Elkhart. As a result, Cosentino perceived that his chances would be improved if he could select jurors who were the exact opposite of the kind normally favorable to the state and, ironically, of the kind he normally chose to hear his cases. An older, male, conservative jury might be ideal for a typical homicide case, but it was unlikely that such a group would be inclined to view a corporation, like Ford, as a criminal capable of committing homicide.

With the help of his associates, Cosentino developed a series of over forty questions. These questions were aimed at unmasking biases that would make the juror "good" or "bad" for the prosecution. They ranged from whether a person owned a Ford vehicle or stock in Ford and believed that a "corporation is responsible for its conduct" to what magazines were read, what T.V. shows were watched, and what health activities were pursued. Lifestyle questions were important, Cosentino believed, because they served as indicators of a person's political orientation and general attitude toward the centers of power in America. Thus, citizens who read *Mother Earth News* rather than *Time*, preferred PBS to CBS, were "into jogging" for their health, and avoided smoking because they believed the government's warnings about its dangers seemed more likely to be critical of Ford's handling of the Pinto. Unfortunately for the prosecution, however, this kind of prospective juror was in short supply in Pulaski County.[18]

Jury selection took four days and involved the tedious questioning of nearly sixty citizens, but by Thursday afternoon, the twelve jurors and three alternates had been chosen. Both sides were pleased with the results and felt that a "fair" jury had been seated.

The jury included seven men and five women, and had an average age of forty-one. All the members were or had been married; all were parents. Although every juror had earned a high-school diploma, few had any higher education. They worked in varied occupations; the jury included two farmers, two housewives, several self-employed business people, a railroad employee, an X-ray technician, a telephone service worker, and a steelworker. One woman, Hans Zeisel was pleased to learn, drove a truck, and half the jury members owned Ford vehicles. Juror Raymond Schramm even had a Pinto, but he claimed this would not bias his views. After all, he noted, "I used to drive a Corvair."[19]

The jury selection process indicated clearly the kind of courtroom battles that would erupt in the weeks ahead. Reporter Lee Strobel observed that only fifteen seconds after the start of the trial, Cosentino and Neal began a dispute over how close a lectern should be placed to the jury box.[20] The opening days also revealed the stylistic differences between the two lawyers. Because this was a homicide case, Cosentino adopted a serious demeanor. He spoke assertively and with an intensity meant to emphasize the gravity of the charges leveled at Ford. By contrast, Neal did not hesitate to use humorous quips to lighten the mood of the courtroom, and he often relied on folksy language to score points with prospective jurors. "From the Ford side of the courtroom," reporter Alan Lenhoff commented smartly during the first week, "the accepted way of addressing the jury seems to be 'you-all.'"[21]

Now that the jury was seated, the small community of Winamac, executives at Ford, corporate America, and legal scholars across the nation waited eagerly for testimony in the Pinto trial to begin. The preview of the "Mike and Jim show," as local residents came to call it, had ended; the curtain was about to rise on the main event.[22]

Preparing for Trial: Documenting Ford's Culpability

Before the trial, the prosecution spent considerable effort on neutralizing Ford's attempt to quash the indictment; they also faced the critical task of preparing their substantive case. In part, this preparation involved analyzing the details of the accident and establishing that a faulty car, not faulty driving, had caused the Ulrichs' deaths. Much more evidence would be required, however, to prove that Ford was guilty of recklessly manufacturing a lethal vehicle and of keeping it on the road despite its obvious dangers. Cosentino would have to penetrate Ford's corporate shield to acquire the documents that would reveal the company's inner workings and allow him to show how executives' decisions, informed by a profit ideology, had led to the marketing of a hazardous product.

As mentioned in Chapter 4, the general campaign against the Pinto made it feasible to secure internal Ford documents. In particular, Cosentino carefully tracked down the numerous lawyers who had civil cases against Ford; many were willing to share whatever damning information they had obtained. Over time, the prosecution became a clearinghouse for data on the Pinto.

Even so, the various threads of evidence still had to be interpreted in such a way that the complex history of the Pinto could be reconstructed and presented to a jury in a convincing fashion. Terry Kiely, the law professor from DePaul who had volunteered his services, assumed much of this burden. His task was to gain the technical expertise that would enable him to sift through the stack of "Pinto papers," as he called them,[23] and to craft the prosecution's account of what had happened nearly a decade earlier, when Ford went about the business of manufacturing "Lee's car."

In a sense, Kiely had plenty of material. The prosecution's digging had uncovered 101 documents, including 35 crash tests, 44 financial documents, and a number of correspondences between Ford and the National Highway Traffic Safety Administration (NHTSA).[24]   Yet this was a "corporate crime"; therefore the method of establishing guilt was quite different and more intricate than required in a typical street crime. It would not be sufficient for Kiely to portray the Ulrichs as "homicide victims" and to equate their charred Pinto with the "smoking gun" found at the scene of a "normal" homicide. Instead, he would have to demonstrate that the origins of the teenagers' deaths rested not so much in the rapid sequence of events on Indiana's Highway 33 as in the cumulative effects of decisions by Ford executives, which caused the company to manufacture a vehicle that it had ample reason to believe was potentially lethal.

After months of poring over his Pinto papers, Kiely believed he had the documents to substantiate five broad observations which, taken together, painted a disquieting picture of Ford's conduct.[25]   First, while the Pinto was still in the planning stages, Ford already had "state-of-the-art" technology which would have allowed it to build a safe fuel-injection system in a subcompact vehicle. Most notably, the company had produced the Capri, a modified version of which later became the Pinto. Ford engineers avoided the problems that would beset the Pinto's fuel system by placing the Capri's gas tank over the rear axle. In European advertisements, in fact, Ford emphasized that the Capri's tank was "safely cradled between the rear wheels and protected on all sides."[26]   Despite this knowledge, Kiely concluded, Ford located the Pinto's "fuel tank behind the axle (3 inches from differential bolts and other hostile sources) and 6 inches from the rear *ornamental* bumper." (emphasis in original)[27]

Second, before the initial marketing date, Ford crash tested four prototypes—a Toyota and three Capris—all modified to have the Pinto's fuel tank arrangement. In these tests, the prototypes were rammed into a wall at approximately 20 mph. In each instance the vehicles leaked fuel and failed the text. Although these results constituted an ominous warning, the company nonetheless "released the Pinto for sale on September 11, 1970 without any further testing of even one production Pinto."[28] Corporate memos indicate that the placement of the tank over the axle was scrapped because it consumed too much trunk space and hence would jeopardize sales. From Kiely's perspective, this decision was clear evidence—drawn from a time before the car was distributed to dealerships—that corporate profits were placed above consumer safety and that Ford had neglected its duty to alter the Pinto's design, even though the corporation knew of the car's inherent dangers.

Third, shortly after the release of the Pinto onto the open market, NHTSA informed Ford of its intention to promulgate standards mandating that all vehicles be able to withstand a 20-mph rear-end collision into a fixed barrier (wall) by January 1, 1972 and a 30-mph collision by January 1, 1973. This mandate led the company to analyze systematically the ability of its products, including the Pinto, to meet these standards. Crash tests confirmed that the Pinto was unable to meet the 20-mph standard, but the investigation also noted that the technology was available to satisfy the forthcoming regulations. Yet, despite continuing knowledge of the Pinto's dangers, the management decided that the costs of altering the fuel system were too great. "Safety," observed Kiely, "is never a consideration and the word does not even appear in the documents."

As an alternative to revamping the Pinto, Kiely continued, Ford's strategy was to lobby the government for a more lenient standard—one that was consistent with an internal company regulation stating that by 1973 all models, including the Pinto, must be able to withstand a 20-mph *moving* barrier crash. (In a moving-barrier test, a barrier is rammed into a car; in the more stringent fixed-barrier test, the car is towed rearward into a wall and sustains greater damage at a comparable speed.) Concretely, Ford's 20-mph moving-barrier standard meant that in an actual highway or car-to-car accident, a 1973 Pinto would risk fuel leakage if struck in the rear at a speed between 26 and 28 mph—less than the speed limit on most city streets. The proposed NHTSA standard mandating fuel-system integrity in a 20-mph fixed-barrier test would have boosted the Pinto's safety level approximately 6 mph, while the 30-mph standard proposed for 1973 models—like the Ulrichs' Pinto—would have required fuel-leakage protection during rear-end collisions at speeds well above 40 mph. Of course, Kiely and the other prosecutors believed that the Ulrichs' car had burst into flames when hit at a speed much lower than 40 mph.[29]

Fourth, though Ford executives chose for the moment to "stand their ground" on the Pinto, they considered developing a solution to the growing prospect that NHTSA would eventually impose tougher safety standards. At that point they weighed the possibility of using a bladder to line the Pinto's fuel tank, and even secured cost estimates from Goodyear and Firestone. Ford management rejected this option, however, in order "to realize a design cost savings of $20.9 million."[30] A memo dated April 22, 1971, five days before Henry Ford II and Lec Iacocca spoke with Richard Nixon in the White House (see Chapter 4), instructed that the manufacturing process allocate space in which a bladder or another protective device could be inserted should NHTSA regulations be forthcoming. By October, however, these instructions were amended so that the Pinto would no longer even be "packaged" or designed for the possibility of an improved fuel system "until required by law."[31] The political climate apparently had become more sympathetic to Ford's corporate interests; therefore the need to make the Pinto more crashworthy was no longer a pressing concern.

Fifth, Ford continued its efforts over the next several years to stifle governmental regulation and to resist revamping the Pinto. In making its argument against more stringent standards, Ford developed its cost-benefit memo, which balanced human lives and injuries against profits—the memo popularized by Dowie in his "Pinto Madness" article (see Chapter 4). Because the analysis contained in this document did not focus on the Pinto, and was related to fuel leakage in a rollover test rather than a rear-end collision, it was not critical to the prosecution's case. Kiely found it relevant, however, because it displayed a mind-set that shaped the thinking of Ford executives and represented the kind of argument that the company made to NHTSA to avoid safety regulations. The memo, suspected Kiely, revealed why Ford did not recall its Pintos until NHTSA prompted it to do so in 1978.[32]

Kiely believed that these five observations, viewed together, demonstrated a pattern that consistently guided Ford's handling of the Pinto: knowledge of the dangers inherent in the fuel-injection system, possession of the technology to rectify the hazards of the tank location, conscious decisions not to improve the fuel system, and efforts to maximize profits by resisting governmental policies that would have mandated safety standards. In Kiely's view, these observations made a compelling case that Ford was reckless in its manufacturing and continued marketing of the Pinto, as well as in its failure to recall the 1.5 million vehicles it allowed to remain on the road. Therefore the circumstances underlying the Ulrichs' deaths were years in the making and were tied up intimately with Ford's way of doing business.

Still, a sticky problem remained. Although the prosecution had numerous documents at its disposal, these were generally copies of originals supplied by lawyers with civil cases against Ford or by former Ford executives. As a result, Cosentino was confronted with the chore of "authenticating" the documents, that is, of proving that the documents in his possession were indeed Ford's and not forgeries. Until this was accomplished, none of the documents would be admissible as evidence.

The prosecution began to address this issue in the summer preceding the trial. Cosentino's opening gambit was to ask Judge Staffeldt to permit the prosecution to have the "right of discovery," that is, the right to compel the defendant—in this case, Ford—to turn over potentially relevant evidence. Cosentino's purpose was twofold. First, if Ford produced the requested documents from its files, it could be argued that they were authentic and thus admissible in the trial. Second, a discovery process would allow Cosentino to obtain copies of damaging reports that he did not currently possess.

Jim Neal moved quickly to neutralize this attack. In civil cases, he admitted, discovery rights were broad and both sides had the obligation to surrender any evidence specifically requested by the opposition. But this was a *criminal* case, Neal reminded Staffeldt; therefore Ford, as a defendant, enjoyed the Fifth Amendment right against self-incrimination. The State of Indiana could not legitimately expect Ford to help convict itself. Cosentino countered that unlike individual defendants, *corporations* did not have the right against self-incrimination. Discovery, he asserted, should be allowed in a corporate prosecution.

This would not be the last time in the case that Judge Staffeldt faced a fuzzy legal issue. The very novelty of prosecuting corporations on charges such as reckless homicide (the very point that would bring news reporters to Winamac) meant that Staffeldt would have few clear legal precedents on which to base his rulings. The small-town judge could seek to break new legal ground at the potential risk of having his decisions reversed on appeal by a higher court, or he could take a safer, more conservative approach and decide issues on narrower grounds. As would be seen, the judge was reluctant for the most part to stray too far from his conservative roots; he did not care to be a trendsetter.

In this instance, Staffeldt was not prepared to grant the prosecution broad discovery rights in a criminal case. He did, however, add one caveat: should Ford request evidence from the prosecution (such as autopsy or police reports), as defendants typically do in criminal cases, the company would have to disclose the materials designated by the prosecution.

Neal, who wished to keep tight control over corporate information, refused to initiate a process of mutual discovery. Instead, he relied on Aubrey Harwell, his law partner, to coordinate an exhaustive and costly pretrial investigation that used more informal means—most notably, extensive interviews—to accumulate information about the accident.   In response, Cosentino appealed to the Indiana Supreme Court. Much to his chagrin, the Court voted 4-1 to uphold Staffeldt's ruling.

Despite this setback, Cosentino did not lack hope or alternatives. He felt that he had enough evidence to win a conviction; thus Ford's disclosure of new materials was not critical. Discovery was primarily a way of authenticating the documents already in his possession; now he would have to employ different means. His first attempt was to subpoena Henry Ford II and twenty-nine Ford executives, asking them to appear in court with the relevant documents. Again, authentication would be achieved by the fact that the documents were produced by Ford officials from company files. This effort was derailed, however, when Wayne County, Michigan Judge Richard D. Dunn rejected the prosecution's bid to have the executives testify at the trial. Cosentino, unwilling to be denied, then served a subpoena on the CT Corporation, a Ford subsidiary designated to represent the corporation in the State of Indiana.

Neal's hand was finally forced, and he offered to provide the requested documents, but only on two conditions. First, any original documents not accepted into evidence must be returned uncopied. Because Ford was facing civil suits, the company did not want any evidence to find its way into the hands of potential plantiffs. Second, although Neal produced the documents from company files, he refused to admit that this act substantiated for legal purposes that the documents were in fact Ford's.

On Monday, January 7, Neal turned over two hefty cartons of Ford materials, but the issue of the documents' authenticity would not be settled until well into the trial, after much wrangling between the defense and the prosecution. Judge Staffeldt was reluctant to resolve the continuing dispute; when he did rule, he leaned toward Ford. "The party offering the evidence," he concluded, "must prove its authenticity."   Undeterred, Cosentino—reportedly at his own expense—arranged for civil lawyers to travel to Winamac; each lawyer would testify that in previous cases Ford had relinquished a specific document and had not challenged its authenticity. Cosentino also knew former Ford executives who could substantiate that they had seen the documents when in Ford's employment and could state that they recognized the signatures on these materials.[33]

Eventually Neal relented on the authentication issue, in part because Ford feared that public opinion might turn against the company for claiming that obviously genuine documents might have been forged. In the end, at any rate, the prosecution lawyers did not believe that the hassle over authenticating documents had a major bearing on the case's outcome.[34] Nonetheless, this issue quickly taught Cosentino that Jim Neal would use every legal maneuver to frustrate the prosecution and to drain their limited budget and energies. As Aubrey Harwell commented later, the firm of Neal and Harwell was a "legal machine" that knew how to use its immense resources to wear down the opposition.[35]

Indeed, Neal wasted little time at the trial before making a concerted effort to cripple Cosentino's case. He filed over fifteen motions *in limine*, that is, motions which attempt to restrict severely the kind of evidence that a prosecutor can introduce. Now that jury selection was completed, Judge Staffeldt announced that he would hear evidentiary arguments at 9:30 on Monday morning, January 14th. Opening statements to the jury would begin the next day.

Among Ford's many motions, two had the potential to constrain the prosecution so severely that the corporation's acquittal would virtually be assured. First, Neal noted, NHTSA had mandated that all 1977 model cars meet the standard of minimal fuel leakage in a 30-mph rear-end crash. In turn, Neal reasoned, this mandate suggested that in deciding whether Ford had constructed the Ulrichs' Pinto recklessly, the jury should consider only this federal standard. After all, as a national company, what would be more reasonable than to use uniform federal criteria to evaluate Ford's conduct? "One would think," Neal asserted, "if we met these standards we would not be subject to prosecution."

Cosentino realized that the entire prosecution was hanging in the balance. He believed that he had enough evidence to show that when Robert Duggar's van hit the Ulrichs' Pinto, it was moving about 35 mph faster than the Pinto. Yet if NHTSA's 30-mph standard was used to define "recklessness," then Ford was clearly off the hook. Neal's argument, however, was not new to the prosecution. In its attempt to quash the initial indictments, Ford had previously contended, though unsuccessfully, that the company could not be held accountable to individual state standards (see Chapter 5). The stakes were high, but at least the territory was familiar.

Bruce Berner, one of Cosentino's volunteer law professors, was assigned the task of arguing this critical issue. Federal regulations, he asserted, were not operative when the Ulrichs' 1973 Pinto was manufactured; they also served merely as *minimum* standards of acceptable conduct. The prosecution was prepared to show that during the Pinto's production a higher standard for fuel-system integrity—one which Ford chose to ignore—was technologically and economically feasible. More broadly, Berner contended that a federal regulation did not preempt a criminal statute in the State of Indiana. A jury of Indiana citizens, not Washington bureaucrats, should decide what constituted reckless homicide in the Hoosier State.

The prosecution was relieved when Staffeldt announced that he would permit the jury to set its own standards for determining whether Ford was reckless. To James Neal, the decision meant that the fight would continue. "If we had won that one," he observed, "we all could have gone home."[36]

A second critical motion remained to be resolved, however. Neal argued that the prosecution should be prohibited from introducing any evidence, including internal Ford memos and crash tests, that did not pertain specifically to the 1973 Pinto—the type of car involved in the Ulrichs' deaths. If Staffeldt accepted this reasoning, the prosecution would have only a shadow of its case. Cosentino did not possess data for relevant crash tests on the 1973 model, and his budget prevented him from having these tests conducted. More important, a ruling in Ford's favor would indicate that Staffeldt did not embrace, or perhaps even understand, the *theory* informing this corporate prosecution.

In a "normal" homicide, the specific characteristics of the murder weapon may be of special significance in establishing the guilt of the defendant: Did the weapon found at the scene of the crime belong to the defendant? Did it carry his or her fingerprints? Did anyone witness a smoking gun in the defendant's hands? In a case like the one against Ford, however, the key evidence was not simply the characteristics of the Pinto that the Ulrichs were driving or what Ford did in 1973 when it manufactured the vehicle. Equally salient, in the prosecution's view, was what the evidence revealed about the nature of Ford's conduct in designing and manufacturing its whole Pinto line and in failing subsequently to recall products—such as the Ulrichs' car—which the company knew were potentially dangerous. In this context, internal corporate documents and crash tests relating to 1971 and 1972 models as well as to later models were relevant, because they demonstrated the process by which the lethal defects in the 1973 Pinto's fuel system were created and then not repaired. In short, this material showed why Ford was reckless and could be blamed for the three teenagers' deaths.

To the prosecution's dismay, Judge Staffeldt ruled to exclude all documents that did not deal directly with the 1973 Pinto. "If I can't get that evidence admitted," Cosentino lamented, "I'll have a lot of problems." Yet not all was bleak; some hope was drawn from the judge's qualification that if Cosentino "could lay the proper foundation," evidence on other models might be admitted during the trial. Further, to the surprise and confusion of both the prosecution and defense, Staffeldt added that on all the day's rulings, he was "subject to changing [his] mind....We'll just take it a day at a time and a motion at a time."[37]

Thus, as Cosentino was about to bring his landmark case before the jury, he and his colleagues faced an uncertain future. After months of preparation, they had accumulated and analyzed numerous Ford memos and Pinto crash tests, and they were confident that with some effort they could authenticate these materials. Indeed, they felt that their case was compelling and that Ford's culpability in the Ulrichs' deaths could be documented amply. As the trial progressed, however, would Judge Staffeldt prove flexible and admit the prosecution's evidence? Would Cosentino have an opportunity to tell the jury the full Pinto story?[38]

Prosecuting Ford: Profits Over Lives

Although engaged in a complex corporate prosecution, Mike Cosentino felt that his case hinged on a simple but powerful truth: because Ford Motor Company had decided that fixing the Pinto was not cost-effective, three teenage girls had suffered needless, horrible deaths. The pictures of the Ulrichs' incinerated bodies had left an indelible mark on the consciousness of every member of the prosecution; they called them the "car wars photos." Despite all the talk of setting legal precedents and the constant media attention (Jim Neal said, "I've not seen anything like this since Watergate"), no one who had viewed the pictures could forget what this case was really about. Cosentino was fully prepared to have the jury face this reality; they, too, would be shown the "car wars photos."[39]

Neal, who knew how damaging the photos could be to Ford, took the offensive with a bold tactic to prevent the jury from seeing any photographs of the victims, living or dead. The defense would stipulate that the Ulrichs died from burns and not from injuries sustained in the crash (as might be expected in a high-speed collision). In light of this concession, Neal reasoned, there was no need for Cosentino to introduce any information about the girls' identities or to show gruesome photographs of incinerated bodies. Such evidence lacked probative value; indeed, its only purpose would be to prejudice the jury. Thus Neal entered a motion to prohibit the prosecution from making "any mention of any and all oral, documentary, physical and photographic evidence of the identities of the victims, their manner of death or the condition of the victims and their belongings during or after the accident."[40]

Learning of this motion on Monday, January 14, Cosentino had only until the next morning to develop a rationale for its denial. Bruce Berner quickly placed a call to his volunteer law students at Valparaiso University, and their research helped to uncover two cases that seemed to put the prosecution on firm legal ground. In one case, over which Judge Staffeldt had actually presided, an appeals court affirmed the judge's admission of gory autopsy pictures as prosecution evidence. A second court decision, handed down just two months before the start of the Pinto trial, was even more encouraging: a mother accused of child abuse stipulated that she had beaten her son, and her lawyer used this admission to claim that four photographs of the boy's battered body, taken at a hospital emergency room, should be excluded as prejudicial evidence. The mother then said that she would contest only the issue of her sanity. On appeal, the defense argued that the trial judge had erred in permitting the jury to view the four photographs. The appeals court, however, did not accept this logic, in part because it believed that evidence on all aspects of the case should be heard "where [the] State in prosecution...did not agree to [the] stipulation that [the] defendant would only contest [the] issue of her sanity."[41] This recent Indiana precedent suggested that unless the prosecution agreed, a defendant could not stipulate facts to prevent a jury from viewing photographs of a victim's injuries; armed with such a precedent, Cosentino seemed well prepared for the next day's skirmish.

In Tuesday morning's oral arguments, Bruce Berner contended that the "State has an obligation and right to prove every material element of the crime....In a criminal case, a defendant has two choices. He can plead guilty or not guilty. He cannot plead partially guilty." Citing the legal precedents uncovered in the prosecution's research, Berner added that regardless of Ford's stipulation, the obligation remained to present evidence on the cause of the Ulrichs' deaths. Staffeldt was unconvinced, however, embracing instead Jim Neal's position that the information on the girls would distract from "genuine issues," create a "melodramatic spectacle," and inflame the jury. Indeed, the judge accepted Ford's motion nearly intact, excluding not only the "car wars photos" but also all other pictures of and information about the girls.

After this session, an angry Cosentino commented to the media that "Ford has sanitized the State's case. We cannot show that they [the Ulrichs] were alive, and we cannot show that they died. We can't show what they looked like before; we can't show what they looked like after. We can't prove anything about the victims themselves and the victims are what this case is all about."

Yet Cosentino could not afford to dwell on this stinging defeat or, for that matter, on Staffeldt's previous ruling, which potentially excluded documents on non-1973 Pintos. A more pressing matter was at hand: in the afternoon session, he would present his opening arguments. This would be his first crack at the jury, and he faced the critical task of setting the proper tone and foundation for the prosecution's case.

In a presentation lasting almost an hour, Cosentino sent a clear message to the jury. "Ford management," he maintained, "deliberately chose profit over human life," and the Ulrich girls "needlessly died as a result of the callous, indifferent, and reckless acts and omissions of the defendant." Although they knew that the Pinto's gas tank was defective and "susceptible to an explosion equivalent to 250 sticks of dynamite," the company decided to market the car and to resist warning owners of the Pinto's inherent and potentially lethal dangers. Indeed, the Pinto "was designed with one thing in mind: profit, not safety."

Jim Neal then rose to unveil, in reporter Lee Strobel's words, "Ford's million dollar defense."[42] He began his 75-minute address by assertively challenging Cosentino's characterization of Ford. Although he admitted that Ford may have made mistakes or may have been wrong in some instances, he denied that "we are reckless killers." Neal then outlined nine considerations that would form the core of Ford's case. Once the defense had elaborated and substantiated these "facts," he declared confidently, the company's innocence would be beyond dispute:

1. The curbs on Highway 33 were badly designed, prevented the Ulrichs from pulling off the road, and thus contributed to the accident. Yet those who planned and approved the road's construction were not being held accountable for their negligence.

2. Robert Duggar, the driver of the van, was the primary cause of the accident, but he, too, was escaping trial.

3. Ford's 1973 Pinto met every government fuel safety standard.

4. For the 1973 model, Ford was the only automaker to have an internal company standard requiring fuel-system integrity for a rear-end crash (20-mph moving-barrier test).

5. The Pinto was comparable in design to other 1973 subcompacts.

6. As an indicator of the Pinto's safety, Ford engineering executives involved in the development of the car furnished Pintos for their wives and children.

7. Government statistics revealed that the Pinto was no more likely than other subcompacts to suffer from fires, and fared as well in collisions.

8. During the 41-day period in which Cosentino had to prove that Ford was reckless in not warning the Ulrichs of the Pinto's dangers, the company was undertaking a vigorous recall campaign.

9. Given the speed difference between the Ulrichs' subcompact Pinto and Duggar's heavy van—which was 50 mph, and not under 35 mph as the prosecution claimed—other subcompacts and many larger automobiles would also have suffered ruptured fuel systems.[43]

In closing his remarks, Neal asserted, carefully emphasizing each word, "*We are not reckless killers.*"

After the opening arguments were ended, Cosentino launched his case against Ford; his evidence would take over a month to present. He intended to prove Ford's guilt by establishing four broad points that, when taken together, revealed how the corporation's recklessness led to the Ulrichs' deaths.

First, Cosentino wanted to show that during the collision on Highway 33, the fuel system of the Ulrichs' Pinto had displayed a disquieting lack of structural integrity. Called to the stand as the State's lead witness, Trooper Neil Graves described how he had found a mixture of gas and water (from the fire hoses) in the front passenger compartment. Apparently, he testified, the fuel gushed into this area through a split in a seam connecting the wheel housing to the floor. The question of origins remained, however: where did the gasoline come from? Graves provided the obvious answer: the Pinto's fuel tank had ruptured. Although it had been filled only minutes before the accident, the eleven-gallon tank was almost empty. Clearly, the fuel had escaped through the "large gaping hole in the left side of the fuel tank." In a dramatic demonstration, Graves illustrated just how large this breach was. With the Pinto's scorched and mangled tank resting on a table before the jury, Graves placed his hand and then his forearm through the hole. After the accident, he said, this was how he determined the amount of gasoline left in the tank.

Mattie Ulrich, the mother of Judy and Lyn, was the prosecution's next witness. Her testimony would corroborate Cosentino's second point: before her daughters perished, the family had not been warned of the Pinto's hazards. Her presence meant more than this, however. For the most part, Neal had indeed succeeded in "sanitizing" the prosecution's case, but with Mattie Ulrich in the courtroom, the jurors would be reminded—concretely and vividly—of the enormous loss suffered in the accident.

"Yes, sir," she replied softly, when asked if she had ever received a Pinto recall notice from Ford. Then, revealing a tragic irony that shocked the courtroom's packed audience, she noted quietly that the company's letter arrived in February 1979, six months after the fiery crash that took her daughters' lives. And if the warning about the Pinto's dangers had come earlier? "I would have gotten rid of it," she answered dramatically. "I would not have let the girls drive it that evening." Her words left the court-room hushed and filled with tension.

Cosentino moved next to support the prosecution's third major con-tention: the difference in speed between the Ulrichs' Pinto and Duggar's van was no more than 30 to 35 mph. This empirical issue was critical to the prosecution's case. If it could be established that a rear-end crash at this relatively low speed had transformed the teenagers' Pinto into a flaming death trap, then a compelling argument could be made that the car's fuel system was designed recklessly and did not meet acceptable safety stan-dards. By contrast, if the speed difference between the Pinto and the van had approached 50 mph—as Neal contended—then the fire could be at-tributed to the force of the impact and not to the fuel system's lack of in-tegrity. Any subcompact hit by a heavy van at that speed, Ford could argue persuasively, would have suffered the same fate.

Cosentino was confident, however, that the prosecution's assessment of the speed difference would be sustained; after all, he had six eyewitnesses to the crash as well as other convincing evidence.

Albert Clark was the first of his eyewitnesses to take the stand. "It was—I'm an ex-GI—like a large napalm bomb," he said, "It just blew up." But what was the crash like? Although the windows were down in Clark's mini motor home, the impact "was not that terrific...I heard no noise...I thought it was going to be a fender-bender." Clark then estimated that Duggar's van was traveling 40 to 45 mph, and the girls' Pinto 30 to 35 mph—a difference of only 5 to 15 mph. "Will you ever forget that day?" asked Cosentino. Remembering the sight of Judy Ulrich as he tried to pull her free of the Pinto, Clark answered softly, struggling to hold back tears, "No...no."

One by one, the other eyewitnesses confirmed Clark's version of the acci-dent. They agreed that the van's speed did not exceed 50 mph. The Pinto's exact velocity was less clear; but everyone agreed that the car was moving at a minimum of 15 mph. The calculations were clear: the maximum speed difference was 35 mph. In addressing the other issue—the horror of the ac-cident—each witness relived that moment, often at an emotional cost. It was "like a bomb blowing up," recalled teenager Yolanda Ihrig. College professor William Martin told a similar story. "I could look directly into the front windshield area of the Pinto," he commented. "I saw a solid mass of orange flames. There was absolutely no air space in the passenger compartment." Later, with the jury dismissed from the courtroom, he told about seeing Judy Ulrich on the ground, "supporting herself on her arms." Visibly upset, Martin added, "It shocked me that a person could be so incredibly burned and be alive."

The prosecution was optimistic; the eyewitnesses were persuasive and unshaken by Neal's cross-examination. The evidence indicated that the Ulrichs' Pinto had been moving when hit and had exploded "like a bomb" at a speed difference that was unacceptably low.

Cosentino wished to maintain the prosecution's advantage by solidifying this image in the jurors' minds. Robert Duggar, he believed, would help him do so. Now twenty-two and a freshman at a small Michigan college, Duggar testified that he had been driving at 50 mph; he had checked his speed after passing a police car equipped with radar. After recounting the moments before the crash—how he had glanced toward the van's floor to locate a fallen cigarette pack, only to look up and find "the Pinto ten feet in front of me"—he estimated the Pinto's speed at 15 to 20 mph. "I hit the Pinto and smelled gasoline," he said. And then what happened? "Before I could think, there was a fire. The whole car was on fire."

Cosentino had one final piece of evidence to support the prosecution's version of the difference in speed between the two vehicles. Thus far, he had based his proof on the subjective assessments of the witnesses to the crash; now he would provide some hard scientific data. When asked to describe the nature and origin of the bodily trauma suffered by the Ulrichs, Goshen radiologist Sean Gunderson testified that no life-threatening physical damage could be traced to the impact of the crash. This conclusion was corroborated by Dr. Robert J. Stein and Dr. James A. Benz, who presented the dramatic findings of the autopsies they had conducted on the exhumed bodies of Judy and Lyn Ulrich. Stein, who conducted Judy Ulrich's autopsy, testified that she had sustained no internal injuries; Benz revealed that Lyn, who had sat in the back seat of the Pinto, suffered only a few minor broken bones and did not show the kind of spinal-cord damage that typically occurs in a high-speed rear-end accident. Thus Cosentino's scientific experts were in agreement that if not for the girls' burns, the girls would be alive. Again, the point was clear: because the force of the collision did not cause serious physical injuries, the crash must have occurred at a relatively low speed.

After two weeks of testimony, Cosentino was satisfied that he had established three key points: during the accident, the fuel system of the Ulrichs' Pinto lacked structural integrity; Ford Motor Company did not warn Mattie Ulrich of the Pinto's inherent dangers until after her daughters' deaths; and the maximum speed difference between the van and the Pinto was approximately 35 mph. Yet, as Cosentino understood, "the meat—the heart of the

State's case" remained. In order to make a convincing case, the prosecution had to support a fourth point: Ford knew of the Pinto's safety hazards and had economically feasible technology to prevent and rectify the fuel system's defects. Byron Bloch and Harley Copp, both of whom had testified in previous civil cases against Ford, could be counted on to lend credence to this contention. Yet the critical evidence—the crash tests and the internal Ford documents that Terry Kiely had analyzed diligently and arranged to tell the "Pinto story"—had yet to be admitted as evidence. Although Cosentino felt that he could fulfill Judge Staffeldt's requirement that he lay a "proper foundation" for these materials, he had also learned that little was certain in a precedent-setting corporate prosecution.

Byron Bloch, a safety consultant based in West Los Angeles, was a veteran not only of past Pinto cases but also of an array of product liability suits. Cosentino intended to use Bloch as an auto safety "expert" who could verify the nature of the Pinto's defects; in his week-long testimony, Bloch undertook this task vigorously. With the help of a rear section of a 1973 Pinto which Cosentino purchased for $100 and brought into the courtroom, Bloch showed the jurors the "hostile environment" that surrounded the car's gas tank and made it excessively vulnerable to punctures, rips, and tears. He also used color slides of the Ulrichs' Pinto to explain how the tank had ruptured and how the "filler tube definitely pulled out of the gas tank," allowing fuel to "whoosh out." Then Bloch asserted that the Pinto's hazards were avoidable. Backing Cosentino's claim that Ford's use of "state-of-the-art" technology would have created a much safer fuel system, he listed a number of models that located the gas tank above or forward of the axle rather than (as in the Pinto) behind the axle and close to the bumper. Most revealing, he observed, Ford itself had used an above-axle or forward-of-the-axle design in its late-1950s Skyliner, its pre-Pinto Capri, and its more recent Fiesta. In light of these considerations, did Ford "deviate substantially from acceptable standards of conduct" in designing and marketing the Pinto? Bloch's conclusion was clear: "Yes. Ford Motor Company did deviate."

Although he educated the jurors about the technical aspects of the Pinto and fuel-system safety, Bloch proved ultimately to be a disappointing prosecution witness. The defense had systematically investigated Bloch's background and testimony in previous product liability cases, and now Neal was well equipped to discredit his "expert" opinions. One strategy was to force Bloch to admit that "95 percent of all American cars had the gas tank flat behind the axle as it was in the 1973 Pinto." If the Pinto was comparable to other 1973 models, Neal reasoned, then how could Bloch claim that it "deviated" from the automotive industry's standards? "They were all bad," was the best answer Bloch could muster—though Cosentino offered a more compelling response: "It's a typical tactic of defendants to say that 'Everybody else did it, so we can do it too.'"

Neal's second line of attack was even more damaging. The defense's research into Bloch's past revealed inconsistencies between the academic credentials listed on his resumé and those he had actually earned. Neal also noted that Bloch had testified as a safety "expert" on a wide range of products (e.g., coffee percolators, garbage trucks, hospital tables, train accidents), and in 1976 had advertised a combination cocktail party and seminar with the promise of showing lawyers "how to expand accident cases into product liability cases." As reporters James Warren and Brian Kelly observed, this evidence succeeded in portraying Bloch as a "mercenary consultant."[44] After all, Neal remarked, "if a man advertises how he can expand accidents into product liability cases, it seems obvious to me he's got an axe to grind."

Heading into the final stages of his case, Cosentino realized that much would hinge on the effectiveness of his next witness, former Ford executive Harley Copp. Now that Bloch's testimony was tainted, Copp would have to convince the jury that Ford knew about and could have restricted the Pinto's defects. Further, Cosentino was counting on Copp's expert testimony to lay the foundation for the admission into evidence of non-1973 Pinto documents.

As mentioned, Cosentino had been thwarted substantially in his attempts to show the jury why the prosecution blamed Ford's recklessness for the Ulrichs' deaths. Until this point in the case, Cosentino's tenacity regarding the evidence had resulted in only one major breakthrough. Over Neal's strong objections, Judge Staffeldt had admitted NHTSA's letter of May 1978 to Lee Iacocca, which informed Ford that it would hold hearings on recalling the Pinto because "when impacted by a full-sized vehicle from the rear, the 1971-1976 Pinto demonstrates a 'fire threshold' at closing speeds between 30 and 35 miles per hour." More controversial, however, was Staffeldt's permitting the jury to see the technical "investigation report" attached to the letter. As noted in Chapter 4, this report contained the crash test data—ten tests conducted on 1971, 1972, 1974, and 1976 Pintos—which led NHTSA to "its initial determination of the existence of a safety related defect." Although apparently he had not read the report, the judge said that he would "take a chance on this one" and let the jury view the letter and report; according to his rationale, the NHTSA material revealed Ford's knowledge that the government believed the Pinto was defective before the Ulrichs' accident. Given the grounds for this decision, Staffeldt also instructed the jury not to assume that the technical information in the report was necessarily accurate.

To be sure, the crash test data were an immeasurable help to the prosecution's case, but these data were only suggestive. In themselves they did not establish the extent of Ford's awareness of the Pinto's dangers, nor did they confirm that its executives had made a conscious decision to place profits over human safety. To prove Ford's motives, Cosentino knew that he would still have to convince Staffeldt to let the jury see the company's internal documents. Moreover, Cosentino wanted the judge to approve his showing the jury movies of rear-end crash tests, in which 1971 and 1972 Pintos exploded into raging infernos when struck at 35 mph. These vivid sights, he believed, would be far more powerful than sterile reports in forcing the jurors to consider why the Ulrichs' Pinto had burst into flames.

Thus, as Harley Copp took the stand, both sides were aware that he held the key to the prosecution's case. Cosentino began by establishing Copp's credentials: he had been employed by Ford since the 1940s, had risen to the number-six position in the company as an executive testing engineer, and had been forced into retirement at age 55, four years earlier, after giving safety lectures critical of the automotive industry. (Ford cited "excessive and unauthorized absences" as the reason for his dismissal.) Clearly, Copp had the engineering expertise and the first-hand knowledge to tell the Pinto story.

Now came the crucial point in Copp's testimony. Asked how new models were developed, Copp explained that automakers use a "cycle plan," in which the car's structure remained the same throughout the model's existence. Apart from cosmetic or stylistic changes, as the cycle progressed only minor structural changes were made based on the car's performance in its earliest years.

Cosentino had the opening he needed: How long was the Pinto's cycle? How long did Ford plan to keep the same fuel system? "I believe it was for the life of the vehicle," Copp responded, "ten years." Copp then discussed the obvious implication of this remark, noting that all Pinto models were essentially the same car. A left-side frame rail was added to the 1973 make; even so, he observed, this rail increased the crashworthiness of the fuel system only from 21 to 25 mph.

Cosentino believed that he had succeeded at last in laying the foundation that would enable the bulk of his documents to be admitted as evidence. After all, it seemed irrefutable that if the Pinto's structure and fuel system remained unchanged, materials on non-1973 Pintos should be admitted as evidence. In particular, crash tests and company memoranda related to pre-1973 models should be relevant because the structure of the Ulrichs' 1973 Pinto had been determined during these years.

Judge Staffeldt, however, remained unconvinced. "I don't know what more knowledge you want [to show the jury] than that they [Ford] produced that [the Ulrichs' 1973] automobile. I don't think that these things should be admitted because they allow the jury to speculate. The only thing important here is if what they failed to warn [about] caused the deaths."

"How can you lay a better foundation than we did with Copp?" Cosentino challenged. "[Ford] built a bomb in '71 and '72 and they know it. That's why they don't want it known." Refusing to budge, Staffeldt countered, "This is a criminal case, not a product liability case. Strict construction should be involved here."

Neal moved to reinforce the judge's view. As news reporters noted, Neal had developed a special rapport with Staffeldt. Whether because of the defense attorney's charm, his reputation, or his ideology, Staffeldt had "become unusually aware of Neal," even to the point of "openly anticipating objections from Neal as Cosentino presented his case." As one reporter quipped, "You'd think we were at an art auction. Maybe the judge and Neal have a set of secret signals." Most important, Staffeldt appeared to defer to Neal and to give him wide latitude in shaping the direction of the trial. "All this," observed reporters James Warren and Brian Kelly, "allowed Neal to define the case almost as he wanted."[45]

Thus Neal bolstered Staffeldt's strict constructionist interpretation of what constituted relevant evidence. "I am concerned this will turn into a broad general examination of how a car is made or should be made," he said. "This is a criminal case." The prosecution, Neal warned, was trying to use criminal charges against Ford as a "Trojan horse" in their effort to criminalize the whole realm of product design. He concluded, "that's why I thought this case never should have been brought."

With so much at stake, the prosecution persisted. Terry Kiely took his turn: "Mr. Neal, Your Honor, would have you believe that they can make this car over the weekend. Ford had this knowledge [about the Pinto's fuel system] for years. They kept it from the public and tried to keep it from the federal government until they were pressured to recall the Pinto." As usual, Neal responded by narrowing the focus of the case. "The issue," he reasserted, "is did we recklessly fail to warn how this car [the Ulrichs' Pinto] was built....We are charged with what this car is, and was—not what might have been. This car might have been a horse." Kiely replied, "Yes, it might have been a horse. But it could also have been a car that didn't incinerate three girls. The issue is what are acceptable standards of conduct."

The prosecution's arguments, however, were ineffective. Staffeldt even remarked "that there has been a lot of [prosecutorial] evidence admitted that probably should not have been admitted." A despondent Cosentino could only comment, "I don't know what I'll do now." Later he complained to the press that out of the plethora of documents, government reports, and internal Ford memos that the prosecution had compiled by the start of the trial—including the materials analyzed by Terry Kiely—only ten or twelve had been admitted. "We are not getting our story told," he continued. "We have a case, but we are being handicapped. It's like fighting a battle with one hand tied behind your back."

Sensing that his opponent was ready for a knockout, Jim Neal was quick to capitalize on the situation. Walking by Cosentino in the hallway of the courthouse, he taunted in a sing-song voice, "Don't lose your cool. Don't lose your cool." Still Cosentino and his crew of volunteers had come too far to throw in the towel. At first, they contemplated requesting a mistrial based on Staffeldt's rulings. This was dismissed as unfeasible; even if it succeeded, the resources simply were not available to support another trial. Instead, they would rely on Harley Copp to tell the Pinto's history. Without the documents, the story would be less compelling, but as a former Ford executive, Copp might have enough credibility to convince the jury of the company's recklessness. After all, Copp had been a devastating witness in Ford's loss of the Grimshaw civil case.

Copp did not disappoint. Following Cosentino's lead, he substantiated the prosecution's key accusations against Ford: because of intense foreign competition and at Lee Iacocca's urgings, the Pinto's parameters were set at an upper limit of $2,000 and 2,000 pounds, and subsequently the car was rushed into production without proper testing. Ford officials knew about the problems of the fuel system, and for $6.65 per car could have increased the Pinto's ability to withstand rear-end-crash fuel leakage from 20 mph to 30 mph. This proposal was rejected on the basis of "cost and the effect on profitability." In short, to enhance company profits, Ford executives allowed an "unreasonably dangerous" Pinto to be manufactured and to remain on the road.

With the help of Copp's testimony, Cosentino had been able to tell the jury the Pinto's story, but once again, this account lacked the depth and force he had anticipated. It remained uncertain how many jurors were convinced of Ford's recklessness and how their inclinations would be shaped by Neal's upcoming defense. Despite these misgivings, however, the prosecution remained optimistic. They had overcome many obstacles before the trial, and now had survived Neal's best attempts to prevent them from portraying Ford as a reckless killer. They hoped the jury might have heard enough to blame the automaker for the Ulrichs' deaths. Indeed, even Judge Staffeldt agreed that the issue of Ford's guilt should be left in the jury's hands; he rejected Neal's motion for a directed verdict of not guilty on the grounds that the prosecution had not proven its case. Ford Motor Company would still have to defend itself against charges of reckless homicide.

Defending Ford: The Legal Machine Responds

As Aubrey Harwell observed, Mike Cosentino was pitted against a "legal machine." He was not only facing one of the nation's best trial lawyers in Jim Neal; he also had to confront a firm with the skill and experience to keep constant pressure on an adversary by using the vast resources at its disposal. Already, Neal and Harwell had shrewdly deployed their assets to defend Ford and keep the prosecution off balance. They had wisely hired consultant Hans Zeisel, who provided testimony that helped to win a change of venue and who assisted in the critical task of jury selection. They retained Lester Wilson, Judge Staffeldt's former office mate, to give Ford a respected local representative. Further, before coming to Winamac, Neal and Harwell's research staff had become a "brief factory," producing the legal reasoning and written documents which later persuaded Staffeldt to limit the evidence that Cosentino could present to the jury.[46] Indeed, though Cosentino was able to fend off several of these attacks, the defense's meticulously planned legal maneuvers had severely constrained his case. As he often lamented, he could not tell the jurors the full Pinto story.

Neal and Harwell would continue to benefit by their demand that nothing be overlooked or left to chance. In the preceding months, the defense's preparation had ranged from costly crash tests to an exhaustive investigation of everyone even remotely associated with the accident. The result was a formidable defense, bolstered at key points by surprising testimony.

On Wednesday, February 13, Neal opened Ford's defense with a dramatic witness, Levi Woodard. Now employed in a Michigan hospital, Woodard had been working as an orderly at Elkhart General Hospital the night of the Ulrichs' accident. Unknown to Cosentino, he had been called to Judy's side when she asked, "Does anyone know Jesus? Can anyone here say Bible verses?" As a Seventh Day Adventist, Woodard comforted her; he also talked with her about the events on Highway 33.

Until this point, no one had explained why the Ulrichs were driving away from rather than toward Goshen, where their church volleyball game was scheduled. Woodard unraveled this mystery. Judy explained that after they had stopped at a self-service gas station, they had left the cap to the gas tank on the roof. Seeing it fly off the roof and roll across the highway, she had made a U-turn to retrieve the cap and had put on her emergency flashers. Then Woodard offered a shocking revelation: Judy said that when hit by Duggar's van, her Pinto was "*stopped* beside the cap to get it." Neal argued that this was why the gas cap was found near the place where the van first struck the Pinto rather than down the road, where the car eventually came to rest. Moreover, Neal reasoned, Woodard's testimony exonerated

Ford: any small compact car stopped on the road and hit by a 4,000-pound van traveling at 50 mph would have exploded.

Cosentino felt that Woodard's story could be disproved by the testimony of his six eyewitnesses, all of whom had said that the Pinto was moving when struck by the van. Yet he was concerned that doubts may have been raised in the jurors' minds and that the prosecution's credibility had been shaken by its obvious failure to interview Woodard during its investigation. A lesser opponent, however, would never have produced Woodard. Indeed, he was discovered only after an arduous search. Operating on a tip that someone named "Levi" had talked with Judy Ulrich, Harwell learned Woodard's full identity only after calling a former Elkhart nurse doing missionary work in Costa Rica; she gave him the name of another person who knew Woodard's name. Because Woodard was not listed in any telephone directory, Harwell dispatched two investigators—Thomas Dundon and former Dallas Cowboy Richmond Flowers—to find their potential witness. As Neal commented, "We traced him to a cabin in the woods near Levering on the first day of the Michigan deer hunting season. Have you ever heard what it's like walking through the woods when Michigan opens its deer season? The guys all wore big red hats. But they finally found Levi—and Aubrey came in with the evidence."[47]

Having started his case with a bang, Neal wanted to establish a key technical point: Ford was not a reckless manufacturer because the Pinto's fuel system was comparable to that of other 1973 compacts. To substantiate this claim, Neal convinced Staffeldt to allow the jury to view the rear ends of four cars (a Dodge Colt, a Chevy Vega, a Toyota Corolla, and an AMC Gremlin) that he had brought into the basement of the courthouse. Douglas W. Toms, the director of NHTSA from 1969 to 1973, was then called in to show the jurors that all the vehicles' gas tanks were located in the same general place as the Pinto's: behind the rear axle. On the stand, Toms testified further that he was "amazed" that the Pinto had been recalled, because it "did not substantially deviate" from acceptable industry standards. "It would be my opinion," he concluded, "that it was a very conventional automobile."

Reinforcing this line of reasoning, Tom Sneva, the first driver to break the 200-mph barrier at the Indianapolis 500, argued that it was safer to place a car's gas tank behind the axle. An over-the-axle design, he claimed, redistributed a car's weight and made handling more hazardous. Moreover, fuel-tank bladders, which the prosecution contended were an inexpensive means of preventing gas leakage, were costly: the one in his racing car cost $3,700.

Ford's next witness, though less famous, was also prepared to defend the company's decision not to fortify the Pinto's fuel system. Donald Huelke, a

University of Michigan anatomy professor and a Ford consultant from 1964 to 1973, observed that deaths from rear-end collisions were rare events and not a major safety hazard. As a result, in his advisory capacity, he did not warn Ford that "fires on rear-end impact were a problem in the real world."

Neal's witnesses had clearly scored points on the technical issues. If nothing else, they had shown that determining where to place a gas tank is a complex decision that requires considering a number of variables. Moreover, Toms had laid the groundwork for a key element of Ford's defense: the Pinto's design was not radically different from that of other subcompacts.

In cross-examination, however, the prosecution was able to minimize the potential damage of this testimony. One strategy, which Cosentino used throughout the trial, was to show that the witnesses had a conflict of interest because at one time or another they had financial ties to Ford. Huelke had been a consultant, Sneva had driven Ford cars, and Toms's recreational vehicle company currently did a "substantial" business with the automaker. In addition, deputy prosecutors Terry Kiely and Terry Shewmaker chipped away at the witnesses' substantive testimony. Toms, for instance, admitted that it was unusual for NHTSA to recommend a recall, that he was not "personally aware" that Ford's Capri could withstand a 44-mph rear-end crash, and that Ford (like other automakers) lobbied against safety standards. Sneva revealed that the use of a fuel tank bladder had limited leakage in one of his racing accidents, and that the Indianapolis 500 Technical Committee had required drivers to insert bladders as a protective measure. Huelke conceded that he had conducted his research on rear-end fires before the production of the 1973 Pinto; furthermore, he did not know that more people died each year from such fires than from airplane accidents.

At this point, Neal decided to call to the stand Ford executives involved in the Pinto's production. He understood well the risks of this maneuver: it would give Cosentino an opportunity to question the executives in an open court before the nation's media. A misstatement or a fumbled answer could lead the jurors to impute culpability to the entire corporation and could result in news reports damaging Ford's reputation. Yet Neal also realized that much could be won if a confident and unapologetic Ford representative came willingly before the court. On the one hand, such an appearance would counteract the jurors' tendency to see Ford as an impersonal corporation; now they would have to ask themselves if the respectable person before them was a reckless killer. On the other hand, Neal feared that if he did not call someone directly associated with the Pinto to testify, Cosentino would ask why "Ford" was afraid to take the stand. Did they have something to hide? The implication would be clear: only guilty defendants remain silent and "seated at the side" of their high-priced attorneys.

Fortunately for Neal, he had the ideal candidate for Ford's corporate representative: Harold C. MacDonald, vice-president of engineering and research. A sixty-two-year-old grandfather of five and church deacon, MacDonald was Ford's engineer in charge of all passenger cars—including the Pinto—built in the United State from 1965 to 1975. In an obvious attempt to counter Cosentino's depiction of the Pinto as Lee Iacocca's car, Neal referred to MacDonald as the "father of the Pinto." He also told reporters that "big companies are made up of people like Mr. MacDonald—good decent people, people doing the best they can in a difficult world."[48] Decent people may make mistakes, but they do not recklessly endanger the lives of teenagers in the crass pursuit of profits.

Showing the human dimension of the automaking industry, MacDonald explained why he had a "great personal concern about the placement of the fuel tank in the 1973 Pinto." In 1932, his father had been burned to death when his Model A Ford hit a tree. The gas tank, located between the engine and the passenger compartment—almost in his "father's lap"—had exploded upon impact. This event convinced MacDonald that the fuel system should be placed "as far from the passenger compartment as possible"; the Pinto, with its tank behind the rear axle, met this criterion.

Personal history aside, MacDonald was proud of the Pinto and ready to defend its record. First, he denied Harley Copp's charge that the Pinto was ever "locked into" the $2,000 and 2,000-pound limits—the rigid standards reportedly dictated by Lee Iacocca. Second, he felt that the car's fuel system was "reasonably safe." After all, the Pinto in question met all 1973 federal regulations, and even satisfied a voluntary internal Ford standard that the car be able to withstand a 20-mph rear-end collision from a moving barrier—a standard that no other American automaker had in force. Moreover, objective statistical data confirmed his assessment of the Pinto's safety. A 1975-1976 federal study indicated that Pintos constituted 1.9 percent of all cars on the nation's highways and were involved in 1.9 percent of all fatal accidents involving fire. Clearly, a recklessly designed car would have been overrepresented rather than represented proportionately in its share of such fatalities. Third, from an engineering perspective, MacDonald believed that placing the tank above the axle was not desirable. The danger of this design, he claimed, was that during a collision, the tank was more vulnerable to puncture by unsecured items inside the trunk. Fourth, and perhaps MacDonald's most convincing testimony that he believed in the Pinto's safety, he drove a 1973 Pinto and had bought one for his son.

Cosentino quickly launched a vigorous cross-examination. He began by demonstrating MacDonald's personal stake in Ford's well-being. In the previous year, he had been paid $195,000 in salary and another $200,000 in bonuses; he also owned nearly $450,000 in company stocks. Cosentino then disputed the Pinto's safety record by introducing statistics indicating that the Pinto was not represented proportionately in fatal rear-end accidents in which a fire occurred—as Ford claimed—but rather was involved in such accidents two times more often than would normally be expected. The data showed that by 1976, Pintos comprised 3.5 percent of all automobiles on U.S. roads, yet were involved in seven percent of these fatal fire crashes. MacDonald responded weakly, "I am not familiar with those statistics." He also admitted he did not know that the Pinto was the only 1973 subcompact recalled by the government. Cosentino continued to score points for the prosecution when MacDonald said that he did not believe Ford could have built a 1973 Pinto that would be able to withstand a rear-end collision at 43 or 44 mph. This statement presented Cosentino with the opportunity to show the jury a 1969 advertisement in which Ford stated that its Capri, manufactured in Great Britain, could indeed safely withstand impact at this speed. Finally, Cosentino made an observation about Ford's internal standard requiring the Pinto's fuel system to have integrity in a 20-mph moving-barrier rear-end crash test: in an equivalent highway crash, the car would begin to leak fuel if hit at a speed greater than 26 to 28 mph.[49] "But," Cosentino asked, "didn't this mean that it could not withstand a collision at the 30-mph speed limit on most residential streets?" And when Ford recalled the Pinto, did they ever warn consumers, such as the Ulrichs, that their vehicles were "subject to fire on rear-end impact" if hit at a speed greater than 28 mph?

In response, Jim Neal called a series of witnesses to repair the damage done by Cosentino's cross-examination. Two Ford engineering executives came forward to testify that they allowed family members to drive Pintos. Particularly effective was James G. Olson, who had bought a 1973 Pinto for his eighteen-year-old daughter—the same age as Judy and Donna Ulrich. "Would you have purchased it if you didn't think it was safe?" asked Neal. "Most certainly not," replied Olson.

James J. Schultz, a twenty-four year Chrysler employee now employed by a California engineering firm, reiterated that the Pinto was "certainly comparable, and in some respects was superior" to other subcompacts. He also contended that his analysis of the evidence led him to conclude that the Ulrichs' Pinto was stopped and hit at a speed of 60 mph. The car's structure, he added, "did quite well in light of the speeds involved." Cosentino succeeded, however, in diminishing Schultz's credibility. He showed not only that Schultz was being paid $41 an hour for his testimony (and that another $24 was going to the firm he represented), but also that Ford's "expert" witness did not know at what speed the Pinto experienced hazardous gas leakages. Further, Schultz claimed that when a 1973 Pinto was hit from behind by a moving barrier at a test speed of 21 mph, the welds on the floorpan would not split and make it possible for fuel to spill into the passenger compartment. This claim contradicted earlier testimony by Harold Mac-Donald, "the father of the Pinto," who had admitted that such splits were possible. An elated Cosentino announced to reporters, "I think the state's case against Ford is getting better with every witness Ford produces."

Engineering vice-president Thomas J. Feaheny was brought forward to explain why Ford recalled the Pinto. He asserted that the company did not recall the car because it was dangerous, but only because adverse publicity about the Pinto's alleged fuel-system defects had become "a critical problem—damaging our corporate reputation." By reaching an agreement with NHTSA on how to modify the Pinto, he continued, Ford felt "it would reassure our owners and the public of the company's good intentions on the matter." To substantiate this claim, Feaheny produced 1975-1976 data revealing that the Pinto had a similar if not a lower incidence of fire-related crashes during that time than five other subcompacts. He also testified that this information was compiled because of escalating public concern, and was presented to Ford's Board of Directors in March 1978. In light of the data, the corporation's "state of mind" was that the Pinto was as safe as comparable subcompacts.

Again, Cosentino was able to blunt the effectiveness of the prosecution's witness. He forced Feaheny to state that he was unaware of government statistics indicating that the Pinto's fuel system was more fire-prone in rear-end collisions than other models in its class. More important, Feaheny conceded that he did not inform the company's directors about Ford's own crash tests, which showed that a 1973 Pinto would suffer fuel leakage at relatively low speeds.

Neal now embarked on a second line of attack against the prosecution's case. Thus far, he had attempted to show that the Ulrich teenagers did not die because Ford had designed their Pinto's fuel system recklessly. The testimony, he hoped, had established three major conclusions: the speed difference between Duggar's van and the Ulrichs' Pinto was so great that any car would have exploded in flames; Ford had complied with all federal regulations and the Pinto was comparable to other subcompacts; and the good people at Ford, including engineers directly involved in the Pinto's production, believed so strongly in the car's safety that they purchased Pintos for their spouses and children. Yet, even if the jurors were unconvinced of these points, Ford's conviction on charges of reckless homicide did not necessarily follow. According to pretrial rulings (as discussed in Chapter 5), the prosecution had to demonstrate that Ford had not only built a dangerous vehicle but also had been reckless in its failure to recall the Pinto during the forty-one days between the implementation of Indiana's reckless homicide statute and the Ulrichs' deaths on August 10, 1978.

Fortuitous circumstances made this side of the prosecution's case especially vulnerable to attack. On June 9, 1978—three weeks *before* the Indiana statute took effect—Ford had agreed with NHTSA to recall the Pinto. As a result, a full recall effort was under way throughout the forty-one-day period in which the company's recklessness was in question. Furthermore, Neal was prepared to show that Ford had done "everything possible" to contact Pinto owners, including the Ulrichs.

Ronald Hoffman, a thirty-two-year-old supervisor with Ford's parts and services division, testified that once the decision to recall the Pinto had been made, he was told to "drop what I was doing and work on this as quickly as possible....We did everything we could, with no cost constraints and no time constraints, in order to get this done as quickly as possible." Although the company worked around the clock and even hired planes to rush parts to dealers, Hoffman noted, the recall was a complicated task that required time to complete. Not only did the addresses of Pinto owners have to be traced, but the kits used to modify the Pinto had to be manufactured. These kits contained sixteen pieces, including a longer filler tube and a plastic shield to prevent tank punctures. These items were not ready to be shipped until August 9, one day before the Ulrichs' deaths. Recall notices were not distributed until later that month. The first person to own the Ulrichs' Pinto was sent a letter on August 22.

Neal's advantage dissipated quickly, however. In a surprise move, Cosentino attempted to introduce evidence that in February 1973 Ford was convicted of 350 criminal counts of filing false reports to the Environmental Protection Agency and was fined a total of $7 million (3.5 million in criminal penalties and 3.5 million in civil damages). This crime occurred in 1972, when Ford performed unauthorized maintenance on test vehicles and submitted falsified data certifying that the emission levels of its 1973-model-year cars (including the Pinto) met the standards prescribed by the 1968 Clean Air Act.

This evidence should be admitted, the prosecution argued, for three reasons. First, although prior convictions normally could not be used in court because they would bias a jury unduly against a defendant, Indiana law stated that such convictions were admissible when they were related to a defendant's reputation for truthfulness, and that a court had no discretion to exclude "anything having to do with false and fictitious representations" by a defendant. Clearly, Ford's attempt to deceive the EPA fell into this category. Second, the convictions were related directly to 1973 models and thus met Staffeldt's demand that the prosecution restrict evidence to the year in which the Ulrichs' Pinto was manufactured. Third, because Ford executives were testifying on behalf of the company—and were portrayed as "churchgoers" and "family men"—the prosecution had the right to impeach

their testimony by introducing evidence regarding Ford's corporate character. "The jury," Bruce Berner told Staffeldt, "has the right to know that
Ford has not been truthful in the past." By contrast, Neal argued that it was
inappropriate to use information about a corporation to cast suspicion on
the testimony of an individual.

After hearing legal arguments for over an hour, Staffeldt announced that
although this was "a novel question of law," he would admit the evidence on
Ford's convictions because it tended to show "the poor reputation of the
defendant for truth and veracity." The jurors were then allowed to read the
details of Ford's earlier brush with the law.

Neal immediately took steps to reaffirm the integrity of Ford's corporate
character. Herbert Misch, a company vice-president, was called to explain
what had transpired. He stated that only lower-echelon employees had falsified records, and no one who had testified in the current case was involved. More instructive, after the matter was brought to his attention,
Misch met with Henry Ford II, who told him "to investigate this and make
it right." In turn, the company notified EPA of the misinformation and
eventually pleaded "no contest" to the criminal charges.

Outside the courtroom, the usually restrained Neal was "openly dis-
tressed" about Staffeldt's ruling. In a "booming voice" he vigorously defended Ford's handling of the EPA situation. Noting that his client "blew
the whistle" on itself, he claimed that this was "not only Ford Motor Company's but American industry's finest hour....All these people [who] go
around talking about immorality should applaud, not condemn us." Privately, however, Neal was worried that even though Ford admitted its EPA
transgressions, the evidence might prove "devastating." As one of his associates commented, "You can imagine what this will do to the jury—to continually hear how we were convicted for lying about our 1973 cars."

Indeed, the second week of the defense's case had not gone well. Although Hoffman's testimony on Ford's recall efforts was persuasive,
Cosentino had effectively cross-examined several witnesses—most notably
Harold MacDonald, proclaimed by Neal himself to be "the Pinto's father"—and had won a rare legal victory on the EPA convictions. Cosentino
had reason to tell reporters that "our case gets stronger and stronger as the
defense continues. The longer this trial goes, the better I feel."

Over the weekend, however, Neal worked to halt the prosecution's mo-
mentum. He captured the attention of the press by promising to close his
defense the following week with a "bomb." Headlines were no longer reporting, "Week's Testimony Shakes Ford's Pinto Defense" or "Ford Lawyer
Becomes Upset." Instead, everyone was waiting to learn "how he would
produce a document this week which would devastate the prosecution's case
like a 'bomb.'"[50] Jim Neal had a history of fulfilling his promises.

On Monday, February 25, Herbert Misch continued his testimony. Building on Hoffman's earlier description of Ford's recall efforts, Misch noted not only that everything possible was being done to notify Pinto owners but also that the whole recall effort was being regulated by NHTSA. Furthermore, if Ford had followed all conditions set down by NHTSA, how could the company have been reckless during the forty-one days in which they had a legal responsibility to Pinto owners?

Cosentino, however, contended that Ford did not simply have an obligation to repair the vehicles but also had a *duty to warn* people like the Ulrichs as soon as possible that they were driving a potentially lethal car. Thus he asked Misch whether Ford's June 9 press release announcing the Pinto's recall told owners not to drive their cars until the defect in the fuel tank could be fixed, or whether the company subsequently had taken television or newspaper advertisements cautioning its customers of the full extent of the Pinto's dangers. In response, Misch asserted that since the Pinto was recalled merely to protect Ford's corporate reputation and not because of any alleged hazards, it would have been "ridiculous" to ask "one and a half million or more people not to drive their vehicles...and the one they'd be getting into would be no more safe than the Pinto." It remained to be determined whether the jury believed that Ford had fulfilled its duty to the Ulrichs by feverishly embarking on a recall effort, or whether the company was reckless because it did not warn owners immediately and publicly that their Pintos might explode when struck from the rear at less than 30 mph.

Now Neal was ready to launch his "bomb" at the prosecution: he had crash test data indicating that the Ulrichs' Pinto was hit at a speed of 50 to 55 mph. John D. Habberstad, a Spokane, Washington mechanical engineer and accident reconstruction expert, had been hired to conduct a series of tests in which a Pinto and comparable 1973 subcompacts were struck by a 1972 Chevy van identical to Robert Duggar's. The price of conducting this experiment was substantial: Habberstad was paid a consultant's fee of approximately $22,000 and each of the nine crash tests cost between $8,000 and $9,000. Nonetheless, winning, not money, was the prime consideration of Neal's legal machine.

Over the prosecution's strenuous objections, Judge Staffeldt ruled that the jury could see films of the crash tests because "any scientific demonstration of the evidence is encouraged by the court." In the key test, a 1973 Pinto sedan was hit by the van at 50.3 mph. Red stoddard solvent, used as a substitute for fuel so that no fires would occur, gushed from the Pinto's gas tank. Moreover, the rear end of the test Pinto was "crushed a little bit less than the actual accident vehicle," suggesting that the Ulrichs' car had been struck by a vehicle traveling above the 50.3 mph test speed; Habberstad es-

timated the speed difference at 55 mph. The implication was clear: the
teenagers' Pinto must have been stopped when hit by Duggar's van.

The jury was shown the films of five other tests which involved four subcompacts—a Vega, a Colt, a Gremlin, and a Corolla—and a full-sized
Chevrolet Impala. In each instance, stoddard solvent leaked from the cars'
fuel tanks. These data, Habberstad concluded, indicated that virtually any
car would be a fire hazard if hit at 50 mph. Further, he claimed that a protective device or plastic shield—such as that contained in the recall modification kit—would not have prevented a fire in the Ulrichs' Pinto. In a high-
speed rear-end collision, fuel does not leak because external objects puncture the gas tank, but because the buildup of liquid pressure inside the tank
causes a rupture. "A plastic shield," Habberstad remarked, "will not prevent a hydrostatic burst."

As reporter Lee Strobel observed, the defense had presented its "most
dramatic evidence" that the Ulrichs' fiery crash "involved an impact more
powerful than eyewitnesses reported."[51] Cosentino scrambled to recoup
the losses inflicted by Habberstad's engrossing crash-test films and expert
"scientific" testimony. To prepare the next day's cross-examination strategy,
he worked far into the night with his staff. He would launch a counterattack on several fronts.

First, Cosentino noted not only that Habberstad was paid a hefty consultant's fee by Ford, but also that he had conducted his supposedly
"independent" experiments at the company's own testing grounds in Dearborn, Michigan. Second, he asked Habberstad if the testimony of numerous
eyewitnesses who saw the Ulrichs' Pinto moving would cause him to change
his assessment. The point, of course, was that it was difficult to reconcile
the test results with the accounts of those who had actually witnessed the
accident. Third, he forced Habberstad to admit that the dummies used to
represent drivers or passengers in a crash test "would be thrown around
quite violently" in a high-speed collision. The Ulrichs, however, had not
been "thrown around" in their Pinto, and they had not sustained the kind of
serious bodily harm one would expect in a 50-mph crash. Indeed, medical
testimony had established that they would have survived the accident if
their Pinto had not burst into flames. In the same vein, why hadn't Habberstad's tests included cameras that filmed what happened to the dummies inside the crash vehicles? Didn't he "want the jury to see that people are seriously injured, maybe killed, without fire at those speeds?" Fourth,
Cosentino noted that if the Pinto had been stopped when hit by Duggar's
van, glass and underbody debris would have fallen to the ground at the
point of the impact; after all, this is what had occurred in Habberstad's
Pinto crash test. Yet the debris found on Highway 33 was scattered 24 to
113 feet down the road, thus indicating that the Ulrichs' Pinto must have

been moving. Fifth, Cosentino questioned Habberstad about a four-page report on "vehicle fires" that he had presented at a 1971 accident seminar in Portland, Oregon. Hadn't he written that "fuel tanks located near the perimeter of a vehicle"—like the Pinto's—were "particularly susceptible to damage during an impact between two vehicles"?

Despite Cosentino's inventive and unrelenting cross-examination, Habberstad was not an easy witness to shake.[52] He claimed, for example, that the Ulrichs may not have suffered serious injuries because "the back end of the Pinto was forced forward 38 inches, which gives you a big sponge, the big cushion that allows the riders to adjust to the change in velocity." Similarly, he disputed the contention that no debris was found at the point of impact between the van and the Pinto. A close examination of the photograph of the accident scene revealed fragments of debris at the contact point; the rest of the glass and underbody pieces could have been propelled down the road by Duggar's moving vehicle. Moreover, Habberstad offered, his examination of the Ulrichs' Pinto indicated that the damage sustained by one of the support posts meant that the car door was open at the time of impact. This fact also explained, he continued, why the gas cap was discovered close to where the Pinto was initially struck and not down the road, where it eventually came to a halt: the car was stopped and someone was opening the door to retrieve the cap.

To be sure, Habberstad did not counter all of Cosentino's attacks. Yet, when taken in conjunction with Levi Woodard's claim that the Pinto was stopped, his testimony might have raised enough uncertainty about the speed difference between the Pinto and the van to create a "reasonable doubt" in the jurors' minds regarding Ford's guilt. Consequently, Cosentino knew that once the defense rested its case, he would have to make the most of his opportunity to introduce rebuttal witnesses and evidence.

Neal had planned to conclude his case with the "bomb" of the crash test films. A late development, however, changed his mind. Once again, his insistence that every possible lead be explored, regardless of cost, proved critical. After Levi Woodard's surprise testimony, Cosentino sent his investigators to Elkhart General Hospital to see if any evidence disputing Woodard's account could be discovered. In response, Neal arranged for a South Bend attorney to "hang around" the hospital in case this new inquiry produced information that supported the defense's case. His hunch was accurate: prompted by the prosecution's investigation, hospital employees started to discuss the accident—a topic that had faded from their daily conversations. Through the grapevine, Neal's representative learned that another person had talked with Judy Ulrich as she lay near death in the emergency room:

Nancy E. Fogo, the hospital's nursing supervisor for the evening shift on August 10.

Fogo testified that after encountering Levi Woodard and hearing his explanation of the accident, she went to talk with Judy. "I told her...'I understand that it was really a bad situation out there on [Highway] 33.' She said,'Yes'." Fogo continued, "'I understand you stopped on 33. Did you have car troubles?' She said, 'Yes I stopped,' and then something about the gas cap."

A startled Cosentino desperately assaulted Fogo's story. Judy had been through a "holocaust" and was under "heavy sedation" from pain killers. How could she accurately recount, Cosentino asked, what had occurred on Highway 33? Fogo noted, however, that Judy was able to provide telephone numbers where her parents and an aunt might be reached to tell them about the accident. Refusing to lessen the pressure, Cosentino observed that Judy's lips had been burned off, and that it could not have been possible to understand fully what she was saying. How could she talk? "Using her teeth," Fogo replied. "I believe, sir, she said, 'Yes, I was stopped.'" Cosentino demanded that she try to say "stop" without using her lips. Holding her lips back and speaking through her teeth, Fogo's muffled response sounded something like "stot."[53]

Outside the courtroom, an elated Jim Neal announced to reporters, "Cosentino challenged us to stop that Pinto. Well, now we've stopped it twice." Meanwhile, Mike Cosentino knew that his case had been damaged, and that winning Ford's conviction would hinge on the effectiveness of his upcoming rebuttal. He was optimistic, however, that he had the witnesses to demonstrate that the Ulrichs' Pinto was moving and that the three teenagers should not have perished in a fiery crash.

The Verdict

Taken together, Habberstad's crash test and the testimony of Levi Woodard and Nancy Fogo presented a strong challenge to the prosecution's assertion that the speed difference between Duggar's van and the Ulrichs' Pinto was so low that only a defective vehicle would have exploded on impact. Clearly, Neal had succeeded in raising doubts about Ford's guilt. In a high-speed collision, deaths might be blamed on careless driving, on an unfortunate sequence of fateful events, or on a market economy that demanded affordable though less safe cars, but the blame could not be placed on corporate recklessness.

To combat this assessment of responsibility for the Ulrichs' deaths, Cosentino prepared a rebuttal case which he felt would show the jury that the speed difference between the van and the Pinto was not nearly as great as the defense claimed. He planned to use Fred Arndt, an accident reconstruction specialist, to counter Habberstad's testimony by demonstrating that the maximum speed of impact was approximately 40 mph. Dr. Robert Stein, the pathologist who had performed the autopsy on Judy Ulrich, could be relied upon to state that her injuries were inconsistent with those typically sustained in high-speed collisions. Neil Graves would also be called back to the stand. He would suggest that Habberstad's test results overestimated the speed difference because the wooden bumper on Duggar's van was smaller than the bumper on the van used in the crash experiments and because the rear end of Ulrichs' car was rusted and hence more susceptible to crushing than the test Pinto. Further, Graves's testimony would be used to show how particular features of the accident scene—for example, the distribution of debris on the highway and the pattern of fire inside the Pinto—supported the conclusion that a defective fuel system and not a high-velocity impact caused the Pinto to catch fire.

Most important, Cosentino had his own "bomb" to drop on the defense: Frank C. Camps, a fifteen-year Ford employee who had retired in 1978. A veteran of over two hundred crash tests on Ford vehicles, Camps was ready to reveal that company personnel had rigged or misreported a number of tests that failed to meet federal regulations, and would "do whatever was necessary to pass a test." The implication was clear: given the company's less than reputable history, could the jury trust crash tests that were conducted at Ford facilities by a highly paid consultant?

Jim Neal moved quickly to insure that the jury would not hear any of Cosentino's potentially damaging rebuttal. Citing a 1959 decision, Neal argued that in no instance was the prosecution permitted to "split its case" by reserving evidence for its rebuttal that could have been presented earlier in the trial. Instead, the prosecution had an obligation to present all evidence on a specific point during its original "case-in-chief" so that the defense would have the full opportunity to dispute the allegation. In light of this ruling, Neal asserted forcefully, "we object to any further testimony as to closing speed" between the van and the Pinto. After all, Graves and Stein had already testified, while Arndt and Camps were available and could have been called to the stand when the prosecution made its case against the defendant.

Bruce Berner retorted for the prosecution that throughout the trial Ford had endeavored to steer the evidence "to the posture they want and then clos[e] off any additional testimony." Further, he contended, the Indiana Supreme Court had ruled that expert testimony at this phase of the trial could "explain, contradict, or disprove" evidence presented by the defense. Rebuttal evidence is not limited to new evidence. Therefore, although it is inappropriate to repeat testimony, the court may admit information that specifically rebuts evidence offered by the defense in its case. On the basis of this principle, Berner reasoned, it became clear why the prosecution should be allowed to call its witnesses: because Neal had introduced crash-test data related directly to the issue of "closing speeds," the jury should be allowed to hear the prosecution's rebuttal evidence on this point.

Both sides anxiously awaited Staffeldt's critical ruling. Calling the decision "probably one of the toughest issues in the trial," the judge stated that it would be "an abuse of discretion if the court permitted the prosecution to separate its case-in-chief and its rebuttal." Consequently, the prosecution would not be allowed to present any evidence that "could have been produced in the case-in-chief and was available at that time."

In effect, Staffeldt's decision scuttled Cosentino's rebuttal case. Once again, Neal had maneuvered to create a legal obstacle that the prosecution could not surmount; once again, the full "Pinto story" would not be told inside the Pulaski County courthouse. In the end, Arndt, Stein, and Camps were not allowed to testify; meanwhile, Neil Graves was forced to limit his comments to several minor points related only tangentially to the issue of the speed difference between the van and the Pinto.[54] Later, Cosentino decided not to place on the stand a statistical consultant who was prepared to dispute Ford's claim that the Pinto was as safe as other subcompacts. Not wanting to "end with a statistical argument," he chose instead to rest the prosecution's case.

After Staffeldt's ruling, a disquieted and frustrated Cosentino refused —for the first time—to attend the daily briefing with media representatives. As one reporter noted, the "state's case had reached its nadir"; indeed, an "angry depression" hung over the entire team of prosecution lawyers as the prospects for winning Ford's conviction seemed to be slipping away.[55]

Cosentino was not one to remain gloomy for long, however; he still had reason to be hopeful. For one thing, though Judge Staffeldt reserved the right to overrule the jury's decision, he had rejected Neal's request for a directed verdict that would acquit his client. "We will submit this case to the jury," Staffeldt commented. In addition, final arguments still lay ahead, and this stage of the trial would present Cosentino with another opportunity to convince the jury of Ford's culpability. "We haven't been able to tell our entire story," he noted, "but I think it will be sufficient when we tie it up in final argument." Outwardly, at least, Cosentino's confidence had returned.

On Monday morning, March 10, Cosentino rose to address the jury for the last time. His remarks were couched on two levels: a technical discussion of the evidence and a consideration of the moral issues at stake. There were sound evidentiary reasons, he claimed, for blaming Ford's recklessness for the Ulrichs' deaths. Even Ford executives had testified that the Pinto could not safely withstand a rear-end crash at the speed limit in effect on most city streets, including downtown Winamac. "Do you know what happens to a Pinto when it's hit at a speed between 26 and 28 mph?" he asked. "It blows up." Moreover, he asked, could the jury really believe Ford's contention that it recalled a car that had "nothing wrong with it"? After all, this company not only was convicted of 350 counts of lying to the government, but also made $1.5 billion in 1978 profits. Yet it would not invest another $6.65 per car to insure that Pintos like the Ulrichs' were free from a lethal fuel-system defect. And what of the defendant's allegation that the Pinto was comparable to other 1973 subcompacts? Well, said Cosentino, "this is like an accused burglar defending his actions because other people burgled."

Most important, however, the impact of the collision on Highway 33 "did not kill Judy, Donna, and Lyn. Were it not for the Pinto, they would be with us today." Ford, Cosentino continued, wished to deflect blame by arguing that any car would have exploded into flames; but what was their evidence? Crash tests conducted by a paid consultant? Conversations with a dying girl who had just been through a "holocaust"? By contrast, the prosecution had offered two incontrovertible facts: a number of eyewitnesses all agreed that the Pinto was moving when struck, and the girls' injuries were consistent with a low-speed collision. "If the crash doesn't kill you," Cosentino asserted, "the car shouldn't kill you."

Yet larger moral issues were also at stake. Waving three death certificates before the jurors' eyes, Cosentino demanded that the jury "give meaning to these senseless deaths." A wrong had been committed and now the scales of justice must be balanced. Nothing could bring the Ulrich girls back to life, of course; but the jury did have the power to prevent others from suffering tragic fates at the hands of socially irresponsible corporations. Indeed, by convicting Ford Motor Company on charges of reckless homicide, Cosentino reminded the jurors, they would be "planting the seeds of needed corporate moral responsibility. You can send a message that can be heard in all the large boardrooms in this country....All America awaits your verdict."

Neal's final argument contested Cosentino's interpretation of the evidence and raised a different set of moral issues. On a moral level, he disputed Ford's portrayal as a big business blindly pursuing profits in disregard of potential human costs. To be sure, the company "may not be perfect, but it is not guilty of reckless homicide." The Pinto was not the creation of crass capitalists but of "honest men who honestly believed the 1973 Pinto was a reasonably safe car, so safe that they bought it for their wives and children." They followed all federal regulations in the car's construction and even went so far as to implement voluntarily their own standard for fuel leakage in rear-end crashes. What other automaker could make this claim? Further, once Ford executives agreed to recall the Pinto rather than lose the confidence of consumers, they acted vigorously. During the forty-one-day period in which the company was legally liable under Indiana's reckless homicide statute, what more could they have done to contact the Ulrichs and give them the opportunity to modify their Pinto?

Neal also warned the jury that their verdict would have profound implications for the future of American business. "If this country is to survive economically," he cautioned, "we've got to stop blaming industry and business for our own sins. No car is now or ever can be said to be safe with reckless drivers [like Duggar] on the road." Particularly dangerous, he continued, was the attempt to preempt federal regulations with the personal biases of local prosecutors—prosecutors like Mike Cosentino. "What chaos it would involve if the federal government set standards, but state prosecutors started saying, 'I'm not satisfied.' How can any company survive?" It was the jurors' moral duty, Neal concluded, to halt the increasingly dangerous practice of vilifying corporations and undermining the nation's economic strength.

Beyond this broader issue, the hard facts substantiated the claim that Duggar's van hit the girls' Pinto at such a high speed that it "made no difference what kind of car" had been involved in the collision. Neal claimed that any comparable subcompact—if not any larger car—would have suffered fuel leakage and a fire. Indeed, all evidence supported the defense's view that the Pinto was not moving. Thus, the car door was open and the gas cap was found close to the initial point of impact, "right where it would have been" if the girls had "stopped to retrieve the cap." Scientific crash tests and analysis corroborated this interpretation, showing that the speed difference was greater than 50 mph. Most important, both Levi Woodard and Nancy Fogo testified that Judy Ulrich had told them her Pinto was stopped.[56]

With final arguments concluded, Pulaski County's crowded courtroom began to disperse. The room had been filled by an odd mixture of people whose social circles touched infrequently—lawyers with small and large reputations, local and national news reporters of all sorts, corporate executives and rural Hoosiers—all drawn together by historical circumstance and a celebrated trial. Meanwhile, the jury faced the task of making sense of 29 days of testimony that resulted in nearly 6,000 pages of transcripts, 22 prosecution and 19 defense witnesses, and 200 exhibits introduced as evidence.[57] It was Monday afternoon, but they would not reach consensus on a verdict until Thursday morning, after twenty-five ballots had been taken.

The first vote was eight for acquittal and four for conviction. The majority voted for acquittal for a variety of reasons. First, they "felt the state never presented enough evidence to convince us that Ford was guilty." They felt a "little shortchanged" at not seeing more of Cosentino's information on 1971 and 1972 Pintos, but they had to decide on the basis of what was presented to them. Second, although they believed that the Ulrichs' Pinto was moving when the collision occurred, they thought the prosecution had failed to establish the exact speed at impact. Some jurors doubted that any Pinto, even if equipped with a recall modification kit, could have withstood the force of Duggar's van. Third, many jurors felt that the Pinto "was not safe enough"; nonetheless, the lack of safety was inherent in small cars and the Pinto was not that much worse than comparable subcompacts. Moreover, "the American public has the right to choose whether they want to purchase that product." Fourth, and perhaps most important, the jurors believed that during the forty-one days in which Ford was legally liable, the company did everything in its power to recall the Pinto. Ronald Hoffman, the Ford employee who supervised the recall, had been a particularly effective witness. As one juror commented, Hoffman was "an average working guy—truthful, honest and straightforward, and he could prove everything he said. He left no doubt in my mind that Ford did all that it could between June and August 10."[58]

As the deliberations continued, support for Ford's conviction weakened. By Wednesday evening, the jury voted ten to two for acquittal. The two jurors in the minority remained convinced of Ford's guilt, and talks continued far into the night. Shortly before midnight, Staffeldt called the jury into the courtroom. He was prepared to read them the special instructions that typically are given only when a judge anticipates a strong possibility of a mistrial. Staffeldt had begun to fear this possibility after learning from Arthur Selmer, the jury's foreman, that the existing deadlock seemed unlikely to be broken.

"If you fail to reach a verdict," stated Staffeldt, "this case will be open and unresolved. Another trial would be a burden on both parties." He added, "There is no reason to believe that the case can be tried any better than it has been...[or] that a more intelligent or competent jury would be selected."

Staffeldt's prompting had an effect. By two a.m., one juror had changed her mind, making the vote 11 to 1. James Yurgilas was the lone holdout, but he was steadfast in his opinion that Ford was responsible for the Ulrichs' deaths. At three, Selmer told Staffeldt that he was "very doubtful" a verdict could be reached. Nonetheless, the judge ordered the jurors to return at ten. If no decision was reached by the end of Thursday, Staffeldt would accept the existence of a "hung jury." He would then have to choose whether to declare a mistrial or whether to issue a verdict himself.

After a sleepless night, James Yurgilas reluctantly changed his mind, although convinced that the Pinto "was a reckless automobile....On the other point you couldn't actually prove they [Ford] didn't do everything in their power to recall it....They got off on a loophole." After more than twenty-five hours of deliberations, suddenly the ten-week trial was over. In a courtroom filled to twice its forty-eight-seat capacity, Arthur Selmer delivered three envelopes containing the jury's verdict, one for each of the three reckless homicide charges.

As Judge Staffeldt ripped open the first envelope, suspense gripped the courtroom. His announcement: "We, the jury, find the defendant not guilty." These words were repeated twice more.

In the presence of reporters from nearly every major newspaper and television network, a triumphant Jim Neal stated that he was "grateful, relieved, and proud, and I thought the verdict was fully justified." He added that "the Pinto has been maligned for years, but we were tried by a jury of twelve people in the heartland of America and all twelve found us not guilty. That says something." At corporate headquarters in Dearborn, Michigan, news of the verdict interrupted a board meeting. Sitting around a horseshoe-shaped table, eighteen corporate directors cheered loudly. By coincidence, the directors had assembled that day to see Henry Ford II retire and relinquish control of Ford Motor Company to Philip Caldwell, the first non-Ford since 1906 to head the company.[59]

Judge Staffeldt was reluctant to comment on the case, only remarking, "I won't quarrel with the verdict. It was the right one." Later he admitted that he might have acquitted Ford if there had been a hung jury, but he would not have overruled the jurors if they had found Ford guilty.

In stark contrast to the jubilation expressed by the defense, Cosentino and his band of volunteers could not hide their bitter disappointment. Asked for his reaction, Cosentino interpreted the verdict as meaning "that manufacturers can make any kind of car they want and it's up to the public to decide if they want to buy it or not." Given some time to reflect, however, he added that the trial would have at least one positive result. "It will make large corporations understand they can be brought to trial with twelve citizens sitting in judgment on decisions of the corporation—that boardroom decisions can be scrutinized by a jury."[60]

Finally, two days after the end of the trial, the Ulrich family wrote to Cosentino to "express our feelings." They thanked him for "being very patient with us" and for "keeping us informed about what is going on." "When we think about all the things that have taken place in the last year and a half," they continued, "and what motivated you and your staff to spend endless hours on the investigation of the Pinto...we admit we ask why us?" They also noted that "God has allowed us to be here for a reason. We are involved if we want to be or not. We realize you were limited in the evidence you were allowed to present. You did very well and need not be ashamed in any of your actions." They concluded, "We also have a moral obligation in the future of other peoples' lives. Our prayers are with you and your staff and families."[61]

Epilogue

It was over.

For more than a year and a half, Mike Cosentino and his fellow prosecutors had been enmeshed in a case that had earned continued national attention. Before the Ulrichs' tragic deaths on August 10, 1978, the members of the prosecution team could not have predicted that historical circumstance would present them with an opportunity to participate in a landmark criminal trial. Further, to a large extent, none of the prosecutors could have anticipated what this trial would have meant for their lives. Their families, their regular offices, and their normal routines were replaced by a pressure-filled, absorbing crusade in which lawyers, a rural courtroom, and media representatives became part of their everyday landscape.

Today the Pinto trial remains a vivid memory, but not a dominant part of their lives. Mike Cosentino still carries the label of the "Ford Pinto prosecutor," and the volunteer law professors now use the case an an example when teaching about product liability and corporate social control. Yet after the flurry of attention immediately following the end of the trial on March 13, 1980 (Cosentino, for instance, appeared on ABC's "Good Morning America"), they largely resumed their former lives. Cosentino returned to Elkhart, where he is still a popular conservative Republican prosecutor with a thriving civil practice; Terry Shewmaker remains his assistant and law partner. Bruce Berner still teaches at Valparaiso University and Terry Kiely at DePaul. Perhaps the largest change took place in Neil Graves's life. Although he continued to serve as an Indiana State Trooper, he became involved in a newly formed white-collar crime unit that investigated offenses such as the illegal dumping of toxic waste products.

The members of the prosecution also had to adjust emotionally. Not only had they experienced a draining trial; they also had to come to grips with a stinging defeat. At first, the bitterness of the loss and the frustration of not having told the "whole story" did not wane. They were plagued by a sense that justice had not been served. In time, however, they were consoled by the realization that while they had failed to prove Ford's reckless-ness, they had succeeded in *bringing Ford to trial*. This success was critical, they believed, because it showed that "corporations can be prosecuted for any crime, including homicide; that corporations can be prosecuted criminally for failing to warn the users of its products of dangers known to the corporation; and that corporations are criminally accountable for their actions, as any other citizen to the people of the State of Indiana sitting as a jury."[62]

For Jim Neal and Aubrey Harwell, the aftermath of the trial took a different direction. To be sure, they too were accorded celebrity status, receiving numerous speaking invitations and giving many news interviews. Yet the importance of the Pinto case soon receded. Although it was significant in establishing their law firm as a leader in defending those accused of committing white-collar crimes, the case lost its importance as they became absorbed in other cases of national scope. Aubrey Harwell, for example, decided that he would make about thirty Pinto-related speeches. He did so quickly when the trial ended, and then largely forgot about the case. In an interview in 1983, it appeared that he had not thought about the details of the trial in years. At first, in fact, he did not remember Levi Woodard's name—the star witness whom he was instrumental in unearthing.[63] By contrast, interviews with members of the prosecution suggest that they can recall the smallest details of the case and, even today, retain vivid memories of the trial.

Since his victory in Winamac, Jim Neal's reputation has continued to grow; *Fortune* magazine labeled him one of the top five "lawyers for companies in deep trouble."[64] When he defends a client, the mention of his name is always accompanied by a list of his accomplishments: the defendant will be represented by Nashville attorney James F. Neal, former Watergate and Jimmy Hoffa prosecutor and defender of Ford in the Pinto case and of Elvis Presley's doctor. After the Pinto trial, Neal was appointed by the U.S. Senate Select Committee to examine the role of the FBI in Abscam and other undercover cases. More recently, he acted as the chief counsel representing Louisiana Governor Edwin Edwards, who was acquitted of charges of racketeering and fraud. He also defended director John Landis on involuntary manslaughter charges stemming from three deaths that occurred during the filming of *Twilight Zone: The Movie* (see Chapter 7). Neal is sometimes rumored to be contemplating a political career; as noted, he chaired Walter Mondale's presidential campaign in Tennessee, and he is considered a potential gubernatorial candidate.

In 1982, Neal accepted Mike Cosentino's invitation to address the Elkhart Bar Association. Cosentino asked him to Elkhart "because he's one of the foremost defense counsels in the country." Neal accepted the invitation because he "found Cosentino extremely competent and a friend—wrong headed, but a friend....I think we both agree it was a very fascinating trial...one of the 10 or 15 most important trials in this century....I think we both agree it arose out of very tragic circumstances. We would clearly disagree as to whether justice was done."[65]

Judge Harold R. Staffeldt died at age 62 on August 30, 1981. He was diagnosed as having cancer during the Pinto case's pretrial hearings—ironically, "during the only time in his career that he was in the national spotlight"—and he suffered pain as he presided over the ten-week case. When reporters faulted him in the midst of the trial for not reading all relevant memoranda before rendering an evidentiary decision, Staffeldt said, "I have been criticized and rightly so. But some people don't understand all of the problems I have." After the trial, he said that if he were retrying the case, he would still decline to admit the prosecution's documents.[66]

Lee Iacocca's career since his stewardship at Ford can be described as a quintessential but somewhat ironic American success story. Fired as president of Ford by Henry Ford II in July 1978, a month after the decision to recall the Pinto, Iacocca became an American folk hero after he was named president of the Chrysler Corporation in November 1978 and rescued the company from bankruptcy. Recently he led a highly publicized and successful fund-raising campaign to restore the Statue of Liberty, and although he denies any interest, he has been mentioned frequently as a possible Democratic presidential candidate. His autobiography, titled simply *Iacocca*, was a bestseller; indeed, it was the top-selling autobiography in the history of American publishing. In the book, Iacocca wrote very little about the Pinto debacle; stating that while he was president the company "resisted making any changes [in the Pinto], and that hurt us badly," he admitted that it was "the fault of Ford's management—including me." He concluded, "It is fair to hold management to a high standard, and to insist that they do what duty and common sense require, no matter what the pressures....But there's absolutely no truth to the charge that we tried to save a few bucks and knowingly made an unsafe car."[67]

The difficulties of Ford Motor Company did not end with its victory in Winamac or with its phasing out of the Pinto. After manufacturing over 2.9 million of these cars, Ford rolled the last Pinto off the assembly line on July 18, 1980 in Metuchen, New Jersey—the same plant that had produced the Ulrichs' 1973 yellow subcompact.[68] Yet the Pinto's demise did not leave the company free from legal entanglements. Ford reached an out-of-court settlement with the Ulrich family in August, reportedly paying $22,500 ($7,500 compensation in each girls' death).[69] (As noted in Chapter 5, Indiana law severely restricted the damages that surviving families could receive in civil suits.)   In addition, the company was confronted with suits from other Pinto owners: Ford reportedly made a $2.1 million settlement to the families of two Fayette County, Pennsylvania girls who died when their 1971 Pinto burst into flames in a rear-end collision. Another case was settled in Texas just one week after the Winamac trial.[70]

Ford also faced litigation over the allegedly negligent placement of the gas tank in its Mustang. A New Hampshire jury awarded a man $821,375 for burn injuries suffered when his 1972 Mustang was hit from behind by a Cadillac. In a 1984 case, a Texas jury went even further, awarding $106.8 million to the family of a girl who perished when a rear-end crash caused her Mustang II to be engulfed by flames; the presiding judge reduced this amount to $26.8 million.[71] Further, Ford came under increasing criticism when charged that defective transmissions in its products had resulted in approximately 100 deaths and 1,700 injuries. Attorneys claimed that the vehicles lurched backward after drivers had placed them in park. In addition, they argued, corporate documents showed "that as long ago as the early 1970s the company was aware of a defect in the transmissions of millions of cars and light trucks and could have corrected it for three cents a vehicle." Ford reportedly paid approximately $20 million "as a result of settlements of court verdicts in about 125 cases."[72] In one case, moreover, the Center for Auto Safety, a consumer group based in Washington, D.C., requested that Wisconsin authorities file criminal charges against Ford: a fifteen-month-old boy strapped into his child-restraint seat drowned when the 1977 Thunderbird in which he was sitting jumped from "park" into "reverse" gear while his mother was opening the garage door, and backed into a pond across the street.[73] The Wisconsin attorney general decided against criminal charges after a coroner's jury determined that even though "the major perpetrating cause of the accident resulting in the death of Michael Cannon was this faulty design and function and the Ford Motor Company's omission of its corrections," not enough facts were presented to establish criminal negligence.[74]

In more recent times, however, Ford Motor Company appears to have rebounded from both its legal problems and the general slump in the automotive industry. In the December 1985 issue of *Fortune* magazine, the cover and the lead story featured "Ford's Comeback." Thanks to innovative engineering designs, forward-looking products, and reduced costs, said *Fortune*, "Ford is back on the track." Company executives' efforts to win back consumer confidence "by making the best American cars" have been rewarded; one survey, for example, indicated that the public voted Ford the "top U.S. carmaker." As the *Fortune* story noted, "Ford's struggle for quality has not been lost on consumers."[75]

Notes

[1] In researching this chapter, we accumulated several sorts of data. First, accounts were provided by author William Maakestad, who attended much of the trial and provided volunteer legal assistance to the prosecution. Second, we had access to nearly one thousand news clippings on the case. These included reports by both the local and national media. Although we compiled many stories ourselves and received others from Brent Fisse and John Braithwaite, most of the clippings were provided by Michael Cosentino's office. It should be noted that not all the news reports given to us contain full bibliographic information; thus we are limited to listing only author and title in some references. Third, Lee Patrick Strobel's *Reckless Homicide: Ford's Pinto Trial* (South Bend, Indiana: And Books, 1980) contained useful descriptions of the personalities of the participants in the trial and of the trial itself. Fourth, in June 1983, Francis Cullen and William Maakestad travelled to Indiana and conducted interviews with Michael Cosentino, Terry Shewmaker, Bruce Berner, and Neil Graves. Maakestad also interviewed local reporter David Schreiber at that time. In November 1983, Cullen and Maakestad interviewed Terry Kiely in Chicago and received documents relevant to the prosecution's case. Additional telephone interviews with Michael Cosentino, Bruce Berner, and Terry Kiely were completed in late 1985 and early 1986. Finally, on July 28, 1983, Gray Cavender interviewed defense lawyer Aubrey B. Harwell, Jr. in the law office of Neal & Harwell, located in Nashville, Tennessee.

Much of this chapter involves reconstructing events and social interactions by weaving together many minor details drawn from a variety of sources. To avoid burdening the text with an inordinate number of footnotes, we have chosen not to provide a reference for each specific detail of the trial. Instead, we have furnished footnotes that list the major sources used to write distinct sections of this chapter. We made exceptions to this general rule when specific information in the text was sufficiently important to warrant a clear citation.

[2] David Jones, "Lawyer James Neal Likes the Big Cases," *Lexington Leader* (February 16, 1981), p. A-1; James Warren and Brian J. Kelly, "Inside the Pinto Trial," *American Lawyer* (April 1980), pp. 28-29; Joyce Leviton, "A Local D.A. Charges the Pinto with Murder—and Watergate's James Neal Comes to Its Defense," *People* (February 4, 1980); "Pinto Attorney Neal Returns for 'Reunion,'" *South Bend Tribune* (May 21, 1982); "Neal Not Bothered by 'Heavy' Image," *Elkhart Truth*; Strobel, *Reckless Homicide?*, pp. 59-62.

3   Interview with Aubrey B. Harwell, Jr., July 28, 1983.

4   David Schreiber, "Defense Attorney One More Pinto Trial Paradox," *Elkhart Truth*; Strobel, *Reckless Homicide?*, p. 63.

5   Malcolm E. Wheeler, "Product Liability, Civil or Criminal—the Pinto Litigation," *The Forum* 57 (Fall 1981), pp. 250-265. See also Wheeler, "In Pinto's Wake, Criminal Trials Loom for More Manufacturers," *National Law Journal* (October 6, 1980), pp. 28-30; "The Public's Costly Mistrust of Cost-Benefit Safety Analysis," *National Law Journal* (October 13, 1980), pp. 26-27; "Cost-Benefit Analysis on Trial: A Case of Delusion and Reality," *National Law Journal* (October 20, 1980), pp. 28-29, 31.

6   Wheeler, "Product Liability, Civil or Criminal—the Pinto Litigation," p. 252.

7   "Summary of Findings," Defendant's Exhibit 37A, p. 5; Strobel, *Reckless Homicide?* pp. 65-66.

8   Strobel, *Reckless Homicide?* pp. 66-67.

9   Information contained in document supplied by Michael Cosentino.

10   Alan S. Lenhoff, "Pinto: The Big Case in the Small Town," *Detroit Free Press* (January 5, 1980), p. 11-D; George Barker, "Neal Counsels Ford in Landmark Trial," *Nashville Banner* (January 7, 1980), p. 22; Jeffrey Hadden, "Pinto Trial Puts Town on Map," *Detroit News* (January 7, 1980); Reginald Stuart, "Indiana Town Astir Over Pinto Trial," *New York Times* (January 7, 1980); Brian J. Kelly, "A Corporation on Trial: Ford Pinto Case Begins," *Chicago Sun-Times* (January 7, 1980), p. 6; Lee Strobel, "Winamac Citizens Find Pinto Trial Trying," *Chicago Tribune* (January 13, 1980), p. 4.

11   Alan S. Lenhoff, "Judge Is Calm Despite Big-Stakes Drama," *Detroit Free Press* (January 6, 1980), p. 11-D; James Wensits, "Ford Trial Not Rattling Judge," *South Bend Tribune* (January 7, 1980).

12   Lenhoff, "Pinto: The Big Case in the Small Town," p. 11-D; Strobel, *Reckless Homicide?* pp. 70-71.

13   Strobel, *Reckless Homicide?* p. 99.

[14] Interview with Michael Cosentino; Fred D. Cavinder, "The Man Who Tried Ford for Homicide," *Indianapolis Star Sunday* Magazine (1980), pp. 6-10.

[15] Interview with Aubrey B. Harwell, Jr., July 28, 1983.

[16] Alan S. Lenhoff, "An Expert Helps Ford Select Pinto Jury," *Detroit Free Press* (January 9, 1980), p. 5-C; Bruce Mays, "Hans Zeisel: The Time of His Life," *Student Lawyer* 8 (April 1980), pp. 23, 37-39; Nina Totenberg, "The Jury Pickers," Parade (May 9, 1982), p. 12.

[17] Strobel, *Reckless Homicide?* pp. 105-106.

[18] Interview with Michael Cosentino, June 1983. We also had access to the document containing the *voir dire* questions used by the prosecution.

[19] Alan S. Lenhoff, "Seven Men, Five Women Form Pinto Jury," *Detroit Free Press* (January 11, 1980), p. 6-C; Dennis M. Royalty, "Jury Chosen in Pinto Death Trial," *Indianapolis Star* (January 11, 1980), p. 27; Jeffrey Hadden, "The Pinto Trial: 'Plain Folks' to Judge Ford," *Detroit News* (January 13, 1980), p. 10-A.

[20] Strobel, *Reckless Homicide?* p. 101.

[21] Alan S. Lenhoff, "Just Folks: Ford's Lawyer Playing the Hick for Rural Jurors," *Akron Beacon Journal* (January 10, 1980), p. B-l.

[22] Lee Strobel, "'Mike and Jim Show' Keeps Pinto Trial Fans Coming Back," *Chicago Tribune* (February 17, 1980).

[23] Strobel, *Reckless Homicide?* p. 75.

[24] Terry Kiely, "Case-In-Chief: Overview of Exhibits—Phase III." Document prepared for the prosecution.

[25] Interview with Terry Kiely, November, 1983; Terry Kiely, "Phase III—Overview (Nutshell)." (Document prepared for prosecution.) It must be emphasized that throughout this section, we are reporting Terry Kiely's *interpretation* of the evidence at his disposal. In the actual trial, Ford would dispute both his interpretation of the corporation's motives and, more generally, the prosecution's reconstruction of the Pinto's history.

[26] Strobel, *Reckless Homicide?* p. 81.

[27] Kiely, "Phase III—Overview (Nutshell)."

[28] *Ibid.*

[29] See *Ibid.* for Kiely's evaluation of Ford's response to the proposed NHTSA regulations. Kiely's "best recollections" are the basis for the figures on how a 20-mph moving- and fixed-barrier test translates into the speed and impact of an actual highway accident. Telephone interview with Terry Kiely, March 3, 1986. See also Strobel, *Reckless Homicide?* pp. 79, 83-84. Further, Ford would note later in the trial that it was the *only* company to have a rear-end fuel-leakage standard for its 1973 models. Similarly, the other automakers also lobbied NHTSA for regulatory relief. It was not until 1977 that NHTSA passed a regulation mandating that vehicles not suffer fuel leakage in a 30-mph moving-barrier rear-end crash. Obviously, this regulation was much less stringent than that proposed earlier in the decade. See Strobel, *Reckless Homicide?* p.89.

[30] Terry Kiely, "Summary of Ford Memo, 4-22-71: 'Fuel System Integrity Program Financial Review (Confidential).'"

[31] Kiely, "Phase III—Overview (Nutshell)."

[32] Terry Kiely, "Summary of Ford Memo, 9-19-73: 'FMC-NHTSA letter requesting reconsideration of FMVSS 301.'"

[33] The section on authenticating documents was based on the following sources: telephone interview with Bruce Berner, November 10, 1985; Wheeler, "Product Liability, Civil or Criminal—The Pinto Litigation," p. 254; "Ford Aides' Subpoena Quashed," *New York Times* (December 8, 1979), p. 8; Strobel, *Reckless Homicide?* pp. 93-97, 139-140, 143-144, 159-161; Reginald Stuart, "Ford Turns Over Papers as the Pinto Trial Begins," *New York Times* (January 8, 1980), p. A-14; David Schreiber, "Pinto Jury Selection Snail-Slow Process," *Elkhart Truth* (January 8, 1980), p. 2; Alan Lenhoff, "Ford Avoids Release of Pinto Crash Data," *Detroit Free Press* (January 8, 1980), p. 4-C; "Legal Arguments Surfacing in Pinto Trial Jury Selection," *Logansport Pharos-Tribune* (January 8, 1980), p. 2.

[34] Telephone interview with Michael Cosentino, November 10, 1985. See also David Schreiber, "Documents Issue at Winamac Trial," *Elkhart Truth* (January 23, 1980), and Jeff Kurowski, "New Method for Evidence:

Cosentino 'Confident' of Document Acceptance," *South Bend Tribune* (January 23, 1980),

[35] Interview with Aubrey B. Harwell, Jr., July 28, 1983.

[36] David Schreiber, "Jury Permitted Own Standards," *Elkhart Truth* (January 14, 1980); Alan Lenhoff, "Judge Splits Decisions on Pinto Motions," *Detroit Free Press* (January 15, 1980), p. 3-B; Reginald Stuart, "Court Turns Back Ford Attempt to Limit Evidence in Pinto Trial," *New York Times* (January 15, 1980), p. A-16; Lee Strobel, "Ford Lied During Probe of Pinto: Prosecution," *Chicago Tribune* (January 15, 1980), p. 3; Strobel, *Reckless Homicide?* pp. 109-111; James Warren, "Ford Loses Key Point in Pinto Trial," *Chicago Sun-Times* (January 15, 1980), p. 20; "Judge: Pinto Trial Shall Proceed," *Elyria Chronicle Telegram* (January 15, 1980), p. A-4; "Judge Restricts Use of Key Documents in Case Against Ford," *Globe and Mail* (January 15, 1980), p. 12.

[37] Lenhoff, "Judge Splits Decisions on Pinto Motions," p. 3-B; Strobel, *Reckless Homicide?*, pp. 107-108; Stuart, "Court Turns Back Ford Attempt to Limit Evidence in Pinto Trial," p. A-16; Warren, "Ford Loses Key Point in Pinto Trial," p. 20; Hugh McCann, "Pinto Trial Judge Restricts Prosecutor on Documents," *Detroit News* (January 15, 1980), p. 14-A; Andy Pasztor, "Ford Loses on Potentially Crucial Point in Pinto Suit But Wins Technical Rulings," *Wall Street Journal* (January 15, 1980), p. 2; "Pinto Data Restricted in Trial," *Cincinnati Enquirer* (January 15, 1980), p. A-7; "Ruling on Evidence Jolts Ford Prosecutor," *Akron Beacon Journal* (January 15, 1980).

[38] As stated in footnote 1, we used a variety of news reports to reconstruct the events of the trial. Listing the individual citations for each fact or event would be a laborious exercise of minimal substantive value, but it seems appropriate to note the major reporters whose works we used in the upcoming sections: David Schreiber of the *Elkhart Truth*, Jeff Kurowski of the *South Bend Tribune*, Lee Patrick Strobel of the *Chicago Tribune*, Alan Lenhoff of the *Detroit Free Press*, Brian Kelly and James Warren of the *Chicago Sun-Times*, Lisa Levitt of the Associated Press, Reginald Stuart of the *New York Times*, and Dennis Royalty of the *Indianapolis Star*. Apart from the stories filed by these reporters, the most comprehensive summary of the trial is contained in Strobel's *Reckless Homicide?* Finally, when specific information is not drawn from these sources or when a contention appears to require special verification, we have provided the relevant citations.

[39] Letter from Bruce Berner to William Maakestad, July 16, 1981. See Chapter 5 for the text of this letter.

[40] Wheeler, "Product Liability, Civil or Criminal—The Pinto Litigation," pp. 255-256.

[41] *Mingle v. State of Indiana* 396 N.E. 2d 399; Interview with Bruce Berner, November 10, 1985.

[42] Strobel, *Reckless Homicide?* p. 117.

[43] "Nine Key Points Outline Ford's Winamac Defense," *Ford World* (February 1980), pp. 3, 10; Wheeler, "Product Liability, Civil or Criminal—The Pinto Litigation," pp. 256-257; Strobel, *Reckless Homicide?* pp. 117-119.

[44] Warren and Kelly, "Inside the Pinto Trial," p. 29.

[45] *Ibid.*, p. 29. See also James Warren and Brian Kelly, "Pinto Case Judge No Sirica? Some Rulings Baffle Observers," *Indianapolis News* (February 13, 1980), from the *Chicago Sun-Times*.

[46] Interview with Aubrey B. Harwell, Jr., July 28, 1983. Harwell noted that the defense's legal briefs were about 75 percent complete before the start of the trial; the remaining 25 percent involved either revisions necessitated during the proceedings or specific responses to the prosecution.

[47] George Barker, "Neal: Didn't Think We Could Win," (March 14, 1980); Warren and Kelly, "Inside the Pinto Trial," p. 29.

[48] David Schreiber, "Neal Hopes Pinto Witness Typifies Ford 'Good People,'" *Elkhart Truth* (February 19, 1980}; Dan Larson, "Father of Pinto Defends Fuel Tank Location," *Logansport Pharos-Tribune* (February 19, 1980), p. 1.

[49] For an earlier discussion of Ford's 20-mph moving-barrier test standard, see footnote 29 and the accompanying passages in the text.

[50] David Schreiber, "Week's Testimony Shakes Ford's Pinto Defense," *Elkhart Truth* (February 23-24, 1980), p. 2; Jeff Kurowski, "Ford Lawyer Becomes Upset," *South Bend Tribune* (February 22, 1980); Dan Larson, "Neal Planning to Close Defense with a Bomb," *Logansport Pharos-Tribune*

(February 24, 1980). p. 11; "Neal May Introduce Pinto Case 'Bomb,'" *Nashville Banner* (February 25, 1980).

51 Lee Strobel, "Pinto Jurors See Crash Films," *Chicago Tribune* (February 28, 1980).

52 David Schreiber, "Ford Witness Hard Man for Cosentino to Shake," *Elkhart Truth* (February 29, 1980); Alan Lenhoff, "State Only Budges Ford Expert," *Detroit Free Press* (February 29, 1980).

53 Dan Larson, "Witness Talked to Pinto Driver," *Logansport Pharos-Tribune* (March 4, 1980). Also, in a closed-door hearing in Judge Staffeldt's chambers, Neal raised the issue of whether the prosecution had illegally concealed the identities of Nancy Fogo and Levi Woodard. Their names were listed in the prosecution's files, and it was the state's duty to give the defense access to any information that could prove its innocence. The charge was dropped, however, when Neal accepted Cosentino's response that "we never checked them out." Our interviews confirmed the fact that the prosecution did not investigate either witness and was surprised by their testimony. See Alan S. Lenhoff, "Pinto Was Stopped, Dying Girl Said," *Detroit Free Press* (March 4, 1980), p. 3-C.

54 In addition to the rebuttal issue, the defense also opposed Camps's potential testimony because he was not in Ford's employment when Habberstad conducted his tests, and because his crash-testing experiences were related to windshield safety and thus did not qualify him as an expert witness on fuel-system integrity. Further, Ford lawyer Malcolm Wheeler denied that Ford had rigged any crash tests required by the government. Compare this view, however, with Strobel, *Reckless Homicide?* p. 249. For accounts of the issues surrounding Camps's relevance as a witness, see Alan Lenhoff, "State Rests Case in Indiana," *Detroit Free Press* (March 6, 1980), pp. 1, 10; Dennis Royalty, "Ford Hid Test Failure Information, Former Designer Says at Pinto Trial," *Indianapolis Star* (March 6, 1980); and David Schreiber, "Ex-Ford Worker Not Allowed to Testify," *Elkhart Truth* (March 5, 1980).

55 Jeff Kurowski, "Prosecution Nadir?" *South Bend Tribune* (March 5, 1980); Alan Lenhoff, "Rulings Deal a Blow to Pinto Prosecution," *Detroit Free Press* (March 5, 1980), p. 4-B.

56 For accounts of the final arguments, see Dennis Royalty, "Pinto Jury Begins Deliberations After Emotional Final Arguments," *Indianapolis Star* (March 11, 1980); David Schreiber, "Pinto Judge Anticipates Jury Report

by Midweek," *Elkhart Truth* (March 10, 1980); Lee Strobel, "Pinto Jury Told: 'Send Message' to Business," *Chicago Tribune* (March 11, 1980); Jim Thompson, "Jury in Pinto Trial Begins Deliberations," *Louisville Courier-Journal* (1980); Reginald Stuart, "Indiana Jury Gets Homicide Case Involving 3 Deaths in Pinto Fire," *New York Times* (March 11, 1980), p. A-16; James Warren, "Jury Hears Final Plea to Convict Ford Over Pinto," *Chicago Sun-Times* (March 11, 1980), p. 2.

[57] Lenhoff, "State Rests Pinto Case in Indiana," p. 10-A.

[58] After the end of the trial, the entire jury held a press conference at which several members explained the reasoning underlying their votes. This section is based on this information. For accounts of the jury's reactions, see Robert Ankeny and George Bullard, "Pinto Jurors Acquit Ford," *Detroit News* (March 14, 1980); "Despite Verdict, Jurors Have Doubts About Pinto," *Bergen County Record* (March 14, 1980); Mary Rose Dougherty, "State Didn't Prove Case, Jurors Say," *Pulaski County Journal* (March 20, 1980); Jeff Kurowski, "The Jury Talks," *South Bend Tribune* (March 14, 1980), pp. 1, 14; "Prosecution Failed to Give Ford Jury Enough Evidence," *Indianapolis News* (March 14, 1980); Dennis Royalty, "Jury Says Ford Is Not Guilty," *Indianapolis Star* (March 14, 1980); David Schreiber, "Pinto Verdict: Questions Remain," *Elkhart Truth* (March 14, 1980); "Some Jurors Still Uneasy About Pinto's Safety," *Columbus Dispatch* (1980); Lee Strobel, "Pinto Jury Acquits Ford," *Chicago Tribune* (March 14, 1980), p. 1; Reginald Stuart, "Jurors Clear Ford in Pinto Deaths," *New York Times* (March 14, 1980), p. 1; James Warren, "Ford Wins Pinto Case: 'Heartland' Jury Clears Ford Co. in Pinto Case," *Chicago Sun-Times* (March 14, 1980); "Why Pinto Jury Found Ford Innocent," *Oakland Tribune* (March 14, 1980).

[59] Jeff Kurowski, "Neal Sees Ford's Acquittal as 'Vindication,'" *South Bend Tribune* (March 14, 1980); Alan Lenhoff, "The Ford Story: Victory in the Pinto Case," *Detroit Free Press* (March 14, 1980); "Ford Jubilant Over Pinto Case," *Cleveland Press* (March 14, 1980), p. A-2; "Ford Acquitted in Pinto Case: Jury Clears Car Firm of Homicide," *Washington Star* (March 13, 1980), p. 1; "Three Cheers in Dearborn," *Time* (March 24, 1980), p. 24; David T. Friendly with William D. Marbach and James Jones, "Ford's Pinto: Not Guilty," *Newsweek* (March 24, 1980).

[60] Lisa Levitt, "'Buyer Beware' Emerges as Lesson of Pinto Trial," *Indianapolis News* (March 14, 1980), p. 1; David Schreiber, "'No Regrets'—Cosentino," *Elkhart Truth* (March 14, 1980); Lee Strobel, "Clear

Ford on Pinto: Indiana Jury Ends Deadlock," *Chicago Tribune* (March 14, 1980); James Warren, "Ford Wins Pinto Case"; "Prosecutor Denounces Pinto Verdict," *Cincinnati Enquirer* (March 14, 1980), p. 1. Also, Cosentino initially indicated that the prosecution might appeal several of Judge Staffeldt's rulings. Since this was a criminal as opposed to a civil case, however, the "not guilty" verdict could not have been reversed on appeal. In the end, the prosecution decided not to pursue any appeals. See "Statement of Elkhart County Prosecuting Attorney and Staff on Pinto Trial Appeal."

61 Letter to Michael Cosentino from Mattie, Earl, and Shawn Ulrich, March 14, 1980.

62 "Statement of Elkhart County Prosecuting Attorney and Staff on Pinto Trial Appeal." See Also Diane M. Balk, "Cosentino Claims Partial Pinto Win," *South Bend Tribune* (March 2, 1981), p. 5; Jeff Kurowski, "'Errors Made in Trial': Views on Pinto Case," *South Bend Tribune* (March 1980), and "Ford Prosecutor Eyes Re-election," *South Bend Tribune*; David Heidorn, "Berner: The Pinto Case," *The Forum*, Valparaiso University, (November 10, 1980), p. 5.

63 Interview with Aubrey B. Harwell, Jr., July 28, 1983.

64 Liz Roman Gallese, "Lawyers for Companies in Deep Trouble," *Fortune* (October 14, 1985), pp. 106-114.

65 Ken Bode, "The Trial of Edwin Edwards," *The New Republic* (January 27, 1986), pp. 19-21; Karen Garloch, "Warner Bolsters His Law Team: Prosecutor in Watergate Trial Lends Expertise," *Cincinnati Enquirer* (September 8, 1985), p. 1; "Where Are They Now?" *Cincinnati Enquirer* (August 5, 1984), p. A-4; "Pinto Attorney Neal Returns for 'Reunion,'" *Elkhart Truth*.

66 Jeff Kurowski, "Cancer Claims 'Pinto' Judge: Winamac Mourns," *South Bend Tribune* (August 31, 1981); "Staffeldt Dead: Had Pinto Trial," *Elkhart Truth* (August 31, 1981).

67 Lee Iacocca, *Iacocca*. New York: Bantam Books, 1984, p. 162.

68 John Holusha, "Ford Conversion to Small Cars: Jersey Plant in Changeover for Post-Pinto Era," *New York Times* (July 28, 1980), D-1; Ralph Gray, "Putting the Pinto Out to Pasture After a Decade," *Advertising*

Age (April 7, 1980). As Fisse and Braithwaite have observed, Ford officials claimed that "contrary to rumor...the production of the Pinto had not been stopped as a result of the publicity about safety, but because the car had come to the end of its planned 10-year cycle." Brent Fisse and John Braithwaite, *The Impact of Publicity on Corporate Offenders*. Albany: State University of New York Press, 1983, p. 48. See also David Schreiber, "Ford Feeling Pinch of Pinto Publicity," *Elkhart Truth* (March 4, 1980).

[69] Thus $15,000 was paid to the family of Judy and Lyn Ulrich, while $7,500 was paid to Donna Ulrich's family. The families never formally filed a civil suit. See Jeff Kurowski and Marti Heline, "Ford Settles in Pinto Case," *South Bend Tribune*; Marti Heline, "Parents of Three Girls Consider Pinto Case Closed," *South Bend Tribune*; David Schreiber, "Pinto Settlement Reported," *Elkhart Truth* (1980); Lee Strobel, "Ford to Pay $22,500 in 3 Pinto Deaths," *Chicago Tribune* (August 6, 1980), p. 3.

[70] "2.1 Million Settlement OK'd in Pinto-Crash Deaths," (1980); "Ford Settles Texas Lawsuit Over Deaths in Pinto Crash," *New York Times* (March 19, 1980), p. 19. Also, as another 1980 report stated, "the legal battle over the subcompact isn't over—similar Pinto crashes prompted suits against Ford, and as many as 50 are pending in various courts." See "2 Years Ago Explosion Shook Auto World," *Tampa Tribune* (August 1, 1980). In contrast, Fisse and Braithwaite have contended that after Ford's "acquittal in the criminal trial, the flow of civil claims dropped to a trickle and a case proceeding to trial in December 1980 was won by the company." Braithwaite and Fisse, *The Impact of Publicity on Corporate Offenders*, p. 49.

[71] William F. Doherty, "Man Burned in Crash Wins $821,375 from Ford Motor," *Boston Globe* (April 15, 1980), p. 19; "Family Gets $27 Million from Mustang Crash Suit," *Cincinnati Enquirer* (September 8, 1984), p. A-6. We do not know, however, whether Ford appealed these decisions, and if so, whether the financial awards were sustained, reduced, or vacated.

[72] Raymond Bonner, "Ford Quietly Settles Transmission Suits," *Cincinnati Enquirer* (February 15, 1983), p. B-5. See also James Warren and Brian J. Kelly, "Ford Recall May Trigger Suits," *Chicago Sun-Times* (June 15, 1980), p. 3; "Ford Transmissions Still Pose Dangers Despite Warning Program, Coalition Says," *Wall Street Journal* (November 30, 1981).

[73] "Consumer Group Seeks New Homicide Prosecution of Ford Motor Company," *Product Safety and Liability Reporter* (April 25, 1980), pp. 297-298.

[74] "Acting on Results of Inquiry, Wisconsin Will Not Prosecute Ford," *Product Safety and Liability Reporter* (May 23, 1980), p. 356.

[75] Anne B. Fisher, "Ford is Back on Track," *Fortune* 112 (December 23, 1985), pp. 18-22.

Chapter 7
Beyond the Ford
Pinto Trial

But it would be naive for Ford or any other corporation to assume that the Indiana case will be the last of its kind. Sooner or later there will be other trials, and if the prosecution makes a stronger case there may be convictions. The precedent has been set—the notion that a corporation can be made to answer criminal charges for endangering the lives or safety of consumers has been engrained in law and public thinking. It's a healthy precedent, and we don't think it should be—or will be—discarded.

> —*San Jose Mercury,* March 14, 1980

Much of our book has been devoted to examining Ford Motor Company's prosecution on charges of reckless homicide. Why did we choose to focus so intensely on this one case?

One reason was that Ford's prosecution constituted a fascinating drama, which earned national attention. We hoped the story would be interesting enough to encourage our audience to read to this point. There was also a practical consideration: because one of the authors had participated in the prosecution (as noted in the preface), we had first-hand knowledge of what happened in Elkhart and Winamac. We believed that this knowledge would allow us to tell the Pinto story—to relay factual details accurately and to capture some of the human elements of the case.

This was not our full rationale for choosing to study the Pinto case, however. If it had been, we doubt that we could have offered anything more than an interesting account of an important prosecution.[1] In fact, we had two additional reasons—more substantive, we hope, from an academic point of view—for making the Pinto case the core of our book.

First, the case provided a means of illustrating our main proposition, developed in Part I of this book, that social and legal changes have combined to fuel an attack on corporate lawlessness and to make even the most powerful members of the business community vulnerable to criminal prosecution. In Chapter 1, we argued that a general social movement, though still uncrystallized and diffuse, has resulted in greater concern about white-collar and corporate crime. Lawyers, academics, and private citizens are no longer surprised by revelations of managerial misconduct; they show little hesitation in supporting the use of criminal sanctions against guilty parties, whether these are companies or individual executives. We argued further that the growing movement against corporate illegality has its roots in wider social changes, particularly those which have taken place in the past two decades. These changes have called into question the legitimacy of existing institutions and, in the words of Seymour Martin Lipset and William Schneider, have created a pervasive "confidence gap."[2]

This framework, we believe, furnishes insight into the origin of the Pinto prosecution. In Chapter 4, we noted that the Pinto case was a "sign of the times," an event produced by the general social movement against white-collar crime. Thus the prevailing social climate provided fertile soil for the growth of a crusade against the Pinto, which resulted not only in civil suits (including the highly publicized punitive damages awarded to Grimshaw), but also in widespread allegations—such as those voiced on *60 Minutes* and in Mark Dowie's "Pinto Madness" article—that Ford had marketed a car it knew to be dangerously defective. This crusade raised consciousness about the Pinto and, in the current social climate, created a context in which Ford's criminal prosecution became feasible.

It was now possible to view the crash that claimed the lives of the three Ulrich teenagers as a "corporate crime" rather than as an example of reckless driving, hazardous road design, or fate. Reporters, engineering experts, and lawyers who had filed civil suits after earlier Pinto tragedies soon told Mike Cosentino that Ford should be blamed for these deaths. Given the social context, the conservative prosecutor did not dismiss this interpretation. He also perceived (if with some trepidation) that his constituents would not consider it farfetched to indict a major corporation. He would also discover eventually that he could rely on talented law professors to volunteer many months of service; they, too, wished to join an attack on corporate crime.

Another circumstance, however, was needed to make Ford's prosecution possible. In Chapters 3 and 5, we proposed that the law had edged increasingly toward holding corporations criminally culpable for socially harmful conduct. Thus Cosentino could argue that Indiana's reckless homicide statute applied not only to individuals but also to corporations, including Ford. In addition, sufficient legal precedent existed to counter Ford's attempts to quash the indictment and to prevent a trial from taking place.

In short, the Pinto prosecution reflects the social and legal changes that have placed corporations under attack. We do not wish to claim too much in our analysis; we recognize that the interaction of many unique factors—such as Cosentino's personality and the peculiarities of the accident—determined why Ford was indicted on reckless homicide charges in Elkhart, Indiana and not in some other jurisdiction. Nonetheless, we are confident in our assessment that the Pinto trial—as well as many other recent corporate criminal prosecutions—would not have taken place a decade or two earlier.

In addition to using Ford's prosecution to illustrate the relationship among social context, law, and corporations, we chose to study the case for a second reason: it provides a starting point for considering what lies ahead regarding the use of the criminal law in the control of corporate conduct. The richness of the case, we believe, allows us to draw lessons about the possibilities for and against future corporate criminal prosecutions.

Of course, it is important to be sensitive to the obstacles that limit bringing and winning corporate criminal cases, particularly when major business enterprises are the target. As our analysis of the Pinto case shows clearly, Ford's lawyers used their ample resources to make Cosentino negotiate an unending obstacle course in his efforts to win a conviction. Many commentators, however, have focused exclusively on the factors which preclude the initiation and success of corporate prosecutions; in doing so, they have neglected to consider the prospects for such prosecutions. Below, we will attempt to offer a more balanced view on this issue. We believe that despite the ostensible rightward shift in American politics and crime policy, the general social movement against white-collar and corporate crime has shown few signs of abating since the Pinto trial ended in 1980.

We will begin our discussion with a review of corporate criminal prosecutions that have either reached final disposition or have been initiated in recent years. We believe that the prevalence of these cases, especially those in which companies and their executives have been indicted for reckless homicide or manslaughter, supports the contention that corporations remain under attack by the criminal law. The second section of this chapter presents what we see as the major obstacles to the prosecution of corporations. We will discuss three kinds of obstacles: ideological, legal, and structural. Then we will examine several circumstances which we anticipate will insure the continuation, if not the escalation, of the movement against corporate crime. Finally, we will consider two issues that commentators debate with increasing frequency: whether corporate entities are deterrable and whether they are appropriate objects for sanction by the criminal law.

Corporate Crime Under Attack

There is little evidence to suggest that the decision in the Pinto case—Ford was not guilty—marked the end of an era. If anything, the case signified the entrenchment of the idea that corporations should no longer escape criminal prosecution. In the aftermath of the Pinto trial, the roster of corporations indicted and/or convicted of criminal offenses has grown. Chapter 2 reviewed several of the more notable cases: E.F. Hutton's checkkiting scheme; General Electric's overcharging on a defense contract; First National Bank of Boston's failure to report large cash deposits; the ESM Government Securities fraud.

Even more instructive is the growing number of criminal cases accusing corporations of *violent* crimes. The most celebrated of these, also discussed in Chapter 2, remains the 1985 homicide conviction of three Film Recovery Systems executives in the toxic poisoning death of an employee. Although similar in some ways to the Pinto prosecution, the FRS case must be distinguished for three important reasons: the charges included murder rather than reckless homicide; the indictment named not only the corporation but also individual executives; the case not only reached the trial stage but also resulted in a conviction (though an appeal has been filed). Again, the FRS trial should not be seen as an aberration, though it broke legal ground; like the Pinto case, it belongs to a pattern of prosecutions that has widened its scope during the 1980s.

Thus, in recent years, a number of corporate homicide cases have been decided by the courts; other cases are currently moving toward trial. Most of the prosecutions which have been completed have not resulted in convictions. Like the Pinto and FRS trials, however, they have added legitimacy to the idea that a corporation and/or its executives are liable to criminal prosecution.

The vast majority of homicide indictments that have been brought against corporate entities and/or executives involve workplace deaths. While the FRS case is not solely responsible for the rapid growth of occupationally related homicide prosecutions, it has received widespread publicity and clearly has shaped the legal strategy in many recent cases.

Cutbacks in OSHA controls may also have helped to inspire these prosecutions. Beginning in 1981, as one agency spokesperson noted, OSHA stressed "cooperation toward manufacturers rather than an adversarial role."[3] In the next four years, the number of OSHA inspectors decreased by 17 percent; both the number of complaints investigated and the amount of fines for violating safety standards declined by 44 percent. In 1984, the U.S. Labor Department reported alarming statistics: work-related deaths had jumped 17 percent in 1983, while occupational injuries and illnesses had increased 11 percent.[4] Although it is risky to claim a direct link between weakened regulatory controls and increased death and injury in the workplace, prosecutors have not been reluctant to make this connection and to cite it as justification for criminally sanctioning corporate offenders. Ironically, efforts to effect "regulatory relief" may have created the rationale, if not the opportunity, for extending the criminal law into the workplace. Thus, in the FRS case, Assistant State's Attorney Jay Magnuson commented, "The more I looked into this, the madder I got. I felt that if OSHA had taken a look at that plant, Golab might still be alive."[5] More recently, after workers at the Pymm Thermometer factory were exposed to toxic mercury vapor, Brooklyn District Attorney Elizabeth Holtzman charged company executives with assault; at the press conference announcing the indictments, Holtzman displayed a poster titled "OSHA's Failure to Protect Pymm Workers."[6]

The following prosecutions are among those that the legal and business communities have watched most closely:

> *Seven construction workers were killed in a 1981 accident at a power plant project near Fresno, California. After being presented with evidence regarding safety standards on the site, a grand jury indicted the Granite Construction Company for manslaughter. The firm sought to dismiss the indictment on the ground that a corporation could not be charged with homicide, but a court of appeal rejected this claim and upheld the indictment—a decision which the California Supreme Court left undisturbed in 1983.[7]

> *In New York, Warner-Lambert Company and several of its officials were indicted for second-degree manslaughter and criminally negligent homicide after a 1976 explosion in the company's gum-making plant killed six workers. The prosecution alleged that the blast could be traced to the failure of officials to install an adequate exhaust system. Although it did not deny the possibility of such a prosecution in different circumstances, an appellate court dismissed the indictment in 1980, stating that the cause of the explosion had been unforseeable.[8]

*In 1984, General Dynamics Corporation was charged with involuntary manslaughter and criminal violations of state occupational standards in the death of a worker exposed to fluorocarbon solvent vapors at its military tank plant in Center Line, Michigan. A state court dismissed the charges, citing the worker's "hypersensitivity" to the solvent, but the Michigan Attorney General's office is appealing the decision.[9]

*In 1985, the California Supreme Court refused to overturn the involuntary manslaughter indictments of movie director John Landis and four other defendants. The charges stemmed from the 1982 deaths of actor Vic Morrow and two children during the filming of *Twilight Zone: The Movie*. Prosecutors claim that negligence during the filming of a late-night scene led to a disastrous helicopter accident. If convicted, the defendants could face two to six years in jail.[10]

*Three officers of Jackson Enterprises, an Ohio cable television contracting firm doing business in Troy, Michigan, were charged in 1985 with involuntary manslaughter in the death of a worker. The employee was overcome by carbon monoxide while working in a van that the firm allegedly failed to maintain properly. Each executive faces a maximum penalty of fifteen years of imprisonment and/or a $7,500 fine.[11]

*S & W Waste Inc. and five present or former officers and employees were tried in Akron, Ohio for a 1984 explosion at a trash-burning plant, which killed three workers. The blast was allegedly caused by sawdust soaked with hazardous chemicals that S & W had shipped to the plant. The company and the individuals—each charged on thirteen counts, including manslaughter and criminal endangerment—were acquitted in 1985.[12]

*After the death of a worker who had suffocated while digging an elevator shaft, Maggio Drilling Inc. and its president were charged in 1984 with involuntary felony-maanslaughter in Los Angeles. The district attorney alleged that the company failed to shore up the trench, provide a safety harness, and monitor the air in the underground shaft. The corporation's president pleaded no contest to the manslaughter charge.[13]

*In 1986, two Austin, Texas companies—Peabody Southwest Inc. and Sabine Consolidated Inc.—and their officers were charged with criminally negligent homicide in connection with the deaths of three workers who were buried alive in two separate construction-trench cave-ins. Once again, prosecutors alleged reckless disregard of on-the-job safety standards.[14]

There also appears to be an increase in corporate homicide indictments against companies charged with recklessness in providing services to their customers, though these cases are not increasing at the same rate as occupationally related cases. Like the workplace prosecutions, most of these cases involve an allegation that the company knowingly or recklessly created—or disregarded—an unacceptably high level of risk which placed users of its service within a foreseeable zone of danger. Three illustrative cases follow:

*Great Adventure Inc. and its parent firm, Six Flags Corporation, were indicted for aggravated manslaughter after eight children were killed in a 1984 fire at their theme park in Jackson, New Jersey. Charged with consciously disregarding the public's safety by not installing smoke alarms or a sprinkler system, the companies were acquitted in 1985 after a controversial trial. Two indicted executives had elected earlier to enter a "pretrial intervention" program requiring one year of community service, after which the indictments would be dismissed and expunged from their records.[15]

*After the death of a 78-year-old patient, the Glendale Convalescent Center in Milwaukee, Wisconsin pleaded no contest to homicide by reckless conduct and to 58 counts of criminal neglect in the care of other patients. While three corporate directors fought extradition, the Center's administrator was convicted of reckless homicide and twelve counts of patient neglect. On appeal, the neglect convictions were upheld, but a 4-3 vote by the Wisconsin Supreme Court reversed the reckless homicide verdict.[16]

*In another nursing-home case, Autumn Hills Convalescent, Inc. and five of its officials were charged in Texas City, Texas with murder by neglect in the death of an 87-year-old patient, who allegedly perished from conditions brought on by poor nursing care. The case ended in a mistrial in 1986. Prosecutors chose not to retry the case because of concern about the potential cost and duration of a second trial and the risk that another jury would also reach a split decision.[17]

While no corporate homicide prosecutions against automakers have been reported since the Pinto trial, several cases have been brought against companies whose alleged pattern of recklessness in leasing, maintaining, and/or operating motor vehicles has led to unnecessary highway fatalities and public risk. Representative cases from three states follow:

*In Frostburg, Maryland, a Michigan executive was indicted for involuntary manslaughter when a truck he had leased experienced brake failure, smashed into fourteen cars, and left three people dead. Prosecutors charged that the executive had repeatedly ignored pleas by his drivers to fix the brakes. Direct Transit Lines Inc., the company leasing the trucks, pleaded no contest to involuntary manslaughter and was fined $3,000.[18]

*In Cambria County, Pennsylvania, McIlwain School Bus Lines, Inc. was indicted in the death of a six-year-old girl, who was struck and killed after leaving a company bus. Although a trial court judge quashed the indictment, an appellate court reversed the ruling. A subsequent jury trial led to the company's 1981 conviction on the charge of homicide by motor vehicle, a fine of $2,000, and an assessment of court costs.[19]

*In a similar case out of Livingston County, Kentucky, the state court of appeals reversed a lower-court dismissal of a manslaughter indictment against Fortner LP Gas Company, Inc. The charge had been filed after a company truck, later discovered to have "grossly defective brakes," struck and killed a six-year-old girl. The criminal case never went to trial, however. A sizeable civil suit judgment against the company and the attendant adverse publicity led the prosecutor to withdraw the indictment.[20]

Corporate indictments for violent crimes are unlikely to diminish. A number of potential prosecutions are on the horizon: a Massachusetts case in which a worker perished after inhaling toxic gas; a Connecticut case in which another worker was killed from exposure to a toxic chemical; an Illinois case in which a worker's death was attributed to silicosis and ruled a homicide by a medical examiner; investigations of construction-related deaths in New Mexico and in North Carolina.[21]

WARNING
THE ILLEGAL DISPOSAL OF
TOXIC WASTES WILL
RESULT IN JAIL.
WE SHOULD KNOW
WE GOT CAUGHT!

Acme Disposal Company

Dear Businesses & Residents of the City & County of Los Angeles

Pollution of our environment has become a crisis.

Intentional clandestine acts of illegal disposal of hazardous waste, or "midnight dumping" are violent crimes against the community.

Over the past 2 years almost a dozen Chief Executive Officers of both large and small corporations have been sent to jail by the L.A. Toxic Waste Strike Force.

They have also been required to pay huge fines; pay for cleanups; speak in public about their misdeeds; and in some cases place ads publicizing their crime and punishment.

THE RISKS OF BEING CAUGHT ARE TOO HIGH—
AND THE CONSEQUENCES IF CAUGHT ARE NOT WORTH IT!

We are paying the price. *TODAY,* while you read this ad our President and Vice President are serving time in *JAIL* and we were forced to place this ad.

PLEASE TAKE THE LEGAL ALTERNATIVE AND PROTECT OUR ENVIRONMENT.

Very Truly Yours,

Acme Disposal Company
(a ficticious company)

Corporate Crime on Display: This Full-Page Notice Appeared in the
<u>Los Angeles Times</u> in 1985 as Part of One Company's Punishment

Further, prosecutors in Milwaukee and Los Angeles have established special units to explore all workplace deaths to determine if corporate criminal charges are warranted. The purpose of the Milwaukee probes, observed County District Attorney E. Michael McCann, is to "heighten existing safety precautions and go after those who take a casual view of worker safety."[22] Echoing this sentiment, District Attorney Ira Reiner estimates that gross negligence by employers is responsible for a "substantial portion" of Los Angeles County's annual toll of 100 workplace deaths. Investigations by the District Attorney's Environmental Crimes/Occupational Safety and Health Division have already led to several workplace prosecutions, and announcements of additional indictments are expected to be forthcoming.[23]

In addition to cases in which reckless homicide or manslaughter charges have been filed, corporations have been indicted on other charges for conduct that allegedly jeopardized human health and safety. In August 1985, Eli Lilly & Company, a pharmaceutical firm, pleaded guilty to misdemeanor charges for failing to advise the government of fatal side effects linked to the arthritic drug Oraflex.[24] Chicago Magnet Wire, an insulation-wire manufacturer, and five of its officials were indicted for aggravated battery and reckless conduct. The charges stemmed from injuries to workers exposed to toxic chemicals. The indictment was dismissed by a Chicago trial court judge and is under review by the Illinois Appellate Court.[25] Another recent criminal case involves Jalisco Mexican Products, Inc., which was fined and given three years' probation for violations of California agricultural, health, and safety codes. The company's president pleaded no contest to 10 criminal misdemeanor charges and was sentenced to a 30-day jail term. Investigations into a massive food-poisoning epidemic that may have killed 40 people resulted in accusations that the company's plant was unsanitary and produced cheese containing bacteria. (The company could not be linked directly, however, to any of the poisoning deaths.)[26] Finally, there have been an increasing number of prosecutions related to the dumping of toxic chemical wastes. Most notably, the Toxic Waste Strike Force of the Los Angeles County District Attorney's Office has launched a number of prosecutions which have sent more than twenty corporate officers to jail.[27] Moreover, environmental cases like these, which attempt to impose criminal liability on individual corporate officers, are no longer limited to state courts. In Orlando, Florida, the owner of several companies that engaged in hazardous waste disposal was indicted in federal court for "knowingly placing employees in danger of death or serious bodily injury" by illegally disposing of chemical wastes and mislabeling waste containers.[28]

Taken together, the cases reviewed in this section indicate that the Ford Pinto trial was not an isolated event but a part—although an important part—of a movement that continues to place corporations under attack.

Yet, as noted earlier, we do not wish to take this line of analysis too far and create the impression that corporate prosecutions are so frequent and so effective that they have become mundane events. If anything, such prosecutions retain interest these days precisely because they are still sufficiently infrequent and novel to make for a good story, whether for reporters in search of a newsworthy piece or for academics in search of publishable research. Indeed, as we will discuss below, several major obstacles remain that limit the truly broad use of the criminal law against corporate illegality.

Corporate Criminal Sanctions: The Obstacles

Although important societal and legal transformations have interacted over the past two decades to make possible cases like Ford's reckless homicide trial, many aspects of the social fabric and criminal justice system have remained unchanged. Legal and social customs, power relationships, and bureaucratic structures are not easily altered, particularly when the agenda is to prosecute corporate actors and other occupational elites. Thus, while the current context encourages corporate criminal prosecutions in some important ways and in some situations, circumstances still dictate that prosecutors must surmount a series of significant obstacles to initiate and win these cases. As Mark Green and John Berry observed recently, "a vigorous, dedicated law-enforcement official who wants to prosecute corporate wrongdoing...must scale [a number of] high walls surrounding a fortress in order to apprehend, convict and punish a suspect sheltered inside."[29] These "walls" which limit corporate criminal prosecutions can be grouped into three general categories: ideological, legal, and structural.

Ideological Obstacles: Thinking About Crime

Much of our analysis is based on the assumption that criminal justice policy has been affected strongly by "what people think."[30] We have asserted that prosecutions of corporate offenders became more prevalent when private citizens, academics, and members of the legal profession began to lose confidence in the trustworthiness of elites, were sensitized to issues of equal justice before the law, and broadened their view of what "crime" might entail. These attitudes, given life by the events of the 1960s and 1970s, have both prescriptive and instrumental implications: upperworld criminals *ought to* and *can* be prosecuted.

The origin of the Pinto case illustrates the importance of these changes. Ford's prosecution was contingent not only on Mike Cosentino being outraged by the alleged link between the Pinto's hazards and the tragic deaths of three teenagers, but also on his defining Ford as a "reckless killer" that he should and could criminally sanction. Had he embraced another definition of the situation—had he thought differently about the relationship of corporations to the criminal law, a likely occurrence ten years earlier—Ford's landmark prosecution would not have taken place.

As we cautioned in Chapter 2, however, there are limits to how much people's thinking about crime has changed. The word "crime" conveys powerful imagery about what is or is not illegal, and about who is or is not an offender. Despite meaningful changes in consciousness about white-collar and corporate lawlessness, "crime" is more likely to trigger the image of the urban poor mugging helpless citizens than of executives fixing prices or recklessly marketing dangerous products. This stereotype is reinforced not only by the way offenders are typically portrayed in news reports and on television programs, but also by the demographics of those processed daily by the criminal justice system. Because disadvantaged persons are prosecuted and imprisoned in disproportionate numbers, the justice system creates a distorted picture of the crime problem: only street crimes are to be feared and only poor people are to be caged. In this sense, the justice system actually supports certain conceptions of crime and helps to create a social reality that many citizens take for granted.[31]

This ideological distortion, however, is not absolute: attitudes have changed and the hegemony of traditional imagery is challenged by the mounting number of corporate crime cases. Nonetheless, such imagery remains consequential, shaping how criminal justice officials define their role and exercise their discretion. Again, the Pinto case provides an appropriate illustration. Although Cosentino eventually decided to pursue Ford's conviction, he did so only after he had overcome reservations about whether it was within the scope of his duties to take on Ford and about whether his community would support his efforts. (Let us recall that unlike the prosecutor in a "normal" case, Cosentino did not try to sway the grand jury toward an indictment because he felt that the jurors would serve as a needed barometer of community sentiments).

Ideological obstacles to undertaking corporate crime cases are likely to be found in most other jurisdictions. Some prosecutors, we suspect, remain actively hostile to the idea of bringing corporations within the reach of the criminal law, believing that such social control is best left to civil courts and regulatory agencies.[32] Other prosecutors, like Cosentino, accept that corporations should not be immune to criminal sanctions. Even so, before launching a criminal case, they will pause to ask a series of questions, any one of which could preclude a prosecution from taking place. Has a crime been committed? Should the corporation and/or its executives really be blamed? Could this incident be handled more adequately through civil or regulatory options? Will the public support a prosecution? To be sure, these are reasonable questions, particularly because a corporate case is often unfamiliar territory and threatens to consume much time and many resources. Yet it is revealing that street crimes do not prompt such a long list of questions, nor do they demand as much thought to resolve whether an indictment is warranted.

Ideology plays even a more fundamental role, however, in restricting the number of corporate crime prosecutions. The prosecutors' and elected officials' views of crime influence how the criminal justice system is organized and how its resources are allocated. To the extent that a narrow, traditional definition of crime is embraced, the enforcement machinery will be geared to catching and processing only street criminals. As a practical consequence of this orientation, corporate misconduct either will escape detection or, when too egregious to be ignored, will not result in an indictment or conviction because the foundation for an effective prosecution, such as legal and investigatory work, was not laid.

When officials think differently about crime, however, the more vigorous prosecution of upperworld offenders becomes possible. As discussed in Chapter 1, the Carter administration's definition of white-collar crime as an enforcement priority created a context in which federal prosecutors sought to advance their careers by bringing criminal cases against members of the political and business elite. Similarly, as noted above, Los Angeles County's recognition of the problems associated with the illegal disposal of toxic wastes led to the formation of a special strike force which has won convictions against numerous corporations and top executives. We admit that these instances, in which changed ideology has resulted in a systematic reallocation of prosecutorial resources and activity, remain the exception; nonetheless, they show how raising consciousness about the full dimensions of the crime problem can remove a major barrier to an ongoing attack against corporate lawlessness.

As we will argue later, there is reason to anticipate that ideological obstacles to corporate prosecutions are likely to diminish in the years ahead. At the same time, the political debate over what constitutes crime—or, more accurately, what constitutes "serious" crime—shows few signs of abating. When Ronald Reagan took office, his administration moved quickly to replace white-collar illegality with violent street crimes and drug trafficking as the Justice Department's foremost priorities.[33] In 1981, Attorney General William French Smith named a Task Force on Violent Crime; five years later, Edwin Meese, Smith's successor, formed a Task Force on Pornography.[34] The reports of the commissions illuminated the dangers of street violence and sexual violence respectively, and offered an agenda for getting tough with those who threatened the public's health and the strength of the moral order. Both reports also received considerable media publicity. It is instructive that no task force was formed to analyze the dimensions of corporate crime and to recommend strategies for lessening this form of victimization.

As suggested in Chapter 1, however, the Reagan administration did not simply dismiss white-collar crime as a social concern. In fact, when criticized for advancing class-biased justice, administration officials were uniformly careful to assert that "the [Justice] Department still regards white-collar crime as a high priority."[35]   Instead, the attempt to shape public thinking about crime proved more subtle. "White-collar crime" was not simply downgraded in importance; the term was now used to cover only certain activities: economic offenses committed *against* corporations and the government, but not offenses, including violent offenses, committed *by* corporations.[36]

This ideological message can be illustrated by examining an FBI official's 1984 testimony to a House of Representatives subcommittee, which was considering the agency's budget requests. The official began his comments by defining white-collar crime as "illegal acts that use deceit and concealment rather than the application or threat of physical force or violence." He warned that the "cost of white-collar crime is enormous in terms of both dollars and lost faith in Government institutions on the part of American citizens," but did not mention any physical costs. He then justified the redirection of agency resources to fight drug trafficking on the grounds that "while many of the white-collar crime investigations are lengthy and complex, they are often not life-threatening situations and may be unaddressed for a longer period of time than other investigations such as narcotics matters." Finally, he stated that "our national priorities within the White-Collar Crime Program are Governmental Fraud, Corruption of Public Officials and Financial Crimes in that order."[37]

This testimony, it seems, lends credence to the view that the criminal law is an ideological construct.[38]   Yet we do not wish to imply that the public's thinking was being manipulated purposefully; the meaning given to "white-collar crime" probably was not evidence in support of conspiracy theory but a reflection of the consciousness of government officials. In any case, this conceptualization of white-collar crime was consistent with the administration's overall agenda to bolster the image of corporate America and to lessen governmental interference in business enterprises. Corporations were portrayed as society's benefactors, not its victimizers, and the urgent task was not to invoke greater surveillance but to provide regulatory relief. In this context, talk of getting tough with corporate crime did not earn a warm response.[39]

Of course, corporate prosecutions took place during the Reagan administration; the E.F. Hutton case is one celebrated example. We believe, however, that such prosecutions emanated not from the administration's crime control ideology but from the circumstances that have fueled the general movement against corporate lawlessness and constrained the actions of those who previously would have turned a blind eye to the indiscretions of the advantaged.

Legal Obstacles

A favorable ideological context is a necessary but not a sufficient condition for a corporate criminal prosecution, as was vividly apparent in the Pinto case. Once Cosentino decided to push ahead with Ford's prosecution, he confronted a series of legal barriers that could have derailed his efforts. As reviewed in Chapter 5, Ford argued that its indictment should be quashed because on a *conceptual* level Indiana law precluded trying a corporation for reckless homicide. Unlike an individual offender, the defense asserted, Ford was not a "natural person," could not form criminal intent, and could not be imprisoned. As we also noted, Ford's lawyers contended that there were *constitutional* reasons for throwing the case out of court. First, because Ford built the Ulrichs' Pinto in 1973 but was indicted under a 1978 Indiana statute, the prosecution violated the *ex post facto* provisions of the Indiana and the United States Constitutions; second, because federal statutes in a comprehensively regulated industry "preempted" local criminal law, Ford's compliance with all NHTSA standards meant that its indictment violated the supremacy clause of the U.S. Constitution. Finally, in Chapter 6, we observed James Neal's use of the constitutional protections granted to criminal defendants—traditionally relatively powerless individuals—to help limit the evidence which the prosecution could show the trial jury.

For Cosentino and the prosecution team, Ford's legal arguments were serious obstacles to reaching trial and then winning at the trial stage. Some of these obstacles were overcome fully (the conceptual and preemption issues), some partially (the *ex post facto* issue, which upheld Ford's potential culpability but limited it to a 41-day period), and others not at all (many of the evidentiary rulings). In all instances, however, dealing with these points of law required substantial legal expertise (which volunteers Berner and Kiely helped to provide), consumed valuable time, and exacted a steep emotional cost as the prosecution wondered if a single judicial ruling would scuttle its entire case.

Of course, the Pinto case is sufficiently idiosyncratic that the legal obstacles faced by Cosentino will not be reproduced identically in subsequent corporate criminal litigation (the *ex post facto* issue and the 41-day ruling added a particularly odd twist). Yet Ford's prosecution is not so unusual that it fails to illuminate the kinds of legal obstacles that will continue to surface and limit the initiation and success of corporate cases.

First, the conceptual issues surrounding corporate prosecutions, especially for violent offenses, are far from settled. As we observed in Chapters 3 and 5, the criminal law has edged enough toward holding corporations culpable that conceptual concerns are no longer insurmountable, although certain statutory definitions must be considered carefully by any state's attorney who is drafting an indictment. Thus, in 22 states, legislatures have passed specific statutes codifying corporate criminal liability (see Figure 1).[40] In other states, corporate prosecutions have been sanctioned judicially.[41]

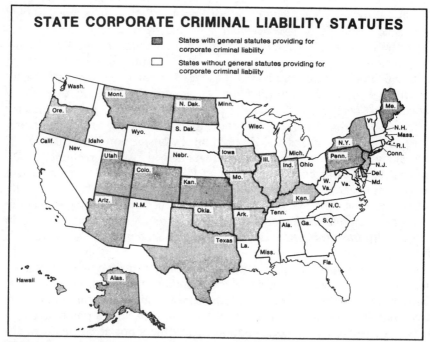

STATE CORPORATE CRIMINAL LIABILITY STATUTES

States with general statutes providing for corporate criminal liability

States without general statutes providing for corporate criminal liability

Figure 1

Under the Federal Criminal Code, however, it is still not a crime for corporate managers or officers to conceal a workplace hazard or knowingly market an unsafe product. In 1985, a bill was introduced in the U.S. House of Representatives, providing for a stiff fine and/or a jail sentence for managers who "knowingly fail" to inform appropriate federal agencies and affected employees or consumers about health and safety risks. It was opposed vigorously by several business groups and never made it out of committee. Although the bill's sponsor plans to reintroduce it, the future of a federal corporate criminal liability law of this type is uncertain.[42]

Other problems, as well, have the potential to derail prosecutorial efforts. As seen in the review of recent cases presented earlier in this chapter, judges at various levels and in various states have dismissed indictments on conceptual grounds, while other cases focusing on these issues are awaiting final decisions. Further, the existence of statutes or rulings permitting corporate prosecutions does not prevent their legitimacy from going unchallenged on appeal, especially when corporate entities or managers are charged with violent crimes. In Texas, for example, corporate criminal liability has been codified by legislation. Nonetheless, in *Vaughan & Sons v. State*, one Texas appellate court held that corporations could not be held liable for homicide because they were incapable of forming and acting with "intent, knowledge, [or] recklessness."[43]

Second, as in the Pinto case, constitutional obstacles continue to threaten the viability of prosecutors' cases. The preemption argument could prove particularly thorny. Although Indiana Judge Donald W. Jones found Cosentino's reasoning more persuasive than Ford's and refused to overturn the company's indictment on the grounds that federal regulatory standards preempted state criminal law (see Chapter 5), it is unclear how judges elsewhere will interpret this issue. Thus, in the Chicago Magnet Wire case mentioned above, the trial judge ruled that OSHA regulations preempted state law, and he dismissed corporate and executives' indictments for aggravated battery and reckless conduct in exposing workers to toxic chemicals.[44] Lawyers for the FRS defendants have also adopted this legal principle and contend that the executives' convictions should be reversed because "OSHA safety standards, even if unenforced, preempt any state laws and that local prosecutors therefore lack the authority to press charges."[45] Illinois courts are now weighing the validity of this reasoning.

More generally, prosecutors will have to contend with the reality—as did Cosentino in taking on Ford—that corporations as *criminal* defendants enjoy nearly the same constitutional protections as individual "persons" (see Chapters 3, 5, and 6). Exceptions to this rule exist—corporations do not generally possess the right against self-incrimination, for instance—but they are relatively rare. Instead, in building a defense and trying to stymie the prosecution, corporations can rely on the same due process protections that more traditional defendants invoke.

This fact places a special burden upon states' attorneys. As John Braithwaite has noted, constitutional "protections were built to ensure that financially weak and politically powerless individuals were not crushed by the prosecutorial might of the state."[46] The irony, as Bruce Berner came to appreciate in the Pinto case, is that corporations like Ford do not lack financial or political resources. "The prosecution is twice cursed," Berner observed, "once for having fewer resources and once for playing by the rules that assume it has more."[47]

Braithwaite is among those commentators who would curtail the rights of corporate criminal defendants:

> The tendency automatically to attribute traditional rights and due process protections to corporations simply because they are available to individuals is legal anthropomorphism at its worst. Corporations cannot have a confession physically coerced out of them under the bright lights at a police station. Corporations do not stand in the dock without benefit of legal counsel. When corporations do suffer at the hands of the state, the suffering is diffused among many corporate actors—shareholders, managers, workers. The extreme privations suffered by individual victims of state oppression which justify extreme protections of individual rights are not felt within the corporations.[48]

However persuasive Braithwaite's remarks might seem, they offer little comfort to current corporate prosecutors. They must obtain indictments, gain convictions, and have verdicts sustained on appeal—all within the boundary of prevailing criminal law. And if the experiences of the Pinto prosecutors are representative, even the most resourceful and talented among them will find this a demanding obstacle course.

Structural Obstacles: The Pragmatics of Enforcement

Many commentators have detailed why corporate prosecutions are infrequent and why, when they do occur, they are unlikely to succeed. Although some of these authors have illuminated the ideological and legal barriers to such litigation, most have focused on how the very *structure* of corporations, the types of crimes they commit, and the prosecutorial role make prosecutions difficult and nonutilitarian. Indeed, at each stage of the criminal justice system, circumstances exist that limit the practicality of using the criminal law to control corporate wrongdoing—even when a prosecutor might wish to launch a case and would be permitted to do so by existing legal statutes. These circumstances often place the greatest burden on county prosecutors like Mike Cosentino, but they can be formidable obstacles to successful corporate criminal cases even for federal prosecutors, who may possess more resources and experience in trying white-collar offenders.

Detecting Crime. To begin with, corporate offenses are difficult to detect, and detection is a precondition for any prosecution. Although it is usually obvious when a traditional crime has taken place, a corporate crime is less apparent. The difference in visibility is tied directly to the nature of the crimes involved in each offense category. Missing property, a mugging, or an assault are forced upon a victim's attention. By contrast, the very structure of most corporate acts insulates workers or citizens from knowledge of their victimization.[49] Typically, corporate offenders are not present physically at the scene of the crime, and the effects of their victimization are diffused over time (as when toxic agents are released into the workplace or the environment) and over populations (as when prices are fixed on consumer products). Thus the offender-victim relationship is distant, if not fully abrogated, and it militates against people blaming corporations for lost income or impaired health.

This relationship necessarily limits the detection of corporate lawlessness. Law enforcement is primarily a reactive process: investigations begin only after citizens report that a crime has taken place. Since many victims of corporate illegality lack the awareness to file a crime report, no state response is forthcoming. Of course, police do employ proactive methods to detect certain ongoing criminal activities—for example, "undercover agents" and "sting operations" when investigating vice-, drug-, and "Mafia"-related enterprises—and these could be used to unmask corporate malfeasance. In most jurisdictions, however, this remains a moot point: criminal justice agencies have neither the inclination nor the expertise to undertake proactive operations in hopes of discovering unlawful corporate practices.[50]

Deciding to Prosecute. "Desirable as it may be to punish the wicked," John Coffee has observed, "one cannot ignore that the supply of such persons vastly exceeds available prosecutorial resources."[51] Necessarily, then, prosecutors must exercise discretion in deciding which cases to pursue and which cases to ignore or refer to other control agencies (e.g. mental health centers, federal regulatory agencies). Notably, prosecutors face powerful disincentives for embarking on a campaign to restore law and order in the business community.

One immediate difficulty is whether the prosecutor can determine clearly that a crime has, in fact, been committed. In the Pinto case, for example, even when Mike Cosentino was confronted with concrete victims and evidence linking the Pinto to the Ulrichs' deaths, he still had to question whether Ford's conduct could be defined as criminal. Similarly, in the Wisconsin nursing-home death case discussed above, Charles Schudson, the prosecutor, commented that seeking a conviction "may be like nailing an omelet to the wall." After the conclusion of the trial, he offered the more general observation that "this initial uncertainty as to whether a crime has been committed may loom as an insurmountable obstacle to the district attorney who must decide whether to allocate resources to an investigation with such uncertain potential for success."[52]

Other circumstances may prove even more influential in persuading prosecutors that the costs of pursuing a corporate case outweigh the benefits. Before deciding to prosecute, they must weigh the feasibility of winning a complex case against a powerful corporation. They must also compute the utilitarian value of devoting substantial economic and human resources to a case with an unpredictable outcome, particularly in light of their constituents' potential reaction and the simultaneous need for resources to process street-crime offenders.[53] We may recall that in the Pinto prosecution, Cosentino tried to overcome these obstacles by requesting a special budget allocation of $20,000, securing a volunteer staff, and keeping a close eye on community sentiments. Other prosecutors, less adventurous or more cautious, have often chosen to bypass the disruption of routines, political risk, and personal cost entailed in attacking a corporation.

Another consideration concerns the relationship between district attorneys' offices and other governmental agencies. Since most allegations of corporate crimes involve activities supervised at least partially by regulatory agencies, the path of least resistance for most prosecutors has been to refer any irregularities to an administrative agency. In fact, when a prosecutor's office does decide to try a corporate offender, officials in regulatory agencies may react as though their "turf" has been violated and may become uncooperative—as did officials from NHTSA and OSHA during the early stages of the Pinto case and FRS case respectively. Though such problems may be overcome (both NHTSA and OSHA eventually provided assistance in the Ford and FRS prosecutions), a prosecutor cannot risk alienating a potentially helpful regulatory agency: in corporate cases, a prosecutorial staff often is overwhelmed by technical documents and jargon, and hence can ill-afford to forfeit the expertise and resources an agency has to offer.[54]

Prosecutors also face the difficult decision of whether to indict individual executives and/or the corporate entity. Legal scholars still dispute this issue on a number of philosophical and policy grounds: Can a corporation form criminal intent? Will the harm incurred by a corporate sanction fall on innocent parties, such as shareholders and employees? Do chief executives create pressures that induce mid-level managers to violate the law, but remain insulated against criminal culpability by their organizational position? Are individual executives or corporations more deterrable?[55]

We suspect, however, that the key issue for many prosecutors is less esoteric and more narrowly pragmatic: whom do they have a reasonable chance of convicting? The presence or absence of obstacles, then, will not only determine whether a prosecution is initiated; it will also pinpoint the target of any indictment that might be secured. Certainly this was true in the Pinto case, where Cosentino determined quickly that he had little chance of extraditing and convicting individual Ford officials. In the FRS case, by contrast, the size of the firm and the nature of the offense made it feasible to attempt to convict both the corporation and individual executives.

Building a Case. Once the initial decision is made to move ahead with a prosecution, the very nature of corporate illegality creates special barriers. In processing street crimes, prosecutors often can rely on witnesses to furnish damning testimony; they saw who mugged them or can identify stolen property found in a suspect's possession. This situation occurs only occasionally in white-collar cases, as when current or former employees—like Harley Copp in the Pinto dispute—become "whistle blowers" and reveal what took place behind the closed doors of a corporation. More often, however, organizational secrecy means that the only witnesses to a corporate crime are the offenders themselves.[56]

Like any defendant, corporate offenders are reluctant to cooperate with their accusers. But in contrast to street criminals, who have little control over the evidence that comes to the attention of enforcement officials, the organizational position of corporate executives gives them the opportunity to obfuscate evidence or to reveal it selectively. As a result, they exert considerable control over both the degree and the kind of information that prosecutors will be able to ferret out.[57]

Moreover, their attorneys help them to deflect prosecutorial attempts to secure incriminating evidence. In his study of white-collar crime defense attorneys, Kenneth Mann discovered that the main strategy of these lawyers is "information control"—keeping "evidence out of government reach by controlling access to information"—rather than "the conventional advocacy task of substantive argument in which the defense attorney analyzes a set of facts and argues that a crime is not proved."[58] These attorneys use two approaches to insure that items such as company records, reports, internal memoranda, and test results escape the prosecutor's grasp. First, in "adversarial information control," they invoke legal rules and precedents to argue that prosecutors should not have access to certain corporate documents. Second, in "managerial information control," they instruct clients "holding inculpatory information how to refrain from disclosing it to the government and, if necessary, to persuade or force him to refrain."[59] The adversarial approach to information control is inherent in our system and can be used by counsel for traditional as well as corporate defendants. The managerial approach, however, is particularly well suited to corporate defendants: they often have considerable control over the very information—technical documents, internal memoranda, knowledge of how decisions were made—that prosecutors require to develop a plausible case against them.

Corporations do not always succeed, however, in maintaining complete control over potentially incriminating evidence. As we saw in the Pinto case, Ford's "corporate closet" was opened over the course of a decade by Harley Copp's revelations, by lawyers in civil cases, by investigative reports (such as Dowie's article in *Mother Jones* and the *60 Minutes* segment), and by NHTSA's testing and inquiries. Even so, building a case against Ford was not a simple task. Once company documents were compiled, it was necessary to decide how this information could be used to convince a jury to convict Ford of reckless homicide. As discussed in Chapter 6, Terry Kiely spent several months developing the necessary expertise to make sense of Ford's reports, reconstructing the Pinto's history, and preparing the prosecution's case for trial.

Similar difficulties are likely to face prosecutors who succeed in neutralizing a corporation's attempts to control information. Because illegalities are embedded within the corporation's decision-making structure and economic function, prosecutors must often devote considerable time to learning about the corporation and about how the criminal enterprise was carried out.[60] Moreover, the skills required to analyze evidence are quite different from those normally employed to build a case against a street criminal. Many corporate documents are couched in highly specialized or technical language, making the necessary research academic, tedious, and dull. Further, reviewing company files and reports can be a formidable assignment; even small corporations can produce a staggering volume of paperwork, particularly if several years' records must be studied. Without a staff of experienced investigators and researchers, deciphering what is salient and what can be ignored safely may not be accomplished quickly or accurately enough.[61]

Thus prosecutors face a double-edged sword. On the one hand, successful information control by a corporation means that too little evidence will be available to win a conviction. On the other hand, access to a wealth of corporate documents may prove a Pyrrhic victory because there may too much evidence to process. Whether the information is insufficient or overwhelming, it could lead a state's attorney to the same conclusion: a convincing case cannot be built and thus the prosecution should be terminated.[62]

Bringing the Defendant to Trial. As the chronicle of the Pinto saga reveals, the time between a corporation's indictment and the trial can determine the character and perhaps the very survival of a case. We noted previously that the defense will raise legal arguments to have the indictment quashed or critical evidence suppressed. Apart from the legal merit of these arguments, practical considerations also apply.

First, does the prosecution have the legal expertise to counteract the defense's efforts to scuttle the case or to limit it severely? Cosentino was able to counteract Ford's briefs with the assistance of law professors Bruce Berner and Terry Kiely, but not all district attorneys will have the good fortune to secure such expert services free of charge.

Second, how many prosecutors have the tenacity for this kind of fight? A corporation's legal maneuverings will consume a great deal of time and exhaust much of the prosecutor's emotional reserve. Many corporations have the resources to absorb the costs of filing legal brief after legal brief and of stretching out the pretrial phase over several years. By contrast, the organizational strength of most prosecutorial offices is limited and the comparative organizational costs of a prolonged legal battle are potentially much greater. Moreover, the brunt of these burdens is likely to fall most heavily on the shoulders of a few individuals—like Cosentino and his small staff—who must sustain a high level of personal involvement and risk in the face of a corporate opponent.

Winning the Trial. As the Pinto case illustrates poignantly, success in bringing a corporation to trial does not mean that the most serious obstacles to winning a conviction have been surmounted. With so much at stake, corporate defendants have a large incentive to retain prestigious law firms—like Neal and Harwell—and give them the resources to formulate a vigorous counterattack. These resources allow such attorneys to conduct investigations that "leave nothing to chance" and to purchase the expert testimony needed to dispute the substantive points of the prosecution's case. Yet if the Pinto case is representative, corporate defense lawyers are also apt to use their legal expertise and staff resources to make continued efforts at information control. At the very beginning of Ford's trial, James Neal filed numerous motions *in limine* to restrict severely the kind of evidence that Cosentino could introduce (such as pictures of the victims and documents on pre-1973 Pintos). As recalled from Chapter 6, these briefs were prepared in the months before the trial and played a crucial role in thwarting the prosecution's case.

Prosecutors must also overcome the problems inherent in presenting a complex corporate crime case to a jury of lay persons, particularly if the defense has used experts (such as Hans Zeisel) to assist in selecting jurors sympathetic to its interests. Unlike specialized corporate criminal defense attorneys who have had significant trial experience, prosecutors often are on unfamiliar ground as they use corporate documents and technical testimony to convince jurors that an intricate sequence of bureaucratic decisions over a number of years culminated in a criminal offense rather than in unforseeable harm.[63] This task is complicated further for prosecutors who must rely on scientific data (for example, test crashes or measures of toxicity of a work environment) to prove "guilt beyond a reasonable doubt." As John Braithwaite and Gilbert Geis have commented:

> Pollution, product safety, and occupational safety and health prosecutions typically turn on scientific evidence that the corporation caused certain consequences. In cases that involve scientific dispute, proof beyond a reasonable doubt is rarely, if ever, possible. Science deals in probabilities, not certainties. The superstructure of science is erected on a foundation of mathematical statistics which estimate a probability that inferences are true or false. Logically, proof beyond a reasonable doubt that a "causes" b is impossible. It is always possible that an observed correlation between a and b is explained by an unknown third variable c. The scientist can never eliminate all the possible third variables.[64]

Beyond these constraints, prosecutors must deal at times with judges—such as Harold Staffeldt—who seem uncomfortable if not antagonistic to the prospect of bringing into their courtroom a corporation and its executives. Part of this reluctance may be ideological. As Leonard Orland has contended, "many judges perceive corporate crime as victimless.... Corporate crime is seen as nothing more than aggressive capitalism—a virtue, not a vice, in a capitalistic system which espouses profit maximization as morally sound."[65] We are not certain that Orland's insight is empirically accurate—we suspect that the tendency, even among judges, to view harmful corporate conduct as morally neutral has declined in recent times—but his point is well taken.[66]

There are other reasons, however, why prosecutors may not fare as well with judges as they do normally. Unlike typical street crimes, which are readily understood, judges must come to grips with the complexities of a corporate offense. Because not all judges succeed at this task, they may hesitate to view a corporation as clearly criminally culpable.[67] Judges also may find themselves in unfamiliar legal territory; prosecutors may ask them to embrace innovative applications of law which the defense counters by filing lengthy briefs claiming rights traditionally afforded to individual defendants. As seen in the Pinto case, at least some judges seek to resolve this ambiguity by relying on narrow or strict constructionist readings of the criminal law that do not allow the prosecution, in Mike Cosentino's words, "to tell the whole story."

Finally, it should be mentioned that a prosecutor's work does not end with a guilty verdict. Corporate convictions can lead to lengthy appeals which involve intricate legal arguments and threaten to consume additional resources. The prosecution may not have the expertise and sustained commitment to win in the appeals court.

We do not wish to claim that we have presented an exhaustive list of the ideological, legal, or structural (or pragmatic) obstacles that limit the initiation and success of corporate criminal prosecutions. Nonetheless, we hope our analysis is sufficient to furnish a sense of the formidable barriers that prosecutors may encounter. At the same time, we do not intend to imply—as some commentators have done—that the obstacles are so great as to preclude or undermine all attempts to sanction corporations criminally. This viewpoint, we believe, leads to two errors.

First, such a perspective ignores the reality that the obstacles vary from one corporate crime case to another, and that prosecutors have varying incentives to launch a case despite the promise of a difficult struggle. Rather than assuming that barriers will deter all but the irrational or the ideological from seeking a corporate indictment, it is more profitable to explore the conditions under which prosecutions are likely to take place.

It is apparent, for example, that the capacity to punish corporations varies across jurisdictions; U.S. Attorneys and state prosecutors in large urban counties (like Cook County) are more likely to have the staff, funds, and expertise to undertake and win corporate cases.[68] This is true particularly when special units have been created to investigate and prosecute white-collar offenders, as in Los Angeles County. In addition, corporate defenders are not equally able to fend off attempts to criminalize them. Not all businesses possess the resources and the stature to attract expert legal counsel, and even when a quality defense attorney is retained, it will be difficult to avoid prosecution if existing evidence clearly establishes the corporation's culpability (as in the E.F. Hutton case). Research also indicates that the seriousness of an illegality is important in determining whether an indictment will be sought. Prosecutors have a compelling reason to give a corporate case high priority when huge sums of money have been obtained fraudulently or, for that matter, when three teenagers perish in a flaming crash.[69] Further, as a number of commentators have observed, attempts to sanction corporations criminally are more likely when regulatory or civil controls either are not available or have proven ineffective. Thus a study of the Securities and Exchange Commission enforcement process concluded that "criminal prosecution is often invoked as a residual response when other options cannot be pursued."[70] As observed earlier, prosecutors have pointed to the absence or failure of OSHA controls as a reason for indicting corporate offenders for harm in the workplace; again, Jay Magnuson, the prosecutor in the Film Recovery Systems corporate murder case in Chicago, stated that he "stepped in because nobody else would do it."[71] We also recall from the Pinto case that one of Mike Cosentino's justifications for prosecuting Ford was his feeling that neither NHTSA nor previous civil judgments had moved the company to fix the Ulrichs' Pinto, and that under Indiana law, the teenagers' parents could have received only limited financial compensation for their tragic loss.

The second pitfall of assuming that the obstacles to corporate prosecution are prohibitive is that this perspective ignores the changing social and legal circumstances that made possible Ford's trial and the other criminal prosecutions reviewed in this and earlier chapters. In the next section, we will discuss why we believe the prevailing context will sustain a continued movement against corporate and white-collar crime and support attempts to bring business offenders within the reach of the criminal law.

Corporate Criminal Sanctions: The Prospects

When we focus exclusively on why corporations cannot be criminally sanctioned, we risk the necessity of explaining prosecutions like the Ford Pinto case as situational, if not idiosyncratic, events. This view has some merit; after all, in most jurisdictions corporate prosecutions are not everyday fare. They arise only when a unique set of factors combine to move someone like Mike Cosentino to seek a criminal indictment. Yet a situational view suffers from the failure to grasp "the larger picture." It does not address why corporate criminal prosecutions, though still relatively uncommon, have become so much more frequent now—even in the face of significant obstacles—than they were several decades ago.

In previous chapters, we offered a framework for understanding this attack on corporate crime. We began with the contention that the Pinto case was not so much an idiosyncratic occurrence as a sign of the times. In particular, we proposed that this and other corporate prosecutions were part of a general social movement in which lawyers, the media, and even criminologists as a profession criticized elite behavior and called for equal justice before the law. This social movement, we suggested, was itself the product of transformations in the nation's political economy and of the "legitimacy crisis" (or "confidence gap") that intensified in the decade beginning in the mid-1960s.

Again, we do not wish to overestimate how much the times have changed. At this stage the movement remains diffuse and uncrystallized, and its general character makes it vulnerable to a conservative political agenda which seeks to replace concern for white-collar lawlessness with a renewed interest in conventional street crime. Still, meaningful changes have taken place. This is why we contend that despite countervailing political forces, the prospects are bright for future attempts to criminally sanction corporate misconduct.

Perhaps the most significant legacy of the past two decades is that people have come to think differently about corporations: about the potential for executives to pursue profits at any cost, about the harm that companies can inflict, about the social responsibility that business should exercise, and about what constitutes a tolerable level of risk as corporate decisions affect the welfare of workers, consumers, and entire communities. In short, society has shifted its moral boundaries between what is considered to be acceptable or unacceptable corporate conduct.

To be sure, ideological blinders remain; many citizens, for example, may not yet appreciate fully the violent consequences of corporate lawlessness. As discussed in Chapters 2 and 4, however, a variety of empirical indicators support the conclusion that the public has grown increasingly critical of the moral status of corporations and their executives. Opinion polls conducted from 1965 to 1975 reveal a steep decline in the public's confidence in businesses. In current polls, respondents continue to give executives "low marks for honesty."[72] Survey data also suggest that the public does not view corporate lawlessness in morally neutral terms but sees such acts as serious and deserving of punitive sanctions.[73] Further, although citizens tend to favor the general idea of relief from government regulation, they consistently oppose policies that would roll back standards for environmental pollution, workplace safety, and consumer protection.[74] "Americans," as Thomas Ferguson and Joel Rogers commented recently, "are profoundly suspicious of big business."[75]

It is instructive that the business community has mobilized to address the problem of diminished legitimacy. College students with corporate aspirations are frequently required to take courses in "business and society" and "business ethics." Indeed, interest in teaching and researching the moral issues facing corporate citizens has grown so rapidly that more books have been published on this topic in the past five years than in the previous twenty-five.[76] Not coincidentally, we believe, there has also been a widespread emphasis on "quality" (quality control, quality circles) and corporate "excellence." Some writers have suggested that we must search elsewhere—Japan, for instance—to find solutions to business's problems. Others have been optimistic that the "passion for excellence" still exists in America, and that we can learn valuable lessons from taking a close look at "America's best-run companies."[77]

Although marginally susceptible to political influence, the prevailing moral boundaries are not likely to shift wildly with the changing ideological winds. As argued earlier, these new boundaries were produced by a series of events that shook the public's confidence in the nation's institutional arrangements. On a general level, consciousness was altered by the familiar list of crises and protest movements that defined the character of the 1960s and early 1970s: the civil rights movement, urban riots, Attica, Kent State, Vietnam, and Watergate. More specific occurrences, however, fostered special enmity and suspicion toward corporate America. Revelations of overseas payoffs, illegal campaign contributions, charges of recklessly endangering workers, and the wanton dumping of toxic chemicals—to name only a few examples—created a dark picture of business executives. In this context, it was not unusual to think that corporations were criminals who should be sanctioned stringently.

This discussion suggests that changes in people's thinking about corporations—or, in our terminology, shifts in existing moral boundaries—are rooted in their social experiences. As Seymour Martin Lipset and William Schneider have noted, this observation carries the implication that reversing an attitudinal trend like this requires people to have countervailing experiences that create renewed trust in a given institutional structure. Such a transformation is not accomplished easily. "In order for confidence in institutions to be restored to a significantly higher level," Lipset and Schneider caution, "we will need a sustained period of good news, far longer than the modest upswings experienced in the past decade."[78]

In short, we are suggesting that the moral or ideological context which made corporate prosecutions seem feasible, if not obligatory, will not be eroded substantially in the near future.[79] Further, we have reason to anticipate that the prosecutions themselves will help to sustain the very context which made them possible. We have proposed that shifts in moral boundaries allowed prosecutors to attack corporations, but the relationship between normative standards and social-control measures may also be reciprocal. When the state punishes a wrongful act, it essentially heightens the visibility of the violated norm and thereby reaffirms the moral boundaries of society.[80] Prosecutions like the Pinto case, then, not only arise from a favorable context, but also sharpen or reify what constitutes acceptable or deviant corporate behavior. The result, which now seems to be in process, is that efforts at social control escalate: corporate trials strengthen emergent moral boundaries, which in turn create new pressures for holding corporations criminally liable.

Prosecutions, particularly when highly publicized, also have practical effects that make subsequent corporate cases more likely. Thus cases set legal precedents, create expertise in the methodology of corporate prosecution, and establish social networks that provide instrumental and affective support to other district attorneys contemplating a corporate indictment. The attention given to the homicide convictions of the Film Recovery Systems' executives is revealing. As an official of the American Prosecutors Research Institute observed, "This case is being discussed all over the country. People are looking at work-related cases in their own areas and drawing parallels."[81]

Prosecutions have the additional pragmatic effect of furnishing valuable information on the political ramifications of undertaking a corporate case. In this regard, we have encountered little data suggesting that prosecutors, like Mike Cosentino, experienced political losses from going after a "big fish."[82] Indeed, Richard Epstein, a critic of the expansion of corporate criminal liability, has gone so far as to suggest that "the current climate of opinion" is sufficiently conducive to attacking business that "it seems almost fanciful to rely upon notions of prosecutorial self-restraint" to achieve "circumspection in invoking...criminal sanctions." After all, Epstein laments, "such self restraint will deny to some what is...the joyous opportunity of both making and seeing the mighty fall."[83]

We should also note important developments in the legal profession. In Chapter 3, we suggested that law played an integral role in facilitating the development of corporate power (though we have also seen that at certain points in history the law has served to restrict unfair and injurious commercial activities). Ironically, however, the legal system now poses a growing threat to many of the interests and practices it has traditionally protected, if not advanced. To some extent, this threat has become real because of the changing status of corporate criminal liability. Even so, the existence of the legal possibility of sanctioning corporations and executives does not mean that attorneys—particularly those employed by the state—will necessarily take advantage of the opportunity to criminalize corporate offenders. Clearly, more is involved.

Part of the inclination for members of the legal profession to attack corporations has historical roots. During the 1960s and 1970s, many students entered law school because they felt that the law could be used as a weapon against entrenched interests and social injustice. For activists, "big business" made an inviting target, and Ralph Nader provided an appealing role model. It is equally instructive, perhaps, that beyond the innovative legal aspects of the Pinto case, Terry Kiely and Bruce Berner did not find the thought of prosecuting Ford ideologically discomforting.

This line of reasoning may help us understand why legal activists and liberal law professors would find compelling the idea of corporate criminal liability, but does it explain why conservative prosecutors (like Mike Cosentino) have increasingly embraced this idea? We believe that it would be wrong to ignore that the tenor of the times also made an important difference in their thinking. Conservatives as well as liberals witnessed

Watergate and other instances of elite corruption, and they were influenced, even if unwittingly, by the changing sentiments of their constituents. Undertaking a campaign to sanction a corporation no longer seemed to present the same risk it might have posed two decades earlier.

Again, however, we believe that more than this is involved. As we discussed in Chapter 1, the development of the legal profession—itself tied up with the growth of modern capitalism—has increasingly emphasized the values of rationality, neutrality, and autonomy. Professional socialization therefore stresses the importance of consistent and logical thinking, norms of equal justice, and independence from economic and political influence. Of course, lawyers have often been accused of irrationality, unfairness, and playing favorites. As argued in Chapter 1, however, such charges—which were voiced frequently beginning in the 1960s—are not viewed lightly. Indeed, they threaten the very legitimacy of the legal profession and typically lead to attempts to show that attorneys are committed to justice and have a fundamental loyalty to the law, not to ideology or special interests.[84]

Two implications follow from these observations. First, professional norms provide lawyers with a common ground. They may disagree on politics, economics, or who will win the pennant, but they share the ostensible commitment to upholding the requirements of the law (not all do, of course, but these tend to be exceptions). On the one hand, this means that whether offenders are rich or poor, corporations or individuals, they have a right to be defended vigorously. Attorneys have the option, if not the obligation, to furnish these defenses.

On the other hand, prosecutors are also mandated to fulfill their half of the bargain and to uphold the law when it is violated. They labor under the constraint of insuring equal justice for all and are assailable if they leave this obligation unfulfilled. In this context, attacks on corporations by conservative prosecutors become understandable. In the face of corporate malfeasance, failing to act would constitute disloyalty to the law, a transgression of implicit, if not explicit, professional norms. Thus Mike Cosentino was no admirer of Ralph Nader, had represented corporations in his civil practice, and felt that the criminal law was inappropriate "99 percent of the time" as a mechanism to regulate economic transactions. Yet when three teenagers perished in a flaming crash and the information seemed to blame Ford for their deaths, he felt that prosecuting the company was the "right thing to do."

The second implication of the legal profession's neutrality and autonomy is that it creates conditions conducive to future corporate criminal prosecutions. If we are correct in our assertion that the moral boundaries between acceptable and unacceptable corporate conduct have shifted toward requiring greater social responsibility, the legitimacy of the legal order hinges on maintaining these boundaries. Evidence that neutrality has been compromised or autonomy has been sacrificed to satisfy special interests will evoke public furor and exact an unacceptably high cost. By contrast, prosecutions that reaffirm moral boundaries have the potential to furnish legitimacy to the legal profession and to the wider legal order. Seen in this light, criminalizing corporate offenders may prove an increasingly rational and utilitarian reaction to changed social circumstances.

Predicting the future is risky business, of course, particularly when we suggest that powerful actors in the society will become more vulnerable to legal attacks. Even so, we believe that the recent numerical trend supports our views. Corporate prosecutions are occurring with increasing frequency and show no signs of abating. It may be equally instructive, however, to examine anecdotal data on two cases—one local, the other of national significance—that reveal the intensity of existing pressures to see that all citizens, including those in corporate settings, receive equal treatment before the law.

The prosecution of local interest took place in Cincinnati. Investigations exposed an ongoing scheme by managers of the city's Riverfront Coliseum to minimize electrical costs by tampering with the facility's meters. At times, their manipulations reduced readings to only thirty percent of the actual consumption. This practice began as early as 1976 and continued until January 1983. The financial loss to Cincinnati Gas and Electric, and ultimately to the customers, who subsidized the loss, reached nearly $750,000.

Once the tampering was uncovered, the county prosecutor not only secured restitution from the Coliseum corporation but also chose to bring charges against the three executives who had rigged the electrical meters. All three pleaded guilty to the charges and were eventually fined and placed on probation.

The reaction to the news of the sentencing is illuminating. Citizens' letters to local newspapers praised the prosecution but denounced the judge's leniency in meting out punishment. The city's conservative daily, *The Cincinnati Enquirer*, ran an editorial reflecting this mood titled "The Coliseum: Yesterday's Sentences Leave Many Convinced Justice Is Not Just." The editorial asked, "Is there one kind of justice for the rich and powerful, as many suspect, and another kind for the poor and powerless?" The writer warned, "The feeling will persist that the sentence was nearly as great an affront to the community as the crime itself."[85]

In a related story, the *Enquirer* reported that the citizens were not the only ones "upset": the judge's colleagues also "decried" the decision to put the "Coliseum electricity thieves" on probation. One jurist, the story noted, felt that the sentence was "just discouraging as hell." After all, the judge lamented, "how do you tell some guy caught running out of [a department store] with a handful of dresses that he's going to the penitentiary when you can tell a guy who stole $750,000 in electricity he's going to be on probation?"[86]

A similar response followed revelations of the disposition of the E.F. Hutton Case. As discussed in Chapter 2, it was discovered that the corporation had engaged in an intricate check-kiting scheme that netted large profits from interest on what amounted to unlawfully obtained loans. In a 1985 plea-bargain agreement with the Justice Department, the corporation pleaded guilty to 2,000 counts of fraud, paid a $2 million criminal fine, and established an $8 million restitution fund for the victimized banks.

In the reaction to the announcement of the plea bargain, there was no sign of the apathy which would suggest that the company's transgression was interpreted in morally neutral terms.[87] No one dared to decry the guilty pleas as yet another attempt to undermine the nation's already beleaguered corporations. There was no collective sigh of relief—except, perhaps, among the executives themselves—that respectable members of the business community would not be housed with more common criminals.

Reaction to the E.F. Hutton Case

In fact, exactly the opposite happened, as the deal struck with E.F. Hutton created something of a legitimacy crisis for the Justice Department. Ralph Nader raised the issue of equal justice before the law, but he was far from alone in doing so.[88] Fifteen Democratic senators forwarded a letter to Attorney General Edwin Meese regarding "the blatant failure to find individual liability." Noting that a poor black woman convicted on a $200 shoplifting charge had been sent "off to the slammer" for thirty days, the senators stated that "the disposition of the E.F. Hutton...case does not bode well for the tone of enforcement, nor for the evenhandedness of justice we can expect from your tenure as attorney general."[89]

Such commentary might be dismissed as political opportunism and rhetoric, but this type of criticism came from both ends of the ideological spectrum. In a column titled "When E.F. Hutton Talks...," conservative William Safire observed that "letting so many white-collar lawbreakers go free was a colossal misjudgment."[90] Newspapers in the nation's heartland echoed this theme. A story carried in a small-town Illinois paper asked, "Does Justice [Department] Have Double Standard?"—and suggested that it does.[91] The lead editorial in the *Peoria Journal Star* ran the headline, "Business Crime: Stealing Money the New-Fashioned Way." The editor wrote:

> If you're going to steal money in the United States, take big amounts and do it with a pen or a computer, not a gun. That's the safest way to do it; you don't have to worry about getting shot by a policeman and you don't have to worry about going to prison if you get caught....E.F. Hutton pleaded guilty to criminal-fraud charges involving an elaborate scheme to overdraw bank checking accounts and deprive banks of millions in interest. The company was ordered to pay a $2 million fine, but no one went to jail...[According to Senator Paul Simon], "The impression is with the public that if you rob a service station of $25 you're going to prison. But if you're with a big brokerage firm and you rob millions of dollars, nothing's going to happen to you." It's not surprising that the public has such an impression. It is based on fact.[92]

In response to this wave of criticism, the Justice Department tried to "defend its stance on white-collar crime" by reaffirming its commitment to equal justice and to deterring lawlessness in the upperworld.[93] "White-collar crime," Edwin Meese declared, "is no less reprehensible an assault on society for being committed with a pencil or a computer rather than a gun." The plea bargain with E.F. Hutton, he noted, was motivated not by sympathy for the offender but by the fear that a costly, complicated trial might have failed and sent "the wrong signal" to corporate America. Instead, a quick, firm sanction sent a message that would not be ignored. "The significance of the Hutton prosecution," he contended, "has not been lost on the financial community."[94] We tend to agree with this final observation, but would add the caveat that neither did the significance of this prosecution escape the attention of the Justice Department.

Corporate Deterrence: Much Ado About Something

In assessing the origins, extent, and future of the attack on corporate crime, we have striven to present a balanced account. Thus we have noted that corporate prosecutions constitute only a fraction of all criminal cases, but that corporations are appearing on criminal dockets, particularly for violent offenses, in far greater numbers than ever before. We have cautioned that, at this stage, the effects of the movement against white-collar crime have been largely symbolic, bolstering the legitimacy of the legal and economic order while bringing about few fundamental institutional or structural changes. Yet we have also argued that it would be misguided to dismiss as unimportant the movement's achievements, symbolic or otherwise: moral boundaries have shifted as the demand for equal justice has intensified; private citizens, academics, reporters, politicians, and prosecutors now think differently about the wisdom of extending the scope of corporate criminal liability; new legal theories have been advanced and precedents set; corporate brushes with the law, like Ford's trial and E.F. Hutton's plea bargain, now come under close scrutiny and receive widespread publicity.[95] And in this chapter, we have attempted to detail the many obstacles to corporate prosecutions, but have urged the reader to consider the conditions that create bright, or at least less dim, prospects for future prosecutions. More generally, we chose the Ford Pinto case as the focal point of our book precisely because it illuminates the poverty of viewing simplistically the complex issues involved in corporate prosecutions—why such prosecutions will or will not be initiated, will succeed or fail, will be seen as morally justified or unfairly intrusive.

Another issue, also concerned with the matter of balance, requires comment. We have proposed that corporate prosecutions are becoming more frequent and will continue at a similar, if not higher, rate in the future. Yet will this attack on corporate crime make any real difference? Will it reduce the victimization of workers, consumers, and the general public? Or is all the talk about prosecuting wayward capitalists really "much ado about nothing"?

Of course, deterrence (or, more generally, crime control) is not the only reason why one might justify imposing criminal sanctions on corporations. For some individuals, exacting retribution is a compelling enough reason to invoke the criminal law. Indeed, as witnessed in the Pinto case, a major motivation for prosecuting Ford was moral, to see that justice was done and the victims' loss not diminished. We suspect that moral considerations will continue to play a large role in future attempts to exact a just measure of pain from corporate offenders.[96]

From a broader policy perspective, however, questions of utility will almost certainly arise. The question of utility is particularly likely to shape policy decision making, because options other than criminal penalties (namely civil and regulatory controls) are available and, it might be argued, are more efficient in compelling corporate compliance. Thus it seems that Herbert Packer is not too far off the mark in asserting that with regard to the "economic offenses" of business, "the case for this use of the criminal sanction rests squarely on deterrence."[97]

A comprehensive consideration of corporate deterrence—specific and general, executive and entity—would require a full chapter, if not a complete volume. Because this task would take us far beyond the issues we have set out to explore, we do not hesitate to leave this large enterprise to others or for another occasion. Nonetheless, given the salience of the deterrence debate, we will add at least a general commentary.

As will become apparent below, many commentators have suggested that corporations are so large and powerful as to be immune from efforts at deterrence by trivial criminal sanctions. In this view, the attack on corporate crime is an exercise in futility; not much will come of it. We disagree with this portrait of the corporation as an "invincible criminal" and argue instead for a more balanced perspective. Rather than assuming that the current attack on corporate crime is really "much ado about nothing," we propose that, at the very least, it is "much ado about something."

Lines of Analysis

The case for the deterrent effects of corporate criminal sanctions can be made along several lines. We will touch briefly on four broad reasons why corporate prosecutions, particularly if they continue to grow more frequent, have the potential to diminish lawlessness in the business community. Next we will focus in more detail on one line of analysis which we believe has been largely neglected, but which suggests that corporations may be less immune to existing sanctions than many people imagine. Our discussion necessarily will be speculative, since research on corporate deterrence is still in its earliest stages. We will note, however, that the limited data available—anecdotal, interview, quasi-experimental—tend to support the conclusion that white-collar and corporate offenders are deterred by criminal prosecution.[98]

Deterring the Rational. Although research has yet to establish convincingly that criminal justice punishment deters conventional offenders,[99] several commentators have proposed that corporate managers are a different breed and thus are more likely to be influenced by the imposition or the general threat of a criminal sanction.[100] For three reasons, the argument goes, executives must be counted among the most deterrable types. First, their illegalities are seldom acts of passion or situational opportunism—as many street crimes are—but flow instead from calculated risks taken by rational actors. As such, they are more amenable to control by policies based on the utilitarian assumptions of the deterrence doctrine. Second, the potential costs of a legal violation are greater for executives than for typical clients of the criminal justice system. They generally have more to lose through a criminal conviction, such as social status, respectability, a comfortable home, and life's amenities. And third, because executives are not committed to crime as a way of life, as many serious street criminals are, desisting from criminal involvement does not entail a loss of social role and change in lifestyle.

This line of reasoning should not be carried too far, as it is based on simple distinctions between disadvantaged and advantaged criminals. Further, it decontextualizes managers and embraces the idea that they are perfectly rational economic actors, whereas organizational life and decision making involve much more than rational thought. These caveats, however, are not meant to dispel fully the notion that corporate managers are sensitive to criminal sanctions. Even if executives are not uniformly calculating and unlike street criminals in many respects, their structural location would seem to rationalize their decisions and provide them with more resources to lose in case of conviction. To the extent that econometric models of crime are valid, then, it is plausible to hypothesize that corporate executives would be more deterrable than actual or potential criminals drawn from other levels of society.[101]

Criminal Sanctions as an Organizational Contingency. Corporations historically have paid scant attention to the threat of criminal sanctions, but this observation is not proof that they still sport such a cavalier attitude. Much of this book has been devoted to showing that in recent years corporations have become markedly more vulnerable to attempts to criminalize them. The objective certainty of punishment may remain low, but without doubt the perceived risk is increasing steadily. Even if corporations have not had recent legal entanglements themselves, their managers have read—in newspapers or in *Fortune*, for that matters—about the growing number of firms and executives being hauled into court.

In short, we are suggesting that times have changed enough that criminal penalties are being viewed as contingencies, which organizations must begin to address. It would seem that prosecutions are no longer seen simply as idiosyncratic legal responses but increasingly as a predictable environmental condition. As a result, there are incentives to undertake organizational reforms that address this legal contingency and minimize the risk of criminal sanctioning. Indeed, it may be a sign of the times that some business commentators now worry that "applying criminal sanctions may result in much more deterrence than is socially desirable,"[102] and that "a marked emphasis on criminal sanctions could scare many firms into taking 'defensive' measures, resulting in corporate inefficiency, higher costs, and rising prices."[103]

This line of analysis takes on some meaning when we examine the E.F. Hutton case, which (as Edwin Meese claimed) apparently has sent a message to the financial community. As *Fortune* reported, "the most visible effect of E.F. Hutton's scandal over cash management has been a surge of interest in the subject by chief executives." Accounting firms "spent the summer attending to clients who suddenly wanted their cash management procedures reviewed." The article concluded by warning, "Send your bank a letter, as some companies recently have, explaining your methods of transferring and pooling cash. Negotiate a formal agreement on your accounts and handling of overdrafts if they occur. And if you're chaining, cut it out."[104]

The Pinto case is also suggestive here. Nine months after being indicted on charges of reckless homicide, Ford took steps to introduce organizational reform. This reform emphasized product "durability, quality, and reliability," and instructed management to "look beforehand at points of no return," such as when designs for fuel systems are finalized and when machines are tooled. The problems besetting the production of the Pinto were to be avoided in the future.[105]

Reform at Ford also included efforts to establish a better system for recording the kind of information needed to defend the company in court battles; thus procedures were instituted requiring more detailed documentation of safety and engineering decisions.[106] These measures may have the expected result of bolstering Ford's legal defenses, but they may also create greater internal accountability and insure the correction of practices that cause undue liability problems. In any case, concern over self-protection reveals Ford's sensitivity to the need for introducing organizational change in order to address the legal contingencies that promise to be permanent features of doing business in today's corporate world.

The Educative Effects of Criminal Sanctions. Criminal sanctions also have the potential to reduce corporate illegality through more indirect means. As numerous commentators have observed, the applications of law serve an educative function in teaching people what is socially acceptable or unacceptable, what is or is not a crime. In short, sanctions allow people to learn the moral boundaries of social conduct and thus provide guides for subsequent actions.[107]

Previously we suggested that corporate prosecutions both resulted from and helped to produce new moral boundaries regarding corporate misconduct. We would add that prosecutors, or citizens, are not the only ones who have learned from these legal encounters. Executives also have had ample opportunity to be educated by corporate crime cases. Some may simply have learned that the threat of sanction has crossed the threshold at which it must be given consideration. For others, we suspect, the lesson has had a moral component. The highly publicized condemnation of corporate schemes has sensitized them to the ethical issues at stake and has impressed upon them the salience of corporate social responsibility. They think and act differently than before.

Accordingly, many corporations adopted codes of ethics in the 1970s, when illegal corporate campaign contributions and overseas bribes were making headlines. These firms often discovered that simply implementing such codes did not always compel ethical conduct. Their subsequent response, however, is revealing. According to Gary Edwards, executive director of the nonprofit Ethics Resource Center, "a lot of them thought the job was done. Now they come in, codes in hand, and say, 'These don't seem to be doing the job.' They want to transform them into management tools—training, communication, education." As a result, an increasing number of companies—including such giants as General Dynamics, McDonnell Corporation, Chemical Bank, and American Can Company—have taken further steps to initiate formal ethics-education programs.[108] Although we cannot infer that a moral revolution is brewing, ethical concerns seem to be gaining increasing importance in corporate boardrooms.

Strengthening Overall Corporate Social Control. We noted earlier that criminal sanctions are often used against corporations when other controls are either unavailable or ineffective. It is equally true that the criminal law sometimes complements other control mechanisms. The threat of prosecution may persuade companies to comply with government standards or to negotiate settlements with regulatory agencies.[109] Seen in this light, such prosecutions have the potential to diminish corporate illegality not only through moralizing messages or direct threats but also indirectly by strengthening the overall system of social control.

The Process Is the Punishment

The lines of analysis set forth above, though grounded in previous literature, remain speculative and await systematic investigation. Taken together, however, they suggest plausible reasons for anticipating that the growing attack on corporations will reduce corporate lawlessness. Now we will take this perspective one step further and offer in somewhat greater detail a final line of analysis disputing the premise that efforts to achieve corporate crime control are "much ado about nothing."

Although several commentators have argued for the possibility of corporate deterrence, the dominant position is that corporations cannot be tamed; the criminal law is impotent in the face of the immense power exercised by corporations. We will review the variants of this thesis that corporations are, in effect, "invincible criminals," and then will explain why we believe the general argument needs modification.[110]

Christopher Stone asserts that truly effective "social control of corporate behavior" can begin only "where the law ends."[111] Legal sanctions, Stone argues, either prove impotent in the face of corporate power or are ineffective because they do not reach and transform the forces in the corporate environment that induce criminal behavior. Business irresponsibility, adds Stone, will continue to flourish unless innovative steps are taken to reform the very structure of organizational decision making and the corporate culture that informs it; most of these urgently needed measures cannot be stimulated by the application of formal legal sanctions.

More radical thinkers take this analysis to a broader level and observe that the relationship between business interests and the state in a capitalist society precludes both the formulation and the application of law that would limit the public's victimization at the expense of corporate profits. In this context, thoughts of deterrence are difficult to sustain. Thus Sheila Balkan and her colleagues have noted that proposals to control corporate lawlessness through criminal sanctions "fail to consider the power wielded by corporations and the close relationship between business and government agencies designed to regulate it."[112] Indeed, it is apparent that "changes in the political economy will have to precede a reduction in corporate and business crime."[113]

Although they agree that corporations are substantially immune to *existing* controls, other authors are more optimistic about the possibility of achieving a measure of law and order in the business world by invoking *new* sanctioning strategies. A leading article in the *Harvard Law Review* states that "corporations will not be deterred by the threat of prosecution as long as corporate fines remain small."[114]   Although this goal may not be accomplished through the criminal law, the article contends that "larger fines, enforced through civil procedures, should better serve to deter proscribed conduct."[115]

In another variant of this idea, sanctions will be effective only if they are directed against individual executives.   The punishment meted out to corporations is either dwarfed by company profits or passed on to consumers and stockholders.   Meanwhile, unscrupulous executives remain unscathed and are left free to use illegal means to accumulate corporate profits and commensurate career advancement.   Accordingly, some commentators suggest that crime could be controlled more effectively by punishing guilty individuals within the corporation with jail sentences.[116]

Thus many commentators support the proposition that corporations are unaffected by attempts to use the criminal law to deter their wrongdoings: some authors envision reform as beginning only "where the law ends," within the corporate organization itself; others portray corporations as invulnerable to efforts at control undertaken within the boundaries of the existing political economy; still others see deterrence as a possibility only if penalties are increased substantially and/or directed against individual executives.   Although these observations contain important elements of truth, they are not beyond reconsideration.   The available evidence, we believe, suggests that corporate entities may be far more vulnerable to *existing* criminal sanctions than commentators have often led us to believe.

We draw support for our position from Brent Fisse and John Braithwaite's detailed study of seventeen cases of corporate misconduct.[117] They used two criteria in selecting their sample: the corporation was transnational (the smallest ranked 268th in the "*Fortune* 500"), and the violation received substantial publicity.   Further, nearly all the cases involved some attempt to sanction criminally the corporate entity, such as a grand jury hearing, a plea bargain, or a trial.   At the very least, civil suits were filed or an administrative inquiry was undertaken.

Fisse and Braithwaite discovered that in all seventeen cases, the action against the corporation and the subsequent publicity produced corporate reforms that promised to "reduce the probability of a recurrence of the offense or wrongdoing alleged (and often other kinds of offenses as well)."[118]   Admittedly, these cases all received considerable media exposure, and the amount of deterrence was neither measured systematically nor anticipated to be equally strong in all corporations.   Nonetheless, the corporations in the sample were the kind of business giants that commentators have portrayed as impervious to any existing sanctions, particularly to those that merely imposed financial penalties.   In fact, in a number of instances, the companies succeeded in defeating attempts to sanction them and were not damaged significantly by any sort of financial loss (either from the fine imposed or from loss of sales). Even so, the corporations uniformly took steps to minimize future legal difficulties. These included disciplining middle managers who participated in the wrongdoing, rewriting company policies, tightening internal controls, improving communication channels with top management, and trying to introduce a "climate of control" into the organization.[119]

Why would corporate giants be prompted to implement the type of organizational reforms that authors like Stone have suggested, particularly if profits were not seriously jeopardized? The key to this puzzle, Fisse and Braithwaite discovered, is that executives are influenced markedly by the disruption to their lives and the tarnishing of their reputations which occur when attempts are made to sanction their corporation. From extensive interviews with executives involved in the cases, they learned the following:

> It was non-financial impacts that executives in all of the companies reported as the factors which truly hurt and which made them want to avoid a recurrence even if it cost a great deal of money to try to guarantee this. In short, at the level of subjective management perceptions, financial impacts were not a strong deterrent, while non-financial impacts—loss of corporate and individual prestige, decline in morale, distraction from getting on with the job, and humiliation in the witness box—were acutely felt.[120]

Again, these non-financial impacts were felt in cases where the corporation and not the executive was sanctioned, as well as in cases in which not even the corporation was penalized. The study reminds us that corporate giants are run by people and that publicized attacks, regardless of their outcome or effect on profits, impose strains on management that are not always dismissed easily. To borrow a phrase used by Malcolm Feeley in another context, for many executives "the process is the punishment," and this process is sufficiently discomforting to move them to avoid future difficulties.[121]

Most commentators have missed this point. Although they realize that an individual prosecution can inflict a range of disabilities on an executive and scare others straight, they have assumed implicitly that sanctions directed at corporate entities leave executives personally unaffected. This assumption shows the reluctance of many commentators to study the range of people who manage corporations. Although a burgeoning literature on corporate crime and its control has been produced in recent years, relatively little of this research has sought to interview or survey executives to see how they view and negotiate the ethically questionable situations they encounter. Instead, much of this literature contains implicitly an oversocialized conception of the corporate manager—the notion that the criminogenic conditions of organizational life turn even the most moral individuals into profit-seeking sociopaths.

Perhaps we overstate our point. In any case, the few available studies support the conclusion that no simple portrayal of business executives is possible. One study, a poll of 1,227 readers of the *Harvard Business Review*, revealed widespread recognition of the legitimacy of the goal of corporate social responsibility. "Those critics who continue to characterize the American business executive as a power-hungry, profit-bound individualist, indifferent to the needs of society," they concluded, "should be put on notice that they are now dealing with a straw man of their own making."[122] Survey data on attitudes toward environmental issues led another commentator to paint a similar picture: "While popular conjecture might place executive opinion soundly and consistently on the side of advocating economic growth over environmental concerns, we find businessmen highly flexible. Far from demonstrating knee-jerk pro-growth responses, executives today are assessing trade-offs individually, and in many cases support the environmental protection option."[123]

To be sure, a general belief in corporate social responsibility may bend in the face of job pressures to maximize profits, but it would be wrong to believe that such an ideology exercises no constraint at all. Notions of social responsibility raise questions of ethics, make it more difficult to rationalize deviance, encourage "whistle blowing," and potentially heighten sensitivity to sanctions. At the very least, such attention to corporate morality furnishes a conducive context for reform.

On this latter point, Marshall Clinard conducted research on 64 retired middle managers from Fortune 500 companies. The former executives, he found, felt that the top management of a company is crucial in "setting the corporate ethical tone." Legal violations were seen to be likely where there was "an aggressive 'go-go' type of top management, especially the chief executive officer seeking to achieve power and prestige rapidly, both for himself and the corporation."[124]

This finding is important in two respects. First, it suggests that most middle managers are aware of ethical issues and feel discomfort when pressured to violate legal standards. In other words, they would prefer to work in an environment where lawlessness is not encouraged, and would not resist reforms aimed at eliminating illegalities. Second, the finding indicates that attempts to deter corporations will be effective if they succeed in influencing the executive elite which "sets the moral tone" for the organization. The nonfinancial impacts of sanctions are especially relevant because they have the potential to tax the energy of the aggressive executive and to help restructure career interests in favor of greater legal compliance.

Of course, we are not unaware of the organizational and broader structural conditions that nourish corporate criminality. Nor are we suggesting that the criminal law is unlimited and can effect a complete solution to the corporate crime problem. Nonetheless, corporations do not appear to be invincible offenders; for a variety of reasons—some direct, some indirect—sanctions directed against corporate entities may play a meaningful role in deterring waywardness in the business community.[125]

Corporate Criminals or Criminal Corporations?

Students of corporate social control have asked increasingly whether individual executives or corporate entities should be the object of criminal sanctions. Is it best to speak about "corporate criminals" or "criminal corporations"? The most common answer is that the preferred statutory scheme provides both individual and entity liability; the appropriateness of each is to be determined case by case by the prosecutor. Accordingly, a wide range of methods, apart from the traditional practice of fining businesses, have been proposed or tried to penalize corporate entities more effectively: mandatory community service, managerial intervention, government contract proscription, equity fines, and especially formal publicity.[126]

Some critics, however, have argued against the application of criminal sanctions to corporate entities, primarily on two grounds. First, they challenge the deterrent effect of the sanction essentially because "corporations don't commit crimes, people do"; second, they question the retributive function because corporate criminal sanctions may actually punish innocent shareholders (by reducing the value of their shares) and consumers (by increasing the costs of goods and services).[127] Although a detailed analysis of each objection is beyond the scope of this chapter, a few comments are in order, particularly because the Pinto prosecution—along with other important cases like the E.F. Hutton prosecution—involved corporate rather than individual defendants. We suggest that, in many instances, sanctioning the corporation is the most prudent and equitable policy, and thus that prosecutors' options should not be confined to imposing individual criminal liability.

The critics' first objection—that people, not corporations, commit crimes—ignores the reality that the labyrinthian structure of many modern corporations often makes it extremely difficult to pinpoint individual responsibility for specific decisions. Even in cases where employees who carried out criminal activities can be identified, controversial questions remain. John S. Martin, a former U.S. Attorney who actively prosecuted corporate and white-collar crime cases, comments that when individual offenders can be identified they "often turn out to be lower-level corporate employees who never made a lot of money, who never benefited personally from the transaction, and who acted with either the real or mistaken belief that if they did not commit the acts in question their jobs might be in jeopardy." Further, says Martin, "they may have believed that their superior was aware and approved of the crime, but could not honestly testify to a specific conversation or other act of the superior that would support an indictment of the superior."[128] Thus a thorough investigation may well lead a prosecutor to conclude that indictments against individuals simply cannot be justified, even though the corporation benefited from a clear violation of a criminal statute. Such a result would disserve the deterrent function.

The existence of corporate criminal liability also provides an incentive for top officers to supervise middle- and lower-level management more closely. Individual liability, in the absence of corporate liability, encourages just the opposite: top executives may take the attitude of "don't tell me, I don't want to know." In the words of Peter Jones, former chief legal counsel at Levi Strauss, "a fundamental law of organizational physics is that bad news does not flow upstream." Only when directives come from the upper echelon of the corporation "will busy executives feel enough pressure to prevent activities that seriously threaten public health and safety." [129] For a similar reason, proponents of the conservative "Chicago School" of law and economic thought advocate corporate rather than individual sanctioning: a firm's control mechanisms will be more efficient than the state's in deterring misconduct by its agents and will bring about adequate compliance with legal standards as long as the costs of punishment outweigh the potential benefits.[130]

The second objection—that the cost of corporate criminal fines is actually borne by innocent shareholders and consumers—also seems unfounded. With regard to shareholders, whether individual or institutional, incidents of corporate criminal behavior may give the owners the right to redress the diminution of their interest by filing a derivative suit against individual officers and/or members of the board of directors. Although the cost and the uncertainty of winning such a suit may be high, shareholders must regard this cost as one of the risks incurred when they invest in securities. Just as shareholders may occasionally be enriched unjustly through undetected misbehavior by their company, it is only fair to expect them to bear a part of the burden on those occasions when illegality is discovered and duly sanctioned.

Finally, it is simplistic, if not untenable, to argue that corporate criminal fines will simply be passed on to the consuming public through higher prices. Stephen Yoder, among others, notes that in such instances, our economic system allows consumers to exert a type of indirect, collective control. If we assume that competition exists in the offending corporation's industry, the firm cannot simply decide to raise its prices to absorb the fine or the costs related to the litigation. If it does so, it risks becoming less competitive and suffering such concomitant problems as decreased profits, difficulty in securing debt and equity financing, curtailed expansion, and the loss of investors to more law-abiding corporations.[131]

Conclusion

As signified by Ford's prosecution for reckless homicide and by the numerous cases discussed in this book, corporations have increasingly come under attack by the criminal law in the past two decades. At present, however, only beginning efforts have been made to explain why corporations have grown vulnerable to criminal prosecution at this particular point in history and where this trend will lead. Much work remains to be done.[132]

To contribute to this work, we have used our discussion of the Ford Pinto case as a heuristic device for drawing general insights regarding corporate illegality. We have argued that the Ford prosecution was part of a larger, emerging movement, itself the product of social and legal transformations which are rooted in the nation's political and economic structure. This movement against white-collar and corporate lawlessness remains diffuse and uncrystallized; significant obstacles still exist to efforts aimed at controlling corporate misconduct. Nonetheless, we have proposed that meaningful social and legal changes have taken place, which not only have made possible cases like the Ford Pinto trial but also are likely to inspire further attempts at bringing corporations within the reach of the criminal law.

We will be pleased if we have convinced our readers of the merits of our general framework and of the specifics of our substantive analysis. At the very least, we hope that our efforts will prove sufficiently compelling—or provocative—to invite scholars to grapple, as we have, with the question of why corporations have come under attack.

Notes

[1] For the best account by a journalist who covered the Pinto trial, see Lee Patrick Strobel, *Reckless Homicide? Ford's Pinto Trial.* South Bend, Indiana: And Books, 1980. See also James Warren and Brian J. Kelly, "Inside the Pinto Trial," *American Lawyer* (April 1980), pp. 28-29.

[2] Seymour Martin Lipset and William Schneider, *The Confidence Gap: Business, Labor, and Government in the Public Mind.* New York: The Free Press, 1983.

[3] John Burnett, "Corporate Murder Verdict May Not Become Trend, Say Legal Experts," *Occupational Health & Safety* (October 1985), p. 58.

[4] Robert McClory, "Murder on the Shop Floor," *Across the Board* 23 (June 1986), p. 27.

[5] *Ibid.*, p. 27.

[6] Jonathan A. Bennett, "'The Assault Weapon Was a Dangerous Chemical,'" *Guardian* (October 29, 1986), p. 5. Two comments deserve consideration. First, though we believe that the general social and legal context has made corporate prosecutions possible, the actions of OSHA may have helped to direct these prosecutions toward workplace incidents. Second, it is difficult to determine whether prosecutors have focused on occupational violence because they are aware that more injuries and deaths are occurring, or whether they have used revelations about weakening OSHA controls and increased risks for workers to legitimate corporate criminal indictments that they have already decided to pursue. Of course, both alternatives are possible and may be operating simultaneously to fuel occupationally related prosecutions.

[7] *Granite Construction Co. v. Superior Court of Fresno County* 149 Cal. App.3d 465, 197 Cal. Rptr. 3 (1984). See also "Why More Corporations May Be Charged With Manslaughter," *Business Week* (February 27, 1984), p. 62.

[8] *People v. Warner-Lambert Co.*, 51 N.Y.2d 295, 414 N.E.2d 660, 434 N.Y.S.2d 159 (1980). More generally, see Stephen A. Radin, "Corporate Criminal Liability for Employee-Endangering Activities," *Columbia Journal of Law and Social Problems* 18 (1983): 39-75; Sharon R. Weinfeld,

"Criminal Liability of Corporate Managers for Deaths of Their Employees: *People v. Warner-Lambert Co.*," *Albany Law Review* 46 (1982): 655-685.

[9] *People v. General Dynamics Corp.*, No. 214667 (Macomb County Dist. Ct., filed August 11, 1984). See also McClory, "Murder on the Shop Floor," p. 32; Rick Kendall, "Criminal Charges on the Rise for Workplace Injuries, Deaths," *Occupational Hazards* (December 1985), p. 50; Cathy Trost, "Bhopal Disaster Spurs Debate Over Usefulness of Criminal Sanctions in Industrial Accidents," *Wall Street Journal* (January 7, 1985), p. 6; Ray Gibson, "Corporate Crimes: Criminal Prosecutions Gaining More Favor," *Chicago Tribune* (September 9, 1984), Section 7, p. 1.

[10] *People v. Landis*, No. 391583 (Los Angeles Mun. Ct. of Cal., filed December 20, 1983). See also Judith Cummings, "Director Standing Trial for Deaths on Film Set," *New York Times* (July 23, 1986), p. 8; Randall Sullivan, "Death in the Twilight Zone," *Rolling Stone* (June 21, 1984), p. 31; McClory, "Murder on the Shop Floor," p. 32; Kendall, "Criminal Charges on the Rise for Workplace Injuries, Deaths," p. 50; Gibson, "Corporate Crimes: Criminal Prosecutions Gaining More Favor," p. 1.

[11] For reports on this case, see "Owner, Aides of Ohio Firm Charged in Worker's Death," *Wall Street Journal* (September 11, 1985), p. 20; McClory, "Murder on the Shop Floor," p. 32; Kendall, "Criminal Charges on the Rise for Workplace Injuries, Deaths," p. 51.

[12] For a report on this case, see Kendall, "Criminal Charges on the Rise for Workplace Injuries, Deaths," p. 51.

[13] *People v. Maggio*, No. A780779 (Los Angeles Mun. Ct. of Cal., filed March 26, 1986). See also Andy Furillo, "Manslaughter Charge After Death in Shaft," *Los Angeles Herald Examiner* (March 27, 1986), p. 11. Additional information about this case came from conversations with Jan Chatten-Brown, Los Angeles County Special Assistant District Attorney for the Environmental Crimes/OSHA Division, during April 1986.

[14] *State v. Peabody Southwest Inc.*, No. 259,254 (Travis Co. Ct. of Tex., November 22, 1985), and *State v. Sabine Consolidated Inc.*, No. 259,257 (Travis Co. Ct. of Tex., November 22, 1985). See also Martha Middleton, "Prosecutors Get Tough on Safety," *National Law Journal* (April 21, 1986), pp. 1, 8.

[15] *State v. Six Flags Corp.*, No. 65,084 (Ocean City, N.J. Super. Ct. Law Div., September 14, 1984). See also Donald Janson, "Great Adventure Owners Cleared of Criminal Charges in Fatal Fire," *New York Times* (July 21, 1985), pp. 1, 20; McClory, "Murder on the Shop Floor," p. 32.

[16] *State v. Serebin*, 119 Wis.2d 837, 350 N.W.2d 65 (1984). See also Charles B. Schudson, Ashton P. Onellion, and Ellen Hochstedler, "Nailing an Omelet to the Wall: Prosecuting Nursing Home Homicide," in Ellen Hochstedler (ed.), *Corporations as Criminals*. Beverly Hills: Sage Publications, 1984, pp. 131-134. Additional information on the case was provided by Judge Charles Schudson in a telephone interview, May 22, 1986. Judge Schudson was the original prosecutor in this nursing-home case. See also John Pray, "*State v. Serebin*: Causation and the Criminal Liability of Nursing Home Administrators," *Wisconsin Law Review* (forthcoming).

[17] *State v. Autumn Hills Convalescent Nursing Home*, No. 85-CR-2526 (Bexar Co. Ct. of Tex., April 2, 1986). Additional information was obtained in a telephone interview with Mike Guarino, Criminal District Attorney, Galveston County, Texas, May 23, 1986. See also "Nursing Home Deaths: From Texas to Florida," *Institutions Etc.* 8 (January 1985), pp. 1-3; "State Rests in Murder Trial Tied to Nursing Home," *New York Times* (December 22, 1985); "Mistrial Declared After 6 Months by Judge in Nursing Home Death," *New York Times* (March 25, 1986), p. 21. The jury hearing this trial reportedly voted 9 to 3 to convict the corporation, but the vote to convict individual officials, said jurors, never totaled more than four.

[18] For a report on this case, see Gibson, "Corporate Crimes: Criminal Prosecutions Gaining More Favor," p. 1.

[19] *Commonwealth v. McIlwain School Bus Lines*, 423 A.2d 413 (1980). Information on the eventual disposition of the case was provided by the Clerk of Court's Office, Cambria County, in a June 17, 1986 telephone interview.

[20] *Commonwealth v. Fortner LP Gas Co.*, Inc., 610 S.W.2d 941 (Ky. Ct. App. 1981). Additional information on the disposition of this case was provided by county prosecutors in telephone interviews conducted in May 1986.

[21] Jonathan Tasini, "The Clamor to Make Punishment Fit the Corporate Crime," *Business Week* (February 10, 1986), p. 73; Kendall, "Criminal Charges on the Rise for Workplace Injuries, Deaths," p. 52.

[22] "Labor Letter," *Wall Street Journal* (February 17, 1986), p. 1.

[23] Kendall, "Criminal Charges on the Rise for Workplace Injuries, Deaths," p. 52.

[24] *Ibid*. p. 50; Steven P. Rosenfeld, "Corporate Crime Was Big Business in 1985," *Peoria Journal Star* (December 15, 1985). p. A-14.

[25] Kendall, "Criminal Charges on the Rise for Workplace Injuries, Deaths," p. 52.

[26] "Tainted Cheese Manufacturer Is Charged," *San Francisco Chronicle* (March 28, 1986), p. 7; "Jalisco Mexican, Officials Charged with 60 Violations," *Wall Street Journal* (March 31, 1986), p. 28; "Jalisco President Sentenced in Sales of Tainted Cheese," *Wall Street Journal* (June 23, 1986), p. 7.

[27] Barry C. Groveman and John L. Segal, "Pollution Police Pursue Chemical Criminals," *Business and Society Review* (Fall 1985), p. 42. See also "Prosecutions Increase in Environmental Cases," *Cincinnati Enquirer* (March 2, 1986), p. E-14.

[28] *United States v. Greer*, No. 85-105-CR-ORL-18 (M.D. Fla., filed December 17, 1985). The charges were brought under the Resource Conservation and Recovery Act of 1976, 42 U.S.C.A., Sections 6901-6987 (West 1983 & Supp. 1986). See Jeffrey P. Grogin, "Corporations Can Kill Too: After *Film Recovery*, Are Individuals Accountable for Corporate Crimes?" *Loyola of Los Angeles Law Review* 19 (June 1986), pp. 1411-1412, footnote 2.

[29] Mark Green and John F. Berry, "Capitalist Punishment: Some Proposals, Corporate Crime—II," *The Nation* 240 (June 15, 1985), p. 732.

[30] We are not alone in asserting that ideas help to shape criminal justice policy. See Michael Sherman and Gordon Hawkins, *Imprisonment in America: Choosing the Future*. Chicago: University of Chicago Press, 1981, p. 73. See also James Q. Wilson, *The Politics of Regulation*. New York: Basic Books, pp. 384-387, 393.

[31] See Jeffrey H. Reiman, *The Rich Get Richer and the Poor Get Prison: Ideology, Class, and Criminal Justice*. Second edition. New York: John Wiley and Sons, 1984, p. 41.

[32] We do not know of any empirical studies that have systematically assessed prosecutor attitudes toward corporate crime control. The recent

spate of corporate indictments and trials suggests that prosecutorial support for use of the criminal law is widespread. Jack Katz's research on federal prosecutors, discussed in Chapter 1, reinforces this conclusion. At the same time, we do not know how intense these sentiments are or, in an exact way, the conditions under which prosecutors would or would not favor taking a corporation to criminal court. Moreover, we suspect that there is still some resistance to the idea of criminally sanctioning corporations. Clearly, not all legal commentators are enthusiastic about this policy. See, for instance, Richard A. Epstein, "Is Pinto a Criminal?" *Regulation* (March-April 1980), pp. 15-21; Malcolm E. Wheeler, "Product Liability, Civil or Criminal—The Pinto Litigation," *The Forum* 17 (Fall 1981), pp. 250-265. Compare, however, with John Braithwaite, "The Limits of Economism in Controlling Harmful Corporate Conduct," *Law and Society Review* 16 (No. 3, 1981-1982), pp. 481-504

33 Bertram Gross, "Reagan's Criminal 'Anti-Crime' Fix," in Alan Gartner, Colin Greer, and Frank Reissman, *What Reagan Is Doing to Us*. New York: Harper and Row, 1982, p. 105; Robert E. Taylor, "White-Collar Crime Getting Less Attention," *Wall Street Journal* (February 1, 1984), p. 27.

34 See Diana R. Gordon, *Doing Violence to the Crime Problem: A Response to the Attorney General's Task Force*. Hackensack, N.J.: National Council on Crime and Delinquency, 1981; "Meese Panel Report Links Porn, Violence," *Cincinnati Enquirer* (July 10, 1986), pp. A-1, A-16; Hendrik Hertzberg, "Big Boobs: Ed Meese and His Pornography Commission," *The New Republic* (July 14 and 21, 1986), pp. 21-24.

35 Taylor, "White-Collar Crime Getting Less Attention," p. 27.

36 David R. Simon and Stanley L. Swart, "The Justice Department Focuses on White-Collar Crime: Promises and Pitfalls," *Crime and Delinquency* 30 (January 1984), pp. 108-110.

37 "Statement of Oliver B. Revell, Assistant Director, Criminal Investigative Division, Federal Bureau of Investigation," in *Hearings Before the Subcommittee on Civil and Constitutional Rights of the Committee on the Judiciary, House of Representatives, on Authorization Request for the Federal Bureau of Investigation for Fiscal Year 1985*. Serial No. 113. Washington, D.C.: U.S. Government Printing Office, 1985, pp. 2-3.

38 See Steven Box, *Power, Crime, and Mystification*. London: Tavistock, 1983, p. 7.

[39] Alan A. Block and Frank R. Scarpitti, *Poisoning for Profit: The Mafia and Toxic Waste in America*. New York: William Morrow and Company, 1985, pp. 319-333; Kitty Calavita, "The Demise of the Occupational Safety and Health Administration: A Case Study in Symbolic Action," *Social Problems* 30 (April 1983), pp. 437-448; Joan Claybrook and the Staff of Public Citizen, *Retreat From Safety: Reagan's Attack on America's Health*. New York: Pantheon Books, 1984; Jonathan Lash, Katherine Gillman, and David Sheridan, *A Season of Spoils: The Story of the Reagan Administration's Attack on the Environment*. New York: Pantheon Books, 1984; Susan J. Tolchin and Martin Tolchin, *Dismantling America: The Rush to Deregulate*. Boston: Houghton Mifflin Company, 1983.

[40] Although variation exists across states, most of these statutes are patterned after Section 2.07 of the Model Penal Code.

[41] One such state is California, where courts have refused to quash indictments in the "Twilight Zone" and the Granite City Construction Company cases. Before these rulings were made, however, it was far from certain that the California courts would affirm the right to prosecute corporations for violent offenses. See John M. Hickey, "Corporate Criminal Liability for Homicide: The Controversy Flames Anew," *California Western Law Review* 17 (1981), pp. 491-492.

[42] The bill, H.R. 2966, was introduced on July 11, 1985 by Rep. John Conyers (D. Michigan), and was referred to the Committee on the Judiciary. For further discussion, see Paul G. Engel, "Pin Stripes to Prison Stripes," *Industry Week* (August 4, 1986), p. 55.

[43] *Vaughan & Sons v. State*, 649 S.W.2d 677 (Tex. Crim. App. 1983). The appellate court's decision to reverse the conviction on this ground has been appealed to the Texas Court of Appeals, which has accepted a petition for discretionary review. Information on the status of this case was provided by Galveston County prosecutor Mike Guarino in a telephone interview, May 23, 1986. See also Linda C. Anderson, "Corporate Criminal Liability for Specific Intent Crimes and Offenses of Criminal Negligence--The Direction of Texas Law," *St. Mary's Law Journal* 15 (No. 2, 1984), pp. 231-252.

[44] McClory, "Murder on the Shop Floor," p. 32.

[45] *Ibid.*, p. 31. See also William J. Maakestad, "A Historical Survey of Corporate Homicide in the United States: Could It Be Prosecuted in Illinois?" *Illinois Bar Journal* 69 (August 1981), pp. 772-779,

[46] John Braithwaite, *Corporate Crime in the Pharmaceutical Industry*. London: Routledge and Kegan Paul, 1984, p. 339.

[47] Quote taken from letter written by Berner to W.J. Maakestad, dated July 16, 1981. It should be noted that these remarks are excerpted from a longer quote presented previously in Chapter 5. However, because they seem particularly appropriate to the point raised here, we have taken the liberty of repeating these insights.

[48] Braithwaite, *Corporate Crime in the Pharmaceutical Industry*, p. 339. See also pp. 340-343.

[49] John Braithwaite and Gilbert Geis, "On Theory and Action for Corporate Crime Control," *Crime and Delinquency* 28 (April 1982), pp. 294-295. See also John E. Conklin, *"Illegal But Not Criminal": Business Crime in America*. Englewood Cliffs, N.J.: Prentice-Hall, 1977, pp. 109-110.

[50] Braithwaite and Geis, "On Theory and Action for Corporate Crime Control," pp. 295-296. This does not mean that there are no efforts to detect corporate illegalities. Obviously, a central task of regulatory agencies is to determine when corporations violate legal standards. However, the relationship between the control efforts of these agencies and subsequent criminal prosecutions is problematic and subject to a variety of contingencies.

[51] John C. Coffee, Jr., "The Metastasis of Mail Fraud: The Continuing Story of the 'Evolution' of a White-Collar Crime," *American Criminal Law Review* 21 (No. 1, 1983), p. 19. Henry Pontell has observed that the criminal justice system has a limited "capacity to punish," but the system's capacity is particularly circumscribed in the domain of white-collar crime control. See Henry N. Pontell, "System Capacity and Criminal Justice: Theoretical and Substantive Considerations," in Harold E. Pepinsky (ed.), *Rethinking Criminology*. Beverly Hills: Sage Publications, 1982, pp. 137-138. More generally, see his *A Capacity to Punish: The Ecology of Crime and Punishment*. Bloomington: Indiana University Press, 1984.

[52] Schudson et al., "Nailing an Omelet to the Wall: Prosecuting Nursing Home Homicide," p. 137.

[53] William J. Maakestad, "States' Attorneys Stalk Corporate Murderers," *Business and Society Review* 56 (Winter 1986), p. 23; Schudson et al., "Nailing an Omelet to the Wall: Prosecuting Nursing Home Homicide," p. 139.

[54] Maakestad, "States' Attorneys Stalk Corporate Murderers," pp. 23-24. By contrast, as noted in our discussion of the possible relationship between weakening OSHA controls and recent work-related prosecutions, the absence of a regulatory option may precipitate attempts to sanction corporations criminally. This issue receives additional comment later in this section.

[55] As indicated in the introduction to this chapter, we will comment on these issues in later sections. For relevant literature, see Braithwaite, *Corporate Crime in the Pharmaceutical Industry,* pp. 308, 319-328; Eliezer Lederman, "Criminal Law, Perpetrator and Corporation: Rethinking a Complex Triangle," *Journal of Criminal Law and Criminology* 76 (Summer 1985), pp. 285-340; Brent Fisse, "The Duality of Corporate and Individual Criminal Liability," in Ellen Hochstedler (ed.), *Corporations As Criminals.* Beverly Hills: Sage Publications, 1984, pp. 69-84.

[56] Braithwaite and Geis, "On Theory and Action for Corporate Crime Control," p. 295; Diane Vaughan, *Controlling Unlawful Organizational Behavior: Social Structure and Corporate Misconduct.* Chicago: University of Chicago Press, 1983, p. 89.

[57] Maakestad, "States' Attorneys Stalk Corporate Murderers," p. 23; Vaughan, *Controlling Unlawful Organizational Behavior*, pp. 98-99; John Hagan, Ilene H. Nagel (Bernstein), and Celesta Albonetti, "The Differential Sentencing of White-Collar Offenders in Ten Federal District Courts," *American Sociological Review* 45 (October 1980), p. 818. See also Jack Katz, "Concerted Ignorance: The Social Construction of Cover-Up," *Urban Life* 8 (October 1979), pp. 295-316.

[58] Kenneth Mann, *Defending White-Collar Crime: A Portrait of Attorneys at Work.* New Haven: Yale University Press, 1985, p. 7.

[59] *Ibid.,* pp. 7-8.

[60] Vaughan, *Controlling Unlawful Organizational Behavior*, pp. 92-93.

[61] Maakestad, "States' Attorneys Stalk Corporate Murderers," pp. 22-23.

[62] *Ibid.*, p. 23. More generally, see Robert C. Holland, "Problems in the Investigation of White Collar Crime: A Case Study," *International Journal of Comparative and Applied Criminal Justice* 8 (Spring 1984), pp. 21-41.

[63] Schudson et al., "Nailing an Omelet to the Wall: Prosecuting Nursing Home Homicide," p. 138.

[64] Braithwaite and Geis, "On Theory and Action for Corporate Crime Control," p. 299. See also Braithwaite, *Corporate Crime in the Pharmaceutical Industry.* p. 342.

[65] Leonard Orland, "Reflections on Corporate Crime: Law in Search of Theory and Scholarship," *American Criminal Law Review* 17 (1980), p. 511.

[66] There is little empirical research that has systematically assessed judicial attitudes toward the use of criminal sanctions in instances of illegal *corporate* behavior. As noted in Chapter 2, however, public surveys provide little support for the view that corporate lawlessness is defined as morally neutral. In light of these data, we suspect that while his assessment is accurate for some judges, Orland has overstated the extent to which jurists see "corporate crime as nothing more than aggressive capitalism." Compare this view with the more complex portrait of judges' attitudes toward "white-collar" criminality found in Kenneth Mann, Stanton Wheeler, and Austin Sarat, "Sentencing the White-Collar Offender," *American Criminal Law Review* 17 (1980), pp. 479-500.

[67] John Hagan and Patricia Parker, "White-Collar Crime and Punishment: The Class Structure and Legal Sanctioning of Securities Violations," *American Sociological Review* 50 (June 1985), p. 313.

[68] Jack Katz, "The Social Movement Against White-Collar Crime," in Egon Bittner and Sheldon L. Messinger (eds.), *Criminology Review Yearbook.* Volume 2. Beverly Hills: Sage Publications, 1980, pp. 161-184; Donald I. Baker, "To Indict or Not to Indict: Prosecutorial Discretion in Sherman Act Enforcement," in Sheldon L. Messinger and Egon Bittner (eds.), *Criminology Review Yearbook.* Volume 1. Beverly Hills: Sage Publications, 1979, pp. 409-410; Schudson et al., "Nailing an Omelet to the Wall: Prosecuting Nursing Home Homicide," p. 138; Bruce L. Ottley, "Criminal Liability for Defective Products: New Problems in Corporate Responsibility and Sanctioning," *Revue Internationale de Droit Penal* (Volume 53), p. 151.

[69] Susan P. Shapiro, "The Road Not Taken: The Elusive Path to Criminal Prosecution for White-Collar Offenders," *Law and Society Review* 19 (No. 2, 1985), pp. 193-198; Jed S. Rakoff, "The Exercise of Prosecutorial Discretion in Federal Business Fraud Prosecutions," in Brent Fisse and Peter A. French (eds.), *Corrigible Corporations and Unruly Law*. San Antonio: Trinity University Press, 1985, p. 182.

[70] Shapiro, "The Road Not Taken: The Elusive Path to Criminal Prosecution for White-Collar Offenders," p. 199. See also Nancy Frank, *Crimes Against Health and Safety*. New York: Harrow and Heston, 1985, p. 63; Coffee, "The Metastasis of Mail Fraud: The Continuing Story of the 'Evolution' of a White-Collar Crime," p. 20; Schudson et al., "Nailing an Omelet to the Wall: Prosecuting Nursing Home Homicide," p. 138.

[71] Magnuson was quoted in Gibson, "Corporate Crimes: Criminal Prosecutions Gaining More Favor," p. 6.

[72] Adam Clymer, "Low Marks for Executive Honesty," *New York Times* (June 9, 1985), Section 3, p. 1.

[73] These survey data have been discussed in Chapter 2, but we can add one further piece of corroborative evidence. The day after the Film Recovery Systems verdict was handed down, the *Detroit Free Press* conducted an opinion poll which reported that "80 percent of those calling in" did not believe that murder was "too harsh a charge for negligent employers." Although polling by voluntary calls is prone to bias (those with the strongest feelings may be more likely to express their views), the "overwhelming" sentiments of the sample suggest, in the words of Vicki Cahan and Daniel Moskowitz, that "corporate America is definitely being put on notice." See Cahan and Moskowitz, "A Murder Verdict Jolts Business," *Business Week* (July 1, 1985), p. 25.

[74] Thomas Ferguson and Joel Rogers, "The Myth of America's Turn to the Right," *Atlantic Monthly* 257 (May 1986), pp. 44-45; "Opinion Roundup: Government in the Workplace," *Public Opinion* 4 (August-September 1981), p. 34; "Opinion Roundup: Taxes and Regulation," *Public Opinion* 5 (October-November 1982), p. 23; Kathy Bloomgarden, "Managing the Environment: The Public's View," *Public Opinion* 6 (February-March 1983), pp. 47-51; Rebecca Poole, "An Enduring Commitment," *Sierra* 71 (November-December 1986), pp. 12-13.

[75] Ferguson and Rogers, "The Myth of America's Turn to the Right," p. 44.

[76] Kelly Conlin, "Business Schools with a Conscience," *New York Times* (August 24, 1986), Business Section, p. 1.

[77] Thomas J. Peters and Robert H. Waterman, Jr., *In Search of Excellence: Lessons from America's Best-Run Companies.* New York: Harper and Row, 1982; Tom Peters and Nancy Austin, *A Passion for Excellence: The Leadership Difference.* New York: Random House, 1985.

[78] Seymour Martin Lipset and William Schneider, "Confidence in Confidence Measures," *Public Opinion* 6 (August-September 1983), p. 44.

[79] As Jack Katz comments, "There is a long-term market in American political culture for the symbolics of white-collar crime law enforcement." See Katz's "The Social Movement Against White-Collar Crime," p. 178. We should add a caveat: some commentators are now suggesting that the public has grown more optimistic and that confidence in "America's future" is running high. See Everett Carll Ladd, "Generation Myths," *Public Opinion* 9 (November-December 1986), pp. 12-14. Even so, public distrust of corporate and political leaders remains great. A 1985 Gallup poll indicated that only 24 percent of a national sample rated the "honesty and ethical standards of business executives" as "high"; this figure represented only a four percent improvement over the 20 percent rating given in 1976. See "Opinion Roundup: An Erosion of Ethics?" *Public Opinion* 9 (November-December 1986), p. 21. Another 1986 poll asked citizens the following: "There's been a lot of news recently about individuals and corporations committing white collar crimes to make a dishonest profit for themselves and their companies. How often do you think this happens?" Fifty-six percent of the sample answered "very often," 39 percent answered "occasionally," and only 4 percent answered "hardly ever." See "Opinion Roundup: The Sore Spots...And the Bright Ones," *Public Opinion* 9 (November-December 1986), p. 22. Figures like these, we believe, bolster our contention that despite some shifts in attitudes, the ideological context remains conducive to corporate prosecutions.

[80] "Each time the community moves to censure some act of deviation...and convenes a formal ceremony to deal with the responsible offender," Kai Erikson observes, "it sharpens the authority of the violated norm and restates where the boundaries of the group are located." Erikson, *Wayward Puritans: A Study in the Sociology of Deviance.* New York: John Wiley and Sons, 1966, p. 13.

81 McClory, "Murder on the Shop Floor," p. 26.

82 Indeed, as discussed in Chapter 1, Jack Katz argued that beginning in the early 1970s, U.S. Attorneys prosecuted white-collar offenders as a way of advancing their own career prospects. See Katz, "The Social Movement Against White-Collar Crime," pp. 174-179.

83 Epstein, "Is Pinto a Criminal?" p. 21.

84 More generally, see Mark V. Tushnet, "Perspectives on the Development of American Law: A Critical Review of Friedman's 'A History of Law,'" *Wisconsin Law Review* (1977), pp. 81-109.

85 "The Coliseum: Yesterday's Sentences Leave Many Convinced Justice Is Not Just," *Cincinnati Enquirer* (February 26, 1983), p. A-10.

86 Georgene Kaleina, "Other Judges Decry Probation for Coliseum Electricity Thieves," *Cincinnati Enquirer* (February 26, 1983), p. C-1.

87 Herbert Packer claims that "antitrust defendants do not go to jail at least in part because judges and juries are not convinced that their conduct is morally bad"; Sanford Kadish asserts that a "problem of moral neutrality" exists in that citizens do not "generally" view business violations as "morally reprehensible." The outcry precipitated by the sentences handed out in the Cincinnati and (as we will see below) the E.F. Hutton cases makes these contentions quite problematic. See also Chapter 2 where we have presented a review of studies on public attitudes toward white-collar criminality. For the quotes cited above, see Packer, *The Limits of the Criminal Sanction*. Stanford: Stanford University Press, 1968, p. 359; Kadish, "Some Observations on the Use of Criminal Sanctions in Enforcing Economic Regulations," in Gilbert Geis and Robert F. Meier (eds.), *White-Collar Crime: Offenses in Business, Politics, and the Professions*. Second edition. New York: The Free Press, 1977, pp. 304-308.

88 Carol J. Loomis, "White-Collar Crime," *Fortune* (July 22, 1985), p. 91.

89 Robert Wagman, "Does Justice Have Double Standard?" *Macomb Daily Journal* (May 1985).

90 William Safire, "When E.F. Hutton Talks..." *Cincinnati Enquirer* (May 16, 1985), p. A-18. Later Safire again criticized the "Justice Department's

incredible policy laid down in the Hutton affair: that on Wall Street, there is such a thing as crime without criminals. Millions for corporate fines, goes the Meese motto, but not one day in jail for individual perpetrators." See "Probing Conflicts of Interest," *Cincinnati Enquirer* (July 10, 1985), p. A-6.

[91] Wagman, "Does Justice Have Double Standard?"

[92] "Business Crime: Stealing Money the New-Fashioned Way," *Peoria Journal Star* (May 23, 1985), p. A-6.

[93] Bryan Brumley, "Meese Defends Stance on White Collar Crime," *Cincinnati Enquirer* (September 19, 1985), p. B-9.

[94] *Ibid.* p. B-9.

[95] For a similar analysis, see Calavita, "The Demise of the Occupational Safety and Health Administration: A Case Study in Symbolic Action," pp. 445-446. More generally, see Frances Piven and Richard Cloward's discussion of "democracy against capitalism" in their *The New Class War: Reagan's Attack on the Welfare State and Its Consequences*. New York: Pantheon Books, 1982, pp. 125-150.

[96] A number of authors argue that ethical considerations must play a role in justifying the use of the criminal law in the control of corporate criminality. See Kip Schlegel, "Desert, Retribution, and the Theory of Punishment for Corporations and Their Agents." Paper presented at the 1985 meeting of the Academy of Criminal Justice Sciences; John Byrne and Steven M. Hoffman, "Efficient Corporate Harm: A Chicago Metaphysic," in Brent Fisse and Peter A. French (eds.), *Corrigible Corporations and Unruly Law*. San Antonio: Trinity University Press, 1985, pp. 101-136; Peter A. French, *Collective and Corporate Responsibility*. New York: Columbia University Press, 1984.

[97] Packer, *The Limits of the Criminal Sanction*, p. 356.

[98] John Braithwaite, "White Collar Crime," in Ralph H. Turner and James F. Short, Jr. (eds.), *Annual Review of Sociology, Volume 11*. Palo Alto, Ca: Annual Reviews Inc, 1985, p. 16; Braithwaite and Geis, "On Theory and Action for Corporate Crime Control," pp. 304-305; Gilbert Geis, "White-Collar and Corporate Crime," in Robert F. Meier (ed.), *Major Forms of Crime*. Beverly Hills: Sage Publications, 1984, p. 154.

99 As the Panel on Research on Deterrent and Incapacitative Effects concluded after an exhaustive review of available research, "we cannot yet assert that the evidence proves the existence of deterrent effects." See *Deterrence and Incapacitation: Estimating the Effects of Criminal Sanctions and Crime Rates*. Washington, D.C.: National Academy of Sciences, 1978, p. 47.

100 See William J. Chambliss, "Types of Deviance and the Effectiveness of Legal Sanctions," in his edited book, *Criminal Law in Action*. Second edition. New York: John Wiley and Sons, 1984, pp. 430-431; Braithwaite and Geis, "On Theory and Action for Corporate Crime Control," pp. 300-305. See also Packer, *The Limits of the Criminal Sanction*, pp. 356-358.

101 For cautionary statements, see Byrne and Hoffman, "Efficient Corporate Harm: A Chicago Metaphysic," p. 11; Charles A. Moore, "Taming the Giant Corporation? Some Cautionary Remarks on the Deterrability of Corporate Crime." Paper presented at the 1985 meeting of the Midwestern Criminal Justice Association.

102 Wheeler, "Product Liability, Civil or Criminal—The Pinto Litigation," p. 263.

103 Remarks attributed to Professor Ann Bertel, Columbia University's School of Business, by McClory, "Murder on the Shop Floor," p. 26.

104 Dexter Hutchins, "Post-Hutton Lessons in How to Manage Corporate Cash," *Fortune* (November 11, 1985), p. 134.

105 Brent Fisse and John Braithwaite, *The Impact of Publicity on Corporate Offenders*. Albany: State University of New York Press, 1983, pp. 52-53.

106 *Ibid.*, p. 53.

107 As Graeme Newman comments, punishment "is intended to enlighten or embellish the significance of the crime both to the criminal and society. The idea is not to frighten individuals into submission (although this may happen), but rather for all to learn together about the evil of the offense committed." See Newman's *Just and Painful: A Case for the Corporal Punishment of Criminals*. New York: Harrow and Heston, 1983, p. 31.

108 Alan L. Otten, "Ethics on the Job," *Wall Street Journal* (July 14, 1986), p. 17.

[109] Braithwaite, *Corporate Crime in the Pharmaceutical Industry*, p. 292.

[110] For an initial attempt to modify this argument, see Francis T. Cullen and Paula J. Dubeck, "The Myth of Corporate Immunity to Deterrence: Ideology and the Creation of the Invincible Criminal," *Federal Probation* 49 (September 1985), pp. 3-9.

[111] Christopher D. Stone, *Where the Law Ends: The Social Control of Corporate Behavior*. New York: Harper and Row, 1975.

[112] Sheila Balkan, Ronald J. Berger, and Janet Schmidt, *Crime and Deviance in America: A Critical Approach*. Belmont, Ca: Wadsworth Publishing Company, 1980, pp. 175.

[113] *Ibid.*, p. 185. See also Richard Quinney, *Criminology*. Second edition. Boston: Little, Brown, 1979, p. 200.

[114] "Developments in the Law—Corporate Crime: Regulating Corporate Behavior Through Criminal Sanctions," *Harvard Law Review* 92(1979), p. 1368. See also M. David Ermann and Richard J. Lundman, *Corporate and Governmental Deviance: Problems of Organizational Behavior in Contemporary Society*. New York: Oxford University Press, 1982, pp. 233-235.

[115] *Harvard Law Review*, "Developments in the Law—Corporate Crime: Regulating Corporate Behavior Through Criminal Sanctions," p. 1375.

[116] Bruce Coleman, "Is Corporate Criminal Liability Really Necessary?" *Southwestern Law Journal* 29 (1975), pp. 925-926.

[117] Fisse and Braithwaite, *The Impact of Publicity on Corporate Offenders*.

[118] *Ibid.*, p. 223.

[119] *Ibid.*, pp. 233-235.

[120] *Ibid.*, p. 243; See Braithwaite and Geis, "On Theory and Action for Corporate Crime Control," p. 303.

[121] Malcolm M. Feeley, *The Process Is the Punishment: Handling Cases in a Lower Criminal Court*. New York: Russell Sage Foundation, 1979. According to Kenneth Mann, the "issuance of a criminal charge" is for a white-collar offender "often the most severe sanction that can be meted

out, even if at the end of the process a short prison term is given by the sentencing judge." Mann, *Defending White-Collar Crime: A Portrait of Attorneys at Work*, p. 9.

[122] Steven N. Brenner and Earl A. Molander, "Is the Ethics of Business Changing?" *Harvard Business Review* (January-February 1977), pp. 68-69.

[123] Bloomgarden, "Managing the Environment: The Public's View," p. 48. See also Ralph Nader and William Taylor, *The Big Boys: Power and Position in American Business.* New York: Pantheon Books, 1986; Rich Thomas, "Has Nader Gone Soft? Two Views of Business," *Newsweek* (June 2, 1986), p. 51.

[124] Marshall B. Clinard, *Corporate Ethics and Crime: The Role of Middle Management.* Beverly Hills: Sage Publications, 1983, p. 145; see p. 157.

[125] As Fisse and Braithwaite note, "this all means that there is a lot to be said for keeping after corporations." See *The Impact of Publicity on Corporate Offenders*, p. 244.

[126] See, for example, Stephen Yoder, "Criminal Sanctions for Corporate Illegality," *Journal of Criminal Law and Criminology* 69 (No. 1, 1978), pp. 40-55; John C. Coffee, Jr., "'No Soul to Damn, No Body to Kick': An Unscandalized Inquiry into the Problem of Corporate Punishment," *Michigan Law Review* (January 1981), pp. 386-459; Brent Fisse, "Reconstructing Corporate Criminal Law: Deterrence, Retribution, Fault, and Sanctions," *Southern California Law Review* 56 (1983), pp. 1141-1246.

[127] A recent exposition of these arguments can be found in Lederman, "Criminal Law, Perpetrator, and Corporation: Rethinking a Complex Triangle," pp. 285-340. For a discussion of these issues as they relate to corporate homicide prosecutions, see John E. Stoner, "Corporate Criminal Liability for Homicide: Can the Criminal Law Control Corporate Behavior?" *Southwestern Law Journal* 38 (1985), pp. 1275-1296.

[128] John S. Martin, "Corporate Criminals or Criminal Corporations?" *Wall Street Journal* (June 19, 1985), p. 30.

[129] Peter T. Jones, "Sanctions, Incentives, and Corporate Behavior," *California Management Review* 27 (Spring 1985), pp. 126-127.

[130] One of the earliest and clearest arguments supporting this view is found in Richard Posner, *Economic Analysis of Law*. Second edition. Boston: Little, Brown, 1977, pp. 165-167. For responses to the Chicago school of law and economic thought, see John C. Coffee, Jr., "Corporate Crime and Punishment: A Non-Chicago View of the Economics of Criminal Sanctions," *American Criminal Law Review* 17 (Spring 1980), pp. 419-476; Byrne and Hoffman, "Efficient Corporate Harm: A Chicago Metaphysic," pp. 101-131.

[131] Yoder, "Criminal Sanctions for Corporate Illegality," p. 55. Note also that if publicity is used as a substitute for (or supplement to) a fine, the collective "sanctioning power" held by consumers is even more direct.

[132] Ronald A. Farrell and Victoria Swigert, "The Corporation in Criminology: New Directions for Research," *Journal of Research in Crime and Delinquency* 22 (February 1985), pp. 88-91.

Index